Bishop Gilbert Haven

Our Next-Door Neighbor

A winter in Mexico

Bishop Gilbert Haven

Our Next-Door Neighbor
A winter in Mexico

ISBN/EAN: 9783337251413

Printed in Europe, USA, Canada, Australia, Japan

Cover: Foto ©Andreas Hilbeck / pixelio.de

More available books at **www.hansebooks.com**

Cars for Chapultepec.   Cathedral.   Sagrario.   Church of Santa Theresa.   Museum.

OUR NEXT-DOOR NEIGHBOR:

A WINTER IN MEXICO.

BY

GILBERT HAVEN.

AUTHOR OF "PILGRIM'S WALLET," "NATIONAL SERMONS," "THE SAILOR PREACHER," ETC.

> "Thou Italy of the Occident,
> Glorious, gory Mexico."
> — JOAQUIN MILLER.

> "The Silver is mine and the Gold is mine,
> Saith the Lord of Hosts."
> — HAGGAI.

NEW YORK:
HARPER & BROTHERS, PUBLISHERS,
FRANKLIN SQUARE.
1875.

Entered according to Act of Congress, in the year 1875, by

HARPER & BROTHERS,

In the Office of the Librarian of Congress, at Washington.

TO

MY MOTHER.

BY THE ELDEST, AND NOW, ALAS, FOR EARTH AND TIME, THE
YOUNGEST, ALSO, OF HER BOYS.
ON HER EIGHTY-EIGHTH BIRTHDAY, FEBRUARY 28TH, 1875.

THIS BOOK

IS FONDLY INSCRIBED.

CONTENTS.

BOOK I.—TO THE CAPITAL.

I.
BEFORE THE BEGINNING.

The Threshold.—From Snow to Flowers.—A Character, and what made him.—Our South and its Ethiop.—The Bay and Blaze of Havana.—Off.... Page 17

II.
A DAY IN YUCATAN.

The First-born.—An Opportunity accepted.—An Index Point.—Cocoa-nut Milk.—The Market-place.—Euchre as a Food.—A Grave Joke.—The Drink of the Country.—The Cocoa Palm.—The Native Dress.—A Hacienda.—A Pre-adamite Haciendado.—Jenequen.—Prospecting.—Almost a Panic.—Done into Rhyme 25

III.
THE SEA-PORT.

Under the Cocoa-nut Palm.—The Plaza.—The Cathedral.—No Distinction on account of Color either in Worshiper or Worshiped.—The Watering-place of Cortez.—How the Palm looks and grows.—Other Trees of the Tropics.—Home Flowers.—July Breakfast in January.—Per Contra, a Norther.—Its Utility.—Harbor and Fort.—Size and Shape of the City.—Its Scavenger.—Its Houses.—Street Life.—The Lord's Day.—First Protestant Service.—The Railroad Inauguration 36

IV.
THE HOT LANDS.

From Idleness to Peril.—Solitud.—Chiquihuiti.—Tropical Forests.—The Falls of Atoyac.—Wild Beasts *non sunt*.—Cordova and its Oranges.—Mount Orizaba.—Fortin 55

V.
ON THE STAGE.

Our Companions.—Vain Fear.—The Plunge.—Coffee Haciendas.—Peon Life.—Orizaba City.—The Mountain-lined Passway.—The Cumbres.—The Last

Smile of Day and the Hot Lands.—Night and Useless Terror.—"Two-o'clock-in-the-morning Courage."—Organ Cactus.—Sunrise.—The Volcano.—Into Puebla and the Cars.—The three Snow-peaks together.—Epizaco.—Pulqui.—"There is Mexico!"... Page 65

BOOK II.—IN AND AROUND THE CAPITAL.

I.

FIRST WEEK IN THE CAPITAL.

Hotel Gillow.—Cost of Living.—The Climate.—Lottery-ticket Venders.—First Sabbath.—First Protestant Church.—A Praise Meeting.—State of the Work.—The Week of Prayer... 89

II.

FROM THE CHURCH TOP.

First Attempt and Failure.—At it again.—The Southern Outlook.—Popocatepetl and Iztaccihuatl.—Cherubusco.—Chapultepec.—Guadalupe.—The patron Saint of the Country.—Round the Circle................................ 98

III.

FROM THE SIDEWALK.

Views from Street Corners.—Chief Street.—Shops, Plaza, Cathedral.—High and Low Religion.—Aztec Calendar Stone.—The Sacrificial Stone.—The President's private House.—Hotel Iturbide.—Private Residences.—Alameda 110

IV.

A NEW EVENT IN MEXICO.

Palace of the President.—The President.—How he looks.—What he pledges.—Former Property of the Church.—Its Consequences.—Corruption.—Pospects and Perils 126

V.

OLD AND NEW AMONG THE SILVER MINES.

A Mediæval Castle.—First Icicle.—Omatuska.—More about Pulqui.—A big Scare.—A Paradise.—Casa Grande.—A Sabbath in Pachuca.—A native Convert.—Mediæval Cavalcade.—The Visitors.—Mounting Real Del Monte.—The Castle of Real.—Gentlemanly Assassin.—Silver Factories.—Velasco.—A Reduction.—Haciendado Riley.—Mexican Giant's Causeway.—More Silver Reduction.—Horsemanship under Difficulties.—Contraries balancing Contraries.—La Barranca Grande.—A bigger Scare.—A Wedding.—Miner and Mining.—The Gautemozin.—The better Investment.................... 131

VI.
ACROSS LOTS.

A drowsy Beginning.—Paradise somewhat Lost.—Trees of Paradise.—A lingual Guess at the Aztec Origin.—Tizayuca.—Zumpango.—The Lake System.—Guatitlan.—Hotel San Pedro.—Into Town.—Tree of Noche Triste.—Tacuba.—Aqueduct of San Cosme.—Tivoli.................................Page 166

VII.
THE TOWN OF THE ANGELS.

Warnings unheeded.—Slow Progress.—Christ in the Inn.—Why Angelic.—Bad Faith and worse Works.—First English Service.—Outlook from the Cathedral.—Tlascala.—The Volcano.—Inside View of the Belfry.—Inside the Cathedral.—Triple Gilt.—Cathedral Service.—La Destruccion de los Protestantes.. 175

VIII.
THE MOST ANCIENT AMERICAN MECCA.

On Horse.—Irrigation.—Entrance to Cholula.—Deserted Churches.—Plaza Grande, and its Cortez Horror.—A wide-awake Priest.—A wide View from the Summit.—A costly Trifle.—The Ride back...................... 191

IX.
A DAY AND NIGHT AT EL DESIERTO.

A Point of View.—The Woods: their Peril and Preservation.—How we got here.—Chapultepec.—Tacubaya.—Santa Fé.—Contadera.—Guajimalpa.—The Forest.—The Shot.—Solitude.—The Ruin.—Its Inquisition.—A Bowl of Song.—Moonlight Pleasure and all-night Horror.—Morning Glories.—Its History.—A more excellent Way.—Home again 204

X.
A RIDE ABOUT TOWN.

The Horse and its Rider.—Paseos.—Empress's Drive.—A Relic of Waterloo.—The Tree of Montezuma.—The Woods.—View of Chapultepec.—Baths of Montezuma.—Tacubaya Gardens.—The Penyan.—Canal.—Floating Gardens.—Gautemozin.—The Café.. 219

XI.
A GARDEN IN EDEN.

A Temptation.—Up the Mountains.—The Cross of Cortez.—Sight of the Town and Valley.—The downward Plunge.—A Lounge.—Church of Cortez.—The Enchanted Garden.—Idolatry.—The Market-place.—The Almanac against Protestantism.—Palace of Cortez.—The Indian Garden of Maximilian.—A Sugar Hacienda.—The latter End.—All Zones........................ 231

XII.

A WALK IN MEXICO.

The Market-place.—The Murder-place.—Mexic Art and Music.—Aquarius.—Ruins, and how they were made.— A Funeral.— San Fernando Cemetery.—The English and American also.—Vaminos .... Page 248

BOOK III.—FROM MEXICO TO MATAMORAS.

I.

TO QUERETARO.

The Start.—First and last Church in the City.—The Game-cocks.—First Scare.—Guatitlan again.—Barrenness.—Gambling and Tortilla-making.—Descent to Tula.—A Bit of English Landscape.—Tula.—Hunt for a Statue.—A silver Heavens and Earth.—Juclites.—Mountains and a mounting Sun.—Vista Hermosa.—Napola.—A stone Town.—An Interior.—The Stables.—Sombrero Walls. — Eagle Tavern. — Playing with the Children. — Gamboling *versus* Gambling.—Cazadero, the Bull Prairie.—Hacienda of Palmillas.—Blacksmith Idolatry.—Misterio de la Santissima Trinidad.—'Tother Side up.—Descent into the Valley of San Juan.—Lone yellow Cone.—Longfellow and Homer.—Elysium after much Turmoil.—A Dissertation on Beggars.—A Market Umbrella.—In Perils among Robbers.—The beautiful Valley of San Juan.—Colorado.—A Turner Sunset.—Sight of Queretaro.—The Aqueduct.—The Bed 267

II.

QUERETARO.

Into the Town.—Maximilian's Retreat.—Capture and Execution.—Hill of Bells.—Factories and Gardens.—Hot-weather Bath.—A Home.—Alameda.—Sunday, sacred and secular.—A very Christian Name.—Crowded Market, and empty Churches.— Chatting in Church. — Priestly Procession.— Among the Churches.—Hideous Images.—Handsome Gardens 285

III.

TO GUANAJUATO.

A bad Beginning. — A level Sea.—Celaya. — A Cactus Tent. — Salamanca.—Irapuato.—Entrance to Guanajuato.—Gleaning Silver.—The Hide-and-go-seek City.—A Revelation 300

IV.

A SILVER, AND A SACRED TOWN.

Native Costume.—Reboza and Zarepe.—The Sombrero.—A Reduction Hacienda.—The Church in Guanajuato.—Its Antipodes.—A clerical Acquaintance.—A mulish Mule.—" No quiere."—The Landscape.—Lettuce.—Calzada.—The Town and Country.—Fish of the Fence.—The Cactus and the Ass.—Compensation.—One-story City.—High Mass and higher Idolatry.—The God Mary...Page 307

V.

A HORSEBACK RIDE OVER THE SILVER MOUNTAINS.

Indian Dancing and Gambling.—A sleeping City.—Wood and Coal Carriers.—Mineral de la Luz.—A Mountain Nest.—Sometimes up, sometimes down.—Berrying and Burying.—The Apple-tree among the Trees of the Wood.—Off the Track.—A funereal Tread.—Lunch in the Air.—The Plunge.—A Napola Orchard.—Out on the Plains.—Valley of the Sancho............. 321

VI.

TO AND IN SAN LUIS POTOSI.

Aztec Music.—Low-hung but high-hung Clouds.—Troops and Travelers.—A big, small Wagon.—Zeal of San Felipe.—Lutero below Voltaire.—Rough Places not smooth.—Mesquite Woods.—Silver Hills.—Two Haciendas.—How they Irrigate.—Lassoing.—The Frescoes of Frisco.—Cleft Cliffs.—The Valley of San Luis Potosi.—Greetings and Letters.—The Church of Mary.—The coming Faith.—A costly and Christly Flag.—Joseph and Mary worshiped in vain for Rain.. 334

VII.

OUT AT SEA.

Leaving Shore.—A hot Companion.—Parallel Mountains.—Parks and Divides.—Hacienda of Bocas.—Gingerbread Pigs.—A ragged Boy Apollo.—Marriageless Motherhood.—The Widow's Reply.—Sierra Prieto.—Mortevillos.—Reveling in the Halls of Montezuma.—Strife of Beggars.—Dusty Reflections.—Venada.—Chalcos.—The Worship of the dying Wafer.................. 351

VIII.

MID-OCEAN.

The "Rolling Forties."—Ceral Hard-tack.—Not so Hard.—Mexican Birds.—Smoking-girls.—Laguna Seca.—La Punta.—First Breakfast in an Adobe.—Hacienda of Precita.—The Spanish Bayonet.—Mattejuala.—Birnam Wood marching on Dunsinane.—The first and last Mosquito of Mexico.—Yankee Singing.—Worse threatened... 359

IX.

NEARING SHORE.

Preparations against a Rancho.—A golden Set.—Bonaventura.—A Rancho: what is it?—Companions.—Aztec or Chinese?—Desolation.—Tropic Thorns and Flowers.—An Oasis.—Hacienda of Solado, and its unexpected Hospitalities.—Freaks of the Spanish Bayonet.—Green velvet Mountains.—The true Protector .... Page 366

X.
INTO PORT.

Sunrise.—Villa de Gomez Firias.—A lost American found.—Flowering Palms.—An unpleasant Reminder.—A charming Park.—Agua Nueva.—La Encantada.—La Angostura.—Battlemented Mountains.—Buena Vista.—The Battlefield.—The Result.—Why.—Saltillo.—Alameda.—Friends............. 375

XI.
MONTEREY.

Songs in the Night.—Open Fields near Saltillo.—Effect of Irrigation.—"The Rosy-fingered Dawn."—Gathering together of the Mountains.—San Gregario.—A Thousand-feet Fall.—Rinconada.—Wonders of Flowers.—A Hole through a Mountain.—The Saddle Mountain.—The Mitre.—Santa Caterina.—A Tin God.—A familiar Color.—St. Peter.—No Bathing after Midday.—The Smallness of Mexican Heads.—Miss Rankin's Work.—Strife between Brethren.—Its Benefits.—The two Dogs.—The Eye of the Town.—Revolutions... 387

XII.
THE BEGINNING OF THE END.

Rancho de Villa de General Trevina.—A Sign of Home.—A misty Escort.—Blistering Morin.—Chaparral.—The changed Face of Nature.—The Yankee Hat and Hut.—Mesas, or Table-lands.—The bottom Rancho; Garcia.—Mier.—Comargo.—The Grand River unseen, yet ever near.—Last Night in a Rancho.—La Antigua Renosa.. 398

XIII.
JOLTINGS AND JOTTINGS.

A Creator and an Imitator.—Church-making and Carriage-writing.—The oldest Church and the youngest.—*Compagnons du Voyage.*—A Brandy-sucker. .—Prohibition for Mexico.—Talks with the Coachman and Mozo.—Hides and Shoes.—San Antonio.—Its Casa and Inmates.—Rancho Beauties.—Women's Rights in Mexico.—Sermonizing in the Wilderness.—A Night on Stage-top.—Fantastic Forms.—Spiritual Phantasms.—Light in a dark Place.—Matamoras and Brownsville...................................... 403

XIV.
THE FINISH.

Coach, not Couch.—A new Tread-mill.—Rascality of a Sub-treasurer.—The same Country, but another Driver.—Live-oak *versus* Mesquite.—A sandy Desert as large as Massachusetts.—Not a complete Desert.—A dirty, but hospitable Rancho.—Thousands of Cattle on no Hill.—A forty-mile Fence.—A Patch of four hundred square Miles.—Mr. King's Rancho and Pluck.—Perils.—Mr. Murdock's Murder.—Corpus Christi.—Indianola.—Good-bye...Page 418

XV.

CHRISTIAN WORK IN MEXICO.

Not yet.—The First Last.—A Telegram and its Meaning.—Perils and Perplexities of Church purchasing.—Temptation resisted.—Success and Dedication.—Curé Hidalgo and his Revolution.—Iturbide and Intolerance.—Beginning of the End.—The Mexican War, and its Religious Effects.—The Bible and the Preacher.—The first Revolt from Romanism.—Abolition of Property and of Institutions.—Invasion of the Papacy through France and Maximilian.—Expulsion thereof through America and Juarez.—The Constitutionalists the first Preachers.—The first Martyr: "Viva Jesus! Viva Mexico!"—Francisco Aguilar and the first Church.—The Bible and his Death.—First Appeal abroad.—Response.—Rev. Dr. Riley and his Work.—Excitement, Peril, Progress.—President Juarez, the first Protestant President.—The chief native Apostle, Manual Aguas.—His Excommunication by and of the Archbishop.—A powerful Attack on the Church.—His Death.—The Entrance of the American Churches in their own Form.—Their present Status.—The first American Martyr, Stephens; and how he was butchered.—San Andres.—Governmental Progress.—The Outlook.—Postfatory........................ 424

APPENDIX A... 455
APPENDIX B... 456
APPENDIX C... 461
APPENDIX D... 466

ILLUSTRATIONS.

	PAGE
Cathedral and Plaza by Moonlight	*Frontispiece*
The Bay of Havana	23
Governor's Palace at Vera Cruz	37
Vera Cruz	45
Fountain at Vera Cruz	50
Old Bridge of Atoyac	59
Orange Grove, Cordova	61
A Peon's House	66
Great Bridge of Mathata	67
View of Orizaba	69
River at Orizaba	71
The Organ Cactus	77
Maguey Plant	82
The Valley of Mexico, from the American official Map	*faces* 89
Mexican Flower-girl	91
First Protestant Church	94
Chapultepec	101
Church of Guadalupe	*faces* 102
The Lottery-ticket	104
Iztaccihuatl	106
The Dome	108
The Market-place, City of Mexico	112
San Cosme Aqueduct, City of Mexico	117
The Palace of Mexico	119
The Aztec Calendar Stone	122
The Sacrificial Stone	*faces* 123
Interior of a modern Mexican House	124
The Palisades of Regla	153
A Mexican General	158
Tree of Triste Noche	171
Garden of the Tivolis, San Cosme	173
Street View in Puebla	177

	PAGE
Ruins of the covered Way to the Inquisition	179
The Cathedral of Puebla	182
Convent of San Domingo, City of Mexico	186
Prisoners of the Inquisition	188
Church built by Cortez	195
Pyramid of Cholula	198
View from the Pyramid of Cholula	200
The Tree of Montezuma	222
The Baths of Montezuma	225
The Canal	227
Floating Gardens	229
Saw-mill	245
Planting Corn	247
Scene in Market	249
A Water-carrier	255
Soldiers' Monument in the American Cemetery	261
Cactus, and Woman kneading Tortillas	270
Mexican Beggar	280
Aqueduct of Queretaro	284
Queretaro	288
A Cotton Factory, Queretaro	291
Church of San Diego, Guanajuato	305
Mexican Wash-house	*faces* 317
Funeral of Governor Manuel Doblado	317
Mexican Muleteer	336
The Virgin	348
Joseph	349
Buena Vista	381
Saddle Mountain	391
Bishop's Residence, Monterey	393
Alameda, Monterey	397
The Itinerary—from Vera Cruz to Matamoras	415
Church of San Francisco, City of Mexico	425
First Methodist Episcopal Church, City of Mexico	430
A distant View of the Church of the Ex-convent of San Francisco, City of Mexico	437
Church of San Jose de Gracia	442
Manuel Aguas	444
John L. Stephens	448
Tower and Castle of Acapulco, Mexico—Scene of the recent Massacre	451

BOOK I.

TO THE CAPITAL.

OUR NEXT-DOOR NEIGHBOR.

I.

BEFORE THE BEGINNING.

The Threshold.—From Snow to Flowers.—A Character, and what made him.—Our South and its Ethiop.—The Bay and Blaze of Havana.—Off.

THERE is properly a path to the front door of a house, or at least a few steps ere its entrance is reached. So every voyage has a preliminary, a before-the-door-step experience. This is sometimes excluded entirely from the journal of the journey, sometimes inserted in the preface—a proper place for the preliminaries (a fore-talk best occurring at the fore-threshold), sometimes made into Chapter First. The latter course is here adopted, though every reader is at liberty to skip the chapter, leap over the threshold, and press instantly into the centre of the house, that is, the volume.

The nearest things are often the farthest off, the farthest off the nearest. This is true of places as well as of peoples. We know more of Bismarck than of our next-block neighbor, of Paris than of many an American town. This law is verified in our knowledge, or ignorance rather, of our nearest national neighbor, Mexico. Few books are written, less are read, upon the most novel land on our continent, and one of the most attractive on any continent. Prescott's "Conquest" is esteemed a sort of historical romance, the very charm of his style adding to the unreality of his theme. And if it be reckoned strict history, it is still history; not a living, breathing power, as is England or Italy, Germany or Russia, but a vivid fact of three centuries and over ago, a mediæval story of marvel and mystery. In fact, Prescott's "Conquest" has made that of its subject, Cortez, to fade. And one is half tempted to believe that the real *conquistadór* was not the strong-brained, strong-limbed, strong-souled Spaniard, but the half-blind and wholly meditative Bostonian. The Achilles and his Homer are worthy of their several fame. Yet the land on which, or out of which, each won his chief glory is still superior to them both. A run along some of its chief paths of interest may make this fact patent to other eyes.

Just as our North was putting on its winter night-robes, which it did not take off for four long months, I packed my valise, three of them, as became a "carpet-bagger," and moved southward.

Snow chased me as far as Richmond; moist, mild June met me at Montgomery; oranges, in clusters, plucked fresh from the boughs, were passed through the cars near Mobile; and New Orleans welcomed me to summer skies, and showers, and flowers. A Northern touch of sharp and almost icy weather made the steamer for Havana less unwelcome. So a glimpse at good friends, and a coming and going grasp of hands, including a coming but not going grasp of hearts, and the steamer and I are off.

A character that I met on the steamer, by its strangeness relieved the sea-qualms, and, if for no other reason, deserves a sketch. He was a type of a vanishing class—few, I hope, at any time, but not without existence. He was a Havana planter, who had come to New Orleans to sell his crop, and was returning brimful of cash and whisky; nay, not brimful of the latter, or, if so, with great capacity of enlargement—worse than some prolix preachers possess over their text. When the captain entered the cabin, he greeted him with a shower of oaths—not in rage, but in good humor—that being almost his only vocabulary. He called constantly for every sort of liquor—beer, gin, wine, whisky. He drank all the three days and nights like a fish, if a fish ever drinks. It never drinks such stuff as he constantly poured down his inflamed throat. The stuff that went in and that came out were alike horrible.

A clever colored lad from Philadelphia was the special object of his contemptuous detestation. He ordered him to get the liquors and hot water every few minutes until near midnight. When the fires were out, and hot water was not to be had, and the bar shut, and the liquors also absent, then he raved at the lad for not waking up steward and purser, and securing the delectable elements. If the boy went slowly to his impossible task, how he cursed him! how he blasphemed his people! how he cursed the Abolitionists for setting them free! declaimed against Massachusetts in particular for her share in this matter, and declared their incapacity for liberty, though the boy was tenfold more capable of freedom than himself. Yet he was as shrewd as any other Yankee, and said that slavery was as good as dead in Cuba, and he had persuaded his wife, and sold off all his "niggers" when he could get something for them. I am sure they were glad to get away from the lash of his tongue and arm, and I pitied the hired hands on whom he voided the rheum of an arrogant disposition, a trained contempt and hatred, a false theory, and a fearful appetite. Nay, his wife must suffer often from that scourge.

He was a good Romanist withal, though without any of the orthodoxy of his Church. He said that he prayed nightly to the Virgin, but he did not believe in her, or Christ, or the Bible, or any thing but God. I said, "If you believe in God, you believe in Christ, for Jesus Christ is God." "Jesus Christ!" he broke forth; "—— Jesus Christ!" It was the worst oath I had ever heard. I called him quick to his senses, and he halted a moment in his mad and profane career. He was a Free Religionist, like three others whom I have met on this trip, two of whom were also European Roman Catholics, one a Bostonian, showing that there is no distinction of clime or race in this anti-faith. Like the others, he showed his free religion and modern theology by most outrageous swearing. It is the true creed of that churchless church, and shows that men who profess to deny damnation, hell, Christ, and even God himself, are most profuse in using terms which show that these are the profoundest beliefs of their real nature.

I pitied the poor rich man, and the system of religion and society that had turned such a creature of holy possibilities into a demon; and I prayed all the more earnestly for the abolition of the devil of drink, and that it might speedily follow to eternal destruction its kindred demon already slain.

What wonderful blessings has Abolition brought to all those who were held, like this rich victim, fast in more slavish chains! Our white brethren will rejoice as much over the liberty it has given them and their sons as in that which it has given their darker brothers. It has made such characters as this impossible. Men may drink yet, and curse Christ and his Church, but they can not be developed into such frightful specimens of diseased humanity.

He made me think of a like character I met on the road from Suez to Cairo. He was a genteel, well-dressed Turkish merchant, with his nice silk jacket "all buttoned down before" and behind, and tasteful silk breeches. He was bringing some Nubian boys to the Cairene market. He kept tormenting the poor lads by touching their arms, cheeks, and legs, anywhere, with the burning end of his cigar. He laughed at their silent cringes, and looked at us as if expecting reciprocal smiles. Had we known his language, we would have cursed him to his face. If such were his jokes, what must have been his treatment of them when roused to madness, as he undoubtedly often was! He was very devout withal, and at the sunset station was first from the cars, and on the wilderness gravel, in sight of all, was making his prostrations and muttering his prayers.

It is this frightful exception that proves the rule, an exception not so infrequent as it ought to have been, as the Rev. Mr. Bleby shows in his late most interesting book, entitled "Romance without Fiction; or, Sketches from the Port-folio of an Old Missionary," in which he gives thrilling illustrations of hardnesses of heart and cruelties of conduct in the English West Indies, and by English gentlemen, and clergymen even, that are harrowing after almost a century has passed since their enactment. All our Sunday-schools, North and South, should read this vivid record of modern martyrdom, not less horrible and holy than that given by Fox, and executed by false Christians upon the true in the Middle and the later ages. The evil that wrought it has ceased — thanks be to God! — in most lands, and will soon cease in all.

All this conduct was simply because this comely lad was colored. I thought I had escaped from caste and all its effects. When I mounted the *Yazoo* I did not expect to see colorphobia in any shape until I had gotten back to our beloved country, when I again expected to see it everywhere, in every shape. But the presence was not to be put by. It seemed even providential; for the first Sunday that I spent in the South, only the week previous, I opened my Testament and lighted upon the passage, "The angel of the Lord spake unto Philip, saying, 'Arise and go into the south country.'" The next verse says, "He arose and went, and lo! a man, an Ethiop." It was, seemingly, a surprise to him that he was sent to this black Gentile. But he was without prejudice of color, though tempted, as a Jew, by that of blood and faith. For these latter reasons he may have hesitated a little, for the Holy Spirit has to enforce the order of the angel, and he says to Philip, "Go and glue thyself to this chariot." As the Testament was being read in course, I can hardly say the passage was selected by lot or of the Lord; yet it struck me very forcibly, and I fancied (was it fancy?) that the ordering in this case was providential. I had arisen and gone into the South country, and had found there the Ethiop, and now heard the Spirit say, "Glue thyself" — this the original means — " to him." I saw in his conversion the regeneration of all our South land and North land, too; for the Lord will uplift the whole nation only as we uplift our long down-trodden brethren into Christian oneness with ourselves. The Ethiop is riding already in his chariot, and as Lowell wittily somewhere, for substance, says, "The white man will be willing enough to run along by his side, and accept a seat with him, when the black man rides in his own chariot."

But our South country was not sufficiently South. So I am sent yet farther into the South country — the " mid country," as the originel hath it — till I find myself where our "Sunny South" is far away to the north, and where even our country is printed on the map "the United States of the North." Much as some of our good neighbors may dislike to be called Northern people, they are compelled to endure that affliction from Mexican lips. This proud and sensitive nation calls itself "the United States of Mexico," and it will not allow another body of commonwealths on the continent to call itself "the United States of America."

If our brethren had achieved their independence they might have been compelled to conform to this nomenclature, and called their country the Central United States. Fortunately, they can and will yet rejoice in the continental title which includes centre and circumference in its all-embracing area.

This experience on the steamer has led to all these musings. Better these than that dreary heaving of the stomach and the sea. How the outside and the inside miserably harmonize! The gray I get glimpses of through that bit of a hole in the side of the ship, as the berth tips over, lets me sickly see a like sick sea. The waves toss wearily on their bed, and I am glad, in a miserable way, that I have even this sort of communion with nature.

The *Yazoo* carries us to Havana and to midsummer in sixty hours. The hot bay seems hotter than New York's hottest. Its round rim is ablaze with direct and reflected burnings. The golden sand-hills shoot back the golden rays in increased fervor and brilliance. The palm gives a shadeless shade, as would an umbrella stuck on the top of a twenty-foot pole. The catcus, least lovely and not least useful of tropical plants, thick sets its quoit-like leaves with thorns. Deep sheds cover the quays, protecting from the fiery blaze both man and beast: which is which, is yet undecided, since both are beasts here, the mule often less so than the man. Under their broad roofs goes ceaselessly on the busy loading of sugar and oranges and bananas, the busy unloading of bales and barrels of Northern fields and mills.

The slave is still here. He is a vanished institution northward across that blue gulf, and already in his last stages of serfhood here. He exhibits, in this decay of brutehood and beginning of manhood, some traces of both natures. Here is a big, oily fellow, lifting freight out of the New York steamer. He is as lithe as a Greek wrestler, and, like him, anointed with fresh oil, his own oil, extracted by the Adamic curse, not from his brow alone, but from his back and breast and legs and arms, even the whole body. Like the precious oil on Aaron's head, it flows down to the bottom of his garments, or would if he had any on, a *couvert* alone composing his wardrobe.

THE BAY OF HAVANA.

He will make a good Touissant, give him education, or a bad one if he has not soon given him liberty. This he is soon to have; and some future visitor may see him clothed and in his right mind, well cultured, sitting in the council chamber or standing in the pulpit, serving in high places as he now serves in low.

This glimpse from the bay is all I can enjoy; for the steamer *City of Merida* is in, and will leave before night for Vera Cruz. The vessel must be off before sundown, or it can not leave for two days; for this is the night before Christmas, and the Church authorities forbid all leaving of ships or doing of any other work on this holiday, except on payment into their palms, professedly into her treasury, of double fees of doubloons; so, to escape committing the sin or paying the price of bribery, the captain is determined to get outside the Castle before sunset vespers ring.

The hot streets are touched; the collector and commandant are paid their demanded and needless fee; the filth and fever of the narrow streets about the wharf are duly interviewed; a coachman lashes his sick horses from officer to officer; a cup of coffee is drank at those best saloons of Spanish-speaking countries; and some ten dollars are spent for the privilege of entering the port and exchanging steamers. Then the black sides of the goodly steamer are scaled, and Havana is left almost or ere it is reached.

"Out to sea the streamers fly."

We leave the port left three centuries and a half ago by a daring soldier-farmer, with his small accompaniment of ships and soldiers, for the land, whisperings of whose wonders had allured the commandant of Cuba to embark his treasures in its discovery and subjugation; and who also, less wisely for himself, but not for the world, had been induced to give command of the fleet to a reconciled foeman, who had made peace with his adversary, that he might thus gain over him the greater victory.

Velasquez, however, began to fear him before he sailed, and had revoked his commission. But Cortez, before he had received official knowledge of the revocation, hoisted anchor and sail, and fled in the night. We follow after at not far from the same hour. The city lights glimmer along the shore ere we lose sight of it and them, and we skim all night along the way that adventurer sailed.

II.

A DAY IN YUCATAN.

The First-born. — An Opportunity accepted. — An Index Point. — Cocoa-nut Milk. — The Market-place. — Euchre as a Food. — A Grave Joke. — The Drink of the Country. — The Cocoa Palm. — The Native Dress. — A Hacienda. — A Pre-adamite Haciendado. — Jenequen. — Prospecting. — Almost a Panic. — Done into Rhyme.

EVERY thing is affected by first impressions. Sometimes they can never be overcome. That like or dislike often abides incurable. The first sight of a foreign shore is a love or a hate forever. How perfect Ireland is in my memory, because it looked so beautiful, rising, a green wave of stillness and strength, out of that sick and quaking sea, over which I had been rolling so long! Egypt is not a river of verdure so much as a strip of blazing sand, for Alexandria, and not Cairo, is its first-born in my experience.

Mexico has its first picture in my gallery. Whatever grandeurs of mountain or glories of forest it may unfold, its first impression will always be that first day in Yucatan. I never dreamed a month before of seeing Yucatan. Even if Mexico itself had crossed the mind as a possibility of experience, Yucatan had never been included in that concept. That prettily sounding name was as far off as Cathay or Bokhara.

Yucatan was, to me, Central America; a museum of ancient monuments; an out-of-the-world corner. In fact, it did not belong to Mexico till Maximilian's time. He annexed it, and they hold together still. We often strike an unknown rock in our sail through life, and Yucatan was the unexpected shoal on which we first stranded. It happened in this wise:

The *City of Merida* makes a landing as near as possible to the city after which it is named. This city is twenty miles from the shore, in the peninsula of Yucatan. It has sixty thousand inhabitants, and is the centre of a vast hemp-producing country. This hemp finds a ready market in New York. Hence the pause at this spot; hence the name of our vessel. It is to land stores for the big city, and to take hemp for the bigger country.

The steamer lies four miles from shore. Wearied with its close confinement, three passengers, two of whom are General Palmer, president of the Denver and Rio Grande Railroad, who, with General Rosecrans, is seeking the extension of that system in Mexico, and Mr. Parish, their European financial representative, propose to spend on shore the day in which we are to remain here. We are met with protestations from various quarters. We are told that we will be sun-struck; will get the *calentura*, or fever; that the fleas will take possession of us; that a Norther will arise, and we can not get back to the steamer; and thus hobgoblins dire are piled on our path. The American minister, returning home, grand and genial, adds his preventive persuasions. But none of these things move us. We go. The captain of the boat which is rowing us ashore enlivens our depressed spirits with encouraging stories about the abundance of monkeys and parrots, of lions and tigers, and deer and wild boars, and every such terror and delight —none of which we see.

We land at a wharf covered with bales of hemp, and brown-skinned natives in their white suits. On it stands a small, pale-faced gentleman, whom we find to be Mr. Tappan, of Boston, the consular agent, and grandson of the minister who wrote the plaintive and pretty verses beginning,

"There is an hour of peaceful rest."

It is almost always fortunate for an American abroad if the United States official be an American. He knows his language, the first important consideration, and he knows what the visitor wants to know, the second and not less important consideration. Our Boston friend is expert in these two excellences. He takes us across the blazing sands of this holiday season to the cool arches of the collector's house. That gentlemanly official welcomes us to Progresso, the name of this new town. This name shows its newness, and also, possibly, that a Yankee had something to do with its christening; for the Mexican has hardly yet learned that there be such a thing as progress, much less that it can be concentrated into a town, though he indulge in titular progress, and put into names what his Northern brothers put into fact.

Our gentlemanly collector leads us through his official rooms into the domestic apartments, and introduces us to his family. He is a Spaniard, his wife a Cuban, and his three adopted daughters are representatives of the three races, so called, that hold harmonious possession of this soil. They consist of a white young lady of Anglo-Saxon lightness of complexion, seemingly of a Northern European origin, her adopted parents being dark to her; another, slightly her junior, whose tint is of that Afric sort that Mrs. Kemble Butler deemed richer than any European, and whose opinion our former aristocracy confirmed by their conduct: and the third was a pure Indian belle, none the less beautiful in contour and complexion, a half-way house between these two extremes of human colors. We did not see the Pocahontas of the family, but the Cleopatra and Boadicea were among our agreeable entertainers. They were dressed just alike, in neat, light, brown-checked muslins, with girlish modesty of array and manner that was cultivated and charming. Our ignorance of Spanish put a barrier between us, but their bearing was sisterly and filial; and we accepted this index of the New America as a token of the superiority of Yucatan over the United States, and a proof of the fitness of the name of the town. Had many an American father recognized, not his adopted, but his actual family, a like variety would have been visible about the paternal board. It will yet be, and without sin or shame, as in this cultivated circle.

The host offered us the milk of the cocoa-nut in large goblets, and grapes preserved in their natural shape. One cocoa-nut makes a tumbler of limpid water sweet and agreeable. His open apart ments let the cooling breezes blow through, and we rejoiced an hour in the shelter from the July heat of December, and the stimulus of a Long Branch July breeze.

Then comes a walk through Progresso. This city, like our new Western enterprises, is better laid out than settled. It has its straight, broad streets running through chaparral, its grand plaza, with scarcely a corner of it yet occupied, its corner-lots at fabulous prices. That corner opposite the custom-house they hold at two thousand dollars. Others a little outside of the centre you can buy as low as fifty dollars. That is better than you can do on the North Pacific, where on a boundless prairie they will stake out a lot twenty-five feet by a hundred, and charge you hundreds of dollars for the bit.

The market-place is a projecting thatched roof over the side of a one-story edifice. On mats sit brown old ladies with almost equally old-looking vegetables. Here are oranges, bananas, black beans, squash seeds boiled in molasses, a sort of candy, and other esculents, to me unknown. Among them is one called euchre. Never having known what that too-familiar word means in the nomenclature of the States, I thought I would find out its meaning in Yucatan, so I invested a six-and-a-quarter-cent bit in this game of chance. I received a piece of the root—for so I judged it to be—looking like a cross between a turnip and a carrot. It was white, of various shapes, round, square, long. My piece was about as large round as a child's wrist, and as long as its hand. I tasted it, and was satisfied with euchre as an article of diet. If others, on one taste of their sort, would as quickly discard it, they might safely be left to make the experiment. But even my friend, the Rev. Mr. Murray, can not effect the prohibition of that appetite in that way. It is likely this would grow with tasting, as the other does, for it was sweet and not disagreeable, being like the turnip and carrot in nature as well as in looks. If it could replace the fatal fascination of its synonym, I should be glad to see it introduced into our country.

The houses of Progresso are of one story, of mortar or thatch, covered with a high roof of thatch. This high roof is open inside, and makes them shady and cool. The sides are also often of thatch, and they look like a brown dwarf with a huge brown straw sombrero pulled over his eyes. Some of those built of mortar have ornamental squares in the sides, where shells are carefully set in various shapes in the mortar, and which make a pleasing effect, the diamonds and other shapes giving the walls a variety that is really artistic. Why could it not be imitated in larger buildings at home? One house had the word "Sepulcro" in large letters chalked along its front. "What does that mean?" asks one of the party. The occupant was sick a long time, and the boys thought it was about time he had died, so they chalked that word along the door to express their conviction of his duty. He ought to be dead—dead he shall be called. A grave joke, that.

Here I first tasted the sort of chocolate of which Montezuma was so fond, and which he took so thick as almost to make it an edible. A brown, brawny woman made us a cup of the same in a bamboo-sided, rush-roofed café. It was worthy Montezuma's praise: Parisian chocolate takes the second place hereafter, and a good way below the first. It is prepared in milk, and is a thick, soft liquid that melts on your tongue and "goeth down sweetly, causing the lips of those that are asleep to speak." That dame would make her fortune by such a café in New York. But, then, she probably wishes for no fortune, and her secret, the secret of all the dames of the country, may never be revealed outside the land itself. You must come to Mexico to know how "chocolatte" can taste.

The fields about Progresso have chiefly shrubs of the cactus order. Beautiful flowers of purple, yellow, and crimson abound. Here grows wild the heliotrope, the fragrant purple flower that is scattered so generally at funerals. The sweet-pea and other cultivated delights of the Northern hot-house and garden are blossoming abundantly.

The cocoa-palm throws out its long spines, deep green, thrust straight out from a gray trunk, that looks as if wrapped in old clothes against the cold. This gray bark is a striking offset to the dark, rich leaves, which are the branches themselves. Where these leaves push forth from the trunk, from ten to fifty feet from the ground, a cluster of green balls, of various sizes and ages, are hanging. This green rind is an inch thick. Then the black shell known to us is reached, and inside of that, not the thick white substance we find on opening it, but a thin soft layer, or third rind, the most of the hollow being filled with milk. Later in the season the milk coagulates to meat, and the cocoa-nut of commerce is completed. It is cultivated extensively here, both for home use and the Northern market.

The people are chiefly Indians, not of the Aztec, but Toltec variety. This is a nation hundreds of years older than the Aztecs, and who are supposed to be the builders of the famous monuments of Central America, and to have been driven from Mexico southward about a thousand years ago. They are of the usual Indian tint, but, unlike our aborigines, live in comfortable houses, are engaged in industrious callings, and dress in a comely manner.

Both sexes wear white, the men and boys having often one leg of their trowsers rolled up, for what purpose we could not guess, unless it be for the more cleanly fording of the brooklets and mudlets that occur. It was a token of neatness, if that was the reason, that was very commendable.

The women wear a skirt of white, and a loose white waist separate from the skirt, and hanging sometimes near to the bottom of the under-garment. This over-skirt, or robe, is ornamented with fringe and borders worked in blue. The head-dress is a shawl or mantle of light cotton gauze, of blue or purple, thrown gracefully over the head and shoulders. One lady, evidently thinking well of herself and her apparel, had a ring on every finger of each hand, and gold ornaments hanging profusely from her neck. I have seen many ladies who, if they distributed the rings singly on each finger, would not find both hands sufficient for their display. This light-brown laughing madam had her limits seemingly, beyond which she would not go—eight rings and no more.

As a proof of the industry and intelligence of these natives, let us go to a hacienda, or farm, a mile out of town. Though it is a short walk, yet having ordered a fly for a longer ride, we employ it on this excursion. We did not take the carriage of the country, which is a basket on two wheels, about the size of a cot-bed, which cot-bed itself lies on the bottom of the basket, and on which sit the passengers. A wicker covering bends over about two-thirds of this bed; the rest is open to sun and rain. Three mules abreast make this fly fly.

Our three little mules drag a sort of covered coach on high springs, narrow and jolty. They run under the whip and scream of the muleteer. The gate of the hacienda is soon reached. A lazy Indian boy opens it. We rush between a green wall of cocoa-trees a score of rods to a thatched-built house, large, well-floored, high-roofed, clean. The brown lady of the mansion welcomes us, and I try to buy a hammock. She asks three dollars. I have no gold, and she despises greenbacks, whether of Washington or Havana. So the bargain fails. The same thing I have since seen offered in Boston for less money. It is cheaper sometimes to buy your foreign curiosities after you get home.

Her boys take us to a cocoa-nut orchard, pluck off the nuts, split them with a sharp cleaver, and pour their milk into a glass. We drink in honor of the host. An old man runs up to us, with nothing on him but a pair of white pants, a cleaver stuck in his girdle behind, and a straw hat. He offs hat with both hands, and bows low to the ground. Had Darwin seen him he would have protested that he was the man primeval, built ages before the English Adam, who is (to Darwin) the height of attained, if not attainable, civilization. His face looked very like a monkey's, and his posture also. Yet this ape of modern false science was a gentleman of fortune, and industry, and sagacity, who had subdued five hundred acres of this wild land, and made himself a property worth six thousand dollars even here, many times that in the States. He raises hemp and cocoa-nuts, and is rich. His manners were gracious, and when he found he could not talk with us, he bid us

3

good-bye politely, and hastened away as fast as if he had a note to pay, and only five minutes more left to pay it in, and no money to pay it with. His boys remained, and waited on us. One of our party offered him a couple of cigars, which he passed over to a little girl of his tenant's, being too much in a hurry, if not too much of a gentleman, to smoke. So our primitive gorilla disappears in a farmer of to-day. So will all scientific humbugs disappear.

The chief business of this place is the raising of jenequen, or hemp, pronounced heneken. It has the thick, green, sharp leaf of the cactus. A large traffic has sprung up in it at this port; not less than five thousand bales are exported annually to New York, or two million pounds. It is used in making ropes, and has a growing and extensive value. It is worth six cents a pound here, and pays about ninety-five per cent. on its cost of culture, so that it is a very valuable article of commerce. Its finer varieties are as soft as silk. It is destined to be more and more a source of union between Yucatan and the United States.

We roll in the warm surf of the sea—a Christmas luxury not enjoyed at Newport and Long Branch, but which was delightful at Progresso—and dine at our friend, the collector's.

There is no church in the place, and this chief man, though a Romanist, invites me to establish our church here. The chief corner of the grand plaza is still unoccupied, and the Methodist cathedral can be built there. It shows our opportunities, at least, and the liberality of this people, though perhaps it is too much like the sort we find in Western towns, where they will give any body a church lot in order to make the other lots the more valuable. Yet these simple-hearted natives ought to have a Sunday-school and Christian teachings, songs, and ordinances; and we hope some time to see the offer accepted, and such a church flourishing at Progresso. Some Christian body will undoubtedly take possession of the field, as a preliminary to the city near by, which is white unto this harvest. Whoever enters into this inheritance will find a pleasant possession.

Our day's delights have kept us beyond the hour appointed by the captain, and we pull for the steamer with fears that she will pull away from us before we can reach her. The wind is contrary, the rowers weary, the night deepens, the waves roll, the lantern on the ship becomes a star. We fire pistol-shots and kindle paper, and they send up colored lights and fire the cannon. Our fires and shots they do not see or hear. Two hours of fear at being deserted, of questionings as to what to do in such extremity, of yet greater fears that the big black waves rolling high about and beneath us will roll bigger and blacker above us, of tests of inward quality of courage and faith, in which the most believing do not always prove the most courageous, and we come up at last, with great rejoicing, to the huge ship, with its many lights and warm cheer, looking like the palace of home and heaven, riding upon the waters of death. So may that palace yet welcome us all!

The stay-aboard company are thoroughly alarmed at our long absence. But when the fear and congratulations at our safety are over, they follow the example of the Irish mother and her lost child, so affectingly depicted by Hood, whose wailings over him lost are speedily replaced by scoldings at him found. To protect ourselves against their retorts, the rhymist of the party prepared, on the rolling deck, a defense, which, like all poetry, has permitted exaggerations mingled with its truth—a sort of wine-and-water fiction and fact that can be easily separated. As a memento of a lazy moment it may be worth inserting here. If one seeks to sing it, he can employ the tune of "My Maryland," which is the old college air of "Lauriger."

> "The scoffer's boat is off thy shore,
>   Yucatan, my Yucatan;
> Our feet are on the collector's floor,
>   Yucatan, my Yucatan.
> His cocoa-milk and grapes are sweet,
> The cooling breezes gently greet,
> His household dames are mixed and neat,
>   Yucatan, my Yucatan.

"The dinners that we find in thee,
    Yucatan, my Yucatan,
Surpass all else in luxury,
    Yucatan, my Yucatan.
There 're monkey tongues and lizard steak,
And parrot's brains and chocolate;
What *cárne* strange and delicate,
    In Yucatan, my Yucatan.

"The jenequen is growing fine
    In Yucatan, my Yucatan,
To make the hemp for rope and twine,
    Yucatan, my Yucatan.
The hacienda, with its trees
Of cocoa fluttering in the breeze,
Whose fruit is tossed us by monkeys,
    That's Yucatan, my Yucatan.

"There Darwin finds his primal man,
    In Yucatan, my Yucatan,
Of monkey looks, but sharp as Van',
    Yucatan, my Yucatan.
He makes his bow with double grace,
His pants alone are in their place,
His gait is a Chicago pace,
    Yucatan, my Yucatan.

"Rings on each finger and each toe,
    Yucatan, my Yucatan;
The ladies ornament them so,
    Yucatan, my Yucatan.
White robes and thin to ankles go;
Night wrapped in day, a pleasant show;
Such are the dames of Progresso,
    In Yucatan, my Yucatan.

"Oh, 'tis a pleasant land to see,
    Yucatan, my Yucatan,
Lying along that summer sea,
    Yucatan, my Yucatan.

Long will its memories linger sweet
Of flowers and shells, and mules so fleet,
In our far-off and cold retreat,
    Yucatan, my Yucatan.

"May churches, schools, and enterprise,
    Yucatan, my Yucatan,
Gladden thy golden sands and skies,
    Yucatan, my Yucatan.
May railroads, built by Palmer Co.,
Carry great crowds to Progresso,
And Parish into parishes grow,
    In Yucatan, my Yucatan!"

III.

THE SEA-PORT.

Under the Cocoa-nut Palm.—The Plaza.—The Cathedral.—No Distinction on account of Color either in Worshiper or Worshiped.—The Watering-place of Cortez.—How the Palm looks and grows.—Other Trees of the Tropics.—Home Flowers.—July Breakfast in January.—Per Contra, a Norther.—Its Utility.—Harbor and Fort.—Size and Shape of the City.—Its Scavenger.—Its Houses.—Street Life.—The Lord's Day.—First Protestant Service.—The Railroad Inauguration.

My friend, Theodore Cuyler, has written many a racy talk for *The Evangelist*, with the heading "Under the Catalpa." He is outdone this time—a hard thing to do. He can not write "Under the Cocoa-nut Palm;" nor can he write, as I might also, "Under the Tulipan," whose great scarlet blossoms are now blushing over my head; nor "Under the Chinese Laurel," which a slight change in my seat would enable me to do; nor "Under the Australian Gum-tree," a tall elm-like tree, first brought here by Maximilian, and which rushes up to forty and sixty feet in a few years, in this hot air and soil. I have made a point on him, though it took many a point by sea and land, and many a mile from point to point, to gain even this slight advantage.

I am sitting on a green slat-wood and iron lounge, such as are scattered about the Public Garden of Boston and the Central Park of New York, though they are not much occupied there after this fashion on this New-year's-day. The Plaza de la Constitution, the only plaza of Vera Cruz, is where this bench is located, a square of about three hundred feet to a side, which is well filled with trees and shrubs of every sort of tropical luxuriance, with flowers of many hues and odors, a large bronze fountain in its centre, and benches girdling its circumference. Carlotta's gift is this, they say, to the city.

The sun lies hot on the house-tops, and wherever it can strike a pavement. The general costume consists of a shirt and pants: the shirt white, short, plaited all around, and worn often by the

GOVERNOR'S PALACE AT VERA CRUZ.

peasantry on pleasure-days as an outer garment—a not unseemly arrangement. Every body is in gay costume, for is it not the first day of the year? And, in addition, does not the daily morning paper, named *El Progresso*, on the ground, probably, that it never progresses, declare that it is an extra festival-day, because on this day occurred the circumcision of Saint Odilon, and the birth of Saint Euphrosyne the Virgin? Who these are, it does not deign to declare.

But that sun creeps round the corner of the church on this seat, and blazes so fiercely that I must fly or be consumed. Another cocoa-nut palm welcomes me; really another angle of the great church on the opposite side of the street.

That church has just concluded its service—a service without song, or preaching, or audible prayer, or aught else but genuflexions and osculations, and mutterings and millinery. Yet it was filled with women and children dressed in their best attire, and in one respect was ahead of any church I have ever seen in America: all classes and colors meet together. On the same bench sits the Beacon Street lady, in her silks and laces, and the poor beggar in her blue tunic, with her mantle carefully brought up on her head in the church, "because of the angels." The Indian, Negro, Spaniard, all are here, often rolled together in one. Not the least dressed and genteel are these Indian dames of high degree. When shall our better type of faith and worship equal this in its one grand principle, "Ye are brethren?" How hideous a mockery must a white and a colored church appear to the Lord, who is Maker and Saviour of us all! The Romanist is putting this fact assiduously before the mind of our Southern caste-bound brothers. It is their only stronghold; God give us strength to surpass them in this grace, as we have in all else. Not doing thus, we shall find our excellent ointment sending forth an offensive savor, and their offensive ointment surpassing ours in sweetness. Among the wax virgins of this sacristy is a negress, the adaptation of this Church to its votaries being thus signally marked.

I have just returned from an excursion to Medillin, some twelve miles into the country, the summer watering-place of Vera Cruz. It is winter now, and out of season. From March to June that Saratoga reigns. The consul-general of Mexico, Dr. Skilton, and the consul of the port, Dr. Trowbridge, were my companions—two physicians who won a high name in the army, and deserve and honor the stations they occupy. The air was soft as June, and our thin clothes, even to seersucker and linen, were all that we needed, and more. Flowers of every hue and fragrance blossomed along the way.

The cocoa-nut palm abounded, of all heights and ages. The older ones had a smooth bark, made of its own dead leaves, crowned with long, bending branches, made up of spines like ribs going out of a backbone. It begins in these spines, and they seem to grow together as new ones shoot out, so that the trunk is itself a leaf. These leaves hang dead and loose in their upper edges, ragged and gray, but bind the trunk at their juncture. Every new burst of leaves gives a new cincture and a new raggedness. The rains wear off the rags, and the old trees stand smooth in bark, with the rings marked upon the bark of these successive growths of leaves. They are of every height, from a few feet to a hundred.

You see on the ride many tall, wide-branching trees of the acacia tribe, with a light gauze leaf; others of deepest green, and wonderful for shade, which are not unlike the maple in shape, but are denser of color and shade. That is the mango, whose apple even the foreigners put as the front fruit of the world, and which, therefore, may have been the very apple that tempted Eve and ruined Adam.

I have not yet followed the example my first mother and father set me, if this be the fruit, and I can not therefore say how strong was their temptation; for though the leaf be green exceedingly, the time of the mango is not yet. The banyan, orange, banana, and other trees, too numerous to mention, especially when you do not know their names, throng the road to Medillin. The convolvulus, or morning-glory, of every color covers the roadside, with its running vine and flowers. And there, on a little marsh, raises its sweet and lovely cup, the water-lily, blooming here just as deliciously, and just as superior to all rivals, on this January the first, as it will blossom unrivaled in the ponds of New England the July following.

A stumpy old man brings a bouquet of roses, common blush and white, for which we pay two reals, or twenty-five cents, and that is as much again as he expected. In this we count thirty-eight large double roses in blossom, with buds many. Had that been bought for a New York table on this New-year's-day, it would have cost nearer ten dollars.

The country people are coming to town; for it is somebody's feast-day, and the railroad opening too. This modern secular and ancient ecclesiastical holiday, joined together, is too much for the Aztec. So he has donned his spotless white, and she her spotless gray; for the female human bird, like the feathered biped, is here less gorgeously arrayed than its male. Off they tramp to the city. His shirt, plaited and polished before and behind, depends over like-lustrous trowsers, well buttoned on the side with tinkling bell-buttons that rattle, if they do not ring, to the music of his going. Some are on horseback. Two trotting near the track get frightened at the cars, and back their steeds from the path. A broad ditch is behind the narrow way, and one of the horses plunges therein and tips his clean rider over into the black mush. A loud laugh is all the consolation he gets for the splash and its ruin of his holiday costume.

Medillin is a town of sheds, roofed with thatch, and a few houses of brick or wood, with broad arcades for drinking, dancing, and gambling. The season not being on, none of these were going on, except a breakfast or two, which were excellent. It certainly seemed out of place to wander round that open garden, full of roses and oranges and all manner of hot-house plants, on this New-year's morning, and to sit in the open hall, eating as delightful breakfast as my "International Moral Science Association" brother of Ireland ever got up at somebody else's expense. But the cool hall was a pleasant refuge from the heat, and we found the watering-place refreshing in January. A river, used for bathing, makes it the favorite resort of Vera Cruzians. Cortez frequented it, and built a chapel there. He seems to have done that everywhere; piety and impiety being nearly equal in him.

As we go to the cars, I measure the leaves of lilies growing wild along the track. From the central joint to the tip, I could lay my arm from the elbow to the tip of the finger—just a cubit, or a foot and a half. The whole leaf was over two feet in length, and of corresponding breadth. This was the size of nearly all of them. An Indian and his wife were gathering oranges. Huge fruit, as big as small pumpkins, hung from bushes not unlike the quince. Such is this land; are you not home-sick for it? If so, let me make you contented to stay where you are, by trying to describe that indescribable horror which you must or may encounter to get here.

I had heard of simoons and cyclones, and hurricanes and Hatteras storms, but till I touched this Gulf steamer I had never heard of a "Norther." I began to hear hints about its possibility, and how, when it raged, no ship could leave Havana or land at Vera Cruz; that it occurred about every four or five days this season of the year, and that every seaman disliked and even dreaded it.

Our vessel had pushed on a swift and even keel to the last day but one. I was about concluding that the semi-qualmish state would not develop any more violent stages, and was even getting ready to follow Byron, and stroke the mane of this wild beast of the world, that rages and devours from shore to shore—even as a scared child, holding firmly to the parental arms and legs, may rub its tiny hand on the neck of the huge dog that has frightened it— when, lo! at five o'clock in the morning, after leaving Progresso, I was slung violently up and down, clinging in desperation to the door of the room, which was, fortunately, fastened back to my berth. The ship seemed on its beam-ends. Up and down she flung herself in a rage of fear or madness. Up and down we followed, sick and scared.

After much ground and lofty tumbling, the berth is abandoned, with great reeling and sickness, for the deck. Perched among the shrouds that lash the base of the mast, or reeling along the side of the drunken vessel, I enjoy the Norther. The sea is capped with foam; the waves leap short and high; the boat goes down these sharp and sudden hills of water, and is hurled back on its haunches by trying to mount the hills coming up on the other side of the hollow. How she staggers and falls down, and picks herself up and is knocked down again, and blindly rears and as blindly falls! Her freight has been chiefly left at Havana and Progresso, and so she behaves worse than she might have otherwise done. I had never seen so crazy a creature on the sea. I thought the long swells of the Atlantic, the short surges of the Mediterranean, and even the chopping waves of the English Channel and the Huron Bay bad enough, but this Mexican Norther excelled them all. Do you wish to pay that toll to see this garden? It will pay; for sea-sickness, like toothache, never kills.

There was not much done that day except to lurch with the lurching ship. "Now we go down, down, downy, and now we go up, up, uppy." Now on your back, and now on your face. Still we contrived to sit it through, and to have a good talk on religion with a Boston gentleman, who, like so many of his city, had no religion to talk about, being not Christian, nor even Pagan, not so much infidel, as faith-less: not anti-believing as non-believing. Like that ignorant backwoodsman who, being asked if he loved the Lord Jesus, honestly replies, "I've nothing agin him." Yet he that is not for Him, having known of Him, is against Him, and so non-Christianity is anti-Christianity.

How much is Christian faith needed in that Christian town! And what a record have they to meet who have taken away our Lord, and given the people a stolid self-reliance, or more stolid fatalistic indifference as their only religion! But our lively friend could sing—what Bostonian can not, since the Jubilee?—and he mingled "Stabat Mater," "Coronation," and camp-meeting melodies in a pure Yankee *olla-podrida*. May this song-gift yet lead the singer to the grace it springs from and to!

Toward night the winds and waves abated slightly, and after midnight they lulled to sleep. But long after the Norther had blown itself away, the waves rolled slow and steady but deep and long, as if they themselves were tired out, and the steamer swung to and fro evenly and weariedly.

As the storm is gone, so that more violent one of sin shall blow over, and the race of man, like a convalescent but tired child in the arms of its mother, shall rock itself to sleep in the arms of its Saviour, God. Cowper's words, so befitting that sick and weary ship-company, are not an unbefitting prophecy. I was comforted with them as I lay in that tossing berth:

> "Six thousand years of sorrow have well-nigh
> Fulfilled their tardy and disastrous course
> Over a sinful world; and what remains
> Is merely as the working of a sea
> Before a calm that rocks itself to rest."

Are our present waves the passing away of this Norther of sin? Is the level sea of universal grace and goodness appearing? It is; but perhaps many a Norther must yet rage before the heavenly and perpetual calm prevails.

A good word may be said for most of God's creatures, and the Norther has its bright side. But for it, Vera Cruz could not exist. It may create qualms on shipboard, but it drives away the yellow fever on shore. Its coming concludes that pestilence, though it is said to also conclude the lives of all prostrated with the disease at its coming, their relaxed system succumbing to its over-tonical force. So we may accept the lesser evil in view of the greater blessings that it brings, and rejoice that Northers rage in the Gulf of Mexico.

The reason why this storm prevents a landing is that there is no real harbor here, and the situation of the port is such that the north wind drives the waves straight on and over the mole, its only dock, which is a few hundred feet long. The waters rise and roll over this wharf, and prevent all landing. Indeed, the waves could hardly allow a boat upon them, were a landing possible, so high they mount. When it is on, communication ceases, and visitors to the ship, or sailors on the shore, have no means of getting to their own place. Yet all this could be cured by a few score thousand dollars. The castle lies two miles, perhaps, from the shore, and reefs extend a third of the way toward it on the northern side. A breakwater could easily be built over the rest of the way, and the harbor of Vera Cruz laugh at the peril of the north wind, and enjoy its refreshment. Some time the government will make this improvement. Yet "*mañana*" (to-morrow), they would say here: their word for all enterprises and duties.

Our Norther has subsided, and we enter the sunny bay, on the last Saturday morning in December, as warm and delicious a morning as ever broke over New York Bay in June, as George L. Brown's painting of that city superbly represents. The walls of the city of the True Cross break on the eye—a speck of superior whiteness amidst the glittering sand-dunes that inclose it, but a whiteness that does not increase as you approach. Small palms scantily scatter themselves among the sand-hills, and thin grass and a parched vegetation, though far-away hills lift a solid terrace of green to your fascinated eyes, and, towering over all, Orizaba raises its snow-capped spear, a peak of unequaled beauty. All the zones are around and before you, from Greenland to Abyssinia.

The harbor is empty of shipping; only four or five vessels lie on its dangerous sea. The famous castle, San Juan d'Ulloa, is a large, round fortress, of a dingy yellow. A castle impregnable, it is said, except to assault, which was never attacked that it was not taken. Cortez professed to expend thirteen millions upon it; and Charles the Fifth, once calling for his glass, and looking through it, westward, was asked what he was looking for. "San Juan d'Ulloa," he replied. "I have spent so much on it, that it seems to me I ought to see it standing out on the western sky."

We anchor off the costly folly, and are greeted by officials and friends. Boats soon put us on the mole, and we are in the sea-port of the United States of Mexico.

This city consists of sixty acres, be they more or less, inclosed with a begrimed wall, from ten to twenty feet in height. Boston Common is not far from the size of Vera Cruz; its burned district

VERA CRUZ.

considerably larger. It has one principal street running back from the shore a single block. A horse railway passes down this Calle Centrale once a half hour or so, and for a real, or twelve and a half cents, takes you the near a mile that street extends. But it takes no one, as all who have money have no desire to leave the block or two about the plaza; and all who are obliged to go from centre to circumference have no money. So the Spanish Yankee fails of success in this enterprise.

One street runs parallel with the Centrale the entire length of the city, and two shorter ones fill out the arc that the rear wall makes. Eight or ten cross these at right angles. That is all of the True Cross, viewed geographically. Numerically, it has fifteen thousand inhabitants, of whom over one thousand are foreigners, and only about five thousand can read or write. The Indian population predominates in numbers, and the Spanish in wealth and influence, though the Mexican is a conglomerate of both, and each in its separate or blended state is without social degradation or distinction.

Its chief street has two arcades, with little markets and tables for brandy or coffee sippers. It has a score or two of stores, some with quaint names, such as "El Pobre Diabolo" (The Poor Devil), over a neat dry-goods house, whose merchant thereby humbly confesses he does not make over "one per shent" on every two. Another has B. B. B. as his initials: "Bueno, Bonito, Barato" (good, pretty, cheap).

The streets are narrow, as they should be in hot countries. Tiny rivulets trickle down their centres, and disinfectants in the sickly season nightly cleanse these open sewers.

Another and a more important source of its cleanliness is the buzzard. I had been taught to detest the buzzard, perhaps because it was black. I had heard how unclean a thing it was, and was exceedingly prejudiced against it. But I find, to my surprise, that here this despised and detested creature is the sacred bird, almost. It darkens the air with its flocks, roosts on the roofs, towers, steeple-tops, everywhere. A fine of five dollars is levied against one who shoots one of them. It is the most privileged individual of the town. The reason why? It is the street-cleaner. It picks the offal from gutter or sidewalk, and nothing escapes its hungry maw. Its business may not be cleanly, but its person is. It never looks soiled, but its black wings shine, and its beak is as white as "store teeth." It looks like a nice house-maid whose service does not make her soiled. It is a large bird, looking like the turkey, though of a different species, and of a broad, swift wing, that sustains it in long flights. It appears very solemn, the priest of the air, especially when it sits on the cross of the churches, one on each arm frequently, and one on the top. Once I saw two thus sitting on the top, one on the other, as quiet and churchly as though each were carved in stone. Hood says,

> "The daw's not reckon'd a religious bird,
> Because it keeps a-cawing from the steeple."

But the buzzard comes nearer that desert, and by its solemn air, clerical garb, and sanitary service, may claim a place in, as well as on, the sanctuary. Perhaps some foes of the cloth might say its greediness and determination to have the last mite, if alive, was also a proof of this relationship. At any rate, unlike the daw, it is the protected if not the petted bird of the city, and helps keep off the pestilence, which has a blacker hue and more horrible nature than the worst of its enemies ever attributed to it. Honor to this faithful black servant of man, as to those featherless bipeds of like hue, that are more worthy of our praise for their more excellent service.

The houses hug the narrow sidewalks, each with a large portal opening into a roofless court, and with windows scantily piercing their second story. They very rarely go higher. Not a building inclosing the chief plaza is above this height. Hotel, warehouse, and governor's residence close with the second story. The third occasionally appears; but fourth and fifth, up to seventh and eighth, with Mansard roofs — two stories more — these Paris and New York luxuries are here unknown. Why? Because the earth gets sea-sick here. Ex-President Hill's theory, that a fire is fed from below, and must be put out by pouring water on its base, and not on its summit, obtains here in regard to earthquakes. The earth shakes from below, and would topple down these towers on the haughty heads that dared to lift them up. So the city well-nigh reaches the Sybarite perfection Edward Everett Hale approves, and is hardly ever over two stories, and is much of it of his perfect perfection of one story. These houses are of mortar or stone, all of them, and very broad of base and thick of wall. They hug the earth so close that she can not throw them off. She must tip herself clean over, before she can turn these houses on the heads of their builders. Those builders' heads were level, and their works are also.

The wind flows through the open windows, cool as the midsummer sea-breeze—never cooler. The streets have donkeys, carrying water in kegs, milk in bottles, charcoal (their only fuel) in bags, grasses for thatch, and other burdens. A carriage I have not yet seen. One is said to exist here, but it is not visible to the naked eye. A few horses are used, chiefly by the haciendados, or farmers, riding into town. Even the ladies turn out on foot to the grand reception to the President on the opening of the railway to the capital. The horse-car is the only vehicle, and that is useless. The city is a Venice, but for its mules and asses.

The fountain at the head of Callé Centrale is a favorite resort for these few beasts, and for many water-carriers. There is abundance of water; and nowhere in this country, or any country, are there cleaner streets or superior baths. Yet buzzard and bath, free fountain and washed street, do not keep off the yellow fever. The walls, some think, cause it, as they shut out the winds—the only thing they do shut out, every foe easily subduing them. They should be leveled, if they kill thus those they pretend to protect.

The business of the city is quite large. Some houses do a million and a half a year; for here come about all the goods of Europe and America that enter Mexico. But the houses that get the trade

FOUNTAIN AT VERA CRUZ.

are foreign, and chiefly German, so that the people of the country are still poor, poorer, poorest.

The Lord's Day is an unknown institution in Vera Cruz. The Spaniards have given it the right name, properly distinguishing between the Sabbath, which they give to Saturday (Sabbato), and the Lord's Day (Domingo). We could follow their example. It would save much debate, and clarify and steady many a conscience, if we could see the Lord's Day in our nomenclature. We should then perceive its sacred delight and obligation. Yet if it turned out with us as with these, the name had better be left unchanged. *Stat nominis sacri umbra;* and only that shadow stands. All else is gone. The shops are open, the workmen busy. The church is attended once, as in the mummeries this morning. Then the circus came riding down the street; the clown and two pretty boys ahead, preparatory to performing outside the walls. It was the first band of music I had heard on Sunday since that which awoke me in Detroit last summer. How sad and striking the resemblance! Shall our German infidelity and mis-education make our land like Mexico? Or shall a holy faith and a holy life make this land like the New England of our fathers? As Mr. Lincoln said, "Our nation must be all slave or all free;" and as One infinitely greater said, "A house divided against itself can not stand;" so America, North and South, the United States and Mexico, must be all Christian in its Sabbath sanctity, or all diabolic.

I walked out in the afternoon to the cemetery, feeling that the best church and congregation were to be found there. The way led over the alameda, or a short bridge across a tiny stream, which is lined with young cocoa-nut palms, and stone seats for loungers. Here Cortez once built a bridge ten feet or so long, for which he charged the government three millions of dollars, making even Tweed lower his haughty front before this Castilian grandeur of thieving. The Church of Christ stood a little beyond, with huts of the poor near it—a church where funeral services are mostly performed. A poor old man was kneeling on a bench near the door, with arms outspread, and agonized face, muttering earnestly. Oh that he could have been spoken to, so that he might have been taught the way of life more perfectly, and might have gone down to his house justified and rejoicing in the Lord Jesus, to whom not one of his muttered prayers was addressed!

The Street of Christ leads out half a mile to the Campo Santo. Well-named is that street, if lowliest people are nearest him, and if the grave is his triumphant goal.

The walls of the grave yard are high and deep. Tall obelisks stand at either corner. The dead sleep not in the open area, which is unoccupied, but in the walls. Tablets cover the recess that incloses the coffin, and words of tenderness rather than of faith bedew the marble. Not the highest faith. No such beautiful words as are found on the monuments of the saintly dead of Protestant climes shine forth here. Northampton has no rival here, that choicest of grave-yards in its simplicity of elegance and richness of Scriptural and Christian quotation. Mount Auburn is surpassed, however. I heard the Misses Warner once say they had found scarcely any motto of Scriptural faith and hope in that cemetery. It is as stony in its faith as in the hewn and polished walls that engirt each tiny lot. It has marble dogs, and granite sphinxes, and bass-relief expressmen, wreathed pillars, and statues of men of renown, but rare is a monument or a line of faith. It will strike others thus. Edwards, and Fisk, and Wayland ought to stand in marble among its statues, and Christianity speak from its faithless, glittering graves. Let those whose believing dead are buried there make them preach their faith from their sepulchres.

Yet in the Campo Santo itself I found food for meditation, if not in its inscriptions. I gathered its flowers, growing wild and beautiful over its area, and returned as from a Sabbath-day's journey, strengthened in the Gospel truth and work.

That evening, through the kindness of the American consul, a congregation of nearly thirty gathered in his rooms, and held a Christian service. "Rock of Ages" and "Jesus, lover of my soul," were sung, and the word spoken from "To you that believe, he is precious." It was the first service the Holy Catholic (not Roman) Church ever held in that city. It was good to be there, as many felt. We found young men at work on the railroad who were members of the Baptist Church. Those who were, in order or education, Presbyterians, Methodists, and Episcopalians, were also present. It seemed as if the day-star was about to arise over this long-darkened soil. If schools were established here by Christian teachers, and a service held regularly in English, the nucleus of a church would be organized, and the work soon be extended to the native population. This first Christian service has not proved the last. Already the Presbyterians have a flourishing mission. Others will doubtless follow.

The city is putting on its best bib-and-tucker, for to-morrow President Lerdo de Tejada is to arrive. and great is to be the rejoicing. The government residences are being tastefully arrayed, and coats of white, yellow, and blue wash are spread over all the buidings surrounding the square. I never knew before how easily and cheaply one can renew the face of a soiled wall. That cathedral looks as if built yesterday. True, if it should rain to-night, it would be badly streaked, but it can not rain, for

> "To-morrow will be the happiest day of all the glad New-year;
> To-morrow will be, of all the year, the maddest, merriest day;"
> For Vera Cruz is joined to Mexico, and Lerdo comes this way.

This last line is not in Tennyson.

To-morrow came, but not the President. Every body dressed himself in his best; the streets were trimmed with lanterns; a green pavilion was arranged at the station; but he came not. Announced at ten, re-announced at five, the soldiers marched down the streets, all colors, officers and privates, and all mixed together, just as they ought to be in the United States. The people fill the balconies, house-tops, and walls. The boys jeer, and hoot, and whistle, as if they were Yankees. Still he comes not.

Somebody drops a real in the passage-way, kept open for him by the soldiers, and a bit of a black boy, very pretty and very prettily dressed, is pushed out for it by older boys, white and olive, who dare not risk the attempt themselves. A soldier holds him back. His mother, a bright, comely lady, stands behind him, watching him with mingled fear and admiration. She is afraid those olive-colored gamins, of fourteen years or thereabouts, full of roguery and rascality, will burn her boy's fingers in pulling that most desirable silver chestnut out of the martial fire.

While all, officers, soldiers, lads, and loungers, are intent on that shining mark, a bright boy, dirty and brown, in the employ of the street lamp-lighters, comes down the path to help locate some temporary lamp-posts, sees the real, catches it, and is off, amidst the laugh of the crowd. So the successful man is often the last on the field of conflict.

It grows dark, and we give it up, and so do many others. At

eight he comes, but nobody sees him, and Vera Cruz has spent a day in waiting, and spent it in vain. The sound of the vesper bells floats sadly into my ears, as I write close under the towers of the Cortez Cathedral. How long before more Christian bells shall sweetly summon more Christian disciples to a more Christian worship? How long?

The opening for Christian work is not surpassed by that of any city. It should be taken possession of by the true Church of the True Cross. The foreign element alone would make a large congregation. They can all understand English. The natives are horribly neglected, and would respond to earnest missionary effort. It is the sea-port of the country, and many sailors visit it. The danger from yellow fever is not great. Gentlemen who had resided there fifteen years laughed at the fear of strangers. It is certainly no greater for ministers than for merchants. It is a good centre of influence and departure. It should be speedily occupied. Let Cortez's dream be fully answered, and Vera Cruz preach and practice the perfect gospel of Christ crucified.

IV.

THE HOT LANDS.

From Idleness to Peril.—Solitud.—Chiquihuiti.—Tropical Forests.—The Falls of Atoyac.—Wild Beasts *non sunt*.—Cordova and its Oranges.—Mount Orizaba.—Fortin.

Vera Cruz soon wearies. Even the generous hospitality of our consul, whose table and couch have been mine for days, could not make it lovely long. The mountains draw like the Loadstone Mountain of the "Arabian Nights." The consul-general comes from the capital, and by due persuasion is enticed not to wait for the president's return, but to climb back after the old fashion, the stage-coach and the robber; for though the railroad is finished, that does not insure one a ride over it. Until the president returns over it, no one can, except he gets passage in a dirt-car, and takes the mountain morning coldness, without shelter, and almost without a seat. How long we may have to wait for his return, *quien sabe?*—(who knows?)—the universal answer here to all inquiries, as *mañana* is to all orders. So we get as far as is allowed us on the railway, and then take to the stage.

There are several reasons prompting us to this course. The stage is a vanishing institution. A week or two hence there will be no staging between the sea-port and the capital. We must indulge it now or never. Then we are told it is exceedingly dangerous. Robbers abound, and they will not fail to lose their last opportunity to black mail the coach. So it will give the romance of peril essential to a first-class excitement. It is also a horrible road, and men affirm that they would endure any torment they or their friends could be subject to, especially the latter, rather than make the trip again—and then go and make it. Why not we?

It has, too, the *cumbres*, or mountain precipices, so steep that we are led to imagine the stage will tumble off by sheer pull of gravitation and centre of motion ; the passengers rolling down, back first, faster by much than they rolled up. The peril of those "who gather samphire, dreadful trade," must be encountered, or Mexico is not truly done.

And, lastly, the ride all night in a crowded coach full of garlic and tobacco and pulqui, and all abominable stenches, is set forth to frighten the novice from the attempt. But it only whets his appetite. The water feeds the flame, which has got so hot,

"The more thou dam'st it up the more it burns."

The ride in a coach full of dirty and offensive natives, over horrible roads, up precipices that incline the other way, they are so steep, among robbers, all night long—it shall be taken, and it is. Any thing to get out of Vera Cruz. That orange is sucked thrice dry.

My companion attends the governor's soirée in honor of the president until two of the morning, and I turn him out of bed at three to take the unwelcome trip. We start at about four, sleepily and snugly tucked away in the luxurious cushions of an English rail-carriage. For night-riding, or any other, this sort is superior to the low-backed seats of the American car, though inferior to our sleeping-coaches. A nice nap, and the day wakes up, and so do we. The landscape stands forth in its summer warmth of color. We are out on the Tierras Calientes, or Hot Lands. They are moderately level, seemingly thin of soil, but probably more dry than thin. The dog-tree abounds, and is in full blossom. Its white flowers look lovely, and make one fancy that something like peach-trees are growing wild over all the country. Solitud, some twenty-five miles out, is a station where coffee, cakes, bananas, and oranges are disposed of to the half-sleepy passengers. It was at this place that the French, English, and Spanish ambassadors held the convention which resulted in the invasion of Mexico by Maximilian. They made but little, in pocket or fame, by that attempt to resist the Americanizing of America. It will be the last effort put forth by Europe for the colonizing of this continent. From Isabella to Victoria, for nearly four hundred years, the attempt has been kept up. The seed is well sown. Its future growth must be from our own soil. The crowned heads must lay their crowns at the feet of this crownless one, on whose head are many crowns. The land lies idle and desolate for fifty miles. It is undoubtedly susceptible of culture, for rich tropical trees, with their heavy foliage, are not infrequent, and the open pastures are fit for grazing, and occasionally feed a few cattle. But the insecurity of property blights all the land. You can hardly cultivate bananas close to your door without fear of losing your crop through the wild marauders of the region. Life is of no consequence to them, compared with a few oranges or cocoa-nuts, and so the region is almost without inhabitant.

At the distance of about fifty miles the mountains draw near, the first terrace above the plains of the sea.

Chiquihuiti (pronounced Chee-kee-whee-tee) rises along the landscape, cutting the edge of the lowlands as sharply as a house-front cuts the land out of which it arises. This is the beginning of the table-lands of Mexico, and of the snow-capped volcanoes of Popocatepetl and Orizaba. We wind up into it, and are astonished by the profusion of its tropical verdure. The scanty gleanings of the lowlands had not prepared me for this superabundance. The gorges are deep, the heights lofty, and from lowest depth to topmost height there is a flood of green. Such trees and leaves I had not imagined possible in midsummer, and this was midwinter. The trees were compact together, some of familiar forms, such as oak and birch, but of unfamiliar richness. Others among them were new members of the family. The acacia-tree was the largest and the most prolific in species, and it spread itself in huge branches, and towered above its fellows as by natural mastery. Yet it is light of substance, and some of these iron-like woods undoubtedly and justly despise their vain brother. Many sorts of these hard woods are here, awaiting the horrid steam saw-mill that shall eat them all up, and ship them to New York, and make this green, grand wilderness a desolation.

How sorry I am to be compelled to think that some Yankee speculator in lumber from Bangor to Brainerd will read these lines, and be up and off in the next steamer for Vera Cruz and the splendid woods of Chiquihuiti! Cortez did not sigh more for Mexican silver than these lumbermen will for these mahoganies, and rosewoods, and other equally polishable delights. Black-walnut will be of no account when the Mexican lumber reaches the Northern market. Give us a good fill, dear ancient forests, of your green delights, for the Yankee wood-sawyer is coming, and you will soon be no more.

The roadside is lined with immense palms, whose leaves are each themselves almost a covering for the body, while the castor-oil-tree spreads its broad wing along the way, hated of all youth, loved of not all doctors.

Convolvuli of every hue throw their vines and flowers over these palms and taller trees. Our old morning-glories were growing wild, and make our path a perpetual "pleached bower" of beauty. The orchids hang on the taller trees, or sit in nests in the crotch, parasitic plants of every color making the tree into nosegays. They are a fungus, and seem to prefer decayed trees; perhaps themselves decay them. Some that are stripped of leaf and bark glow like a June rose-bed in the radiance of these curious plants. There are hundreds of varieties, and have attracted of late much attention from botanists, and have even got into literature.

About ten miles up, the road winds round a gorge that sinks hundreds of feet below, and whose upper side comes together in the Falls of Atoyac.

This is one of the most beautiful water-falls I have ever seen; I might say the most beautiful. It is not stripped of its trees, as is Minnehaha, who sits shivering in her nakedness, as unhappy as the Greek Slave. Nor does it come, like that, from a level landscape. The hills rise all around it a thousand feet and more.

The sides of these hills from base to peak are densely covered with trees, whose leaves are almost a solid mass of green. The white water leaps from this green centre a hundred or two feet, into a curling, foaming river, and into a darkling mirror of a pool. The whole scene is embraced in one small circumference, and you seem to pause trembling on the bridge that spans a side of the ravine, before you plunge into a tunnel, hanging hundreds of feet

OLD BRIDGE OF ATOYAC.

above the lovely spectacle, with an admiration that is without parallel in any small fragment of American scenery. May the Mexican Government preserve the Falls of Atoyac and their enchanting surroundings from the knife and the factory of the spoiler.

Are there monkeys or wilder beasts in these woods, or parrots, or birds of paradise? Of course they will all tell you that they abound. But when you ask one if he ever saw any, he shrugs his shoulders,

One gentleman says: "I ate armadillo steaks in a cabin on top of that mountain overhanging the Falls of Atoyac;" but he did not kill the choice lizard, and so I receive his assertion with some incredulity. Every body says monkeys are here, but nobody says he has seen them. They say that they have retreated away from the railroad, a sad reflection on Darwin's theory; for should they not accept the higher life to which their posterity have attained, and begin themselves to build railroads, and cut down timber, and speculate in corner lots, and eat armadillo?

The parrot is here, but does not flash his plumage among the trees. Only on the perch of the ranchos do we see his beauty and hear his ugliness. The cougar is reported present; one gentleman, and he a man of veracity, declares he saw a young tiger, or old cat of this species, as he was resting his stage legs by a tramp up another spur of these mountains. But I think the real sight was when he sat at meat that day, and beheld on the table a roasted creature, with a great gray-yellow eye staring at him, and saying, "Come eat me, if you dare." Asking the waiter what it might be, he was answered, "*El gato del monte*" (the cat of the mountain). Like they of the Rimini story, who read no more that day, he ate no more that day. That cat was a reality. Whether the cougar was or no, you must judge. *Quien sabe!* and a shrug is all I say.

A run of a few miles through verdant fields, by coffee-haciendas and banana-groves and orange-orchards and tobacco-fields, and Cordova is reached.

This ancient city of Cortez lies in an open plain, surrounded by mountains. The railroad leaves it a little to the right, and in a deeper vale, so that only its dirty church towers and domes are visible to the eye. It is a decayed town, but under the stimulus of the railroad may revive, especially if pure Christianity can come in here to energize and educate its people. Pure Christianity has come in. The Methodist Episcopal Church has already lay preaching in this city, and a society well gathered. The redemption of this fine old Spanish town is begun. Let it go on to a millennial completeness.

The fruit-sellers at the dépôt give us six oranges for three cents, and as many bananas for the same money. A picayune goes a good way. The oranges are very delicious. Havana and even Joppa are dry to these juicy Cordovas. They bleed at every vein. It is almost impossible to prevent their flowing over your lips on to your garments, like Aaron's oil. Could they be got into our Northern market, they would drive the mean little sour Messina

ORANGE GROVE, CORDOVA.

and the thick-meshed fibrous Havana from the fruit stalls. And why not? Vera Cruz and Cordova are nearer New York by twenty days than Messina, and not two days farther off than Havana. The fruit-boats that go to the Mediterranean of the Eastern Continent should come to the Mediterranean of the Western. Five thousand miles against a little more than five hundred, and this rich fruit against that lime, falsely called orange. Here lies the tropical garden of our land. Let us make it commercially our own.

This commerce is increasing. One haciendado, or farmer, west of the city of Mexico, sends to market one hundred and thirty thousand cargoes of oranges annually from his plantation. A cargo is a donkey burden, and weighs three hundred pounds. This makes almost twenty thousand tons. I give this tale as it was given to me. If you ask whether or no it is true, I answer, after the country's fashion, *Quien sabe?* You must remember that a hacienda often covers many square leagues, so that if devoted exclusively to this fruit, it could produce a vast quantity. Whether that statement be true or not, it is true that the fruit is the best of its sort I ever tasted, and that it could control the markets of America.

The plains about Cordova are very rich, and bear all manner of fruits the year round. The scenery is as grand as the soil is fertile. Mountains thousands of feet high rise on the west and north, green at the base, bare and black at the summit, while just before you, as you look and move westward, stands forth that perfect Orizaba.

I never remembered hearing of this mountain before, though a cultivated fellow-traveler informed me it was frequently referred to by English and Spanish writers. This statement set the memories and the wits of the listeners a-running, and a mass of quotations, as well adapted to this market as the "quotations" of change are to it, were fished up from the English poets. Probably a like knowledge, or ignorance, would have given like results from Calderon, The Cid, Lopez de Vega, and other like celebrities. For instance, had not Byron said,

> "Orizaba looks on Marathon,
> And Marathon looks on the sea?"

and also told us,

> "He that would Orizaba climb will find
> Its loftiest peak most clothed with mist and snow."

And Scott tells of his experience here, in the well-known poem beginning

"I climbed the dark brow of the tall Orizaba;"

though its brow is whiter than a blonde Caucasian's; and Sheridan Knowles makes Tell say,

"Orizaba's crags, I'm with you once again."

Emerson's "Monadnock" and Lowell's "Katahdin" are misprints for this splendor of a mountain. Surely English poetry is full of this name. Strange that one never saw it before.

It is worthy of its fame, for in this hollow among the hills it puts on especial majesty. You are well up to its base. The distant ocean and sea-port view is exchanged for one near at hand. Though still sixty miles away, it seems to rise at your very feet. How superbly it lifts its shining cone into the shining heavens! Clouds had lingered about it on our way hither, touching now its top, now swinging round its sides. But here they are burned up, and only this pinnacle of ice shoots up fourteen thousand feet before your amazed, uplifted eyes. Mont Blanc, at Chamouni, has no such solitariness of position, nor rounded perfection, nor rich surroundings. Every thing conspires to give this the chief place among the hills of earth. None these eyes have seen equals or approaches it in every feature. It will yet win the crowd from Europe to its grander shrine.

It is not difficult of ascent, in this being inferior to Europe's Mont Blanc, if that be an inferiority which makes its summit and the view therefrom accessible to ordinary daring.

The three Mexican volcanoes have been often under foot, though not till Cortez came was this achievement known. His men, in the exuberance of their superiority, scaled the peaks near the city, and astonished the natives by their feat. They brought back sulphur from the crater for the manufacture of powder, thus bringing the fatal mountain in more deathly shape home to the poor Aztec.

A run of five miles brings us as far as we are allowed to travel by rail; and Fortin concludes the luxurious cushions of a first-class car, and transfers us to the hard seats of a *diligéncia*. Misfortin it might be phonographically called, for here exit ease and pleasure, enter peril and pain.

V.

ON THE STAGE.

Our Companions.—Vain Fear.—The Plunge.—Coffee Haciendas.—Peon Life.—Orizaba City.—The Mountain-lined Passway.—The Cumbres.—The Last Smile of Day and the Hot Lands.—Night and Useless Terror.—"Two-o'clock-in-the-morning Courage."—Organ Cactus.—Sunrise.—The Volcano.—Into Puebla and the Cars.—The three Snow-peaks together.—Epizaco.—Pulqui.—"There is Mexico!"

BEHOLD us at Fortin, paying eleven dollars for our stage fare to Puebla, and three more, lacking a quarter, for three valises of moderate weight; eating a hasty plate of soup and nice cutlets, with fried slips of potatoes, washed down with Mexican coffee, which is usually first-rate; not so here. "Stage is ready!" jabbers in Spanish a brown boy. All boys are brown here.

Our seats are taken in a Concord coach made in Mexico, a big, tough, lumbering, easy affair when the roads are easy; when they are rough, it jolts and jumps as if the spirit of the paving-stones inspired it with their madness when they are whirled by a mob. But it is made to stand the jumping as well as the rocks that rock it, and tosses its human contents as unconcernedly as a juggler his balls. There are only five passengers, the first giving out of the dismal programme so faithfully served up to the affrighted appetite. These five men were the two Yankees, who, of course, had neither garlic nor tobacco about them, though one of them smoked all the time, but they were the best of cigars, and three Mexican gentlemen, on their travels to see the inauguration, one a son of a senator from Yucatan, and one an archæologist, and his friend, a light, German-looking gentleman, who had just been exploring the regions of Ixmail, which Stephens has so well described and illustrated. So the second terror disappears. The gentry chat freely with the Spanish-speaking Yankee, and all goes merry as the presidential reception the night before.

The road that was said to be so fearfully and wonderfully not made, is broad and smooth the first ten miles. It winds down a steep hill for two or three miles. The torrid January sun pours its heat fiercely on the coach. The driver and his boy are in their shirt-sleeves, and the passengers wish they were. The drivers have skin and hair-covered overpants for the coming Cumbres and midnight. Cottages line the roadside, half hidden amidst huge

A PEON'S HOUSE.

banana and coffee bushes, tall mango-trees, and flowers of every hue. The cottages are chiefly of cane, with sides not over four feet, and roofs rising ten to twenty feet, some even taller, giving them much coolness and airiness, the great desiderata. Brown women are busy at their household tasks, and brown children lie, like beetles, lazily in the shade or sun. The parrot screams and jabbers, and picks its handsome coat of its unhandsome parasites, poised on perches at times, but not always put in cages. Nature is jammed full of life. Who dreams of the snow-fall of death that now covers all that north country, and makes the poor so poor, shivering over their scanty fires? Are these poor not the poorer? you will ask. I fear the answer will be in your favor. And yet that does not make one like the ice and snow and zero atmosphere any the more. Give these poor New England's religion, and they will be vastly her superior in climatic conditions.

GREAT BRIDGE OF MALTRATA.

We plunge down the steep road, a race of the horses' heels with the coach's wheels as to which shall touch bottom first. The heels touched bottom all the time, and of course reached the bottom of the hill ahead of the wheels, but only a length ahead. High along the side of this exceedingly steep hill creeps the railroad, making some of its most surprising feats of engineering as it winds and leaps across this chasm. It becomes almost circular in its twists and turns.

The coffee haciendas line the roadside. The bush is usually small, not over six or eight feet high, and spreading out like a barberry-bush. The berry is scattered over it, having a reddish tint, sometimes quite light. It is picked of this color, and ripened to its familiar brown by exposure on mats. You see it spread out in the door-yards, for this is its harvest-time. The sun is too hot for the coffee-tree, and so they plant bananas and other taller and thick-leaved trees among it to shade it from the direct rays. It wants heat, but not light.

The Mexican coffee is among the best in the world, the best Colima berry at the west coast selling as high as a dollar and a half a pound. It is prepared very strong, and then served up with two-thirds hot milk, if you are not acclimated. As you become so, the proportion of milk disappears, until it is well-nigh all coffee. But the coffee-house boys always bring two pots, one of coffee, one of hot milk, and pour at your pleasure. Here, too, one of Dr. Holmes's proofs of the millennium is satisfactorily settled:

> "When what we pay for, that we drink,
> From juice of grape to coffee-bean."

The juice of grape is still here a fabulous beverage. Logwood is too plenty, and grapes too few. But the coffee *is* coffee. As Thurlow Weed says he always eats sausage serenely in Cincinnati, because there hog is cheaper than dog, so here coffee is more plentiful than chiccory or peas, and one can feel assured that he tastes the real article. It will become more and more an article of export, and replace the Rio berry, to which it is far superior in flavor and softness, even if it does not rival the Java and the Mocha. Among the beverages that will drive out the gross intoxicants, lager and whisky, is this pleasant Mexican coffee.

Orizaba has such an entrance as gave our critical companion a right to justify his charge against the road. The stones that once paved it lie knocked about on the surface. Deep holes abound.

VIEW OF ORIZABA.

and the stage reels to and fro among the stones and pits like a very drunken man, and the passengers follow its example. A half mile of such a tumble and we strike the pavement, which is not much better. The whipped-up mules fly over its boulders, and we jump up and down like a small boy on a high-trotting horse. The street is long — very long it seems to us — the houses of one story, and of no especial beauty that we could see in our unseemly dancing.

At last, "after much turmoil," we fly ferociously up to a long high wall, pierced with long high windows, well protected with long high bars, a single story, and striped prettily in fancy colors. At the big portal we stop, with a jounce worse than all that preceded, and beggars of every degree welcome us to the Hotel Diligencias of Orizaba. How they whine and grin and show off their horrid rags and sores! What a commentary on Romanism! It breeds these human vermin as naturally as the blankets of its worshipers do the less noisome sort. The more "piety," the more poverty; the more of workless faith, the more of this idle work.

The pieces of our broken bodies are put together after a fashion, and we stretch our legs an hour about the town. A live mill keeps the town chattering, and gives it an unusual Mexican activity. But for that, only earthquakes, of which it has a goodly share, and the arrival of the stage-coach, would make it sensible of motion. The houses are all of one story, because of these earthquakes. A Southern gentleman told me that once, when here, a wave came, and he rushed into the court, and clung to a post for protection, while the ground rocked like a sea. He never was so frightened in his life. Well it may cause fear, for the still and solid earth is about all the basis most people have for faith or any thing else.

The church here has a picture on its façade of a priest stopping with his hands a pillar half fallen, and a motto, which was too far up for my dim eyes to read, that probably told how he had by prayer prevented the falling of that church. Mr. Tyndall will have to come down and correct these errors of faith, for as Pope, modified, says (one might prove thus that he also knew of the great volcano near),

"If Orizaba totter from on high,
Shall gravitation cease if you go by?"

Why not? Here a church seems to have been upheld. If not churches, souls certainly have. The overfaith of Romanism is no worse than the underfaith of Tyndallism. Between the extremes lies the middle path of truth and safety.

A ravine goes through the town, luscious with tropical foliage and fruit. Above it hangs the chattering mill, which on its edge catches its water and busily makes the native wheat into flour. It was the first factory I had seen in Mexico, and therefore doubly interesting. Twenty-five dollars for a barrel of flour should generate more grist-mills and wheat-fields, if protection is the true policy. The narrow lanes run through banana gardens to the open fields, and grand black mountains rise close around, while the huge peak that gives the town its name towers, white and smiling in that golden midday, far above the clouds.

RIVER AT ORIZABA.

Orizaba is the favorite resort of the gentry of Mexico. Being on the railroad, it has outstripped its rivals, Jalapa and Cuernavaca, and bids fair to be the winter home of the big city. Some of the finest estates in the world are perched on its hills and hidden in its hollows. They enjoy the perpetual luxury of every tropical produet, with the pyramid of ice ever cooling the fancy, if not the air. It will be the favorite resort as well of wanderers from the United States of the North.

The cars here begin to really climb the Cumbres; four thousand feet they accomplish in less than thirty miles. It is holding on by the eyelids.

> "The boldest held their breath
> For a time."

As they go, step by step, up the sides of these gorges, which "ope their ponderous and marble jaws" to swallow up that smoking, puffing insect which crawls like a beetle, its rings each separate car, along the almost precipitous sides of the huge *barrancas*, a hand thrust out on one side would touch the mountain, on the other stretch out over thousands of feet of empty space between it and the rocks below. The road is the finest bit of engineering on this, if not on any, continent.

The stage-road twenty miles from Orizaba is the grandest I have ever traveled. It is smooth and pleasant of itself. The crazy Mexican ponies that it took so long to start are off, at last, with a leap and a whirl, and the one-storied, if not one-horse, town is left behind. The way is nearly straight, very level, and lined on each side, at the distance of a mile or two, with a succession of cliffs. They stand out of the valley as sharp as if lifted up in frame-work by human hands. Their origin is clearly volcanic. The sharp cut, the iron-like look, the wave shape, the striated lines, like the lava of Vesuvius, all prove their origin. They are two to four thousand feet high, I should say, on a passing glance. The valley between is rich in every fruit and flower and shrub. Here is a river gliding along, fringed with heavy willows, larger and compacter of leaf than their temperate-zone brother, but of the same bending and hugging nature. No English river bank was ever more lovely in adornment, or more hidden from the passing eye. The hills are mostly rock, without the possibility of culture, but on some of them grasses and trees have sprung up, and goats and sheep find pasturage and shelter.

The pass is without parallel in any spot of Europe or America for its symmetry and grandeur. Interlachen has taller mountains, but not so perfect a valley. For a score of miles you never leave these mountain walls. Like the sphinx-lined pathway to Theban temples, they seem to guard the road to the distant capital. They end fittingly in true Spanish and Mexican grandeur, which is stately from beginning to end.

The Cumbres are their stopping-place. These, too, had been a part of the sup of horrors forced down the resisting will by those who would compel it to abandon its purpose.

We enter upon a still more romantic experience. The path winds up, back and forward, so frequently as almost to make it look from beneath like a series of parallel lines. This wall concludes the valley as completely as if it had been built by nature as a dam across its green river. There is a perfect pause. No way out of the valley in this direction but up this wall. It is not of rock, but of hard earth burned in this ceaseless sun, and supporting a little herbage and a few trees. They also conclude the Tierras Calientes, or Hot Lands, of the shore and its first wide terrace.

The valley itself terminates exquisitely. It lies, a basin of green, between the hills, a mile or two wide, the most of it under culture, and cut into tiny strips of varied tint, brown, green, golden, according to its products. A bit of a village, with a small, dingy white church, is on its southern edge. As we climb the steep face of the mountain this smiling *parterre* lies lovely below. It looks not unlike the meadows of Northampton from the top of Holyoke, only our height is twice or thrice as great, and its breadth is not a fourth as large. The setting sun looks lovingly on this bit of rescued nature among the black and bare hills, and as we wind our way up, every new ascent makes it look the lovelier, as it grows the more diminutive. It is a baby landscape, and all the more charming for its infantile littleness.

The sun goes down as we go up, and by the time the top is reached, the baby, in its cradle of lofty hills, has gone into shadow and approaching sleep. A light twinkles from a window far down there, like the smile of the eye before it closes in sleep, and the mountain valley of Orizaba, with its *petite* perfection of a termination, disappears from our view, perhaps forever; for the stagecoach gives way to the rail-coach, and leaves this grand defile on a side-track. Its path is on the northern side of these hills, through a like but not more lovely valley.

This summit properly concludes the Tierras Calientes. They are of two classes. The low flat belt which lies along the sea, and which extends back some fifty miles to the base of the mountains, and the first terrace of the hills. This terrace is about three thousand feet above the sea. It seems to engirt the whole Mexican range. It extends from Monterey to Oaxaca. Pronounce this "Whahaca," and you will find it easier to handle than it looks. On this shelf, not quite half-way up to the level of the capital, is found the most fruitful section of the country. Here are perched along the eastern side of the country such towns as Monterey, Jalapa, Cordova, Orizaba, Cuernavaca, and Oaxaca. This is the best region for the production of the banana, orange, coffee, sugar, and other semi-tropical fruits. The cocoa, pine-apple, rubber-tree, and other more tropical products belong to the plains by the sea.

This terrace, too, contains the favorite gardens of the land. Its cities have been the winter retreats of the rich men of the capital ever since the country was occupied by the Europeans. Jalapa lies the lowest, being sixty miles north-west of Vera Cruz. It is said to possess the finest view of gulf and mountain of any city. It was on the high-road to the capital before the railroad took a more southern route. Cortez passed up its pass, and Scott followed. To-day it is on a side-track. Its jalap, pronounced as it is spelled, brings grief to those children whose doctors adhere to the old practice. Should you adopt its Spanish pronunciation of halapa, you would avoid that disagreeable reminder.

Cordova and Orizaba are on the same side-hill, and are to-day the favorite resort of the Mexican gentry, the latter especially. Here, too, are the repair shops of the railroad, so that quite an English-speaking population is growing up about this spot. Cuernavaca, to the south, is on the same rich belt, and was the chosen seat of Cortez. We are yet four thousand feet from the top level of the land, though the crawl of an hour or two up the face of this dam has lessened that altitude.

Our mules have rested while this lesson on topography was being given, but they must now hurry forward, for night and danger are on us. Give your last glance into that deep south valley, that mountain-lined passway, that last of the villages of the Hot Lands.

A group of horsemen passed us when we were half-way up, red-jacketed, broad-and-slouched-hatted, well armed, dark, and dangerous looking. Were they spying out the contents of the coach? We easily change them into robbers; not so easily, however, as they may change themselves into that shape. Night comes swiftly down. One realizes the rapidity of the flight of Apollo in Homer —he came like night—in these tropical countries. Our three Mexicans are left at Orizaba, and their places are taken by a revolutionist general, with his carbine, and a Frenchwoman who had been hostess at a hotel most frequented by robbers on the pass from Puebla to Mexico, between Popocatepetl and Iztaccihuatl— not very encouraging comrades for weak nerves. Our first station is a great robber haunt. The Red Bridge it is called—whether from paint or blood, who knows? Fear says blood; fact, probably, paint.

The lady offers me a cigarette, which is graciously declined. She is offered in return a rich Cordova orange, hanging on its stem and among its green leaves. This is even more graciously accepted. But extremes meet. The next morning the orange was found knocking about the coach. So both the cigarette and Cordova failed of reaching the lips to which they were proffered. She lighted, and smoked, and expectorated as perfectly as the rebel general before her, and showed she was all ready to lead a revolution or vote for Lerdo, as circumstances and *pesos* might offer. The latter is the stronger circumstance here, as everywhere. Dollars outweigh scruples, whether of conscience or of the apothecary.

The unsuccessful revolutionist said the people were getting sick of Lerdo. He did nothing. They wanted railroads and emigration; he opposed both. He was Spanish, and not American. When some one told Diaz, the rival candidate, that he would be the next President, "No," said he, "there will never be another President. By that time I shall be an American citizen." This is, much of it, the talk of the outs against the ins—mere bosh—Diaz probably being as little of an American as Lerdo after he gets elected. Yet some say that railroad enterprises will receive a check, and that the new President will install himself with the Church and reactionary and anti-American party. I doubt it. He is too wise. If so, the revolution is only the surer, swifter, and completer. I believe he will verify his antecedents, and lead the country in liberty, education, and improvement.

Our general debarks at the next station, and leaves the stage to three of us. Each takes a seat and stretches out *ad libitum*. Dust piles in on us as a covering, and, through the mouth, covering the inside as well as outside of the body. The moon shines clearly. "*Tres jolie pour le voyageur*," says the French lady. (Very pleasant for the traveler.) Indeed it is. The hills stand out clearly. The cactus hugs the dusty road, as thick-set as an English hedge or New England bramble-bushes on a country roadside. Its tall leaves tower like huge crowns, and show not so much the richness of the soil as the intensity of the heat. The organ variety is quite frequent, and looks, as it lines the road in the gray moonlight, as if we were riding through Springfield Arsenal. This does not make the terror less, unless we change the feeling, and fancy our road is through a vast organ. That changes the night to music, though we can not quite complete the quotation, and say,

> "The cares infesting the day
> Have folded their tents like Arabs,
> And silently stole away."

Cares, or fears, which are the soul of cares, still encamp about. A few shots from the sun will scatter them all. Here we are, six or seven thousand feet above the sea, and here flourish the huge-leaved plants that only hot-houses can raise in the upper States, and they at their best in but a puny shape. Crosses at the roadside show where some have been murdered, and help along our fears and faith with their *memento mori*.

THE ORGAN CACTUS.

The moon goes down as we drive at ten o'clock through the still streets of Saint Augustine, as still as when we leave them three hours later. Not a person or creature is abroad. The adobe huts are all closed, and every donkey ceases to bray and every dog to bark. The court-yard welcomes us, and a supper, not over-relished or over-relishable, and a bed, exceedingly relished. Out in that court-yard the tropical plants are diffusing their fragrance on the dark, soft, summer January air, as we hie us to our wished-for couch.

Three hours, and we are roused up, and are soon off. The mule-boy, well clad now against the cold, waves his flambeau, and the coach rattles out of the sleeping town.

The host has loaned us blankets and pillows, and we make our beds on the racking seats. The roads are bad here, and no mistake; at least they seem so in that two of the clock in the morning. Napoleon said that two-of-the-clock-in-the-morning courage was the most difficult to find. I agree with him. For the first time since starting I began to wish I had not come. The coach was cold, and knocked us about; the road was rough; the flambeau burned out; and aches and chills, and sleepiness without sleep, and perils by robbers, all made a mixture that required more than that sort of courage to face.

But we were in for it, and there was no retreat. Like Cortez, when climbing this same range, we had burned our boats behind us. *Nulla vestigia retrorsum.* So on we drag our slow length. The mules seem terribly lazy. We are sure that the mule-boy does not stone the head ones enough, nor the driver lash the rear ones. I had enjoyed (I fear I must confess it), when sitting on the top in the afternoon, seeing the boy shy stones at the three front mules. There are three tiers of mules—two in the thills, three before them, and three in front. The three leaders can not be reached by the driver's lash, and so the boy who accompanies him picks up a bag of stones, and lets them drive, one at a time, hitting the creature every time, and just where he aims—flank, neck, or ear. They did not seem to mind it much, cringing a little, and picking up a little, but not much of either.

The robbers do not make their appearance, the only disappointment we suffer. The weary hours drag along from two to five, when

> "Night's candles are burned out, and jocund day
> Stands tiptoe on the misty mountain-top."

How great the change that comes over the tired half-sleepers! My companion had fulfilled one Scripture, and I, having compelled him to go with me to Orizaba, went twice the distance of his own accord. He wakes and chatters. Madame the cigarettist rouses and rises. As a fond lover said on a fonder occasion, "Up rose the sun, and up rose Emily," so is it here. Popocatepetl puts in his appearance and Iztaccihuatl. (I want you to learn to pronounce these, so I keep inserting them. Do not skip them; they are very easy when you get the hang of them. Take them just as they look, and look at them that you may take them, remembering that "hu" is like "*wh*.") How quiet and grand they look in their glittering whiteness; the former a rounded dome of the Orizaba type, the latter a range of peaks, with less form and comeliness.

"Our Em'ly" lights her cigarette, and smokes as calmly as the smoking mountains, which do not smoke. I have seen no sign of a volcano in any of them. She is from near Strasbourg; and when she was told she was no longer French, but German, "No, no!" she exclaimed; "*Français toujours! L'Allemand barbare.*" But she was not French forever, and if Germany is barbarous, it succeeds.

The Indian village of Tepeaca is soon entered. A town when Cortez landed, and all Indian to-day, as is about all the rest of the country, it was a favorite place for him to retreat upon, and had no small influence in deciding his fortunes. It looks to-day as if it never could have influenced the fortune of the lowest nature, much less that of this lordly invader.

Soon the flame-shots come. The sun breaks suddenly and superbly on the black and weary night. Never before did I so feel the power of that other verse sung at the grave's mouth, the beginning of the night of death,

"Break from thy throne, illustrious Morn!"

What a shout will ring through the universe when that day triumphs forever over that long, long night of dusty death!

A cup of chocolate and a fresh roll, served by Indian dames, and we rattle down hill twenty-five to thirty miles, to Puebla. The fields open wide to the bases of the P. and I. aforesaid. You can pronounce them if they are not printed in full. Corn-stalks are standing in the fields, and in some instances the corn is being gathered. Melinchi, a high mountain anywhere but here, rises on our right, opposite the snow volcanoes. It is named for the favorite Indian mistress of Cortez, who, more than all other persons, helped him to conquer. It is the haunt of robbers, and its caves are dens of thieves.

We stop only once to change horses and to buy some pretty steel trinkets, pushed into our faces by boys and men, who seem to find the only patronage for quite extensive steel works in these passing travelers. They offer little flat-irons, spurs, cuff-buttons, and other well-executed articles of embossed steel.

The towers of Puebla soon come to view, and a long, wide, dusty thoroughfare, poorly kept up, leads us to the vale where the sacred city lies, seemingly close at the base of Iztaccihuatl, but actually sixty miles from it. We pass the fort over which French and Mexicans fought, by churches and churches and churches, into narrow, busy, well-paved streets, to our hotel court-yard, whence, after the immeasurable dust has been measurably removed, we go to the dépôt and start for Mexico. As we shall return here again, we leave it for the present undescribed.

If you want to know that luxury of modern civilization, the rail-car, put between the beginning and ending of your journey a twenty-two hours' stretch of staging in a mountain land. Then you will relish it. How vast these plains outspread themselves! What a change from the narrow terrace of the coast and the tumbled-up steepness of the intermediate country! We climbed seven to eight thousand feet from the base of Chiquihuite to Tepeaca, a distance of not over one hundred and fifty miles. It was all Cumbres. Here we have prairies as flat and broad as those of Illinois, but not as rich; yet, unlike them, bounded with magnificent hills, snow-covered and smoking, and black and comely. What would not Chicago give for just one of them? The road runs about a hundred miles through a dry, and lean, and level land.

At Epizaco, the halting-place and half-way house between Mexico and Puebla, we get a glimpse of the three snow peaks, the only place where I have seen them together. Orizaba lies low; his stony British stare being seen just above the horizon, while his upland rivals stand out in all their proportions. He is lower, not because of actual inferiority, but because he is farther down this orange of earth. They are all of nearly equal height.

Here, too, we get not only our last look at Orizaba, but our first at a filthy habit of man. Old folks and children thrust into your noses, and would fain into your mouths, the villainous drink of the country—pulqui. It is the people's chief beverage. It tastes like sour and bad-smelling buttermilk, is white like that, but thin. They crowd around the cars with it, selling a pint measure for three cents. I tasted it, and was satisfied. It is only not so villainous a drink as lager, and London porter, and Bavarian beer, and French vinegar-wine, and Albany ale. It is hard to tell which of these is "stinkingest of the stinking kind."

How abominable are the tastes which an appetite for strong drink creates! The nastiest things human beings take into their mouths are their favorite intoxicants. If administered as medicines, they would never taste them, except under maternal and uxorial constraint. And yet the guzzlers of England, Germany, America, and Mexico pour down huge draughts of sour or bitter stuff, all for the drunk feeling that follows.

The pulqui is a white liquor found in the maguey, a species of the cactus. It grows eight years uselessly as a drink. That year it becomes yet more useless by depositing in its centre a bowl of this juice. If picked then, all right, or all wrong, rather. Just as this central bulb is beginning to swell with its coming juices, it is scooped out, and a hole big enough to hold a pail is made in the bottom of the middle of the plant. Into this cavity for three or four months the juice exudes, and is taken out by the pailful daily. If the plant is left alone, this bulb shoots into a stalk ten to twelve feet high, with a blossom. It is this blossom which is exhibited in our States as the century-plant—a seven to ten years', and not a hundred years', blossom. Then it comes to seed and naught.

The chief traffic of the road is in carrying this stuff to Puebla and Mexico. It lies at the station in pig-skins and barrels, the pigs looking more hoggish than ever, as they lie on their backs and are tied at each leg and at the nose, stuffed full of this foolish stuff. It ferments fiercely, and the barrels are left uncorked and the pigs' noses unmuzzled to prevent explosion. You will see the natives sticking their noses into the hog's nose, and drinking the milk of this swinish cocoa-nut, even as they are dumping it on the platform. Never was like to like more strikingly exhibited than in such a union of hogs and men.

MAGUEY PLANT.

Thousands of acres are set out with the plant, a few feet apart, in every state of growth, from a month to its octave of years, when it sees its corruption, and the people begin theirs.

So have I seen, as Jeremy Taylor would say, the Connecticut Valley filled, from Hartford to Brattleborough, with a like large and deep green shrub, growing each by itself, putting forth broad leaves, not for the bowl of juice at its heart, but for the leaves themselves, which are not for food or drink, but for smoke. Shall the deacons and class-leaders and vestrymen of the only New England river valley find fault with these untrained and unchristianized Indians for making their soil to bring forth only one article, when they are in the same condemnation?

And worse—for this maguey plant is useful for many things, though it has one failing: the tobacco plant is useful for nothing. They use its leaves for all sorts of purposes: twine and paper, even needle and thread, roof and shelter. It is the good demon of the Aztec house. Though it does get drunk once in eight years, it is sober all the rest of the time. Our maguey is nothing if not narcotizing. True Christianity will, we trust, cure that defect, and make Mexico and New England and the West, in its abuse of barley and rye, alike free from the perversion of the gifts of God to our own unrighteousness.

The train sweeps round the mountain range of P. and L., and we come to their western side. Puebla is on the east of them. The sun pours a flood of glory over yet more western summits. Our friend quietly says, "There is Mexico."

It does not take long to look and admire. It lies under the blaze, a dim mass of points of fire. Its surroundings overcome us with their grandeur. Twelve miles away, where he spoke that word, is the eastern extremity of the lake on whose western end the city is situated. The brown spurs of Iztaccihuatl lie close to the edge of the lake. The land about it is almost on a level with it; salt marshes, in which the white alkali makes them look like snow. All round the farther sides of the lake black mountains stand. Other lakes lie hidden from our eyes about their bases. The water flashes in the setting sun.

Up these lowest spurs close beside us Cortez climbed and saw the wondrous valley and its waters, prairies, hills, purple and snow mountains, and resplendent city, and he vowed that it should be subdued to the Cross. With fearful expenditure of blood he accomplished his purpose, and gave it a bloody cross, instead of bloody sacrifice of human life. Looking from a like point out of this car window, the product itself of true Christianity, may we not imitate Cortez, and pledge the city that lieth like the very mount of God, in magnificence unequaled by any capital of earth, and all the surrounding region, not to a persecuting and debilitating Christianity, but to one that comes without a sword, comes with an open Bible, a joyful experience, a holy life, education, comfort, refinement for all, the true Cross and Church of our Lord Jesus Christ, who created this scene and its inhabitants for His own praise and glory? May they soon all glorify Him!

Soon Otumba appears, where Cortez fought his greatest fight, without a gun, or pistol, or horse, reduced with a score of reckless followers to the level of his foes. As he debouched through yonder western hills on this broad plain, after the Noche Triste, he met here hundreds of thousands of the Aztecs in solid rank. Cutting his way through till his arm and sword failed, seeing the palanquin of the chief, rushing for it, and striking him dead, he sends a panic into the multitude, who let him through to these lower spurs round which we have just run, on whose farther side, looking toward Puebla, or Cholula then, dwelt his faithful allies, the Tlascalans, who received him, and helped him organize a victory that has continued until now.

Not far from Otumba stand forth two pyramids of earth, like those of Cholula, called the Sun and Moon, each several hundred feet square and high, on a geometric line with each other as perfect as a Hoosac Tunnel engineer could have carved them, each now surmounted with a tiny chapel, emblem of their conversion to the Roman faith. They are the only Aztec remains of mark in all the valley; and they are probably Toltec, an ante-Aztec race, to which that warlike people were indebted for all their arts and refinements, perhaps also for their horrid barbarities of worship.

Guadalupe now appears on the right, a sierra not three miles from the city, the most sacred mountain of Mexico or America, and the most profane. A *via sacra* ran from it to the town, on which the penitent myriads walked upon their knees. Now our train rushes along it, regardless of shrines and kneelers and other vanities of faith. The worshipers have accepted the situation, and ride to and from the favorite seat of their goddess in the railway car, even as pilgrimages are now going on over Europe in first and third class trains. The times change, and we change with them.

The city glitters in the light of the setting sun. Its last beams are gathering on the peaks of the silent Alps that stand forth on our eastern sky, as they had stood on the western when at Puebla. We have run clear round them. They change their light to color, grow rosy in that flush sent from between the saws of Ajusco on the west, and then turn to the awful white of death.

Ere that the Hotel Gillow has welcomed us to its comfortable chambers, and we are housed like Cortez in the Aztec capital.

BOOK II.
IN AND AROUND THE CAPITAL.

THE VALLEY OF MEXICO, FROM THE AMERICAN OFFICIAL MAP.

I.

FIRST WEEK IN THE CAPITAL.

Hotel Gillow.—Cost of Living.—The Climate.—Lottery-ticket Venders.—First Sabbath.—First Protestant Church.—A Praise Meeting.—State of the Work.—The Week of Prayer.

Mexico begins well, though perhaps a good beginning may result in a bad ending. It was Saturday evening, at setting of the sun, that we landed at the Buena Vista station, just outside the city. The last rays had left the top of Popocatepetl, but were lingering yet in a rosy cloud above the snowy deadness of Iztaccihuatl. These two giant guardsmen are set to watch this lovely valley that circles beneath them, a girdle of hundreds of miles, itself encircled with a lower but not inferior range of mountains. The drive into the city is through a long avenue of green trees, past the Alameda, or park, half a mile square, well crowded with trees in their best June apparel, down the streets of San Francisco and Profesa, round the corner of the elegant Church of the Profesa, into the Hotel Gillow, a new hotel built on a part of the convent property belonging to the Church of the Profesa, and confiscated; but in this case built upon by the gentleman whose name it bears, whose son is a priest of this convent, who manages, if he does not own, the building, and who thus assists in desecrating a portion of the estates of the Church.

If a clergyman of the Roman Catholic Church may build, or control, and even give his family name to a hotel on sacred soil, a clergyman of the Holy Catholic Church may occupy a room in it without danger of profaning either it, or himself, or his church, or his landlord. So I enter a somewhat too sumptuous apartment for my means or my church. Yet, as it is the only one opening on the street, I take it till a less ornate one is vacated.

That is already done, and this writing is in a square and handsome parlor, for which the sum of forty dollars a month is paid; too costly for a long stay, but as Methodist preachers never continue in one stay, it may answer for a temporary sojourn.

Yet, costly as it is in this city, it is less than half, if not less than a third, what a like apartment could be rented for in a city of the States. With board at its *fonda*, or restaurant, at thirty-five dollars a month—four meals a day if you wish, and all you ask for at each meal—the whole expense is less than two dollars and a half a day, better for room and food than could be got in New York for four dollars a day. This may be reduced a little, yet not much. Board can not be much less, this ranging only at about one dollar a day; but rooms, unfurnished, may be had for a fourth of this amount, and furnished, if you take one looking on a court instead of the street, in any of the hotels, for about one-half. In this hotel they are twenty-five dollars; very clever rooms, too.

This long preamble is given for two reasons: first, to give you assurance of the practical nature of our mind, so that any fantasies of eulogy over Mexico and its environs into which we may subsequently fly may be considered exceptional, and not normal; and, second and chief, that any of our ice-bound, snow-driven, sleet-covered, cold-racked, and so-on-suffering friends of the North, who may have made more money than they are willing to give the Church, though not more than they ought to give, may know where to come and spend it and the winter.

It is a paradise of climates. The air is just right every day. A light cape is all you want across your shoulders, and that is to be worn in the house rather than out-of-doors, for the houses are cooler than the street. Flowers and fruits are everywhere, and very excellent in taste and looks. Great bouquets of violets and other delights, packed in the mechanical French fashion, learned, it is said, from the French, and improved on by the Aztec, are offered you for a York shilling and upward. The flower-girls stand or sit at the corners of the streets, sometimes old men and women, with their big and little bouquets on the sidewalk about them. Strawberries, blackberries, and green peas are cheap and good, blackberries fifteen cents a quart, and others in proportion, while bananas and oranges, and the fruits less familiar to us, are piled up on the table and forced upon a gorged appetite.

MEXICAN FLOWER-GIRL.

My windows stand open as I write, and the street cries come up into my ears. If I knew Spanish I might perhaps interpret them, but since, although I know English, I never can understand the street cries of New York, I fear all the Spanish I can ever learn will not give me the inside of the calls of the street. I suppose this I hear the most frequently is from the lottery-ticket venders, who stand along the sidewalks, and are the most numerous class of operators in the city. They call the various lotteries the holiest names: Divina Providencia, Virgin of Guadalupe, St. Joseph, The Holy Spirit, The Trinity, Purissima Concepcion, and such like. The most popular of these is that of the Virgin of Guadalupe. The venders wear a badge bearing their number, and for a *medio*, or six and a quarter cents, you can run the risk of getting or losing from one to ten thousand *pesos*, or dollars. These lotteries are largely operated by the Church, and are one of its sources of income. The sale of indulgences is another. The right hand and the left rob in the name of God, feeding the poor victims with false hopes of a fortune in this life, and with falser hopes of a fortune, thus acquired, in the life to come.

The morning after my arrival opened, as every morning does here, bright, mild, charming. The bells rang merrily, and my spirits were in corresponding mood. The Church of Jesus drew my steps to its door. This church worships in a chapel of the old Church of San Francisco. You pass through a garden full of beautiful shrubs and flowers in full bloom and leaf, making the courts of the house of the Lord fragrant with these lovely creations of the Lord. This garden is about thirty feet wide by a hundred long. Our Lord lay in a garden of like sweets. Here he dwells to-day. And as we pass through we breathe that beautiful thought, from one whose pen we hope again to see serving the Lord:

> "And as Thy rocky tomb
>   Was in a garden fair,
> Where round about stood flowers in bloom,
>   To sweeten all the air,
>
> "So in my heart of stone
>   I sepulchre Thy death,
> While thoughts of Thee, like roses' bloom,
>   Bring sweetness in their breath."

The chapel we enter on the side near its lower end. It is high arched, prettily frescoed about the altar, and is seated with chairs for about four hundred. It is nearly full. The worshipers are chiefly native, not over ten or fifteen Americans being present. They are dressed mostly with some attempt at cleanliness, their garb of the week being changed for the Sabbath. A few are in the soiled clothes of their daily toil. They are dark-colored, Indian in whole or largely, and all sit as promiscuously as they ought to do in more enlightened congregations. They are singing "lustily." John Wesley would have declared that they kept that word in his Discipline. They all sing, and sing with all their might. I never heard camp-meeting excel them in this heartiness and gusto. The words were simple and sweet, and the tunes likewise. None of them were familiar till the last one, in which I detected an air I had known, and, after a little, found it was, "I'm a pilgrim, I'm a stranger." I give you a verse of this. You can all sing it, and will find it not difficult to translate. It begins, "I am going to heaven—I am a wanderer—to live eternally with Jesus:"

> "Voy al cielo, soy peregrino,
>   Viveré eternamente con Jesus.
> El me abrió ya veraz camino
>   Cuando murió por nosotros en la crus.
>
> CORO.
>
> "Voy el cielo, soy peregrino,
>   Viveré eternamente con Jesus."[3]

They sung some four or five times, as often as in an American social or prayer meeting, intermingling their hymns with prayers read by the minister from a small pamphlet, with readings from the Old and the New Testament Scriptures, four Psalms, and a short, earnest sermon on The Wise Men—a recognition of the calendar of the Romish Church, which makes this the Sabbath of the Epiphany. The two ministers who officiated were dressed in white robes; one of them was white, and one an Indian. That was a good sight, these two brethren of diverse colors associated in this service. When shall the like be formally established in our more Christian America? I was gratified above my expectations at the spectacle.

The bedizened altar furniture was gone, and an open Bible occupied the place of the idolatrous host. Above it, in a circlet of immortelles in silver letters, was the name of JESUS. The service of song was full of Him. The prayers, lessons, and sermon were alike possessed.

Whatever the ultimate form of this movement, it undoubtedly has the right beginning, Jesus Christ Himself being the chief corner-stone. It needs direction, organization, education; but, as an outburst against a system which has so long suppressed this vital

> "I am going to heaven, I am a stranger,
>   To live eternally with Christ.
> He opened me the true way
>   When He died for us upon the cross."
>
> CHORUS.
>
> "I am going to heaven, I am a stranger,
>   To live eternally with Christ."

FIRST PROTESTANT CHURCH.

ity, it is divine. The Virgin is not here. The Son of God is alone, as becomes His nature and work. It is a protest against that false mediation and intercession. He has taken the work into His own hands. They sing His praises, they implore His salvation.

It is noticeable, too, as an incident of this movement, that they all are so full of song. The Roman Catholic Church does not cultivate or allow in its service congregational singing. It is as gay of plumage as tropical birds, and as songless. A trained choir gives elaborate masses and compositions with wonderful power in a few great centres of its worship, but its people do not sing. These converts are full of song.

It was delightful to taste the freshness of this spring of salvation, breaking forth from this long-parched ground. It was like Elijah's little cloud brooding smilingly over a land from which the rain of grace had been shut off, not merely for three years and six months, but for three centuries and a half. May it soon burst in blessings over all the land!

I stepped over last evening to a chapel opposite my hotel, where one of these congregations was holding service in connection with the Week of Prayer. It was after nine, and the regular meeting had closed. But there stood a group of twenty or so in the upper corner, "going it," like a corner after a revival meeting, in these same songs of Zion. Their leader appeared to be a young brother of twenty (the regular pastor was not present), and they all put in with all their heart and voice, a few sitting about on the benches enjoying the exercise. It was so perfectly Methodistic that I wished to go forward and tell them it seemed just like home. But a slight difficulty, somewhat like that which troubled Zacharias on one occasion, and which would last about as long if I staid here, prevented my making myself known and helping on the melody. I might have sung, however, for the tune I had heard the Sunday before, and the words I could pronounce, if not translate. The favorite hymn, which both congregations sing with great gusto, has this for its chorus:

> " No os detengais, no os detengais,
>   Nunca, nunca, nunca ;
>   Christo por salvanos dió
>   Su sangre cuando El murió."*

The way they bring out the " Nunca, nunca, nunca," is a lesson to many a languid and fashionable quartette and choir, a feebleness that has replaced and half destroyed our hymnal vitality. A half-dozen, who sing only a trifle better than the congregation, take away its office. Let these Mexican Christians lead them back into the divine way. They allowed parts to be sung by two or three

---

* " Do not detain us, do not detain us,
    Never, never, never ;
    Christ for our salvation gave
    His blood when He died."

voices at San Francisco, and the whole congregation joined in the chorus. It was an inspiration and a lesson to our degenerate worshipers.

No one will fail to recognize the spirituality and scripturality of these outbursts of grace in their long-oppressed souls. It is of the Lord, and, like all His doings, is directly and vitally antagonistic to the prevailing superstition. That prays to the Virgin; this to Jesus. That never allows the Bible to be read or heard of; this makes the reading of the Word of God a prolonged portion of the service. That suppresses the singing of the people; this powerfully employs that service of Christ. That has the prayers muttered in an unknown tongue; this repeats them jointly with the congregation in their own language. That has no sermon in this country, or very rarely; this puts the pulpit and its teachings as a part of every service.

I should judge that regular training, visiting, and educating were needed, that the work requires the culture, system, and force of a regular Church order; but I hope no forms or forces will ever repel, but only increase, the ardor and joy which inspired the hearts of these worshipers on that glad morning of the New-year.

The afternoon was spent in an English service, the second in that language ever held in this city. Rev. Dr. Cooper, of Chicago, conducted it. It was in a private house. He is an able and experienced divine, and his word that day was sweet unto the taste of the little company gathered in that upper room, a handful of seed on the top of this mountain-land, the fruit whereof shall yet shake like Lebanon.

A suggestion was made at that service that the Week of Prayer be observed in this city. It was a novelty, surely, that this Week of Prayer should be kept in this lately most hostile town, where five years ago one could have hardly kept erect when the procession of the Holy Ghost passed through the streets without endangering his head.

But a change has come. The Presbyterian missionary, Rev. Mr. Phillips, opened his parlors, and an Episcopalian, a Methodist, a

Congregational, and a Presbyterian minister joined with a few laymen and sisters in offering daily prayer, according to the programme set forth by the Evangelical Alliance. It was good to be there day by day, to hear the songs of Zion in a strange land, to feel that we stood at the fountain-head of this river of life which is breaking forth here at the touch of God for the cleansing of this nation.

The Congregational minister is Rev. Mr. Parks, sent out by the British and Foreign Bible Society to scatter that divine seed over this barren soil. He is a sower going forth to sow. He finds all sorts of soils. One colporteur in a three months' tour could not sell a single Bible. He contrived to give away a few hundreds. Another was beaten and driven out of Puebla, the second city of the country. Others find soil less rocky and less hardened by the wayside treading of centuries of Bible hatred, and some good soil is discovered, as these new movements show, which is yielding fruit already—some thirty, some sixty, and some a hundred fold.

Among those that attended these little meetings was Mr. Petherick, a devoted Wesleyan, and Colonel Rhett, a Confederate officer, in command for a time of the defenses of Richmond, who, though he perhaps can not yet see that slavery is a sin, being a South Carolinian (which people, like their kin in Massachusetts, never change), still is willing to let that system "go," and is devoting himself with a praiseworthy zeal to general Christian activity.

This Gospel Week will not be forgotten in the history of the Church in Mexico. It has shown to every foe of our Christ that the charge they may make against the division of Protestant Christianity is not true. Most of its leading bodies have here harmoniously sung and spoken and prayed. They are a unit in aim and endeavor, in spirit and in life. They are less separated than the orders of the Romish Church; Jesuit and Carmelite, Benedictine and Franciscan, being more hostile to each other than any of our American Churches. This Union Week foretells the Union Year and Union Age of the Church in these United States of Mexico. May it be more and more one in faith, in work, in reward, here and over all the world!

II.

FROM THE CHURCH TOP.

First Attempt and Failure.—At it again.—The Southern Outlook.—Popocatepetl and Iztaccihuatl.—Cherubusco.—Chapultepec.—Guadalupe.—The patron Saint of the Country.—Round the Circle.

THIS is the highest of all the man-built places from whence I have ever tried to talk. I am sitting on the top of the finest church in this city, except the cathedral—that of the Profesa. It adjoins my hotel, and is easily accessible from the azatea, or flat roof, of that building. The sun is burning his way down the western sky, setting masses of clouds on fire with his effulgence.

Two little girls, children of my landlady, have led me hither, and they are woefully frightened at a man in the belfry fixing the bells. In broken English, the older of the two makes known her fears, "Will he make nothing of me?" she cries. I relieve her, and soon she says her little sister calls her a "false fool" for being so alarmed.

Though the place is excellent for composition, the children keep me so intent upon their perilous pranks that I have no leisure for sketching. And so I sit and see the sun roll down behind Ajusca, the highest of the western hills, and behold the reflex glory on the white brows of the two south-eastern volcanoes, with their terrible names, flushed with the opposing sun, as the brow of death glows with the light from the sun beyond the vail.

The sun gone, the glory is gone; no twilight lingers here, as winsome as a morning nap. Abrupt beginnings and abrupt endings are characteristics of clime and people, with very gay and gracious interludes. The air grows chill as the sky grows dark, and the children and I climb the chancel roof, peep into the dome, and down into the church; that is, I do; they are too timid or too well trained. All is dark and silent save the ghastly pictures on the roof of the dome, which are silent but not dark. We slide down the smooth sides of that chancel roof, scamper along on the broad-backed ridge of the nave; that is, they do, not I; alas! for this proof of a vanished childhood, and get ourselves upon our own roof, which is attached to that of the hotel, and into our own rooms. Our bird's-eye view, though viewed like all such views of real birds, stays, like theirs, undescribed.

The easel is set up again at the same spot. It is morning now. The sun is up these two hours, and pours a strong flood of warmth and light on this page. The noise of the street carts comes muffled up to this house-top. The morning trumpet-clang and drumbeat of the soldiers mingle with them, and rise above them, clear and steady, a sign that this government is more military yet than civil. Frequent bells put in their heavy musical notes, sometimes rapid; there is one now striking the half-seconds, sometimes slower, but all alike calling a heedless city to an almost voiceless service.

The birds send up their pretty chatterings among the bells, the trumpets, and the rattling carts, those true babes in the wood, and babes in nature, whose very songs are the laugh of childhood threading the graver tones of maturer nature. How deliciously their treble laugh breaks on the ear! Do you not wish you could hear them, poor ice-bound citizens of the Arctic North?

This is a royal place to see this royal city. Never had a town such grand environment. Athens has mountains and sea, but scanty plains. Rome, plains, but no water, and low-browed hills. Jerusalem, mountains, but no plains nor sea. Modern cities are without the least trace of scenic loveliness. London, Paris, New York, Philadelphia, Chicago, New Orleans, and Berlin, how cheap their panorama! It is a map and not a picture that one draws when he paints these capitals. Boston and Baltimore make a slight approach to hill effects, but only a hundred feet high are their mountains, and no plains to set off even these.

Look here; turn your eye (and body too, or you will leave your head on this slippery roof-side), and take in this scene. Everywhere a green valley, everywhere dahlia hills—the true dahlia—that deep purple sliding into black, and yet never losing its royal bloom, the finest color of all for the garments of men and women, as well as for Greek and Aztec mountains.

I am now looking southward; so may you. The city lies all about us, its limits being equidistant in all directions. Its flat roofs extend for a mile, domed twice or thrice with spacious churches. Then comes a flat gray field for several miles: it is probably more than ten miles, but distances are as deceitful as is every thing else in this clime. It is sprinkled with trees, especially to the west, and at its farther termination. To its right, or westward, the trees grow denser, and evidently line thoroughfares and fill gardens. A village glistens under the hills in which it is ending. Then comes a mass of dark and rugged peaks, soft in their ruggedness, and light in their darkness, the fields creeping well up their sides, and sometimes, but rarely, climbing on and over their heads.

This southern route was the one chosen by Cortez and Scott for entering the town. Between the two snow volcanoes they came over a lofty pass, around the western edge of that broad, flashing lake, by the side of the canal that you see stretching out, lined with trees and floating gardens. Along well-built causeways, amidst a frightened mass of living people, the invaders marched. Cortez had more than one bloody fight on that passway; and Scott made a rough lava height and Cherubusco, a not wide plain, famous with his victories. There, too, you note a purple hill, two hundred feet high, where the Aztec priests kindled the sacred fire at the close of each half century. They thought the world had come to an end. Light was never to come again; everywhere it was extinguished. The people march in solemn procession from the city to this hill; the priests take the chosen human victim to its summit. His heart is extracted. A new flame is kindled upon it. It is transmitted to waiting torches, and sent through the whole nation, re-illumining the face of society, and keeping fresh the hope and heart of man. One can hardly fancy that low and silent and shrubless peak to have been so long the scene of such a sad and memorable festival.

Keep your eye and head moving westward, and you see the same city, landscape beyond, and tall hills in the rear. Almost due west lies Chapultepec, the favorite haunt of the rulers of this people from

CHAPULTEPEC.

Montezuma to Juarez, a superb park, palace, and picture. It is a fortress and a garden, a sort of Windsor Castle set down with its hill-top, forests, and views, three miles from London town. It deserves a visit and a page of its own, and so we now swing round the circle, leaving its yellow walls, a little haughty in their frowning at our presumption to come and go without more obeisance.

On getting round toward the north, the girdle of nearer hills dips down, giving glimpses of mountains beyond. The level lands stretch out farther, fifteen and twenty miles, before the passes are touched. The country is full of trees, which are also full of greenness. Church towers peer above their tops, and white and drab specks appear among the interstices, the proofs that this wide area has villages amidst its verdure.

To the right still, the landscape narrows to its closest limits, and the sierra of Guadalupe comes within three or four miles of the town. It is a range fifteen or twenty miles long, that casts its nearest and highest battlements over against the city. It is woodless, bright, of purple bloom, without a shady retreat, save such as recesses may give.

At its easternmost edge, just where it drops into the plains nearest the city, you notice several domes and towers massed together. That is the group of temples dedicated to the Virgin of Guadalupe, the most famous, popular, and powerful of all the virgins of America, if not of the Church that worships her. That spot is a curious evidence of the manner in which Romanism adapts itself to the people it governs. The Indians were sullen and unsubdued after Cortez had conquered their nation. They were a dangerous element, being, like the subjects of the East India Company, a thousand to one more numerous than their rulers. How shall they be subdued? Their priests and worship were gone, but not their faith in both.

They had a seat of worship in this spot. An Indian coming over the mountains, seeking for a priest at a church built by Cortez, a mile or so from its base, is met by the Virgin, who tells him to build a church to her in that spot. He flees affrighted to the priest, and tells his tale. It is not idle words to not empty ears, though it is so assumed. He is repulsed by the priest, meets her twice again, asks a sign, has his soiled blanket filled by her hands with flowers from these barren and burning rocks, which when poured out at the feet of the incredulous archbishop are no more flowers, but

"A fair maiden clothed with celestial grace,"

even the maiden mother herself. Her flowers had changed to a flowery Madonna, with a bud of a boy in her arms, as on a branch.

If you doubt this they will show you the greasy blanket with her form upon it, over the high altar at Guadalupe, in a frame of solid silver, located just where she spread it, and she filled it with herself.

I agreed to accept the miracle if they would show the flowers as fresh to-day as when they were picked. This they could also do; for flowers abound in this latitude, and beautiful enough to turn any dirty blanket into a Madonna.

That miracle settled the case for the Indians. They had a señora of their own. Our Lady of the Remedies was a Spanish mother. This was an Indian. It was a success. The Virgin of Guadalupe became the goddess of Mexico. Divine honors were paid to her. Temples went up everywhere, and shrines in every temple. Her picture on its blanket hangs in every house and hut, above the counter of the merchant and the bar of pulqui dram-shops, over the forge and over the bed, here, there, everywhere. Books by the thousand and sermons by the tens of thousands have been written and preached upon her virtues and her powers. In one of the books in the library of Vera Cruz she is gravely said to have "got around God." Undoubtedly she got around this people, and effectually took them in, or those personating her did; for the blessed Virgin is in Paradise, and has no connection with this idolatry.

The upper of these three churches, where she first appeared, is reckoned the most sacred. Here are the tombs of the chiefest dignitaries of church and state. The ascent is lined with trophies of her ability to save; one a solid mast and sail of stone, erected by a worshiper whose life was saved from shipwreck, as he believed, through her interposition.

The next is near the foot of the hill, and incloses a chalybeate fountain, which burst forth when she lit there on her foot. "The iron entered her sole," irreverently remarked an American sinner as he gazed upon the fountain. A blaze of gilding covers the chapel connected with this beautiful legend of the fountain. Its walls are

"Thick inlaid with patines of bright gold."

THE LOTTERY TICKET.

Raffle one thousand four hundred and seventy-six.

RAFFLE 1476 IN BEHALF OF THE SANCTUARY OF OUR LADY* OF GUADALUPE.

Fifteenth of December.   *Price one real.*

Eighth of a ticket for the Raffle one thousand four hundred and seventy-six, which is to be celebrated in Mexico the fifteenth day of December, one thousand eight hundred and sixty-five.
$91,000.   Oct. 7.

One thousand eight hundred and sixty-five.

---

* "The Sanctuary of our Lady" would be better translated freely "The Church of the Blessed Virgin."

The largest church, where her blanket portrait hangs, is a few rods farther out on the plain. There is the chief outlay of gold and silver and precious stones. Two solid silver railings with silver banisters lead from the altar to the choir, a hundred feet at least. On its wall is an inscription to her as the Mother of God, Foundress and Savior of the Mexican People.

But the priests of the Virgin have an eye to the main chance. They turn her into lottery speculations, and make her useful to their often infirmities. At the door-way an old servant of the temple sold her pictures, beads, and other ecclesiastical knickknacks. A picture that I bought of her was wrapped up in a lottery ticket like that shown on the opposite page, with its translation.

This lottery of the Virgin is one of the most flourishing. The monthly drawings draw daily pennies to their purse. It makes the priestly pot boil. Time was when luxuries were theirs; but these are hard times now for priests, and so they have to thus turn an honest penny to a dishonest use.

But these popular orgies are fading out. True, each December witnesses multitudes from over all the land attending her annual festival. The Indian honors it with the dances of the ancient times. The rites are more Aztec than papal. Yet the Jesuit begins to say that faith in the Virgin of Guadalupe is not essential to salvation. The Bible will replace the Jesuit, and the trick by which he has held their souls captive these three centuries and a half will cease to possess them more. Christ the Liberator is coming. He is nigh—even at their doors. This old blanket, like that of Bartimeus, will be thrown away, and the people will come to Jesus and be healed.

Let us leave our Lady of Guadalupe, if you can, with all this shrewd but shallow faith and policy, and look more easterly. Here lies the vision that charmed the Toltec twelve centuries ago, the Aztec eight centuries ago, the Spaniard three centuries ago, and the French, Austrian, and American conquerors of our own day. From my post it spreads out into a plain that loses itself in a sun-mist forty miles away. Across the plain threads of water stretch themselves, sometimes spreading into bayous, or lakes.

IZTACCIHUATL.

The lake and level end in a ridge that rises from the surface as modest as the tiniest slope, but grows and grows, not fast, but steadily, like a true fame, into a sharp, brown edge, well lifted up, slides down a little on its continual ridge, and then rises again, still not sharp nor sudden, nor seemingly very high, but into a ragged rim covered with snow. You are surprised to find so low a horizon covered with perpetual ice. Yet there it lies, not so low after all. It is ten thousand feet above this seat, and nearly eighteen thousand above the gulf, that reclining Lady of the Skies, who rejoices in the unpronounceable name of Iztaccihuatl. I have heard all sorts of people seek to speak this word, and never heard two agree. So call it as it looks, or call it Big I, which it undoubtedly is. You see her head, neck, chest, robes, and feet, white-slippered. "with the toes turned up at the daisies" of the stars, with a long trail sweeping beyond, as becomes this White Woman, which that hard name means.

The southern side of this snow range drops off to a sharp and snowless ridge, where the pass lies over which Scott and Cortez marched. Narrow as it looks, it is probably several miles before that valley is crossed and the magnificent dome and peak of Popocatepetl rounds itself up into a superb cone of lustrous ice. Down it glides on the farther side into those brown rims on which we first gazed, and thus sails round the circle of this view. These snow-peaks are thus a not extravagant part of the landscape. They do not stretch suddenly and extraordinarily above their fellows. They are *primi inter pares*. A fall of rain here at this season will make all this high ridge snow. It was so last week, but the snow was gone ere noon, except from the two head centres. The king and queen reign (or snow) perpetually.

The torrid sun, it would seem, ought to burn off their mantle. You can not sit in it now half an hour. It burns on the knees like a burning-glass. I must retreat to the shadow of a tall stone bass-relief lifted up at the front of the roof, and at the foot of a headless statue, once a Magdalene, I judge, conclude this portrait.

It shows how high they are, and how distant also, not less than sixty miles away, if you notice that range of cliffs that lies between them and us. They, too, are well lifted up, and they crouch as lions at the base of these mighty powers.

See the volcanic origin also. The craters are visible of these

THE DOME.

lower hills. Some look just like a bowl upside down, with its bottom cut off—a round hollow.

You have seen the valley of Mexico. On that north-eastern edge of the snow range, a few feet above the lake, you remember, Cortez stood and viewed the landscape over, and said, "I must subdue this exquisite region for our Lady and her Christ." What a job he undertook he hardly then dreamed. How much labor and loss of life, fightings without and fears within, before he rode a conqueror through these streets, which he had made without inhabitant, and almost without a dwelling-place. Inch by inch he leveled off the Aztec city. Two years and over he plotted and fought, and fought and plotted, ere the prize was his.

The bloodless battle now being fought for the recovery of this same land to Christ, how long will that take? How many will fall? Not so bloodless, perhaps, after all. A more cunning enemy than Montezuma, a more daring one than Guatemozin is to be subdued. He may kill many ere he himself is slain. But conquer Christ will. This earth in all its beauty is His. These people in all their lowliness are His. The Church He has saved with His most precious blood must come hither bearing the true cross of personal holiness, and by patient continuance in well-doing bring up this population to the level of Christian probity, piety, and peace.

It is a grander work than any ever before devised. It is worthy of the Church and its Divine Head. Let it be steadily prosecuted. Match Cortez in his patience, perseverance, persistence, and it will be done.

The sun grows hot and hotter. The shelter of the bass-relief is gone. A deep recess below gives a stone seat in the corner, just fitted for shade and air. The breezes of Popocatepetl glide coolingly over the leaf and the writer. You have seen Mexico from the house-top: let us take a new page, and show you Mexico from the sidewalk.

III.

FROM THE SIDEWALK.

Views from Street Corners.—Chief Street.—Shops, Plaza, Cathedral.—High and Low Religion.—Aztec Calendar Stone.—The Sacrificial Stone.—The President's private House.—Hotel Iturbide.—Private Residences.—Alameda.

The dizzy church top from which we swung round the circle of the town is not half as agreeable as this sturdy and simple pavement at its foot. After all, there is nothing like the solid earth under your feet. Even this not too solid earth is better than all airy spirits and domes and azateas. Not too solid, because you remember Mexico is located on a dry, salt marsh, which was a salt lake when Cortez conquered it, and which is yet a lake a few inches below the surface, and often, in its sewers and odors, upon the surface also.

These odors sometimes surpass those of Cologne, but, unlike those of that fragrant town, are not especially pestilential. The high altitudes preserve it from this peril. Nor is it altogether blamable for this defect. Drainage is hardly possible. The flat plain surrounded by high mountains prevents any sufficient descent for sewerage. When the street is opened for such purposes, you see the moist mud not two feet below the pavement. Efforts are being made, or rather being talked about, for opening channels to the Tulu River, some forty miles to the west, and thereby getting up a movement of this sort from the centre. But it is not likely soon to be.

Turning away our eyes, if we can not turn up our noses, from this offense, which is not very offensive on the chief thoroughfares, let us note the map and the traits of the town.

The first peculiarity you will observe is the romantic outlook almost every street corner affords. You look straight through the

THE MARKET-PLACE.

city, and bound your vision by the purple mountains, whichever direction you gaze. Take any corner where the streets pass clear through the town, you see, north, south, east, and west, or as near that as the lines run, the all-embracing mountains. They are from three to thirty miles distant, some even sixty miles, and yet they look as if only just down to the farther end of this telescopic tube of a street. They rise from two to ten thousand feet, and so are never diminutive, often very magnificent.

No city I have ever seen has any equal cincture. Athens approaches it. Her chief streets look out on Pentelicus and Hymettus; but she is not level herself, and so can not get up these vistas; nor is she large, and does not, therefore, match her mountains. They overpower her, not she them. Mexico is equal to her grander mountains. Popocatepetl is not ashamed to call her sister, nor is she unworthy of such a companionship. Athens historically overtops all its peaks. Mexico in its present proportions well fits her magnificent frame. One never tires of this resting-place for the eye. It is so exquisite in calm and color, that it seems as if made on purpose for exhibition and exhilaration.

This fact, too, seems to put the city in your grasp at the start. Most towns of this size you find it somewhat difficult to master. They are so tossed up and down, or stretched out, or have no perceptible limits, that one is a long time in getting hold of them. Though a dweller in Chicago for a month, it still bewilders me to arrange the streets of its west and south sides. Its north side I never attempted to subdue. I left that for the fire. Boston, every body says, except its own people, is untamable. Even the fire got tired of running round and round its narrow and crooked thoroughfares, and gave up in despair, especially when it drew near its narrowest and crookedest portion. Philadelphia's perfect rectangularity is equally bewildering, while Washington makes the head swim, no less in its everlasting radiations than its political plannings. As for New York, Brooklyn, London, and such like villages, they are all under the same ban as their superior sisters.

The real reason of this is, they have no perceptible boundaries;

nothing to which they can be adjusted. Cincinnati, held in a pocket of hills, is much more easily grasped than Chicago, on a walless prairie. Jerusalem is seen at a glance, despite its crooked and narrow alleys, for it is on a hill-top, with higher hills inclosing it. But Mexico is pre-eminent in this respect. You know the town at a glance. There are large portions of it I have not visited, yet I have seemed to see it all at any corner. There it lies, each four of the ways straight to the mountains.

It is not crooked. Every thoroughfare is straight, and the blocks regular. William Penn in 1680 did not surpass Hernando Cortez in 1522. Unlike his ever-stretching, never-girdled town, this city has its natural metres and bounds that put the whole under the eye at once. It is like the observation of a witty judge to a brother lawyer on Hempstead Plains. When urged to stop longer, and see the country more thoroughly, after a brief ride, he stood up in the buggy, turned himself slowly round, and said, "I have seen it. Drive on." So at this corner where the Church of the Profesa stands, you have only to look in four directions, and can say, "I've seen Mexico. Drive on." But if the general appearance is the same, the special and nearer views are varied, novel, and attractive.

Take the spot at the base of our church-tower of the Profesa. It is simply a corner in a city street. The names of the streets are devotional enough to make us pause; for here come together the Street of the Holy Spirit and the Street of St. Joseph, the Royal. You can see north to the Guadalupe range, west to Tacubaya, south to Ajusca (called Ahusca), a tall, dark, purple range, and east to the giant peaks of snow. The mountains are indeed round about Mexico as about no other capital, while the town lies as level at their bases as Chicago by its lake.

The Aztec priest, himself probably a prince and warrior, announced by divination that where they should see an eagle on a cactus, holding a serpent in his beak, there their city should be planted—located rather, for it would be difficult to plant a city on the sea. Such a sight was asserted to be seen at the southern end of Lake Tezcuco. The city was placed there for military protection, whatever were the divinations of the priests; for, being on the water, it was not easily assailable. They took the eagle with the serpent and cactus for their national symbol, and the conquerors accepted that national coat of arms from their subjects. Some irreverent Yankees assert that a more appropriate symbol would be a Greaser sitting on a jackass drinking pulqui. But so they could retort that our symbol could better be a whisky-jug and a turkey than our like chosen eagle.

The city thus laid out has since had the water dry up from beneath it sufficiently to give it solid streets. The water of the lake was in it, in canals, and close to it, in its own shallow waves, when Cortez captured it. To-day it is two or three miles from its outer most eastern gate. While the streets are straight, but few are noticeable, and only two or three are really attractive. The chief thoroughfare from the dépôt to the plaza and its two nearest parallel streets are the main avenues of the city.

The San Cosme Avenue starts out from the station very broad, but it narrows as it passes the Alameda, and enters the thick of the town, where it terminates at the eastern end of the Grand Plaza. This is the very street over which Cortez made his famous escape from the infuriated town, rendered doubly mad by the interference of his lieutenant, Alvarado, in his absence, with the bloody rites of human sacrifice. The town woke up before they were well started, roused by a sentinel, chased them along this dike, which is all this then was, crossed with rude and frequent ditches, and inclosed on either side with water. The multitudes dragged them off the narrow causeways, caught them as they tried to clear the chasms, their pontoon train being pressed into the mud of the first broad ditch, so that it could not be taken up. The band of adventurers lost their arms, ammunition, horses, precious metals, and gems, and all but a score of their men were left along the ravine, a prey to the destroyer. They assembled a few miles up, under the cypress-tree still standing, and a few days later, with their good swords and strong hearts cut their way through two hundred thousand men, swinging down upon them from the Sierra of Gaudalupe, in the plains at Otumba. The avenue is now solid, and Alvarado's famous leap across one of these ditches is an undistinguishable bit of the hard highway. Over the same road marched the American army into town, Scott and Grant and Lee, the known, and the then unknown, being in the little host of later conquerors. If we are seeking a like and larger, bloodless and better, conquest, we can properly pass to our quarters over the same path. It may be ominous of a bloody retreat under the uprisings and assaults of reigning superstition, but it will only thus be prophetic of ultimate and perfect victory.

A parallel street to the central thoroughfare goes out from the western end of the same plaza, and is heavily shaded at the start with covered arcades, like a deep sombrero, behind which shop men of all sorts ply their trades. It runs straight to the luxurious northern hamlet of Tacubaya. Between these two is the street at whose corner you have been standing. It lies between the green plats of the Plaza and the Alameda, each of which appears at either extremity. This street is the busiest and most fashionable of all in the town. It is half a mile long, forty to fifty feet wide, about three stories high, faced with stone or mortar, but, except three or four buildings, without especial ornament. It bears the names of Calle del Plateros (or Street of the Silversmiths), Calle de Profesa, and Calle de San Francisco. It is, however, one in every respect but its name. They have a way here of giving almost every block a name of its own, which in a long street is as perplexing as the multitude of names given to a royal heir would be if he were called by a different one of them every day.

This street is lively with hackney and private coaches; carts with three mules abreast; burros, or donkeys, with their immense burdens; and men and women with theirs almost equally heavy, the women with rebosas, or blue or brown fine-wove mantles, wrapped about their shoulders, and half hiding the faces; the men with their white blankets with bright-colored borders, or with only their dirty white shirts and trowsers, carrying heavy loads on their trained shoulders.

SAN COSME AQUEDUCT, CITY OF MEXICO.

Fashion also flows up and down the streets, on sidewalks, and in carriages. The highest fashion is never to appear on the sidewalk, not even to shop; but the grand lady, sitting in her carriage, has the goods put in her lap, and daintily indulges her feminine passion.

Come up to the plaza, the old centre of the city. It is only a few rods—an eighth of a mile, perhaps. You pass a few dry-goods stores, two or three, in this chiefest resort of the ladies and the trade; many jewelry stores, into which the former silversmiths that gave their name to the street have changed; tobacconists, who have only smoking-tobacco, the chewing variety being here unknown. Their cigarettes are done up in paper of different colors, and so packed as to make the shop look tasteful as its Parisian rival. Shoe stores abound, containing very pretty gaiters, and almost the only cheap article in the city.

Two or three of the old silversmith establishments remain, holes in the wall, where a few manufactured articles of silver, very neat and cheap, are hung up on the sides of the wall above the little old counter, and sometimes a tiny forge is plying its fires at the rear.

The plaza is hardly less than a thousand feet square. In its centre is a large garden, planted by Carlotta, and well filled with trees and flowers, in full leaf and bloom. On the west and south sides are deep arcades, filled with all manner of knickknacks of much show and little profit.

The Government Palace extends along the entire eastern side, a stately but not superb edifice. In its ample courts large numbers of the soldiery are stationed, and even a great quantity of ammunition is stored. The hall of ambassadors is the chief room, stretching along nearly all this front, and adorned with portraits of the leading generals and presidents of the republic, among whom place is found for Washington and Bolivar alone, of other nations. We have no such hall in Washington, though the East Room in its height and breadth is of yet greater grandeur.

The north or chief side is occupied with the cathedral. This immense structure is approached by a very broad esplanade of its own, and is of large and even grand proportions, though its towers are not especially effective. It stands on a plateau, raised several feet from the pavement of the plaza, has adjoining it the sagrario, or parish church, profusely carved without and gilded within, the carving cheap and the gilding faded. It is cut up to fit divers crowds. The altar by the chief entrance is usually thronged. The choir behind it is a stately mass of carving. Two beautiful balustrades, of an amalgam of gold, silver, and brass, connect the choir and the high altar. So rich are they that an Englishman offered to replace them with silver, and was refused. Beautiful figures of like precious metal hold candelabra along this walk. The dome is of impressive proportions, and the high altar is set off with polished alabaster, and profusion of pink and green images, while the altar behind it is one blaze of gilding, from floor to ceiling, with a multitude of gilded images in niches along its broad and shining face.

THE PALACE OF MEXICO.

The area in front of the cathedral is full of people selling their wares—never so full as on Sabbath mornings. Here is the lottery-ticket vender, most numerous and most busy of all. Male and female has this church created them, chiefly old people. All their sales have a percentage of benefit for the priest. The sellers are each numbered, and the church keeps steady watch over this important revenue.

Here is a velocipede course, and children enjoy it. The match-boy, pert and pretty; the cigar-boy; the ice-cream vender of a very poor cream, as I knew by a week evening's trial; the print-seller—every trade that can, is disposing of its wares before this sacred portal. How much is a whip of small cords needed here and now for those who make this house a house of merchandise! But merchandise of souls goes on within. Shall not that of lesser wares consistently proceed without?

I saw high mass performed here two weeks ago in the presence of the archbishop, the most elaborate and ornate religious display I ever saw. I hardly think Rome herself equals this grandiloquence of dress and posture. A throne was set on the side of the altar, and the archbishop, in costly gold and silver vestments, was installed under the crimson velvet pall, whose only defect seemed to be a piece of unpainted frame with white wooden pulleys, by which the top of the velvet back was let out over the head a yard or more as a roof. It was evidently made so that this projection could be hauled up to a line with the back, when it was to be carried to the sacristy, or depository, of the sacred garments.

On either side of this king of priests were many pompously arrayed vassals. Before him were three officiating ministers in like gaudy apparel. On the archbishop's head was a tall, ornate, gilded mitre, which he changed for a less gilded pasteboard in the more penitential portions of the ceremony. A dozen boys, in black and white, swung incense and held candles. One of them was the keeper of his grace's handkerchief, which he once called for by touching his nose. It was handed him, a dingy brown and red silk bandana, clean and folded, however. He took, opened, used, re-folded, and returned, and the service went on. I am surprised so fine a gentleman does not use a white linen handkerchief, or one with a gold border. Is that *en règle?* I saw an officiator at the Madelaine in Paris blow his nose upon a like huge and dirty-colored silk. It jarred badly with his golden robes. So did this with these.

Do you wish to know how the archbishop looks? He is from fifty to fifty-two, short, thick-set, full-fleshed, full-faced; has a strong, loud voice, a bland and meaningless smile, a polished and easy manner, and is evidently trained in the art of government. He preaches every Sunday morning to a large audience in the sagrario, who sit or kneel upon the floor. He is not an orator after the impassioned sort, but, like most high officials, is evidently a manager rather than a talker. The interests of his Church will not suffer in his hands, so far as policy and push can favor them. He seems also very devout in the mass, and goes through that ceremony as though he believed it, which most do not.

A small image, set in a golden base, was carried round the church by four blue cotton-robed peons, the image, I believe, of St. Philip, as it was his day; and the choir followed singing, and the clergy, and a crowd of irreverent gazers and worshipers treading almost on the sacred robes and their more sacred wearers. The crowd was very ill-dressed and ill-mannered; and as for religion— well, the stream can not rise higher than the fountain. Poor Philip did differently with the eunuch than these his worshipers when he ran along by his chariot, and preached atonement and salvation by simple faith in the Lord Jesus Christ. Ah, if that able and accomplished gentleman who is the head centre of this display could only get out of this pomp into that simplicity of faith, how different would this worship be!

The singing was magnificent, as far as elaborateness goes. After the pomp had finished, they disrobed the archbishop, in the presence of the congregation, of about half a dozen garments, and put on him a scarlet robe. It was all grandly done; but to what intent? Those poor crowds of half-dressed spectators, what did they learn by this display? Ah! Christ, Thou art needed in this temple, to teach Thy professed ministers how to feed Thy famishing flock. Hasten Thy coming! He has come!

Let us get out of this holy smoke, and odor and blaze and glare and tinsel, and the nasty, ragged crowd of spectators, and take to the street again. You notice, as you leave the church, a round slab at its northern corner. That is the Calendar Stone of the Aztecs. It was saved from the ruins of the teocallis that stood here. It is a specimen of the learning and art of those people, and shows that but for their religion they might have longer held sway. Their present religion, poor as it is, replaced a poorer. This cathedral, grand as it is, is not too grand to occupy its seat. It is of the Lord.

THE AZTEC CALENDAR STONE.

Turn from the cathedral southward, enter the street opposite that by which you entered the plaza, pass by the President's palace and the post-office, and you come to a museum of antiquities. In the centre of its court lies a huge, round, red granite stone, twelve feet in diameter, four feet high. This stone is covered with amor-

phous figures, and is deep stained as if with blood. Where the cathedral stands, a teocallis stood—five terraces, and two hundred feet high. By a fivefold series of stairs in one corner, and fivefold circuit of the mound, the teocallis was mounted. On its top was this stone. Around the sides of the teocallis and up its steps they led their victims—men and youth by the thousands—made them pause before this stone, stretched their chests over it, so that the heart was strained over its edge, cut the flesh over the heart opening to it, plucked the heart forth, laid it reverently before the god, and hurled the body down the sides of the teocallis to the multitude below, who took it up carefully, cooked it, and ate it as a religious banquet. The cathedral is better than the teocallis, and the genuflexions and millinery of priests and bishops than the sacrifice of bloody hearts and the sacrament of cannibalism.

Turn northward again. We pass up the street of San Francisco, by the modest house of President Lerdo, a two-story city front, with green blinds, without pretense or cost; past the Hotel Iturbide, once that emperor's palace, now the Hotel Diligencias, the costliest edifice on the street; past the chapel of San Francisco and the pile of buildings which made that famous convent. Nearly opposite the chapel and its gardens are the residences of the two wealthiest Mexicans, Barron and Escandron. The brother of the latter once gave his check for seven millions of dollars. He began his fortune by establishing a stage-coach system all over this country. Mines, railroads, and other operations keep it growing. Their residences are plain without, except the latter's new house, which essays pillars and bronze dogs and lions on its roof. Within they are sumptuous. Courts, flowers, long suites of long parlors, everything the heart craves is there, except that which it craves preeminently—the grace of our Lord Jesus Christ. Between their houses is an old structure, faced with porcelain, blue-and-white blocks, four inches square, of various figures. Within is a court with carved pillars. It is a very fanciful structure, and originally cost much. Across the way from these dignities, in pleasant apartments, is the residence of the American consul general, Dr. Julius

A. Skilton, who won large repute for courage and skill in our war, and none the less for his sagacity and courage as a reporter of the *New York Herald* during the close of the French occupation. Whoever comes to Mexico will be sure of a handsome welcome in this American home.

INTERIOR OF A MODERN MEXICAN HOUSE.

A Mexican house is all beautiful within, if anywhere. It is not so, certainly, without. You enter through a large high door, wide enough to admit your carriage, into a patio, or open paved court. Around this are rooms for servants and horses, on the first floor. Handsome stairs lead to the upper stories, light balconies run around them, and rooms open into them. They are not allowed to open on neighboring estates, so they must open on court or street. The last commands usually only one of the four sides; so most houses have three-fourths of their light from the court.

These rooms are as cool and airy as those built after our fashion, though they usually have only one inlet for air and light. They are much higher in ceiling than ours, and are tastefully set off in frescoes. The balustrades are often of brass, and the work has a more finished look, even in common houses, than the best in the States exhibit. On the street side are small balconies for sight-seeing. There are more disagreeable dwellings by far than a first-class Mexican house.

A few rods farther north and we reach the city park, called Alameda. It is a pretty shaded inclosure of about forty acres, lying between the two thoroughfares of the San Francisco and the San Cosme. Its trees are large, thick together, and perpetually green. The leaf hardly falls before the young one presses itself to take its aged place, so that even the deciduous sort never get reduced to a Northern nakedness. Their new spring robes, like a snake's, an eagle's, and an Easter belle's, are assumed or ere their old ones are dropped.

These trees are interspersed with open plats, where flowers of every size and sort gladden the nerves of sight and smell. These are again interspersed with fountains, and circular centres lined with stone benches, and open, hard parterres for children and bands to play. The trees and flowers are shut off from approach by high fences; the circles about the fountains and graveled squares are alone accessible.

This park needs only one addition to make it a perpetual delight —safety. One can not walk there in midday without peril. Almost every day robberies occur. A gentleman walking with his wife saw another man being robbed, and declined to interfere, though he had a revolver, on the ground that it might alarm his wife.

We may rest here from our sidewalk studies, if we are tired, and it is not too dark, and talk on what this city needs to make it as safe as it is lovely.

IV.

A NEW EVENT IN MEXICO.

Palace of the President.—The President.—How he looks.—What he pledges.—Former Property of the Church.—Its Consequences.—Corruption.—Prospects and Perils.

THE first official recognition by the head of the Mexican nation of any other Church than the Roman Catholic, which was till within a few years the only possible religion, was so frank, cordial, and free as to show how complete is the executive and, therefore, political and constitutional changes in this important republic.

At 4 o'clock, Tuesday, Jan. 14th, the American minister, Hon. Thomas H. Nelson, accompanied by his secretary, Mr. Bliss, son of Rev. Asher Bliss, long missionary among the Seneca Indians, a gentleman of remarkable scholarship and hardly less remarkable wit, took three Americans into the presence of the President of Mexico. One was General Palmer, the Philadelphia representative of the Mexican railroad movement; another was Mr. Parish, of Europe, co-operator abroad in these American enterprises; and the third was a Methodist minister, come hither to arrange for the planting of the Methodist Episcopal Church in this country.

The palace occupies a side of the Grand Plaza on which the cathedral fronts. Through long and handsome apartments we are led to one richly furnished in its hangings, marbles, and paintings, chief of which is the portrait of Emperor Iturbide, who more than any other man was the Washington of Mexico, and secured her independence.

The President soon enters. A small man, with small, well-shaped head and features, hair thin, well-nigh to baldness, with pleasant, bland smile, tone, and manner. We are introduced by Mr. Nelson in a graceful and dignified form, and the President addresses each by turn. On the introduction of the clergyman, he said he had often heard of the antecedents of the Church he represented, and welcomed him to the supervision of her work in this country. No one Church was recognized by the state as of superior claims to another. Toleration of all faiths was the law of the land. This movement might not be looked upon with favor by bishops here: but the civil power would protect it, if it became necessary, in defense of its rights and liberties. I thanked him for his offers, but said I hoped no such case would arise as would call for the protection of the state. We had no hostile relations to other religious bodies. Our mission was to build up our work in our own way, by education of the people, and by organization of churches of our own faith and order.

He responded yet more at length, re-affirming his readiness to support our churches in any exigencies that might arise in the prosecution of our work, so far as they were imperiled by any unlawful opposition. He repeated his welcome to the land, and his good wishes for our prosperity.

This interview means more than the recognition of one Christian Church. It is the formal and, to a degree, official announcement of the policy of the nation. The President is a scholar and jurist of large repute. He had charge in his earlier years of a school in this city, and in later years was president of the courts, where the question of Church property has been often in consultation. In all his public life he has thus met with Church matters. He has been affirmed to be in more sympathy with the Church party than Juarez, and some of its leaders have dreamed that their former prerogatives were to be restored under his administration.

This strong and unequivocal affirmation of the law of the realm and of his cordial support of its principles, even to the aid of the civil power, if need be, shows how impossible it is for any single Church government to again possess exclusive jurisdiction here and the support of the national arm.

The Roman Catholic chiefs are recognizing this fact, and are said to be favorable to annexation, because they can get yet larger liberties under our government than are allowed them here. No one is permitted to appear in his official costume in the streets of this city. Religious processions are proscribed. The holy wafer is carried to dying people no longer in a gilded coach, but in a private carriage, the bared head of the driver being the only sign by which the faithful can know it, and can fall on their knees on its passing by. So great has this irreverence grown, that a native gentleman, pointing to the sagrario where this coach is still kept, said to me, "They keep in there what they call 'the Holy Ghost coach,' but I call it the hell-cart." Could disrespect go further?

The confiscation of Church property was an enormous loss of Church power. It held two-thirds of this city in its possession. It held mortgages in as large a portion of the country. Letting its money at a low figure and on liberal and long terms, it gradually became an enormous savings-bank, and controlled the whole landed interest of the country. Its convents covered hundreds of acres in the heart of the city, and were adorned in the highest degree that art and wealth could devise. Gardens, lakes, parks, pillars elegantly wrought in polished marble, churches of splendor in construction and ornamentation, were the unseen luxurious abodes of the world-denying friars and nuns. Corruption of the most startling sort abounded; and money, the sinews of the state, was in the hands exclusively of the corrupted and corrupters.

Good men may have been involved in this arrangement, may have presided over it. Good men have been connected with every controlling evil that the world has ever seen. An Orthodox Congregational minister called his burning satire against New England's demoralization under rum "Deacon Giles's Distillery," and the slave-holding system of English West Indies was supported by rectors of the Established Church, and of our own land by ministers of all churches in the South. So we are all in condemnation, and none can throw stones at the former growth to financial power of the Roman Church in Mexico.

Indeed, it has its eloquent advocates to-day. A lady of high social position and an ardent Papist, as she proudly calls herself, but yesterday was declaring that the former system was far better than the present; that the Church leased its buildings cheaper than landlords do now, and was far more merciful to its debtors; that great suffering had followed the overthrow of its moneyed power. All of this was undoubtedly true. So we have heard of the suffering to the emancipated class in our own land arising from their liberation, and not without foundation is that complaint.

A sudden change in the weather, whether from heat to cold or cold to heat, is attended with loss of life to those whose enfeebled condition can not bear extremes of any thing. If the "Norther" kills every person sick of the yellow fever in the hospitals of Vera Cruz, it drives the fever out of the city, and saves the lives of all that are well. So the old never changes into the new without some sense of loss. But it changes, nevertheless; and it changes for the better. Mexico is far better off under ecclesiastical liberty than under ecclesiastical bondage. New England is vastly improved religiously by the abolition of her State Church, which governed her till within a half a century; as England will be equally advanced in morals and religion when her national Church is disestablished, and lawn sleeves cease to flutter among the black coats of the House of Lords, unless they flutter on the white arms of the ladies of the realm.

So Mexico has sprung up in newness of life through this emancipation from the fetters of an enforced ecclesiastical system. The Roman Catholic Church has yet large control of her people; and will have more, if possible, by the new relation of liberty of choice in which she will stand to them and they to her. Other Christian Churches are springing up, and all the leading bodies in America will be earnestly active.

The prospects of their success are excellent. The people are free in this city and its environs, and are protected in their freedom by public sentiment and the civil power. Consequently, the new churches are well attended, and priests and subordinate church officials are joining them. A doctor of divinity, who was offered a bishopric if he would remain with the Romanists, has left their ranks and joined himself to the new movement.

In some other cities persecution yet abounds. At Toluca, the capital of this State, a riot broke up lately one of these congregations, in which three persons were killed. At Peubla, the chief city next to the capital, a preacher was mobbed from the town for daring to speak in the name of Jesus. But these ebullitions will grow less, I trust; and, if they increase, it will be but for a moment. Like our Ku-Klux outrages, they are the dying blows of a dying evil. They will grow fainter, and then cease. The new order has arisen on this grand country—the order of religious liberty. It has followed the advent of civil liberty here, as it followed it in our own country. It will enlarge and uplift this land, as it has our own.

Honor, then, to President Lerdo for his cheering words! He will not, we hope, be called to put those into effect which promised protection in the courts and by the power of the state. The leaders of the dominant Church will have to accept the situation, and allow the new forms and forces of the Church of Christ to operate undisturbed, except by such friendly rivalry as they may see fit to put forth.

Since this event, interviews have been granted other clergymen, and like assurances been given. The laws of Congress have been liberal and right. But persecutions have broken out, and murders committed in Puebla and elsewhere. One missionary has fallen. But no punishment has been meted out to the murderers. Unless this is done, promises and edicts will be idle words. We trust it will be done. If not, should not America protect her own citizens in these rights as much as she would protect her merchants trading there? Toleration is the first word, Protection the second. Will the wise Lerdo de Tejada give us both?

V.

OLD AND NEW AMONG THE SILVER MINES.

A Mediæval Castle.—First Icicle.—Omatuska.—More about Pulqui.—A big Scare.—A Paradise.—Casa Grande.—A Sabbath in Pachuca.—A native Convert.—Mediæval Cavalcade.—The Visitors.—Mounting Real Del Monte.—The Castle of Real.—Gentlemanly Assassin.—Silver Factories.—Velasco.—A Reduction.—Haciendado Riley.—Mexican Giant's Causeway.—More Silver Reduction.—Horsemanship under Difficulties.—Contraries balancing Contraries.—La Barranca Grande.—A bigger Scare.—A Wedding.—Miner and Mining.—The Gautemozin.—The better Investment.

ONE need not go to Europe to find one of its best mediæval towns. Let him visit Quebec. So one need not go back to the Middle Ages to see a fine specimen of feudal times. Let him come to Pachuca. I have been pleased often at the ingenious way in which Mr. Hale contrives to get allusions to the Old and New in the introductory pages of his magazine. They are by far the best part usually of its contributions, and not the worst specimens of his own ability. But were he where I am to-night, and had he enjoyed what I have these last three days, he would have material for a most piquant page of his preamble. I have never seen there yet, to my surprise, Lowell's line,

"Old and new at its birth, like Le Verrier's planet."

Perhaps it has been quoted. This experience was old and new at its birth to those that were privileged to enjoy it.

The place where I am writing is a castle of the Middle Ages in its important features. Its huge door is kept closed. Beside the entrance armed men are constantly to be seen. An iron gate within prevents the passage of the enemy if the first door is penetrated. The roof is surrounded with a battlement, pierced with loop-holes and slit with turrets, and crowned with a tower, projecting into the sidewalk, and well adjusted to hurl grenades and shoot rifles at assailants below.

The open court, into which the entrance instantly leads, is often full of armed men and horses, called to accompany their leader on his official excursions. The rattling of spurs on its pavement, and clinking of the ornaments of the horsemen and their horses, are familiar sounds. The patio is European and antique; an elegant stairway to the upper story begins opposite the entrance; a balcony runs around that story, well faced with exquisite flowers of every tropical delight, and rooms open from it, spacious and elegant. Everywhere wealth and refinement prevail. The luxurious air of Mexico is about us, and the old times are yet more around us. How did we get here, and why? Thereby hangs a tale. Let the city walks and rides rest a while, as we unfold the panorama of this our first excursion into the country. That, as every thing else here, is attended with danger.

"Dangers stand thick through all the ground,"

we have to constantly sing, and not only sing it, but "sense" it, as the backwoods thinker strongly puts it. One must look sharp, or he will be in the condition of the lepers in Samaria, who were in danger of perishing whether they staid in the city or went without the walls. There seems to be about an equal danger of being robbed, kidnaped, and otherwise abused, whether you remain in the city or go into the country.

For instance, right opposite my hotel, a gentleman of a rich family was kidnaped a few months ago, as he was returning from the opera at an early hour of the night, not later than ten, and confined in a room not far from the Grand Plaza for nine days, being put in a hole in the ground, and knives so placed that any movement of his body would thrust them into him. So it is not without peril even to remain in the hotel, or, rather, to go to the opera, a possibility also elsewhere, but of another sort. He was discovered by the tell-tale of a woman, who had the sweet revenge of seeing four of her masculine comrades executed in twenty-four hours after her revelation.

But there is no less danger in leaving the city. The country is full of robbers. Stage-coaches are rifled on every road. The Government is powerless to protect life or property. Yet one might as well die by the robbers as be scared to death through fear of being robbed. "Faint heart never won fair lady," or any thing else.

> "Let us, then, be up and doing,
> With a heart for *any* fate,"

a great thing to say, if we mean all it includes, though many trip over the distich as though it were only pretty poetry.

Our point objective is Pachuca. You have heard of the silver mines of Mexico. Who has not? Curiosity and churchianity led our first steps to these treasures. We wanted to see what had made Mexico so attractive, and how she could be made more so. Miss Kilmansegg would not have been worth much without her precious leg, and Mexico would have been let alone as severely as the Central African governments, but for her precious legacy. But these treasures are useless to this country unless Christ go with them and before them. They have poured forth hundreds and thousands of millions into the lap of earth; they have enriched thrones and subjects in all lands; they control the merchandise of China and India to-day. Yet the nation that produces them is poor and ignorant and blind and naked; a nation peeled and robbed by its own masters; a nation of blood and strife and desolation. How its splendid ceremonials of service, and magnificent altars and vestments, and golden shrines, and silver altar railings, and unbounded pomp and parade are rebuked by this poverty and peacelessness of its people! Christ must come to Mexico. Even so, come Lord Jesus, and come quickly.

The text for this sermon was Pachuca and Real del Monte, or Royal Mount. If a pun were allowable, it might be anglicized into Mount of Reals, the silver York shilling of the country, or worse yet, and more Englishy, into the Real Mount, for most people would fancy that that mount only had reality which was a mount of silver. The two are properly one, Pachuca and Real del Monte, the former being the city, the latter the hills behind it, many of which are regularly and largely mined, and the topmost one of which, six miles from the city, and the seat of several mines, being known exclusively by that title.

Here, too, are about three hundred English people, seventy-five workmen, and overseers, with their families. Two Spanish Protestant congregations are here gathered. The threefold cord of silver mines, and English and Spanish Church work, was too much for revolvers and robbers to overcome, and so we are off for Pachuca.

That Saturday morning on which we started was January 18th, 1873. Perhaps you remember it where you lived. I doubt not that it was stinging cold, for even here it was cool enough for an overcoat when rushing along with the open windows of a fireless car. One of the party picked up an icicle of a hand's length and half its breadth, at a station a few miles from the city, the only bit of ice I have seen growing all this season. The sunny side of a house was pleasant that morning. That was all. Long before noon it was sultry. Overcoats were off and umbrellas up, and we wilted under the torrid sun. How was it up your way?

Pachuca lies about sixty miles from Mexico to the north, and a little to the east. Our railroad takes us forty miles to Omatuska, where a breakfast and a stage await us. The first ate—and a goodly one it was to eat—the second is mounted. The party is four: two ministers, and two railroaders, a general, and a banker, leaders in one of the projected Mexican invasions. The stage-ride is about forty miles, the distance this way being a third greater than straight across the country, but a third less of coach-ride. The morning is splendid. The sun has warmed to his work at this ten and a half o'clock, but not fierce in burning. The road passes through a landscape of beauty and wealth and emptiness. Two or three haciendas, or plantations, cover almost the whole of the distance. The first stretches for six or eight miles, and is given up almost entirely to the culture of pulqui.

It is pitiful to see these miles and miles of acres surrendered to this pestiferous production. Yet it is pleasant to look upon, as was the fruit Eve tasted and Adam ate, man being generally greedier in crime than woman. The fields are laid out with mathematical exactness. The maguey plant, for that is the name of the pulqui bearer, is a large aloe, with grand, broad green leaves, very broad and very green. The plants stand about ten feet apart, in rows twenty feet from each other, so that the field looks like a nursery of dark, lustrous green bushes. You can see down these green alleys sometimes for miles in this clearest of airs. They radiate regularly from every plant, a perpetual chess-board of tropical luxuriance. They are of various stages of growth, from the infant of days to the patriarch of seven to ten years.

The latter is about to yield his white heart for the delight and ruin of the people. He is about four feet high, sometimes more, and spreads over as much or more from the short, thick, bulb-like stem. Sometimes he is ripe at eight years, more usually ten. The owners thus gather a crop from one-eighth to one-tenth of their shrubs annually. When it is ripe, they thrust the knife near or into the root, so as to prevent its farther growth. The leaves fall over, the bowl-like centre swells with the juices pressing into it. It looks of the capacity of a couple of water-pails. This is of a milky look, and sweet, it is said, at this time. It is taken out twice a day for four months, so that one good plant yields four or five hundred gallons of this substance.

This is put into ox-skins, a little of the old pulqui is added for fermentation, and the new is made worse. So delicate is this substance at the start, that a pinch of salt or any other mal-affinity will destroy the whole crop if it is put into one of these skins and gets passed from one to another. An overseer, being dismissed, took this sweet (or sour) revenge on his master, and by one drop of acid, or salt, spoiled a crop worth a thousand dollars. He was arrested and imprisoned for this petty but powerful revenge.

If it is so sensitive when young, it gets bravely over it, for a more disgustingly smelling and tasting substance than it is when old the depravity of man has never yet discovered. Rotten eggs are fragrant to its odor, and pigs' swill sweet to its taste. I wish that overseer would go into the business of spoiling the crops, and drive the whole iniquity from the face of the land and the face of the people. It has a sweet cider taste in the days of its youth, but rapidly corrupts as that does, only worse, the climate being hotter, into a sour, stinking, abominable beverage.

What would Dr. Bowditch do with this tropical drunkenness? He says lust is the vice of tropics, liquor of the temperate zones. As he would encourage, with modifications, the latter in Boston, of course he must the former in Mexico. Yet here is drunkenness as bad as any in Ireland, Germany, England, or the United States, and on a tropical plant of the country. He had better move his Board of Un-health here, and proceed to sit on this phenomenon. It will all be owed, I suppose he will say, to the lofty height of this table-land, which puts it in a temperate zone. "Logic is logic, that's all I say."

Another peculiar and proper quality of this plant is its animal productions; at least so I was informed, but I doubt the information. These are said to be three: a white rat, a white, and a brown worm. These nice creatures are made great, like Cæsar, by what they feed on; and, according to these people, are ahead of Cæsar, for they are not only great but good. They are served up as delicacies to rich and poor. Fried worms and broiled rat would make a proper accompaniment to pulqui. My informant rejoiced himself in the name of Julius Cæsar. He was also a famous cook. The punster of the crowd objected to this Diet of Worms. But it was rat-ional.

Hills rise on our left, as we move north by east, well clad in the hot and purple sunlight, well stripped of all other drapery; an aqueduct half a mile long strides across a deep gully, bearing water after the high Roman fashion, from Pachuquita, or Little Pachuca, to Omatuska. The half-way station is only a stopping-place under the trees, with a pulqui shop and a fruit-stand on the ground, of bananas, oranges, and pea-nuts. A cavalcade of horses drives up. Are they robbers? Here is where they congregate. They look enough like them "to fill the bill," as they say out West. Well got up in light-brown leather trowsers, with silvered buttons and loops closely running up the sides, wide, gray felt sombreros, silver trappings on horses; they evidently need money and have not much. Will they make our littles into their mickle?

They turn out protectors rather than robbers, a mistake made often in this doubting world. They are a blessing in disguise. The road is dangerous a few leagues onward, and they are sent as an escort. Poor escort they prove, for they gallop on ahead, and that is the last we see of the gay riders.

The next hacienda, where the danger chiefly lies, is owned by the governor of the State of Hidalgo; and, it is said, by way of slander undoubtedly, that he lets the robbers pillage the coach along the line of his farm, if they will leave that alone. Even so, I remember it was correctly reported at a seminary where I once served, that a shrewd old farmer of the neighborhood was said to have kept his orchards untouched by leading the students, who had too much of the old Adam and Eve in them, to the choicest apple-trees in his neighbor's orchards. At any rate, his splendid orchard never seemed touched by that school frost, and the others often were. Whether the story of this governor or that farmer is true or not, *quien sabe!*

All I know is, that his place, like the other's orchard, is by far the finest in the country. The maguey plant stretches for miles in perfect order and beauty. Barley and wheat, and other crops green with youth, or yellow with age, spread out lovely to the eye. A rich, dark hollow of earth, circled by a darker if not richer rim of earth, five to eight miles across, a piece of landscape held in the hollow of your eye, if not the hollow of your hand, made a gem in centre and setting, such as one rarely sees, especially when the flashing Southern sun, pouring through a brisk and stimulating atmosphere, in this rare ether over eight thousand feet above the sea, made the gem yet more radiant and transparent. I well-nigh envied the governor his spot, robbers and pulqui included.

A few miles round a spur brings us in sight of Pachuca. Real del Monte had long been visible, and the high, dark range of which it is a mere point of silver. A lowlier range hid the city. It appears now, lying along the base of that black and treeless mass, a collection of low, white roofs, with a church or two towering with dome and steeple; they use both always here, though the steeple never terminates with a spire. The only decent object in these cities, sometimes the only visible object seen from a distance, is the church. Every thing is unduly abased in order that that may be unduly exalted. Our school-houses, capitols, and tall dwellings and stores, make our beautiful spires chiefs among associates, not solitary masters of an enslaved population.

But Pachuca has one sight that outshines its churches. In front of it lies a valley of exquisite beauty. The trees and plants stud it thick with emeralds. A paradise the Persians would call it—why not we? The verdure spreads out for a mile or two, and perfectly completes the picture of the tall, brown mountains that overhang the town, and the white walls that hug their lower declivities. Brown, white, and green glow together in this summer afternoon of January. Oh, ye frozen and sepulchred home folks, a white cemetery of Nature, with icy winds raving over it, how rapturous this delicious landscape! How I regret that you are not here to enjoy it —that the North could not be transported, body and business, to this dulcet clime for six months of every year!

You are needed; for this exquisite paradise is as full of devils as the primal one, when man had gone over to the enemy. It is not very safe to walk its streets on Sunday, and hardly possible at midnight. So "the trail of the serpent is over it all." You may prefer your icy atmosphere and snowy covering with peace, safety, comfort, and prosperity, a life in death, to this tropical glory, with its assassinations and robberies, a death in life. All things are equal, after all.

We ride to the hotel, but are met by Mr. Comargo, the superintendent of the mines, who invites us to the Casa Grande, or Grand House, belonging to the company, at which place this story began.

We pass under its heavy portal of barred gates of wood and thin iron, and past the large guard that, armed and equipped, protects the entrance, into a large, square, open court. Up the broad stairs, with their gilt and burnished balustrades, among rich tropical plants and flowers, we ascend to the balcony. Here the conductor, as he is called, meets us, a small, gentlemanly person, and makes his house our own. Elegant apartments open on every side of this court, and abundant flowers line the entire balcony.

"We have lighted on our feet," exclaims one of the party. Nobody, for once, disagrees with the observation, the only point of agreement in all the journey.

Dusty garments are brushed, and dusty faces washed, and we mount horses for a ride up the side of the mountain to a mine. Horses before us, horses behind us, horses to the right of us, horses to the left of us; thus we march into the narrow streets and up the narrower slips of the hill-side. A cavalcade more numerous than attends a European monarch accompanied these every-day travelers. Reason why? Not that we were more than monarchs, but Pachuca is less safe to the conductor of its mines than Paris ever was to Napoleon. He would be a prize to the kidnapers.

We inspect the outside of the mine, from the crushing of the ore to the smelting of the silver, and return to a sumptuous dinner, a lively reunion, and a luscious bed. In its comfortable embrace we dream of Elysium, although

> "We should suspect some danger nigh,
> Where we possess delight."

Our first peril is past, Pachuca is reached. Our second cometh quickly.

Just after we reached the town, on Saturday afternoon, we passed a building near the little plaza with "Miners' Arms" over its door. It looked Englishy English to the last degree. Some equally Englishy English persons stood before the door. They noticed we were strangers, and one of them, a tall, plainly-dressed person, came across the street and spoke to us. He had heard that a Methodist preacher was coming to spend the Sabbath, and he made a dash at random at this couple, hoping to bag that game. He succeeded. It was a Mr. Prout, for whom I had a letter of introduction. He accompanied us to the Casa, and then sought out an elder member, Richard Rule, Esq., who for years had had preaching and class-meeting at his house. To show the peril of the place, that night he was sent for to come and see about arrangements for Sabbath services. Guards were sent to accompany him to the Casa, and to accompany him home again. Yet in the day-time there is but little if any danger.

The next morning I attended a class-meeting at Richard Rule's. It met at eight o'clock. But the long ride and the late night made me a little late, and the venerable leader was at prayer when I entered. It seemed strange to hear the voice of prayer in a Sunday-morning class in this far-off land in our own tongue. And yet it seemed not unnatural. A full and devout petition it was, covering all the ground, as if the fewness of the number present allowed larger liberty to each utterance. It was eminently Scriptural in form, as all English prayers are, and rich in faith, in humility, and in assurance. The one other English peculiarity it also exhibited, devotion to fatherland. He prayed for the "favored land of their birth" and "for the benighted land" in which they dwelt. That feeling is wrought deeper in English nature than in that of any other people. America unconsciously copies it, but does not surpass it.

Four members, all males, gave testimony to a present and a full salvation, and responses showed the warmth of the heart still on fire with God's love.

It was good to be there. No mine in all this richest district of the earth was so rich as this, nay, was infinitely less rich. These had searched for wisdom as for hid treasures, and had found her:

> "Wisdom divine, who tells the price
> Of wisdom's costly merchandise?
> Wisdom to silver we prefer,
> And gold is dross, compared with her."

How rich these poor men were. Only one possessed any means or mines. Yet all were rejoicing in eternal and infinite treasure-houses, laid up by the same Redeemer who stored these mounts with silver, in that Mount of God, His Royal Mount, the Real del Monte of the heavens and the universe, for all those who love and serve Him.

The house of Mr. Rule stands in a garden, with large, luscious plants blooming about. The oleander, banana, fig, and unknown trees and blooms fill the retreat with life and loveliness. High walls hide it from the passer's eyes. It is secluded and central. I have quite fallen in love with these dead walls without, and beauty, luxury, and comfort within. I am not sure that it is not an improvement on our system, more open without, and less secluded within. Not as you are in your winter-bound firesides,

> "Shut in
> By the tumultuous privacy of storm,"

but by a privacy which makes a perpetual summer for your private pleasure, though this sometimes shuts out a tumult worse than snow ever creates. It makes the street unlovely, but not the home. These rough walls and gates open on luxury and repose. The high wall is not needed to make this picture. The gardens might be open to all eyes, and the court-yard only be for home consumption.

At eleven o'clock Rev. Mr. Parks, the Bible Agent, preached to a goodly congregation on "The love of Christ constraineth us;" and at two, another full house gathered to attend the third service of the day. "Whom having not seen ye love," is the text dwelt upon, the counterpart and complement of the morning's discourse. The baptism of three infants, and the administration of the Lord's Supper to seven persons, prolongs the service till four o'clock. The full house sits solemn and reverent to the close.

A service in Spanish follows, conducted by Dr. Guerro, a physician of the place. It is not so full as usual, owing to the length of the preceding meeting, but there is a fair assemblage. Some fine-looking young men participated. The service has been compiled by him from that of Dr. Riley, and is entitled "El Culto de la Iglesia Reformada en Pachuca." It is orthodox and devout. But the service needs more liberty extemporaneously, and besides needs additions of prayer, and social and class meetings, and Sunday-schools. It is the seed, but not the flower nor fruit.

The conductor of the meeting is a Protestant against Romanism, and, like most of that class here, has not yet advanced much beyond the first principles of that protest.

The elaboration of the Christian system, independent of all the previous errors and formalities, into a life and being of its own—this work is yet to be done. It needs organization, Church order, breadth, life. It will come, and that speedily. It was delightful to find in this mountain town, and among this degraded and depraved population, a godly few casting off the shackles of a false culture, and forming a reformed Church. May they speedily regenerate the town.

We come back to our agreeable quarters across the plaza, which from our first crossing it in the morning until now has been crowded with sellers and buyers. The pavement is lined with rows of merchant-men and merchant-women with every sort of ware—fruit, fish, flesh, coal, grasses, trinkets, muslins, toys—a Vanity Fair of Sunday desecration. The stores under the arcade are equally busy. The church is open, and has its two services a day, but the crowds are in the market-place, and the devil holds his service all the day.

He is represented in a huge, gross picture in the church on the plaza with a smashing tail, a good deal longer than his body, driving the sinful ghosts to hell. He is out here in calico and cloth, in a white, dirty woolen blanket, dropping down before and behind, with a slit in the middle, through which the head is passed, in thin blue cloth mantillas that cover the woman's head and shoulders and mouth. Here he is buying and selling, and getting gain and loss. Let the true Church of Christ arise and abate this crime that smells to heaven.

I was not a little wearied with this long day's work. From

eight to five, with scarce an intermission, had I been attending to the Lord's business. A summer day, sultry as August, yet not oppressive, it has been a day of delights, "where no crude surfeit reigns."

The hills look soft in that sacred setting, and the fields did not strive in vain to look gay. They looked so without striving. The air was blessed, and I rejoiced to think that this ancient and rich realm would yet be the mount of the Lord, and its silver flow forth for the salvation of the world.

Monday comes, and with it the old again, to offset the new of yesterday. The champing of bits and trampling of steeds below is a signal that we are invited to a ride. A ride is a small affair ordinarily in America, and even in Europe to-day, but not at the Casa Grande. The lord of the casa, Señor Comargo, descends the stairway, with pistol in his belt and a girdle of ball-cartridges about him. His horse has gun and sword hanging at its saddle-bow. Five visitors follow — two less powerfully armed, and two with no weapons save their tongues. Three horsemen precede this company, and twelve follow. A carriage and four mules are provided for any two of the party that may wish to accept the new style instead of the old. Thus protected and equipped, we ride through the awakening town.

Why all this display? Not for display. This is the old, because here the old still exists. This city is full of robbers, and so is the country. It is the chief mining centre of this region, and has only one equal in all this country. The building is the headquarters of the mining company. It has two hundred thousand dollars in its vaults every fortnight. This it must transport sixty miles to Mexico. The reckless marauders of these hills long for these hid treasures more than for those still concealed in the earth all about them. They have attacked the building once and again, and sometimes in large force, three to four hundred men. They would attack the commandant, or conductor, as he is the chief representative of the company, and his capture might be worth many thousands to his kidnapers. Only last week, in company with four of his horsemen, he broke through a band of thirty-five robbers, under a famous bandit leader, killing one and wounding several others.

This company has some valuable nuggets for such marauders. Here is the president of the nearly finished Vera Cruz Railway, Mr. Gibbs, of England, as witty as he is wise, and wise as he is witty, one of the least "stuck up" of well-educated Englishmen I have ever met. He is a representative of Oxford scholarship and London business. He can scan Greek lines or Mexican landscapes with equal accuracy. He confesses to England's aristocratic detestation of the Yankee until the war compelled her to see, first, that we had pluck; second, success; and third, and logically, that we were right. That is the usual construction of an Englishman's syllogism, pluck first, principle last. Then, of course, we ceased to be whittling, nasal Yankees, and turned into gentlemen. He breaks forth at the mouth, like all punsters, and makes fun for the million (of dollars) that rides at his side.

The head of the house of Rosecrans, a rival railroad enterprise, is also here—General Palmer, self-contained, ready to thrust the point of an argument into his antagonist, as whilom the point of his sword, and that as this without malice, though now as then unto the death.

Mr. Parish, the learned and traveled member of the party, is at home equally in the best modern languages and modern society. It is a striking evidence of the union of culture and business, these polished and highly-educated gentlemen on railroad thoughts intent. It shows, what ought to be the case more and more, the best university training a preliminary to the entrance into every profession.

The agent of the British and Foreign Bible Society, a Congregational clergyman, is the fourth; whom, as he is lying awake on his bed in the room where I am now writing, it will not answer to say much about, or I should see the sheeted living, as Cæsar did the "sheeted dead," walking the floor and squaring off. England and America, despite Geneva decisions and the peace societies, would be at war. He is well satisfied with England, at least when talking with an American, though I doubt not he will set forth all those American arguments as to Britain's conditions and needs when he gets back to "Our Old Home," and will forget, perhaps, to put in the quotation marks. He is doing an excellent work here in planting the Bible over the land.

The last who mounts the horse, and who rides *muy mal* (you do not know but that that means very good, and I shall not tell you that it means very bad), is not, perhaps, representing his fellow-ministers so much in their horse-riding reputation as in eating and enduring. He is seeking out this land for the Church, as his associates are for the Bible and the railway, a threefold cord which is not easily broken, and which will yet make this beautiful clime " bound with gold chains about the feet of God."

The road ascends the mountain side. For two thousand feet and two leagues it winds and climbs. The basin of Pachuca lies below, soft in the brown morning, yet unkissed of the sun, which yellows the eastern sky, but does not glow upon its mountain-tops. The green trees, flowers, and maguey plant make a garden of beauty of that basin, lying low in the hollow of treeless hills, " rock-ribbed and ancient as the sun." It is less luxuriant than the woods and ferns of the Hot Lands, but its contrast with the inclosing hillsides and the brisk September air makes its verdant loveliness all the more lovely.

The mountains are without forest, but a purple verdure covers them — a royal mantle of sunlight and shadow, dewy, tender, velvety. Not since I looked on Hymettus and Pentelicus have I seen such a rich hue clothe barren mountains. The composition of the rock has something to do with it; the purple of porphyry imparts its color to the hills.

Iztaccihuatl glitters on the point of its snowy lance. There is some debate as to which of the three ice mountains it is, and so the poet of the company — for "we keeps our poet," like Day & Martin — breaks forth in rhymes on each of the trio. First, he exclaims,

> Why all this palaver
> About Orizava?*

Then adds, toastingly and drunkenly,

> We'll tip the brandy-bottle
> To old Iztaccihuatl.

And teetotally concludes,

> We'll drain our water-kettle
> To Popocatepetl.

Of course he would have gone on thus all day had he not been held in. He was pouring forth the terrible rhymes as if they were avalanches. "Slaver" it was found would rhyme and reason with this Orizava, and "throttle" had to be put to the voluble neck of this Iztaccihuatl; while a lot of mispronounced rhymes, such as "settle," "met ill," "nettle," and so on, were being mustered into the service of the grand old monarch of Mexico. It was time to stop the rhymed nonsense, and it stopped. Sober debates on temperance and other good themes came to the front.

The light slides down the mountain ("coasts," as a Yankee ought to say), down its smooth and lustrous sides, and soon fills all the hollow of the hills with splendor. The soul sends its shafts of light upward as those of the soulless world fall downward, and in silent prayer and praise ascribes the honor, and glory, and dominion, and power thus seen, and the infinitely more and greater not seen, unto Him that sitteth on the throne, and to the Lamb forever.

One side of the roadway leaps down sheer and profound, and the other opens ravines, or descends in mountain slopes, where easily "the robber rends his prey" from the slowly-climbing coach and rider. There is a thicket of bushes at one of these bends, which is their favorite haunt, and yet no one thinks of the simple remedy of cutting up that ambuscade. Fifteen minutes and a hatchet would destroy that fortification. Why is it not done? *Quien sabe?*

---

* "B" and "v" are pronounced exactly alike by the natives; so the word Orizaba is pronounced as in this couplet.

Two hours of such slow and steadfast climbing bring the feudal cavalcade to the Real Castle, or the Castle of the Real.

Here a yet more feudal incident increases the delusion. We draw up to a high, huge dead wall without a window. The gate opens, and we enter. The warder draws near and makes his obeisance to the conductor, a gracious action on the part of each. A low room, not loftier than those usually seen in the ruined castles of the Rhine, welcomes us, and refreshments are served up. The company then proceed to inspect the castle. They kept saying to each other, "How completely feudal!" "Was there ever any thing more perfect?" "This is the real article." "As it should be on the Real," keeps up the execrable punster.

At the entrance of the building proper is a well with a windlass over it. To the ropes of this windlass were attached pieces of maguey or hemp sack, a quarter of a yard wide, made into a sort of seat. In this seat sat the workmen, and, clinging to the rope, were let down ten or twelve hundred feet, "*poco mas y menos*," as they all say here to every thing ("a little more or less)." They are let down and dragged up every day.

Still fancying I had entered a castle, and a little bewildered by this mode of treating its inmates, I was led to a court with rooms long and wide opening out of it, and long benches stretching on either side against the walls, which had that horrid odor that belongs to the wards of a prison, and which is unlike any other smell. Another step, and a barred door, heavy and thick, made of crosspieces that let in the light and air, but not liberty, revealed the fact that this mediæval castle was indeed a prison. So its looks did not deceive itself. That well was to let down criminals to work in the mines.

It took off the edge of our vanity a little to learn this fact. The castle is reduced in vocation, though not in manners. Don Quixote can fancy it a castle, though it be only a *presidio*. Those straps of maguey fibre, in which they were let down that thousand feet, were homœopathic in their nature. Pulqui brought them here, and the fibre of its leaf drops them there. I had seen pits like this in

European castles, as black and bottomless seemingly, where they dropped their victims, to be brought up, not as these are at nightfall, but in the morn only of the Resurrection.

In two of the cells were three leading bandits of the country awaiting execution. I only saw one of them. He was a youth of twenty, fair-faced, smooth-faced, with calm manners and a mild dark eye: so pretty a lad one rarely sees. Is it possible that he is a chief murderer? Even so. Appearances here, as elsewhere, are deceitful. Yet not so. Leaders are rarely demonstrative men. Byron was not at fault in describing human nature when he painted his chief cut-throat as

> "The mildest-mannered man
> That ever scuttled ship or cut a throat;"

and describes him on a balmy eve as he leans over the taffrail and

> "Looks upon the flood:
> His thoughts were calm, but were of blood."

This youth's mien and meditation were alike calm and bloody. He would have put a shot through the warden as briskly and gayly as through a bird. He was trained in crime, and, though still beardless, was gray in guilt. How many of our worst offenders accomplish their end before they reach a ripe manhood! The gallows has more victims under thirty than over. Sin ripens fast, and the lad of fifteen who casts off parental restraint and plunges into vice, before he is twenty-five is apt to die a debauchee or a demon. Christ and the devil recruit their forces from the youth. A Christian or a criminal is the decision usually made before the twenties are touched. Despise not the converted boy. Nurse his childish piety, lest it become youthful impiety ere you are aware.

Sadly we left the fair young face, so soon to be mould and dust, and came into the bright sunshine. How gloomily glowered that sun! The prison was no longer a palace, but a tomb. We gladly mount and ride away from the grim recesses. You have had enough of the Old; now again for the New.

As we emerge into the outer air our eyes light on chimneys, tall and numerous, scattered up and down the steep hill-sides. My English companions thought they had seen the like in Yorkshire. Yet the chief if not only likeness is in the chimneys, and in the fact that they are used in running steam-engines of immense bulk, which are engaged in pumping water out of the mines. This was the New. No such contrivances had the cavalcades of the Old times ever seen. One of these engines, of two thousand horse-power, is beautifully lifting its ponderous arms, as polished and quiet as is its Manchester builder. It is an evidence of the superiority of our age. Two thousand horse-power there in that engine, twenty in this escort: one hundred times is the New above the Old!

It is a *festa* day, and the natives are idling round. But the engines are busy, being worked by Englishmen, who know no *festas* but Sundays and Christmas. A bull-fight is to come off, and especial stir among the natives is evident. If they would fight their sins, and idleness, and errors of faith, and other infirmities, half as zealously as they fight the harmless bulls, they would "get on," as our English friends say, vastly more; but religious error stifles all energy, order, and improvement.

These immense engines teach us the costliness of the mining business. It may be an easy matter to prospect a mine, but it is not so easy a matter to work it. That costs a fortune, and reduces this royal business to the common level of farming and shoe-making. After looking over the works at this spot, we take to our horses, I gratefully getting a seat in the carriage, and whirl down to Velasco.

Six miles of rapid descent it is, winding round and round the spurs of handsomely wooded hills, which woods the steam-devil, as the Mexicans call the steam-engine, is fast devouring. In its locomotive form it devours miles; in all forms, forests. The hills are not unlike those of Vermont, but steeper, deeper, and grander, with warmer, thicker-leaved, and darker-tinted woods. Some of the gorges are sublime. Opposite these ravines tower high, blank, black mountains, some of which are curiously crowned with basaltic rocks, that look like towers, laid in order far up into the air. At times these columns take possession of a stretch of ridge, and make a series of fortifications not unlike Ehrenbreitstein, or a range of towers like a cathedral. They had shot their straight, hot barrels up through the various molten rocks of porphyry and granite, and capped the climax with their rounded finish.

Velasco is a fortified hacienda, where the ores of Real del Monte are reduced. These ores, being less inclined to yield to water than those of Pachuca, are here calcined, ground to powder, dropped from hoppers through leather tubes into strong barrels, which are also filled with water, quicksilver, sulphate of copper, and other chemicals, and a quantity of round stones about the size of small paving-stones. These are sent whirling round and round until the dissolution of the silver from the soil is effected, when the contents are drawn off. Below you see the residuum of the barrel, flowing out over troughs into bowls slightly inclined, whose lower edge holds the heavy white quicksilver, and upper, the lighter and slower precious stuff which it costs so much labor to secure.

Attached to these works is a handsome house, deserted. No officer dare live in it. Not long since its walls were scaled by a robber band, though they could find but little booty. Its garden is full of flowers, and I pluck a half-dozen rose-buds and blossoms as a specimen of the middle of January, which I commend to my frozen brothers of the North. They may retort that that robber thorn is worse than their frozen buds. I do not deny it, but hope when the railroad and the churches of America get possession of the land that the Mexican will be changed into a Methodist, or better, if better there be, as most of these Englishmen have been, and you can then have no excuse for shivering below the zeroes, instead of enjoying perpetual spring and summer, from October to April, among these torrid altitudes.

Three leagues more over hill and dale, amidst an opening and entrancing landscape, now by barren water-courses, now along high uplands, over which canter our horses. I am on the back again, and likely to be on my back with this fierce and unused riding. So we go gayly on to Regla.

The hills are well stripped by the charcoal vender and the steam-engine devourer, and look like some of the brown, barren, rocky sides of New Hampshire in July. The sun pours a midday torrid heat upon us, and makes us like that too-willing lass of whom it is said that, when her lover said "'Wilt thou?' she wilted." So did we, though the heat that wilted us was from without, and not within. San Miguel shone out on the plain below, said to be one of the prettiest of Mexican towns. Our road lies to the left, and its beauty is left also. The plains in which this beauty lingers stretch far away to the east and north, bounded by tall dark mountains that seem to jealously guard the sleeping beauty below. At the hour of noon our tired steeds and more tired selves enter the gates of the hacienda of Regla.

This hacienda lies in a ravine, with a high wall going up to and on its outer edge, and with entrances well barred and guarded. Before its gate is a fine fountain, set in the side of the hill, flowing through a lion's mouth inserted in the rocks. Around the carved stone rim of the basin women and children are filling their water-pots. The water tastes delicious after our hot and dusty ride; far better, I doubt not, than the brandies and other "hot and rebellious liquors" would have done, which are still too freely offered, and far too freely imbibed.

The English have brought valuable money and men to this country, but have not yet brought total abstinence; and too many Americans are still ashamed of that teetotal excellence which, though it has not entirely conquered that land, has given its laborers and leaders more than half the prosperity and comfort they enjoy. If it could come here and drive out the legion of devils which the cup of inebriety introduces, it would be a blessing of blessings to all the people. Amen, so let it be!

Leaving our horses at the gate, we are led by the house where dinner (they call it breakfast here) is awaiting us, under vast arches, alongside of a paved brook, now nearly waterless, and whose blocks look like Broadway, so smooth and even and slippery are their shape and aspect. A few rods farther, and we reach the upper section of the chasm.

The Mexican Giant's Causeway is before us. We had regretted that Britain had one advantage of America in her celebrated Fingal's Cave, and now we are satisfied. Even that crown is transferred to our favored land. The columns of basalt rise on each side of the ravine from seventy-five to one hundred feet in height. The opening is a few hundred feet wide at the mouth, but comes together at the upper edge, with only a slight chasm, which lets out the waters of the river, that tumbles, a pretty cascade, some two-score of feet into a pretty pool below. You are fifty feet or so above the pool. The columns rise one hundred feet sheer over your head. They are five-sided, and fit each to each as close as bricks. Some of the outer ones are split and otherwise marred; one or two seem to have lost both their head and their heels, and hang to their place by a sort of attraction of adhesion. If that gave way, the attraction of gravitation would topple them over upon our heads—a not very attractive attraction. The débris of their fallen fellows lies all about us. Each reveals a round core of light slate-color, that seems to have been built around after the pentagonal model. Where that core came from, and how it was grown around, I leave to those who find sermons in stones to ascertain. I prefer less hardened subjects.

There seems to be no end inward to the serried ranks. They are packed close, and each shaft reveals others that inclose it, and that are ready to take its place should sun and shower cause it to fall. If they could be utilized by some Yankee for house or monument building, we should soon see an end of the exquisite ravine. They are slaughtering the like tall living shafts that have stood together these centuries and centuries from Maine to Michigan, and Michigan to Mexico. Thanks many (*muchas gracias*, to be very Mexic) that they can not cut these down, saw them into stone lumber, and cart them away for Chicago and Boston burnings. Just penalty was that, for that sin of ourselves and our fathers?

THE PALISADES OF REGLA.

This spot, unheard of by me unto this hour, unmentioned by any tourist I have read (and I never read one on Mexico), is now formally introduced to the American public. If you come to Mexico, come to Pachuca; and if to Pachuca, to the basaltic ravine of Regla.

We lean over the balcony of our hospitable quarters, awaiting breakfast, and see the horses tread out the silver. A yard eighty rods square, *poco mas y menos*, is laid down to this work. Beds of black mud are located over it, to the untrained eye precisely like the earth about it. But how different to the eye that is trained! This black mud is silver, mixed badly with other earths, mixed also with salt, sulphate of copper, and quicksilver, that, under the painful pressure of tramping steeds, are to liberate it and make it the beauty and joy of man—and plague also, as are most beauties and joys. Two hundred horses are engaged in tramping out the silver. Their tails are shaven, the mud has splashed up on their heads and backs, and they look so woe-begone, as if their labor were degrading, that it is hard for the uninitiated eye to believe they are horses at all. Mules, and even asses, they get degraded to. The making of silver seems to be as debasing as much of the spending of it is. Eighty of these march round one circle, five abreast, close together. Four such circles employ over two hundred horses and mules. Over three hundred and fifty are owned by the company, and sometimes all of them are put into service at once. The barrel system of Velasco is also employed, and water, barrels, and horses make the ore into silver.

After a most sumptuous breakfast, served by Mr. Rule, the Superintendent of Regla, a breakfast cooked in the best English fashion (and there is none better), we start for the last and not least of the points of interest that have drawn our feet and eyes this way. The horses that are brought out for us, how different from the shorntailed nags that are swinging around those circles! The gayest and handsomest is most unwisely but generously offered to me. He is a fine sprinkled white sorrel, and he has been in the stable many days.

The best seat at the table, and the best dishes upon it, a minister may get used to. A Methodist minister certainly ought to be ready to accept the best horse, for has not much of his success come from his gifts and graces in that favorite department of human enjoyment? He has abolished the parson's jog, which was as well known as the parson's coat, and made the "Gid-up" of Holmes's "One-horse Shay" as dusty a nothing as the shay itself. When the first itinerants drove into the country village on their smooth, fleet steeds, the eyes of the loafers about tavern and store were opened very wide. "Who is this feller who rides such a handsome critter?" was the general inquiry. And when they found he was a preacher, their amazement grew like Fort Garry wheat in July. They had never seen it after this fashion. They would go and hear the minister, whose horse could beat the fastest racer of the Corners, and they did go and hear, and found he could preach as well as he could ride. The way to a man's heart is through a horse, as those fathers found.

I ought, too, to have been inspired by modern examples. I bethought me of that presiding elder way down East, whose little beast used to leave all meaner things behind; and who (the man, not the mare) was accustomed to say to all gayly-dressed horsemen, who rode up in buckskin gloves, shiny hat, horse and harness and all, as if to leave their dust upon his sorry team, ere he quickly passed out of their sight, " I beg pardon, sir, but I treat all alike."

Alas! that this dear, delightful brother so suddenly fled to the world above. Riding into his yard from his wide circuit, struck there with death, disembarking, and pausing by this companion of many a long journey, he drops suddenly, never to rise again. The Pale Horse and its paler rider bear him swiftly away. Nay, the flaming chariots of Israel and the horsemen thereof sweep him heavenward.

I might also have bethought me of that other presiding elder in the Far West who, when his black ponies in an unwashed buggy slid by a costly, stately team, newly bought and burnished, turned to their crest-fallen owner as he passed, and suggested that he put those horses in the lumber-yard.

But not the fathers nor the brothers could give me courage. I preferred to fall into the extravagance of Bishop Soule, of whom Bishop Roberts once remarked that he heard "he had sold his horse down South, and was coming home in a stage-coach," and he regretted the degeneracy of the Church, and the passing away of its heroic epoch. But that epoch had its vices as well as its virtues, and the perils of horse-jockeying worry the Conference now in the passage of the ministers' characters far less than of yore.

I get on my star-dusted steed—silver-dusted I ought to say in this country—and he leaps, and dances, and whirls, and plays his fantastic tricks. And I pull on the curb, and that cuts and maddens and makes him more antic, for that is the purpose of the curb here.

Every thing goes by contraries. You unlock your door by turning the key to the lintel, and not away from it; you open it outward. Your boots are made so that left seems right, and right left, and look so after they are on. You take the same side in the street as your opposite, and so does he, and thus you go bowing and bobbing, neither able to get on or away. You eat your breakfast at noon, or later, and take your midday dinner about seven in the evening. So the curb, instead of steadying the horse, sets his mouth a-bleeding, and that makes him dance, which is very beautiful to riders and lookers-on. A knife thrust into his belly by the spurs, and into his mouth by the curb, gets up just the right degree of pain and madness that makes him lively and lovely.

Mine has no spur, for which all thanks. The curb is enough. He scampers up the hill, among the rocks, regardless of rider: flies down a steep rock slide, as if he would never stop; caracoles along the edge of a ravine, or barranca, five hundred to a thousand feet deep, "like he knew," as they say in my Southern country. I was "awfully scared," lest he would just shake himself when on the edgiest edge, and drop me overboard. But when we got up, and down, and up this rough lane alongside of the gorge, and the splendid park opened out for miles, hard, smooth, carpeted with short, dry grass—how he did fly! So did my coward lips from their color. I was in no danger of witching this world with my horsemanship. "Muy mal" (very bad) was the muttered judgment of my score of Mexican escorts, and so was it mine.

A MEXICAN GENERAL.

There was a general in our troop — called Heneral here (another specimen of the contrary style of this people, for Cock-eral would be by far a more proper designation). This G—, H—, or C—eral was a cavalry officer all through the war. He had noticed what fine horses I had got, and how poorly I rode them, and he had had a suspicion that this one would fall to him; so he had offered early to exchange his easy pacer for my furious charger. In a fit of vainglory I had declined. But that park, grass, and gamboling were enough for me. I was willing to swap horses in crossing this stream. I dismounted and gave my wayward steed to the Heneral. He rode him well. They flew together, mile and mile. I can not say that I felt very bad when I saw him, on returning, dismount and lead his horse for a long stretch, almost over the very ground where it had tossed me so. The frisky fellow was blown. The high altitude and his high spirits were too much for him, and he had run himself out. The short-lived glory died away, and this very short horse was very soon curried.

That park on which we ascend is engirted with high purple hills. It is level, and hard as a dancing-floor, and the horses all dance as they touch it, and have a gay gallopade over it. It was my ignorance, probably, of that sort of floor practice that made me make so poor a display. The Coloradoist of the party said it was very like the parks of that country. It is fine for grazing, though I judge it is too high and dry for most other culture. A half hour brings us to its abrupt close.

La Barranca Grande opens at our feet. You do not know what a barranca is? Nor did I till that day. I wish you could learn it the same way. Conceive of a level plain forty miles wide, with a border of mountains. Ride along over it leisurely and rapidly, a little of both, chatting or singing as the spirit moves, when you halt, without reason so far as you can see. You move on a rod or two slowly, and down you look two thousand feet (ten times the height of Trinity steeple or Bunker Hill Monument), down, down, down. That is no black chasm into which you are peering, but a broad garden, green and brown. Here a hill rolls up in it, a mole scarcely noticed on its handsome face. There a bamboo cottage hides itself without being hid. The green forests are full of deer. Bananas, oranges, every delight is flourishing there. A river trickles through it, picking its glittering way down to the Gulf, two hundred miles away. The walls on the opposite side rise into wild, rocky mountains, and both sides come seemingly together forty miles above—though it is only seeming, for the cañon takes a turn, and goes on and up between the mountains. Eastward it has no visible end. It descends, it is said, through to the Gulf.

The sunlight of a warm September afternoon, so it feels, pours over the whole, glowing grandly on these mountains, pouring a flood of light on the upper terminations where the hills clasp hands over the valley, and glistening sweetly from the home-like landscape below.

One would not tire of gazing, or of going down, though the latter is an hour's job, the former a second's. It is wonderful what great gifts God spreads out on the earth for his children, and how solitary the most of them are. Bryant could not make solitude more solitary than in those lines of his,

> "Where rolls the Oregon and hears no sound
> Save his own dashings."

So here sleeps this wonderful ravine, with its towering mountains, in sun or moon, in midnight blackness or midday splendor, and rarely looks on the face of man. Does not the Giver of every good and perfect gift enjoy His own gifts? "For His pleasure they are and were created." Then the Barranca would be satisfied if no mortal eye ever took in its beauty. It smiles responsive to the smile of its Lord.

Long we hang above the picture. At risk of life we creep to the outermost twig, and gaze down. It stands forth a gem of its own. No rival picture intermeddleth therewith. "It is worth a journey of a thousand miles," said a distinguished traveler to me to-day, "to see the Barranca Grande and the Regla Palisades." And I say "ditto" to Mr. Burke.

We are back to Regla and off to Pachuca none too early, for it is four and one-fourth of the clock ere we leave our too-hospitable friends of the valley, and turn homeward our horses' heads and our own—well-turned these latter be already by what we have seen. It is dark at six, and the ride is five hours, and the country full of robbers. Dark falls on us before we reach Velasco—thick, soft, warm. We begin to climb the mountains and pass the lower entrance of Real del Monte, when I get a bigger scare by far than that which frighted us near Omatuska.

I had just been talking with the builder of the Vera Cruz road. He had expressed fears of an attack, and as he had been long in the land, his fears were well grounded, at least to me. He had been describing how a French friend of his was lately cut to pieces on the hill we were soon to cross. So I was in an excellent condition for a fright. He had ridden ahead a rod or less, and was chatting Spanish with the conductor, Mr. Comargo. It was pitch-dark. Horsemen had been passing us quite frequently, lively with pulqui, and the bull-fight of the day. They were all in good fighting trim. Suddenly a number of them rode in among us, wheeled round their horses, and drove up to the conductor. I heard them speak his name. "It is come now, I am sure of it," I thought. These fellows are going to seize the conductor, and pistols and rifles will instantly flash and fire. As I had neither rifle nor pistol, I was not expected to take a very prominent part in the mêlée. I could see them dimly speak to the leader, and awaited the fire. It did not come. What does it mean? One second — ten — thirty elapsed, and no cry, no grapple, no shot. I turned to one of the escort at my side, and summoning up all the Spanish at my command, I said, "Nosotros ombres?" "Si, señor," was his calming reply, and the scare was over. They were gentlemen from Real del Monte, who had ridden down to escort us through the town. My escort, who said "Yes, sir," did not rebuke me for my bad Spanish. But when I got back to Mexico, and was telling the adventure to some Yankees, they laughed at my language, and said my question meant "We friends?" instead of "Our friends?" which I meant to say, and that I ought to have said, "Nuestros ombres?"

I insert this, so that if you are equally frightened you may be sure and be grammatical, otherwise your stay-at-home friends, who know just a bit more than you, and not your Spanish comrades, will be sure to make fun of you, even as those who never write a book or an article can cut up the grammar of those who do. Lindley Murray did not write Shakspeare, nor Goold Brown edit the *Atlantic*; but how much more they know about correct writing than mere geniuses!

Down hill, on the box with the driver, I go, for my friend, the general, begs the loan of my horse; and, pitying his ill-luck with the former steed, I relent and grant the second favor. The driver responds to my American Spanish with a ceaseless "Si"—not "sigh," as you might properly suppose, but "see." Especially when I say "Ablaro" (another blunder) "Espagnol muy mal" ("I speak Spanish very bad"), you ought to have heard him put the emphasis on that "*Sí, señor*."

We wind around the gulfs of the mountain-side. A white rim about a black sea the road appears. Robberless, and now fearless, we greet the lights of Pachuca, drive through its narrow streets, and, at nine and a half, ride under the fortified arches of the Casa Grande.

The Old and the New accompany us even after we get within the safe and luxurious inclosure; for I am no sooner seated at our ten-o'clock dinner than word comes that a couple await my presence at a wedding, and the guests also. So the dinner is left half done, so far as the appetite goes, and the guard is followed to an English residence, that of the superintendent of the mines. Here we wait two hours for the arrival of the clerk of the city, who must be present to make the clerical work of any value. A supper of English tea, cheese, bread, and buns breaks that two hours in pieces, and half an hour after midnight the Cornwall youth and maiden are duly and truly married by a Mexican officer of state and an American clergyman. So ended the day, when the clock struck one, and I struck the couch, satisfied with this full cup of the Old and the New.

And now, having taken you over the ride, you may like, as practical Yankees, to know what all this is for. You can not be much of a Yankee not to know. Look at that silver dollar! Ah, I forgot! You live in a country where the silver dollar is unknown. A country that pays off its debts, has good credit everywhere, pays its employés regularly, soldiers and clerks and officers, and yet does not clink the silver. Here all is silver and bankruptcy. No currency but coin, and no credit at home or abroad. General Butler's argument for a paper currency based on the credit of the government is the practice of America, whatever be its theory. Mexico has sent out three thousand millions of silver, and is still a silverless country. The Real del Monte mines, as all this group is called, have been known almost from the invasion of Cortez. They have been regularly and valuably worked for over a hundred and fifty years, though with some intermissions, caused by the water getting into the mines.

The most successful operator was Pedro Terreras, a muleteer, who found a shaft about 1762, worked it, and grew so rich that he gave Charles IV. of Spain two vessels of war, and promised him, if he would visit America and Regla, that he should never put foot on the New World, but only on the silver from his mines. He was made Count of Regla, and his family are still among the wealthiest Mexicans. The present yield of the mines is about four millions annually.

We went into an "adit," or passage by which the tram-way drags out the ore. It is the Gautemozin mine, and properly named for the last Aztec emperor, who bravely but vainly sought to keep these riches from the European clutch. It is the richest in the country. A mile or so by mules, careful not to put out your arm and to get too lifted up in your head, and you come to a higher hole in the mountain, and a deeper one also. Here ladders descend for fifteen hundred feet. We take that for granted, climb a hundred feet, and see the steam-engine working in the bowels of the earth. I had heard that this was an English invention. I find it an American discovery. Here we see it growing. It looks strange, this fierce fire in the heart of the mountain, and some of our companions fear it as typical of the place we do not go up to.

These engines everywhere are to draw off the water. They are run by Englishmen entirely. The ore comes up in long iron boxes, is dumped into carts, is divided off in bags, one in ten of which goes to the miner, besides six reals a day. The ore is worth about as much more; a dollar and a half a day is quite a fair day's wages. They search every workman three times as he leaves the mine, from hair to shoes. He has only two garments—a short linen jacket, and a pair of trowsers without pockets. These are carefully shaken. His hat and slippers are pulled off, and equally searched.

The ore does not look very lustrous, but yields about one hundred dollars to the tun. It is crushed, then washed in circular troughs by mules, then trodden out, as at Regla, with chemicals, then baked, then shipped to Mexico, where it goes through a half-dozen bakings and brewings and rollings and stampings before it gets into your pocket for a moment. The other minerals, zinc, copper, antimony, etc., give it more or less difficulty of reduction, but in a country where transportation is cheaper, and the markets nearer, would themselves be preserved, and made to pay in their own value the cost of reducing the richer minerals.

But few of the mines are valuable, and though from three to four millions is the annual product, there are no dividends. The Real del Monte mines proper have not paid expenses within two hundred thousand dollars a year for the past ten years. Those of Pachuca do better, but do not do much. Many mines are worked at a loss. Much expense is necessary for drawing off the water. Miles and miles of "adits" run under the mountain. So that the vast receipts are swallowed up in the vaster expenditures. Yet they expect the costly works will be paid for, and then we will all be changed from mule-driving Pedros to Counts of Regla. If it were not for hope, the heart would break, and silver-mining companies also. They do in spite of hope, as more than one poor minister has found, from Massachusetts to Minnesota.

The conductor says, "Do not invest your money in silver mines. A share or two, if you can lose it, may be well enough; but it is a less certain crop than wheat." He is a good man to follow. Yet one success carries a thousand failures, and a millionaire a century ago will make beggars of all the generations following, as they attempt to discover what he discovered without any attempt. Motto for silver mines: "Be content with what stock you have."

Our ride to Pachuca was for veins of ecclesiastical silver, richer than all this ore. These we found, and were well repaid. Four churches already exist, the fruits of that trip and the subsequent faithful followings of better men. A lady from the States has opened a Spanish and an English school, and Pachuca bids fair to be the silver circuit of the Mexican Conference not many days hence.

Invest in these operations. They are as Old as God and as New—from everlasting to everlasting. Put your money and your prayers into the soul silver mines, and you will lay up treasures in heaven, where no Mexican robbers nor thieves of worldliness ever break through or steal, and where you shall be receiving increasing and immeasurable interest on these human and earthly and present investments for ever and ever.

VI.

ACROSS LOTS.

A drowsy Beginning.—Paradise somewhat Lost.—Trees of Paradise.—A lingual Guess at the Aztec Origin.—Tizayuca.—Zumpango.—The Lake System.—Guatitlan.—Hotel San Pedro.—Into Town.—Tree of Noche Triste.—Tacuba.—Aqueduct of San Cosme.—Tivoli.

Do you want to know where I am writing this? In bed, on my side, by the light of a candle, very dimly burning. Sitting on a bench, by its side, are a brass bowl and a brown pitcher. One chair is the only other piece of furniture besides the bed. It is the Hotel San Pedro, the chief hotel of the place.

I had gotten so far when eyes and fingers gave out, and the candle followed. Nothing like tired nature to overcome disagreeable surroundings. The boy on the top of the mast can sleep as soundly as on a hay-mow, one of the best places ever got up for sleeping purposes. It only needs a sufficient degree of hunger to make any food palatable, and a sufficient degree of drowsiness to make any couch restful. The best bed I ever had was the planks that incline from the platform of the Jersey City dépôt to the floor of the dock. Getting off there about two in the morning, with a regiment of soldiers, we stretch ourselves on the floor for sleep. I was fortunate enough to get the slope that is a substitute for a step or two. The inclination was perfect, and I have often thought that was my bed of beds. I could get out a patent for a bed after that fashion which would do away with pillows, and, if one is sufficiently sleepy, with mattresses and other softnesses as well.

I was going to describe my quarters at Guatitlan, when sleep came down for my deliverance and yours. So I will bring it in at the right place now, and begin at the beginning.

We had done Pachuca — mines, rides, feastings, and worship.

The time came for us to go. It always comes to blissful or painful sojourners. Four nights and three days had we traveled and chatted, and prayed and preached, and mingled all the good things of both lives happily together. "How to make the best of two Lives" is the title of a good book. One might answer, "Go to Mr. Comargo's, the commandant of the mines at Pachuca, and spend a Sabbath and two week-days in and about that romantic spot." General Palmer had engaged a mule-team to take him and his Philadelphia - Paris *compadre* across the country. He generously offered me a seat in his "waggin," as they pronounce it here. You would never dream how it was spelled from that pronunciation. I do not know now. It sounds like a corruption of our word wagon.

The offer is gladly accepted, and we pass out of the narrow streets of the city of silver at about sunrise, into the paradise that incloses the town on its southern side. Paradise always looks a little more paradisiacal when at a distance than on closer inspection. Shall we be disappointed in heaven? Disappointed in getting there, I fear. As Dr. Watts said, "disappointed at three things: at seeing some there whom we did not expect to see, and not seeing some that we did expect to see, and especially disappointed at seeing ourselves there." May this happy disappointment be ours, every one.

Our Pachuca paradise is as green as it promises from the hill-top, looking down. The road runs amidst trees, a brown river with greenest banks. The favorite tree is called the Peru-tree, of slight green leaves, bearing a red berry in clusters; not unlike in look to the checker-berry, as it is called in New England, but very unlike in taste, for this berry is puckery in the extreme. Yet birds like them, and so every thing has its uses. It makes a pretty ornament to the landscape, its varied colors making the fields into an aviary of cardinals—an appropriate effect for a papal land. The maguey flourishes in all its greenness, and very handsome it is in its sweep of leaf and depth of hue. The mountains rise on our left, near and dark and cool. The fields spread out, a level upland, limited by ranges near on the left and rear, remote on the front and right—a prairie of scores of square miles.

We scamper over the plain in the brisk Septemberish morning, finding our shawls and capes no incumbrance. The land is very fertile, and quite generally cultivated. We pass haciendas where barley is being reaped and wheat sown, and all the offices of nature going on all the time. The chill morning air melts before the hot sun, and an August noon fits on to a fall sunrise.

We breakfast at the snug little town of Tizayuca. The funniest thing about Mexico is the names of the towns. It is a sport that is jaw-cracking. It is the punishment the Aztecs inflicted upon the Spaniards, almost equal to any they suffered. As compared with the rich vocabulary of Spain, or the sounding words of more Northern tribes, they are horrid. They sound Chinese and Japanese, and are another of the hints toward the solution of the problem as to where these races came from. Japanese junks now drift on to the western Mexican shore. This people look and act like those Asiatics. They are equally imitative, patient, subdued, industrious. They have a likeness of language. Their habits are Asiatic. There is more indifference to propriety in these Aztec women than in any of the peasantry of Europe or Egypt. It is Eastern Asia that they reproduce. So their consonant names are a like production. All of which is respectfully submitted to the learned societies of Asia and America.

Tizayuca, which brought on this *excursus*, seems incapable of bringing on any thing else. It slumbers like any American cross-roads at midday. Not a breath nor whisper, not a buzz nor a bite, except of invisible fleas and too-visible dogs. The church absorbs the town, which consists of one-story adobe huts, hidden among useless Peru-trees and more useless maguey.

The breakfast was served from twelve to two, and was the best thing in the place, except the pleasant-voiced woman that served it, her pretty children, and the church aforesaid. It is surprising what good meals they get up in these out-of-the-way places. Beef-steak, thin-sliced fried potatoes, chicken-stews, and chocolate or coffee of the best, make us long and lovingly remember Tizayuca. You can remember it by saying, "'Tis a—favorite game of gamblers or food of these natives."

The power of the Castilian to manufacture derivatives was funnily shown by our hostess, who, when scolded at for her delay in bringing on the chocolate, responded, "Ahouta-ta-ta-ta-ta." "Ahouta" meant "immediately." Every added "ta" shortened the time. Could one have been made to say "quickly" in any prettier manner? It is a pleasant privilege, and makes the family and friendly diminutives very cordial and delightful.

Ten miles, and Zumpango is reached. These miles go through a road but slightly traveled, and across fields susceptible of high culture. We cross the divide between Mexico and Pachuca, a hardly noticeable swell, and find ourselves in the rich valley of the capital. Zumpango is a pretty and lively town of five thousand souls. A noisy crowd of chanticleers are keeping up great disturbance. They prove to be some four hundred fighting-cocks, which are brought here for sale. "Elegant-looking birds," said one of my companions, who saw them. More elegant-looking now than when torn, bleeding, from each other's embrace.

This place lies at the head of the lake system which imperils Mexico. Three lakes flow down upon that capital. The remotest one is that of Zumpango. It lies at the base of a range of mountains, and stretches along the rear of the town for several miles. Its hill-sides, opposite the town, look as if it would be a delightful winter resort for Northern people. It is over twenty feet higher than Mexico, and about thirty miles distant. To preserve it from inundating the city, a huge dike or wall, ten feet high, is built along its southern side. This dike is repeated more elaborately at the next lake, San Christoval; and so the last lake, on whose edge the city sits, rarely rises above its proper level. Millions of dollars have been expended on these works, and they are yet unfinished. They need a drainage from the lowest lake into some river flowing down to the Gulf. This is projected, and will be accomplished, "mañana?"

The ride from Zumpango to Guatitlan, where this story began, is very pretty. The haciendas grow frequent; cattle fill the fields; grains are being harvested; and some fields, well irrigated, look wondrous green. The acres are lowly, and often wet. Great herds of cattle and horses are grazing in the drier meadows, while the huge snow-mountains rise higher than ever before from this half-watery base. Iztaccihuatl is more beautiful than from any other position. Both that and Popocatepetl are grand diamonds, flashing solid light in that sun-bright sky. What other fields of earth have such a guardianship?

As we enter the town, it seems certain that it must be an American summer village. Trees line the roadside, lustrous in July verdure; fields equally lovely lie behind the trees; flowers blossom on the wayside. What better place possible to spend a night? Alas! for the vanity of human expectations. The street is busy, and the two boys who are driving our mules, well loaded with pulqui (the boys, not the mules), are greeted by another, more loaded, if possible, than they. He misdirected us; but hung round for his medio, or half a real (six and a quarter cents), till the foot almost followed the voice in ejecting him. The Hotel San Pedro admits us to its ample yard, and that is about all.

Not to disappoint you, when Rosecrans's railroad takes you to this hard-named city, let us take you now to its chief hotel. Imagine a square yard, three hundred feet across. Around it are one-story, low-roofed sheds of adobe. At its entrance is a small fonda, or restaurant. On its rear are some steps going up to a second-story veranda, low-browed and wide, on which are six small rooms, with brick floors and bare bedsteads, with a chair, a table, and a bench as their furniture.

There are the quarters for fastidious guests, the first-class cars for unseasoned Yankees. They are remote from the house, if house that single room can be called which provides your meals alone; and they are easily assailable by any body in the spacious yard, and there are many bodies there. A range of huge mule-wagons is backed along the rear of the yard, just under our balco-

TREE OF TRISTE NOCHE.

ny, and morning reveals the muleteers sleeping soundly under their wagons. Their women find beds under the shed or under the canvas of the wain. An Indian and his wife are stretched, asleep, on a common blanket, on the common ground, under the shed near the gate-way. So we have plenty of comrades inside the gates to rob us of our slumber and our watches. The watch we left at Mexico, fulfilling (this once) the command against putting on of gold and costly apparel; and the slumber they left undisturbed. "I both laid me down in peace and slept, and I awaked; for thou, O Lord, sustained me." David laid himself down and slept in a caravansary not unlike this. His condition, protection, and comfort are ours to-day. How true is it that our Lord is the same yesterday, to-day, and forever!

The morning rays creep in at our doors. We are up and out and off. How splendid is the weather! They never talk of the weather here. It changes not. The sun comes exquisitely up over Guadalupe. The fields beneath the hills are very like the farms of the West, all except the mountains. Culture and comfort seem to nestle in these shaded retreats. The sierras of Toluca and Guadalupe come together in a narrow and not lofty pass, which our engineering associate is easily surmounting with his gauges and his trains. Over it, and we are in the Valley of Mexico. The city lies fifteen miles off, a garden of foliage being our ceaseless escort to its gates. We move moderately through village and town, examining churches, olive-groves, plazas, riding under broad-spreading branches, slowly wading through droves of burdened mules and asses, going to town with the "truck" of the country.

The morning is delicious, and our spirits hardly less so. We could not help exclaiming, although it was not Mexican—inspired, doubtless, by the Massachusetts memories of Samuel Adams and Hancock, on the morn of the battle of Lexington, "What a glorious morning is this!" Yet they have them here all the time and all the day long; although the peculiar preciousness of the Lexington morning is not yet fully transferred to this rare clime.

Just before we reach Tacuba, a few miles from the city, a big old tree, walled in and inscribed, stands almost in the road-way. It is the tree under which Cortez collected the little remnant of his soldiers in that "noche triste" (sad night), when they had been driven from the city by the uprising natives, determined to extirpate the invaders, avenge their gods, and save their country. It was a terrible night. None more terrible in the history of battles. The Indians had rushed upon them in the dark from boat and marsh and at the open crossings of the dike, until but a handful was left to tell the tale. These gathered here a moment on retreat to the victory which another year saw accomplished.

It is a huge and gnarled cypress, with scant boughs and foliage —old then, and held in great veneration to-day by the Spaniards. How do the Mexicans regard it? If New England were to-day three-fourths British, and they were held in subjection, how would they regard the Lexington Monument? But the natives are

GARDEN OF THE TIVOLI, SAN COSME.

mounting to place and power; and so the tree may be allowed to stand, like our battle monuments. A fire almost consumed it last year, and it is preserved with as great difficulty as the big tree on Boston Common.

Tacuba is passed — not pretty in its high, inclosing walls, but lovely in its opening glimpses of gardens and groves. The Street of San Cosme is entered, and its solemn-looking aqueduct passed. This aqueduct, built after the "high Roman fashion," on stately arches, rises gray and black and moist. Its sides drip with coolness, and are flecked with mosses, grasses, and tiny shrubs. It seems a projection of Antechristian times into the bustling present. Along these arches fought the men of Scott against the men of Santa Anna, inch by inch, to the plaza and the palace. Along them now the horse-car flies, the ass tugs under his big and bulky burden, the peon toils under his relatively bigger and more bulky loads. The whole broad avenue is full of life, while by its side stalks the majestic aqueduct, a Roman legion slow marching into Rome. It is as artistic a line of beauty as ever strode along a busy city pathway. It brings the Chapultepec waters to the town, an old-fashioned water-way, but far grander than our modern counterpart of hidden pipes and siphons.

The Tivoli gardens open on this avenue, and just below the terminus of the aqueduct. There we pause for a breakfast, amidst foliage, birds, and summer delights. This is a favorite resort for out-of-door dinner-parties, and has every conceit for such tastes—bowers, boxes, and even tables up in the trees. We can there eat, and chatter like and with the birds. That is high living, at not very high prices. Try it when you go to Mexico. The few deciduous trees are putting forth fresh foliage, and every thing is lovely. How lovely! Oh, that grace and goodness kept step with nature! Where do they? In you?

The perilous journey of sixty to seventy miles is passed without peril, and a new and pleasant chapter added to the book of experience.

VII.

THE TOWN OF THE ANGELS.

Warnings unheeded.—Slow Progress.—Christ in the Inn.—Why Angelic.—Bad Faith and worse Works.—First English Service.—Outlook from the Cathedral.—Tlascala.—The Volcano.—Inside View of the Belfry.—Inside the Cathedral.—Triple Gilt.—Cathedral Service.—La Destruccion de los Protestantes.

WHEN Cortez was told he must not go in a certain direction or to a certain place, he always went straight thus and there. His success was in no small measure due to that quality of his nature. When he came to the wall of Tlascala he went through its gates, not around it. His battles with the Tlascalans assured his success with their Aztec foes. So when they told him he must not go to Cholula, since the priestly city was too cunning for him, into it he marched.

If when in Rome one must do as the Romans do, in Mexico it is worldly-wise to follow the footsteps of Cortez. Puebla had been held up as an especial object of fear. "It is very fanatical," they said. "It got up a riot, and drove out the Protestants three years ago. It is a city of priests, and the sacred city of Mexico. Keep away." So we went to Puebla. Where should a clergyman go but to the city of clericos? Where an angel of the churches but to "The Town of the Angels," as it is always called?

It was Friday, the 7th of February, that two of us essayed to take the eleven o'clock train for a ride thither of about one hundred and twenty miles. The time had been changed to twelve, and we occupied it in lounging through a park adjoining the station, which has swings, dance-sheds, a little amphitheatre for gymnasts and theatrical performances, and a level tract of open prairie, edged with trees. This is a great Sunday resort, and is then busy with dancers, drinkers, and dissipaters of every sort. To-day it is as empty as a Protestant church on week-days. A sluggish canal girds it, covered thick with green scum, which, but for the height of the land, would breed a deadly miasma. As it is, the tropical vegetation goes on harmlessly, and, once used to the sight of it, not disagreeably.

Twelve comes, and a pulqui train also. Said train is a heavy line of freight cars, two stories high, with barrels of the detestable drunk-drink of the country piled close in each compartment. The company makes its chief profits out of this business, and so every body and every train have to give way to its demands.

We wait till three before we start, tacked on to these empty pulqui cars. The engine gives out, and leaves us forty miles out, itself or its engineer overcome with pulqui. Delay follows delay, as one sin breeds another, until it is after four in the morning ere we reach Puebla, where we should have been at seven the previous evening. The cars are not made for night travel, nor our clothes. The night is cool, and our capes are light; the windows of the cars will not stay up, and, all open to their uttermost, let in the sharp air of the snow mountains. We shiver, and seek to sleep. The earth shivers too, either in sympathy or from some other cause, and quite a quaking occurs at three o'clock, sufficient to send the people of Puebla out of their beds and chambers. Our shakes from cold were so great as to make us insensible to the responsive shiverings of the earth. At five we get to our hotel, and under blankets, and into warmth and sleep.

Puebla lies on the opposite side of the snow range from Mexico. Popocatepetl and Iztaccihuatl are west of us here, east there. They are closer here, it being only about half the distance, or thirty miles, to the chief of these from this city, while that Popo, etc., is sixty miles from Mexico.

Our hotel was once a college or theological school, and has over the graceful iron gate-way that opens on the second, and properly hotel balcony, the unusual initials, "I. H. S."—unusual for an inn. "Jesus, the Saviour of men," has at last found his name over the

STREET VIEW IN PUEBLA.

gate-way of the public-house from which He was driven before He was born, and into which He has never found official entrance since. When I first saw this gracefully-wrought monogram, on my way to Mexico, over this portal, my heart rejoiced at this rare expression of piety in a tavern. The rejoicing disappeared when I was told that it had been part of a convent, and that was why the sacred letters were here. I found that even Roman Catholics, who put the cross upon every thing, from the bells of the donkeys to the pulqui plant (for you will often see a cross in a pulqui field, two white bits of straw in this shape stuck in the edge of a leaf, that it may be blessed with fruitfulness) have never yet presumed to erect this sign upon a tavern. It only got in here by a change of use. Having got in surreptitiously, may it stay in, in spirit as well as letter! That it is likely so to do will be seen further on.

The balcony on which we rest incloses an open court, and is wide, high, shaded, and enjoyable—very. It was a school or college in what devout Romanists feel were the good old days of convent and Church power, and therefore has a learned air about it even in its transformation. A sleep till late in the morning, a breakfast as good as the sleep, and we sally forth to take the town. That is not so easy a matter to do, for this town is the seat of the Church power of Mexico. And it happened on this wise:

When Cortez invaded the country, he found Cholula the sacred city. There were the chief priests, and the chief temples, and the chief gods. A population that he put at three hundred thousand thronged its mud-walled streets, and beggars by the myriad made it look like old Spain.

After the reduction of the country it was thought wise, in that wisdom which has always characterized the Roman Church, to get up a Christian city over against the heathen metropolis. So Puebla, or "The Town," was founded six miles from Cholula, and its walls were said to have been erected amidst the singing of angels, an improvement on Thebes of old, which only had Orpheus to harp up its walls. As a proof that this was actually the case, the full name of the town is Puebla of the Angels, "*Puebla de los Angelos.*" Is not that proof positive? Q. E. D.

Such a town, of course, is religious. It is nothing else. It was built for religion. It has been sustained these three hundred and fifty years on religion. Its churches are grander than those of Mexico, its convents and ecclesiastical institutions relatively far more numerous and wealthy. Of the twenty-five millions of its valuation a few years ago, twenty millions was the share which the Church possessed, almost a complete reversal of the tithe principle —four-fifths to the priest and one to the people. Then a gold and silver chandelier hung in its cathedral, and these materials were more common than brass. They were nothing reckoned of in those days of priestly glory, the Solomonic reign of this Church. The chandelier is gone—at least I did not see it—and the cathedral is shorn of much of its gold and its glory.

RUINS OF THE COVERED WAY TO THE INQUISITION.

Such a city, so built, so owned, so occupied, would naturally be faithful to the Church. It could not well be otherwise. All its people get their living, as did Demetrius of Ephesus, by making silver shrines and such like for their goddess Maria. Their devotion was as great as their interests were close. They must approve and defend the Church in which they lived and moved and had their daily being. They must oppose all beginnings of opposition to her, whether local or national. So they cast themselves into the breach, and in the war upon the Church have always been found in the front rank of her defenders. This city has been the seat of her power. Mexico, a political capital far more than a religious, has been indifferent to the fate of Romanism. Puebla, which is nothing if not religious, has been indifferent to every thing but Romanism.

Of course such a stronghold of that order was not considered fruitful soil for anti-Romanism. "Very fanatical," every body says, "is Puebla." It has proved this faith by its works. Among its residents is Mr. Blumenkron, a Jew, born in Philadelphia, raised in Europe, but a citizen of Mexico these twenty-five years—a Jew more outwardly than inwardly, a gentleman of pluck and persistence. In the breaking up of their convents he secured a slice of the Santo Domingo for himself, the Convent of the Inquisition. He also bought a church. This last he offered to the evangelists.

Rev. Gabriel Ponce de Leon came down from Mexico to preach in it. The people rose upon him, three thousand strong, rushed into the little church, hurled stones at his head and those of his associates, who fled upon the roof, and from roof to roof, and so escaped out of their murderous power. I have never heard that the grave and gentlemanly Bishop of Puebla ever publicly disapproved of these proceedings, or that the less grave, though not less gentlemanly, Archbishop of Mexico ever censured the Bishop of Puebla for not condemning the conduct of his own church members. I fear that when, the next Sunday, he and these rioters repeated the Litany with exceeding warmth and fullness of response, they did not pause at that prayer, "From battle, and murder, and sudden death, good Lord, deliver us," and think how earnest they had been the Sabbath before to inflict murder and sudden death upon an innocent preacher of the Gospel of the blessed God. When will the Protestants become like bloody murderers of those who oppose them? Have they not been so in some of their branches? "Let him that thinketh he standeth take heed lest he fall."

That riot made the few English residents timid, and, though we went to the houses of two English families, we could not get either of them to open their doors to an English service. Disappointed, we returned to the hotel. After dinner an American gentleman, Dr. Tinker, spoke to us; we told him our failure. He said we could hold a meeting in the hotel. It was doubted. He immediately applied to the landlord, who instantly offered his best and biggest room, and there, at three on Sabbath afternoon, just seven persons assembled, including the two ministers, and service was held—praise, prayer, and preaching. It was a goodly season, and one long to be remembered. May all who attended it be found in that perfect congregation of which this number was the perfect though *petite* unit: seven, the beginning, a multitude that no man can number, the consummation.

The Town of the Angels is beautiful, and, what is rare in the cities of men, exceedingly clean. It lies foursquare. Its streets are paved in broad blocks, which look as if washed daily, so lustrously they shine in this burning sun. They are wide enough, the streets as well as the pavements; the passion for broad thoroughfares declining as you enter regions where the rays of the sun must be well mixed with shadow to make them endurable.

Most of the streets are raised at the crossings on each side of a narrow channel that runs through their centre under a single broad flat stone, which channel lets the torrents in the rainy season flow to the river without disturbance of travel. It is an improvement on the stone blocks put in the Baltimore crossings for like purposes. The then clean streets are washed by rivulets from Iztaccihuatl, which seems to lie right over our heads, though thirty miles away. How superbly sleeps that snow range above this green meadow and gray town! Were it not too sad a reflection, one might fancy it a body shrouded and laid in state on that high catafalque, ten thousand feet above our eyes.

The straight streets terminate in green groves or brown hills, which look as if they were gates, so close they meet the eye in this bright air. They give a very pleasant effect to the vista that opens to you whichever way you gaze. The streets stretch no little distance before these green and brown gayeties are reached, for there are sixty thousand people in this basin, and these are not packed closely together.

Let us climb the cathedral tower, and take in the whole spectacle. The outlook is both lovely and grand. The city diminishes from this height, but its environs make up for its loss. The fields are better cultivated than those about Mexico, or, rather, are more open and more farm-like, those of the latter being devoted to trees and towns. They are very green and attractive. Irrigation is

THE CATHEDRAL OF PUEBLA.

easy, as the mountains near by keep the streams from becoming dry. The hills to the east go down to the Gulf. Orizaba's white dome flashes among them, the most perfect and most dazzling pyramid that nature has tossed up into the sky for the envy and the despair of ambitious mortals. What is Cheops's gray hill to this polished marble glory? How petty even Emerson's lines sound here:

> "Morning opes with haste her lids,
> To gaze upon the Pyramids."

What cares morning for that five hundred feet high of matched granite? As much as the proudest statesman for the infant's house of cards or blocks. It is a pretty specimen of childish ingenuity, and that is all. Nature in every line leaves art as matchless as God leaves man. She is its offspring, and what are our petty imitations to His creations? No. Morning sees Orizaba and Blanc and their co-creations not only long before, but with far deeper emotions than it looks on our feeble products, even such as may seem very grand when compared with our meanest efforts.

To the north of east rises Malinche, brown and green to its summit, and sometimes white there also, and red even, and black, when the smoke and fires of the volcano mix their colors with its snows and sides. This was named by Cortez for his Marina; his Indian interpreter, and himself also, being known to the Indian allies and foes by the name of Malinche. It is the only one of the volcanoes that lost its old Indian name. The three grander ones preserved their original titles while they changed owners. It lies nearest Puebla, and looks not five miles off, though it will be twenty ere you reach its base, if you gallop from this plaza.

Farther to the north, and trenching a little on the west, is a range of whitened cliffs, without any vegetation seemingly, at this distance, or possibility of any. These scarred bluffs, that look as if made of salt, are Tlascala, the next most famous spot in Mexico to Mexico herself. For there was the little republic of mountaineers that never submitted to the Aztec yoke; whom Cortez first conquered, and who never failed to be his allies afterward; on whom he relied to carry him through all his perils, and to whom he gave his banner, that still hangs in the church of the town; to whom also he gave political liberties that have never been taken away. A railroad station is not three miles from their city, called by the name of the pluckiest, worst, and best specimen of the Mexican of to-day—Santa Anna. So closely is Cortez linked to this present.

It was from that hill fortress that he marched on Cholula because they told him not to; so his line of march is visible to the eye from this tower. Across these low spurs of these inclosing mountains his band of less than four hundred footmen, and a score or two of horsemen, moved slowly upon the priestly town, confident in their arms, their horses, their faith, their leader, and themselves —a five-fold cord which was not easily broken, though often attempted in the terrible strain of the eighteen months which followed.

One feels a growing respect for that general as he stands among these scenes of his career, even if one American traveler has sought to belittle his achievements, and to make his conquest of the Aztecs a mere brush of trained troops with untrained savages. Our trained troops had many years of hard service ere they rooted out the untrained savages of Florida, and have not yet subdued those of the West. But this general in a year and a half brought these organized and warlike Aztecs into such submission that they have never raised their heads in rebellion since. And they are vastly superior in every respect, military included, to the Indians of our frontier. They are the soldiers of the republic, and can fight as well as the soldiers of France, as they showed in this very Puebla, where they won one of their brilliant battles against their invaders, and made the 5th of May famous in their annals. It was something to subdue such a people.

Turn now due west, and fill your gaze with the grand Snow Range. It is all embraced at a glance. Unlike the Alps, which you can never see around, these Mexic Alps are all compassed at once. You can see where they leave the plains, and where they come back to them. You can ride clear around them if you please. From the first breaking of the soil on the east, between Malinche and Tlascala, you go gradually up to Iztaccihuatl, descend enough to allow a pass across to Mexico—the pass which Cortez and Scott crossed—climb again the steeper, taller, smoother, and handsomer sides of Popocatepetl, and "coast" down his western side into the valleys and lakes that come between him and the Toluca range, of which Ajusca is the chief peak—a range that shuts in Mexico city on the south.

I leave you looking at this complete picture while I look at this grand bell and its half-dozen smaller sisters; for the clock is about to strike. Three times a power below pulls back that huge copper hammer before it lets it fall on the huger rim, to send forth a thunderous tone that makes us look to our ears, and almost fear that we shall have no further use for these rudimental wings, as Mr. Darwin might call them, did he choose to detect in man a descent from angels rather than from apes. The power that slowly and thricely swings the hammer ere it strikes the blow, seems so labored and so human that we are sure it must be man. It is so, we find, but man changed into a machine—oiled, and burnished, and operating like clock-work exactly.

You will notice here the number of the churches. Though French cannon have blown some of them to pieces, and Mexican changes have opened streets through others, still the domes and turrets are very numerous, much more so than the needs of the city. Chief of these are the Campaña, or Jesuits' church, and the San Francisco, which stands near the eastern gate, over against the Alameda, with its paved court along the street-side, covering an acre or more; its deep arcades once used for priestly refreshment, now as barracks for soldiers; and its tall, square, ungainly towers, that look as if they could stand many an earthquake and bombardment, as they have already done for a hundred years and more. They all have one model: a dome over the centre of the cross, and two towers at the front or long end of the cross. That is the model of the Mexican church; no pinnacle, no shaft, no Gothic arch—Moorish and Spanish, and that only.

Descend and look at this cathedral. It stands, four feet above the street, on a raised pavement that is of vast proportions. It is not less than three hundred feet before you reach the church from the beginning of this rock-built terrace. The effect is very majestic. A plaza spreads beyond this outside church floor, with a garden and flowers, surrounded by a street, and inclosed by a very wide and shaded arcade, filled with curiosity seekers and sellers.

The side wall of the church rises vast, almost windowless and pillarless, a naked wall of dark gray rock. Enter. The effect is grand and profound; more so, I think, than in any edifice I have seen on this continent, and surpassed by but few on the other. The towers rise in grand proportions, and the bells drop down the richest fruit of melody. Its pillars are of the same dark porphyritic rock, but are built up in stones about two feet in width, laid in white cement, which relieves the pillars by regular lines of light.

These vast columns, ninety feet high, support a vaster roof, that seems almost aërial in its height and grace. The springing arches bend like a hand of heaven, each ridge a finger, above the prostrate worshipers. The altar is of polished pillars of marble, with each groove edged with gold plate. The effect is very brilliant, the play of gold on the variegated marbles being strange and striking. One could hardly tell if they were not all gold. Inside these flashing

CONVENT OF SAN DOMINGO, CITY OF MEXICO.

columns is a mass of polished green and almost translucent marble, and above and around it hang all manner of images: popes and ecclesiastics, angels and apostles, and, over all, Mary, God blessed forever in this ornate idolatry.

The chapel in the rear of the high altar is a mass of gilded and graven images, as are all the chapels in the chief churches in all the cities. None is more resplendent than one in the old Church of Santo Domingo near at hand. Every crevice of the large chapel is covered with carved wood, tossed up into airy forms like the filigree work of a gold setting, and every bit of this carved wood or clay, on roof, wall, side, and every spot but the floor, is covered with gilding. It is a little antique, but when first opened it must have well-nigh blinded the eyes of the worshipers. So yet are some of the chapels of the cathedral in Mexico. One can but feel, as he looks on all this display, the fitness of one of Hood's puns:

> "Just like a button is his soul,
> All cased in triple g(u)ilt."

This church, in its service and its life, its doctrines and devices, is very like these gorgeous gildings,

> "All cased in triple g(u)ilt."

That Santo Domingo is a specimen. Come with me out of that dazzling chapel into this corridor of the convent to which that chapel is attached. Here was another like glittering room, where a rich Pueblano paid four hundred dollars to have his body rest a night on its way to the grave. Back of this gorgeous preliminary to the sepulchre and the worms, you see this closed-up hole in the wall. Knock it open. There is a room there, if room it may be called, where two or three can crouch, and none can walk or hardly stand, with a stone bench, and a hole big enough to pass a piece of bread through. In that wall were confined those suspected by the friars of St. Dominic, who said mass so ornately in that golden chapel. Here they were fed, and here, when the order came, food ceased to come, and they ceased to live. Buried with Christ were these his saints—buried alive.

Close by that living tomb a hole was broken in the wall, and out of it rattled a heap of skulls and other human bones, which had been tossed into a vault at an opening above, and which bottom of the vault was thus opened to the light, and all their deeds became manifest that they were wrought of the devil and not of God.

This Convent of the Inquisition was located in the very heart of the city. The stone whence the town radiates is opposite its entrance. A new street was cut through it, and a portion of it, including that place of sepulture and revelation, has been purchased by the Missionary Society of the Methodist Episcopal Church. That is a sweet and sacred revenge, and the martyrs will feel that their sufferings are truly avenged, when the place of their living burial becomes the seat of a living Church, preaching the faith for which they suffered even unto the death.

PRISONERS OF THE INQUISITION.

The service at the cathedral Sunday morning seemed dry and husky. The robes of the officiators were faded, the young preacher was afraid, and the singing as hollow as if performed in some non-Roman churches I wot of in Boston and New York. But the evening service, which the bishop conducted, was intense enough. It showed how fervid yet was the faith of Puebla, and how easily it might burst into a volcano of persecution. The audience was not over four or five hundred, but they gathered round the pulpit on their knees, and repeated the Litany as I never heard it before —so intense, so united, so devotional. The tents and altars of camp-meetings do not surpass them in earnestness of response.

Some of their utterances were so powerful that my companion asserted that the organ accompanied them. This I denied, and though we both sat directly under that instrument, it is a disputed point between us to this day whether there was any sound but the human voice. I heard none but that was full of deepest and strongest and most united exclamation. Puebla is very religious, as was Athens, and very superstitious, and worships the unknown God with a devotion worthy a clearer faith. May it soon attain this needed grace!

It is likely so to do. The brisk business men begin to see that it needs closer relations with the outside world. It was left thirty miles off the track when the road from Vera Cruz to Mexico was laid out, though it was offered direct connection if it would build that thirty miles. Its refusal to make this investment is charged to its priesthood, and that does not make them any the more popular. It will make connections with other routes, and regain some of the trade it is losing. This ambition makes it more willing to tolerate all faiths, and to adjust itself to the future of Mexico. Still that toleration in this town will be slowest of the slow. Persecution must precede such liberty.

That Sabbath night the crowds in the Alameda showed little thought of the bitter wailing of the cathedral company. A multitude in carriages, on horseback, and afoot, thoughtless, fashion-following, were without God, if not without hope in the world. The golden glory on the snowy brows of the mountains—was it a sign of a new advent that should make the Sabbath a delight, holy unto the Lord, honorable?

There is a cross to be taken here by the saints of the Lord ere that grace dawns. On the show-bills, at the entertainment for the next Sabbath night at the Theatre Hidalgo, was a play entitled "The Destruction of the Protestants" (*La Destruccion de los Protestantes*). I do not know but that I would have overcome two scruples, visiting the theatre and breaking the Sabbath, had I been there that Sunday, in order to have seen of what spirit some of the Pueblanos yet are, and how they would have received the portrayal of a Saint Bartholomew's day. The two scruples have been overcome once and again, though not at the same time, since I have visited a theatre, for religious purposes, on Sunday, and have witnessed Sunday-school exhibitions which imitated the theatre in every thing but artistic excellence and success.

That this was a sort of Sunday-school exhibition was clear, from the fact that that Sunday night the play was to be "Samson." So even in their sports the angels of Puebla are pious. Probably their Sunday bull-fights are with the sacred bulls, such as Egypt once worshiped; not those of the pope—these they never fight.

That play shows what their earnestness yet is, and what Protestants may have to suffer ere the city is truly redeemed to Christ. Yet they are willing to suffer. Twelve brethren and sisters gathered round their beloved minister when the storm broke over him of pistols and paving-stones. Sixty gathered to hear the Word. They will come together again. The government must protect liberty of worship, and Puebla be indeed, in heart as well as in name, the City of the Angels; religious with a happy religion that does not wail with ceaseless confession, *Mea culpa, mea maxima culpa,* "My fault, my greatest fault," but exclaims in joyful confidence,

>"My God is reconciled :
>   His pard'ning voice I hear ;
> He owns me for his child,
>   I can no longer fear.
> With confidence I now draw nigh,
> And Father, Abba, Father, cry."

May that soon be the blessed experience of this City of the Saints and the Angels!

VIII.

THE MOST ANCIENT AMERICAN MECCA.

On Horse.—Irrigation.—Entrance to Cholula.—Deserted Churches.—Plaza Grande, and its Cortez Horror.—A wide-awake Priest.—A wide View from the Summit.—A costly Trifle.—The Ride back.

PUEBLA is a modern and made-up Mecca, an imitation, and not an original. Let us to the true. Horseback is your only mode of riding here, and the horse is made for the business. In the States you run small chance of getting trained steeds for such service. Here you find none else. In Mexico city are fancy teams, but even there the back is the favorite part of the horse. Especially is it so everywhere else.

Mr. Marshall, an American Englishman, whose two sons were educated at Lowell and Chicago, furnishes us with horses, four in all. A gentleman and his wife accompany us, with the guide, an old gentleman, whose pantaloons, like Mr. Grimes, the ancient's, coat, are all buttoned down, though not before, but on the side, silver buttons too, and as thick together as it is possible to place them. Some of these garments, it is said he has, worth five hundred dollars. It would better pay his wife to wear the breeches than in ordinary cases of uxurious usurpation. His horse was as much thought of as his pantaloons, and the one danced and the other shone, and warmed the cockles of the old man's heart, so that he sang love-songs with a voice approaching the childish treble and a sentiment equally infantile or senile.

The morning was magnificent, as all mornings are here, when this company of ten galloped through the yet empty streets of Puebla. The country is soon reached, and the volcanoes rise up before us as only a mile or two away. How grand they glowed in that coming sun! The new paseo is paced, a pretty park and drive, whose trees were leveled to let the French balls in and the Mexican out. The road runs straight to the pyramid of Cholula, which looks as if it hugged the base of Popocatepetl, though it is twenty-five miles therefrom.

Irrigation makes the fields green; not here, as Bryant found it in Berkshire, where he wrote his "Thanatopsis," and where he says are

> "The complaining brooks
> That make the meadows green."

There is no complaining in these brooks, albeit they do "a heap" more business than those that make "a heap" more of complaint, as is the case upward through beast to man. The howling cat catches no mice, and the brawling woman that Solomon was so afraid of, and to whom in his establishment he was able to give a wide house, is not the one he describes in the last verses of his Proverbs. So this land is changed from a brown and barren desolation into beauty and abundance by trickling a few inches of water along a shovel-wide path. That is all. It is the little that makes the muckle here and elsewhere, in this and in every thing.

A ride of an hour and a half brings us to the mud-brick huts that begin the once magnificent city of Cholula. I fear the huts were about the same sort when the city was at the height of its magnificence. The pepper, or Peru, tree grows thickly and uselessly, except to the eye and the birds—the redness of its berry pleasing our vision, and its bitter pungency their taste. The maguey grows yet finer to the eye and yet worse to the taste. It stretches out superbly over these black and level fields. No wonder the dwellings are of dirt, where pulqui and pepper are the chief products of the soil.

We cross a spur of the pyramid, but leave its exploration till the end of our trip. That spur through which the road is cut reveals the artificial nature of the mound, for its layers of thin brick and thick mud are visible on either side of the road, and far up on the chief side to where the strata are lost in the trees and brush that grow upon them.

On this rising edge of the mound you note the number and size of the churches that once replaced in this now deserted city the old idolatry with the new. Churches are everywhere and of every size, hidden away among the trees, standing out to view in the plaza, and on the hill slopes surrounding the town. There is about one apiece for every family, if not for every soul; though in this latter list, if dogs were included—and John Wesley hints that they may be—the churches may not be too numerous, even now. All church and no people seems to be the present character of the town.

This was either a proof that the town had left the churches, or that Cortez and his successors were not content alone with building Puebla, or with having the angels do it, but thought it good policy to fill the old Aztec and Toltec city with their new gods. Whatever prompted them, the fact remains—and it is about all that does remain—that domes and towers rise everywhere in open fields, and pastures without inhabitant. I doubt if such a sort of desolation exists elsewhere on the earth.

We drive a short distance along a line of adobe huts, a single story high, and mostly opening on the street, sometimes used as little shops and stores, and sometimes containing a whole and not a small family in a single squalid room. The opposite side is a part of the inclosure of a gigantic church. A few moments and the Plaza Grande opens on us, as large as that of Mexico, but void of gardens, foliage, and folks, in all of which that place abounds.

Here or hereabouts occurred the cruelest massacre of all that marked the march of Cortez. The cunning, priestly city welcomed him timidly, but with seeming cordiality. Forced by the superior warlike nature of the Mexican rulers, the officials plotted a surprise, making pits in the streets for his horses, and arranging the house roofs for assault. Malinche learned the secret through a wife of a cazique, and revealed it to Cortez. He had the plaza filled with the authorities and thousands of packmen, to see and help him off; and on just such a calm, sweet, glorious morning as this, poured his musketry and cannon upon the harmless, helpless mass, slaughtering them by the thousands. Cannon also commanded the approaches to the place, and swept down all the excited masses that attempted to enter and rescue their brethren. That deed gave him free egress from this city and free ingress to Mexico; for it inspired the country with great fear of these invaders, who could learn every secret and master every opposition.

The plaza gives no sign of this terrible history. Two sides of it are occupied with churches, one with small shops and stores, and one with a long, wide, handsome arcade, as empty of people, however, as a handsome head usually is of sense. A few Indian women, descendants of the poor fellows who were here done unto the death, sit on their mats among their beans, bananas, oranges, water-melons, and other summer fruits, and do a little trading for the little town.

A high wall incloses the immense area assigned to the great church, which fills all the eastern side of the plaza and goes back for several acres, an empty court and church and convent, except a corner occupied by soldiers. The smaller church on the north side was erected by Cortez, so it is said, and contains the little image of the Virgin which he carried in all his campaigns. It is a small church, and not rich in any of its trappings. I did not know that the Cortez's Virgin was there, and so, if I saw it, saw it not. It shows the tact of this general, that he should put his battle banner in charge of the fighting Tlascalans, and his worshiped image in charge of the praying Cholulans. *Suum cuique.* Each had its own, and the country saw, Spanish and Mexic, the fitness of the appropriation.

A ride through one of the half-dozen occupied streets, and that but poorly inhabited, carries us by the door of an exceedingly fresh and pretty chapel. It is flush to the sidewalk, and brilliant with all manner of stucco and fancy-colored washes. It is not paint, but water-colors, that here set off the houses. Puebla is being thus rewashed under orders of the governor, who declares if each house is not thus refreshened within a certain time he will make the owner pay a fine and the expenses of its recoloring. So that city is busy in rewashing its walls in all manner of pretty stripes and tints, almost the only business in which it is very active, though it is not especially dull. Such washes hold several years, and are a cheap and pretty way of dressing up a town.

Service is going on in this only renewed church of Cholula. We dismount and enter. It is exceedingly pretty; gold, and blue,

CHURCH BUILT BY CORTEZ.

and green, and crimson, and all manner of dainty hues flash from its walls and ceiling. Stucco, in images, scrolls, and other delectable patterns, shines whitely and brightly from every "nook and coigne of vantage." A score or two of pious sisters, with here and there a brother (just like the Protestants in that respect), are worshipfully following the old priest at the altar in his sacred mumblings. How much better a dear, delightful prayer-meeting, even in a less glowing chapel! Yet I confess to a liking to these bright colors, and know not why they should be kept out of the house of God. His own house, builded by His own hands, whether of the earth about us or the heavens above us, is thus arrayed, only far more splendidly. And Moses and Solomon each set forth their Tabernacle and Temple in gorgeous hues and dyes, and gold and precious stuffs. Let not the worshiper worship the array, and he can adorn it after his pleasure and his purse.

That old padre would make a good Methodist in one respect, perhaps in others; he knew how to take a poor appointment and make it a good one. That is more than many a Protestant can do. He did not grumble when sent to this "finished" town. Western readers know what that word means. The East has none such. He came and saw, and did not like the dilapidated condition of affairs, and set himself to work to get up a new church, or to make an old one as good as new. There was not much money here, as there is not usually where such preachers are stationed. But he gets what he can at home, and pushes abroad; begs it, brick by brick, and tint by tint, and penny by penny, *poco poquito*, little and least, till he gets the money and work, and finishes his cozy box for his half a hundred worshipers. A hundred would jam it. That is the only non-Methodistic part of the procedure. But in a town which is full of big and empty churches, he may have thought that it was well to make an exception, and so he chose "a little house well filled."

I hope he may yet be found among the Protestant ministers. He will be one of the most useful when he does come.

We ride a mile farther, past a big church ruin—which my party offer me for our church, but which is respectfully declined in favor of the gay little box just left—and, going through a stretch of green fields, ascend a slight hill, ride up a string of broad stone steps, and halt at the closed doors of the Church of Guadalupe. There are many of that name in this country, the Divine Virgin near Mexico not being one-childed in respect to temples or idolaters, if she was, as the Romanists assert, in respect to her married family.

The view is beautiful, but desolate. Streets run straight in all directions, but without a house. Churches besprinkle the vacant landscape. The maguey makes the fields green, and grasses more fit for man and beast cover some of the pastures with their early beauty. The mountains are about us, vast and lonely, and "all the air a solemn stillness holds." It is not so much a church town as a church-yard.

Before us rises the famous Pyramid. We came here to get the right point of observation for that curiosity. It comes forth out of a very level plain, and is evidently built up from that base. Some fancy that it is simply a hill enlarged, but a glance from this spot will change that theory. It covers over forty acres, and is two hundred and three feet high. So the measurements by Lieutenant Beauregard attest; and he was a good scholar then, if not a good citizen afterward. But he has become that also lately, and makes his beginning and end harmonious in patriotism.

Mr. Beecher says somewhere that one can understand the labor involved in making a mountain by shoveling and wheeling and dumping a few barrows of earth in his own lot. The Cholulans shoveled, wheeled, and dumped (though, indeed, they did not wheel, but carried it on their shoulders and heads) not less than a score or two of millions of such barrow-loads, to make a temple for their chief god, and on which many of those who built it, or their children, were offered in sacrifice. It is a big as well as a bad faith that would thus make multitudes erect joyfully their own funeral pyre.

This pyre, with a base of forty acres, is of the size of Boston Common. Conceive of those free-religion Puritans leveling off that sacred place, and bringing loads of earth from Brighton, Brookline, Dorchester, and Somerville to erect the whole leveled square into a pyramid as high as the pine-apple knob of its State-house! Up, up, up slowly creeps the mighty plateau, growing narrow as it grows tall, like many uplifted men. Yet when above the tallest house of Beacon Street, it is twenty acres across; and when it reaches the dome of the Capitol, it is ten acres across; and when it stops at the pine-apple knob, it is two or three acres across. And all this for faith, and a faith which involved their own immolation, or that of their nearest friends and kindred! How happens it that Boston goes to Buddha for its god? He lies nearer home on these Aztec plains; he is a native American, the better suiting their national conceit; he shows us a faith that makes Buddha's nirvaña tame, for suicide is always baser than submission to another's knife. The pyramid of Cholula is the shrine that should draw these worshipers. Here is the eleventh religion that should swallow up all their ten, for it is more majestic than any save the One that builds its temple in the skies, and offers up its one Victim, the

PYRAMID OF CHOLULA.

Divine Author thereof, freely and of His own will, for the world's salvation.

The pyramid that rises before us is one of the chief illustrations on the surface of the earth of the piety and powerlessness of man. Its base is twice the width of Cheops, though its height is less than half. It has another disadvantage: its Egyptian kin are placed on the edge of a flat plain and of low hills, both of which they easily overmaster. This is on the edge of a plain, but is under the shadow of the tallest mountains on the globe. Not thirty miles distant are their peaks, not five, the beginning of their upheavals. It was a daring thought to put a growth of man by the side of these stupendous domes, and as a work of man it deserves the greater commendation for the daring.

The Chicagoans are contemplating transferring some boulders

to their boulevards. They may find encouragement in this Cholula labor of love and faith, done probably at small expense, for love and faith work cheap: done in the long-vanished centuries, when love and faith, if no holier and warmer than now, were none the less active and powerful in their ignorance—more so, I fear, than ours is, with all the light of the Gospel shining straight upon our hearts. Shall these poor blinded worshipers, like the men of Sodom and those of Chorazin, rise up in the judgment against us, saying, "If we had seen your day we should have accepted it in gladness and fullness of heart?"

We ride round the church where we have been looking and moralizing, witness the verdant and magnificent desolation on every side, pass through the still, deserted town, and climb the sides of the man-made hill. The ascent convinces you of its artificial construction and of its remarkable proportions. These forty acres are piled up in valleys and hill slopes, irregular and natural to-day. The path is cut under steep and lofty cliffs, on whose exposed side is a mass of stratifications, brick and clay, in regular layers. Trees grow along the path, tall and old; fruit and flower trees of the tropics, brilliant in colors and green with fruit. Orchards open half-way up; ravines drop down close to the summit. All the traits of natural hills appear.

The pyramid once stood, evidently, near the heart of the town. From it, in every direction, straight and comely avenues still proceed. From these, equally straight streets stretch for a mile or more in all directions. These streets, except a square or two about the plaza, are entirely void of houses, except the churches. These stand forth on all sides, near and far, some skirting the bases of the mountain range, whose edge comes within two or three miles of this spot. We counted forty-one of these edifices, and some were omitted even then. Almost fifty churches still stand about this pyramid, many of them large and elaborate structures, all of them erected at no small cost by the conquerors and their successors. The Indian Mecca is gone, but these efforts to subdue it to the true faith remain.

Not content with these ancient efforts to hold Cholula, the attempt is yet kept up. This summit exhibits its most striking expression. The church that long stood here was cast down by an earthquake not long since, and another is nearly completed in its place. It is small, not over fifty by twenty. The tiny chancel may be a few feet wider. Five altars are in this box, one each side of the entrance, one each end of the chancel, and one at the usual

VIEW FROM THE PYRAMID OF CHOLULA.

place, in the rear end of the chapel. On this bit of stone and plaster are lavished more beauty and luxury than on any like structure I have seen, here or elsewhere. It is not covered thick with gold-leaf, as is the chapel in the Church of Santo Domingo in Puebla, or some of the chapels in Mexico. They are old-fashioned. This is up with the times. Delicate tints, abundant enamel or porcelain in various colors, carved work in green, and scarlet, and blue, and gold, choice paintings, frescoed marbles that make the real look cheap, real marbles that hardly make their counterfeits cheaper, everywhere "a gem of purest ray serene." The work has cost thirty thousand dollars, and much of it has been given, both of labor and of substance. Not less than fifty thousand dollars is its actual cost, and that is half, at least, what it could be done for in the States.

And all this for a box that will not accommodate one hundred people, and that no hundred people will ever visit at one time except when it is dedicated, and possibly some feast day or two during the year.

It is a specimen of Romanism. Every thing for effect. A superb little chapel on the top of this pyramid was essential to the predominance of the system, possibly, in all the State. So the funds of the Church are lavished on it without stint, and Our Lady of the Remedies, to whom it is dedicated, is to be complimented by the prettiest bit of useless jewelry that has been laid at her shrine for many a day.

This pyramid, it is said, was dedicated to the worship of the white and benevolent god, Quetzalcotl. He it was who gave the people many good lessons, and left for the East, saying he would return again. It was his expected return that made so many of the people accept Cortez and his faith as the fulfillment of that prophecy. And, despite the cruelties of the Spaniards and the imperfections of their faith, there is no doubt that the benevolent god did return in that invasion. The horrid human sacrifices that took place on this very summit to this same god—twelve thousand a year, it is said—show how needful was that advent. Seventy thousand persons were sacrificed to the god of war in Mexico in the year 1486—only thirty-five years before that city fell. It was time for it to fall.

This summit, and many lesser ones about it, smoked daily with these victims. Their hearts were being cut out, three every hour of every day, year in and year out, and their bodies served up in daily religious and sacramental repast. Was it not time that it came to an end? True, a low type of Christianity replaced it; but any type is infinitely superior to that intolerable barbarism. The natives were oppressed afterward, yet no more than they had been, while they never after fed an altar or a banquet. The poor family remained poor, but it remained united. The Virgin and her Child were a tender grace in idea and worship compared with those awful demons. And to-day this people are getting ready for the purer form of Gospel truth that is coming to their doors. They will reject all idolatry as they did those devouring devils. They will accept the whole Gospel with more heartiness than they did that imperfect expression of it. The mound of Cholula shall be consecrated to the Saviour of Remedies, the Divine and only Physician, and these natives shall use their rare gifts, not in ornamentations which lead astray, but in elevating contributions to Him who gave their gifts, and will rejoice in their befitting consecration.

Our ride wound through gardens where the peach-tree hung full of blossoms, where the crab-apple was yellow ripe, where oranges flourished, and all other tropical delights. It seemed a very paradise, and it was. Only man — how poor, how hapless his lot! What huts he hid himself in; what sorry outfit for life! Table and chairs has he none, nor bedsteads, nor beds; just a mat on the floor, a bowl to steam his beans in, and a platter on which to fry his tortillas. No books, no papers, no apartments, parlor, kitchen, nor bedroom.

Is there not a chance for the Gospel here? The New Testament and a fine-tooth comb have been suggested as the form this coming revelation should take. They are a good beginning, but a vast structure of society and soul must be built thereupon; a structure of beauty not like that on the pyramid, simply useless, and therefore vain, nor like that of the pyramid itself, solid but earthly, but a structure of truth, of virtue, of culture, of sweetness, of every thing included in the Gospel of Jesus Christ.

One can see the answer of Romanism in this ruined Cholula and flourishing Puebla. These sacred cities have not advanced these natives one iota in culture. The untutored, undeveloped native that first looked on Cortez, it was, in dress and mien and nature, that bowed about the bishop in those Sabbath vespers. Three hundred and fifty years, nine generations of Roman Catholic culture, have not advanced him a step, except in abolishing human sacrifice, and that the mass of the people accepted rather than approved. Shall the other forms and forces of Christ have no better report in their trial of centuries? If not, God will reject them, as he is evidently rejecting this long dominant religion. Not centuries, not years even, hardly months, should elapse before these people give evidence of the radical change the true Gospel works in its believers. They are showing it already. They will more and more. The better clothes they wear to Protestant service is a sign of the inward change. Cholula and Puebla will be crowned with a coming Christian civilization that will make all their past barbaric. Amen and amen!

IX.

A DAY AND NIGHT AT EL DESIERTO.

A Point of View.—The Woods: their Peril and Preservation.—How we got here.—Chapultepec.—Tacubaya.—Santa Fé.—Contadera.—Guajimalpa.—The Forest.—The Shot.—Solitude.—The Ruin.—Its Inquisition.—A Bowl of Song.—Moonlight Pleasure and all-night Horror.—Morning Glories.—Its History.—A more excellent Way.—Home again.

Let me have Turner's pencil for a moment. How your black and white would burn! On this rock, high and lifted up, come and sit. You are panting from the long pull and the steep pull up the gorge; but you forget it all in the landscape, near and remote, that lies under your eye. It is torrid and temperate at a glance. Could we see round that lofty point, we could add and frigid also; for there sit the snow peaks that bring the north pole to the equator. But these apart, the scene is one of exquisite beauty and grandeur. The gorge beneath us is lined on both sides with munificent pines, firs, and hemlocks; not stinted and spindled, as they are on our northern hills, nor clipped and shaven, but in all their original, untrimmed, uncut magnificence. In the midst of them sits a castle-like ruin, such as the Rhine seldom affords, England seldomer, and other lands never. Its gray walls, thick and high, its several domes and turrets, its archways and entrances are of the best Rhine quality. It is on a cleared point that is well above the bottom of the valley and yet well below our towering observatory. It is a reminiscence of feudal times in looks and situation, and one could easily transfer himself almost three hundred years backward, when its foundations were laid.

It is not a castle, though very like a castle; but a convent, built in 1606, the year before the first permanent English colony was planted on this continent, and quite a while before *the* English colony was planted on a rock—the colony that has colonized the whole continent down to Mexico, and will yet colonize that and all south of it.

This elaborate building was then erected in a country that for eighty-five years, nearly a century, had been under European sway, culture, and religion. So the Pilgrim Rock must abase its head before the rock-built walls of El Desierto. I would like to see it lowering its crest before any thing.

Beyond this grand forest and its romantic ruin lie the plains of Mexico. The sun blazes over them, making it all a lake of golden mist, out of which rises many a bold and brown sierra, that at our height and in this radiance looks neither bold nor brown. For forty or sixty miles this open landscape stretches. A matter of twenty miles is of no consequence in this country, so clear is the atmosphere. Emerson's " Brahma " is here fulfilled in one of its lines.

"Far and remote to me are near."

The basin is of treeless land, salt-marsh, irrigated meadow, and shallow lake, with knobs of hills embossed upon it. Just round the corner of that neighboring point of pines, to our right, lies the central spot of the park—not a rude upheaval of mountains, but a fair city, with its towers and domes and roofs flashing in the setting sun. We saw it often in our ascent hither. It is a city that perhaps best of all on earth fulfills Tennyson's description,

"Sown in the centre of a monstrous plain,
The city glitters like a grain of salt."

The monstrous plain and the dazzling sunshine envelop this town, and make it blaze like a diamond amidst diamonds.

This writing, begun at sunset on the mountain-top, is being continued before the convent walls, not long after sunrise. The rest of the party, gentlemen and gentlewomen, are practicing their pistols on the walls. Small success have most ; but one, the guide and guardian of the band, puts his bullet through the mark every time. I content myself with telling Lessing's fable of the Jupiter and Apollo who went out on a shooting-match. Apollo put his arrow through the centre of the bull's-eye. "I could beat that if I had a mind to try," says Jupiter, and stalks haughtily home. Many a critic of shooting guns and ideas is equally contemptuous, critical, and careful, and so maintains a reputation that one shot or one book of his own would utterly destroy. "Critics are men that have failed," says the sarcastic Disraeli, in "Lothair." They would fail if they tried. This Jupiter critic of sharp shots did try, foolishly, and landed his ball way up the side of the wall. Content, he retreats to his mossy seat by the side of the fountain, and resumes his pen and his true vocation.

How would I love to sit for hours and days on the stone fountain where this is being written, and under the grand cypresses that tower above me with less spreading branches than their twin hemlock of New England, or on the broad parapet that makes a low wall for the front of the cloister. "The sound of the going in the tops" of the pines and hemlocks, which David heard in the tops of the mulberry-trees, comes solemnly on the ear, the same sad wail that they have given forth to the like mortal ear since first these forests were pierced and these walls arose.

How sad are the voices of Nature. The moan of the forest and of the ocean have often been noticed. Was that part of the note of lamentation sent forth from Nature when man fell—that groaning after restoration which she and all that her inhabits still unutterably utter? Why should they not be pleasant sounds, full of music and mirth too? Why should they not laugh for joy? The hills skipped for gladness when their Lord came. So may the whispering of forests be yet full of joyousness. When the earth is redeemed, and man is all holy and all happy within and without, the trees shall clap their hands, and every flower smile audibly its fragrant bliss. Could you mix senses better than in that sentence, Mr. Critic? Mrs. Browning is an authority for part of it; for does not she say of the angels,

"I ween their blessed smile is heard?"

These woods, I fear, will never see the leaf-clapping day; for the Yankee is around, and a forest of primeval grandeur affects him precisely as a company of first-class negroes used to affect "a good old Southern gentleman, all of the olden time." Mr. John M. Mason, Buchanan's minister to France, met the Haytien minister at an imperial levee. As he carelessly contemplated his ebon equal, in all the pomp and circumstance of ambassadorial dignity, he was asked what he thought of his sable associate. "I think he would be worth eighteen hundred dollars in Richmond," was his prompt reply. So the American of to-day says, when he sees these magnificent trees, "I think they would cut into so many thousand feet, and be worth so many petty dollars." Let us enjoy them while we may, for they are soon to vanish.

Has not General Palmer and his troupe of engineers been up this very pass exploring for a route from Mexico to Toluca, and so to the Pacific? The railroad is coming, and these trees must prepare to go. Only one thing can save them — a camp-meeting. Maximilian tried to buy them, and could not, though he offered eighty thousand dollars for the place. The Methodists may get a few hundred of the acres by the grace of General Rosecrans, including, I trust, the old convent, and so preserve a bit of this grand picture for future generations. They are about the only conservators of our forests. Their presence is timely here. With the railroad that comes to level these original woods let the Church come to save a portion thereof from devastation.

It is well located, too, for such a service. Less than twenty miles from the capital, easily accessible by the multitudes, we may yet hear the voice of prayer and praise ascending in its newer and better forms from these most venerable cloisters and forests.

Let me tell you a little more fully our visit to each of these choicenesses. Taking to horse, we cantered merrily through the silent streets of the city at six o'clock of the morning of Tuesday, the 11th of February. No shawl or overcoat burdened our shoulders or stifled the breathing. A summer morning, soft as July, it was. Just as we were pacing through the Alameda, and had entered the paseo, or fashionable drive, the sun met us, and smiled responsive to our smile. The road ran along the arches of the aqueduct, looking very Roman, and hiding under them robbers, who not unfrequently here waylay coach and horseman, which is very Roman also.

A half-hour, and we pace along the base of Chapultepec, standing high above the aboriginal pines and cypresses that skirt its base and climb its steep sides. Tacubaya is next passed, a pretty suburb, with superb parks and grounds of Mexican millionaires. Here, a few Saturday nights ago, one of these chiefs, Señor Escandron, gave a *fête champêtre* to nine hundred persons, at an expense, it was said, of forty thousand dollars. Dancing and drinking were the chief amusements of the Sabbath-breaking hour and its preliminary preparation; gambling and gorging were the interludes. These grand pavilions and gardens are so infested with robbers that none of these gentry dare spend a night here except they are strongly guarded. So safe is this country in a large village not four miles from the palace of the President!

Now comes a long pull of a dozen miles up a broad and dusty road, amidst mules and men equally heavy-laden and equally sad-faced—mules often diminishing into donkeys, and men into boys. The human beasts of burden carry on their backs huge crates filled with earthenware and other commodities, weighing, one would guess, several hundred pounds. These are held to their backs by a broad strap going over the forehead, and the hair is left thick, and made to grow thicker over the eyes, in order to make a matting for this strap. I have seen stones and bricks so carried that weighed, I was told, four hundred pounds. Their heads bow to the burden, and they trot along under their huge loads as fast as a horse can walk.

The road ascends the spurs of the Toluca range; through Santa Fé, a string of adobe huts; through Contadera, where a body of troops are stationed that eye us soldierly, that is, quietly and searchingly; and at last leaves us at the venta of Guajimalpa, a wayside station for changing mules on the stage to Toluca.

Here we turn off the dusty highway and climb a smooth, open, steep hill. The water rattles gayly down a brisk stream, which a mile or two back we had turned aside into a pasture path to enjoy. The smooth upland soon becomes rougher and more wooded, and after a mile or more we enter a cleft in a smooth-faced wall of a venerable look, and are in the grounds of the Convent of El Desierto.

The woods grow thicker in numbers and in size. No needy knife-cutter has been allowed to ply his trade in this sacred inclosure. For two hundred and sixty-nine years they have been let alone. Only the path, of a single horseback width, has been cut through them. This path winds along the sides of lofty hills and deep ravines, densely shaded, now climbing, now declining, for a mile and a half; then, winding up a steep acclivity, it emerges upon the open space on which the convent stands.

One notices in this location the same taste that governed the abbots of England and Europe. They always chose the most beautiful spots for their retreats. They had an eye to the beauty of nature, all the keener, perhaps, because they were forbidden to look upon all other beauty. They knew how to make a wilderness blossom like the rose, but they selected the wilderness most susceptible of such blossoming. This rare combination is one of the best. Few ever equaled; none, we believe, surpassed it. Their whole area was nine leagues square—three miles in each direction; and all encompassed with a choice brick wall, that still survives in large part and perfect form.

The clearing is narrow, woods hugging the buildings closely on either side, removed not a hundred feet in the rear, but opening on the front to the breadth of a single pasture lot, a slope of five or ten acres.

Was ever solitude more solitary? In this bright, warm morning not a creature is stirring except the visitors and visited. Not a bird or insect, or man or beast. In fact, I only saw one insect in all the woods and walks, and that was a wasp, that had fallen on the ground, and fluttered and fainted from sheer loneliness. The birds were alike absent. A black hawk sailing over the black wasp was the only representative of that tribe, except the cock and hens of the court-yard.

How near akin seem our very dogs and horses in the dense loneliness. One easily detects in these favorites of man a yet closer affinity, and wonders why, when horses are admitted to the revelator's heaven, dogs are excluded. They must be the ugly dogs of Eastern countries, and not their developed associates of Christian men. No animal seems to have acquired so much from the Gospel as the dog. Every other creature seems unchanged in nature in every estate of man. The ancient horse was as proud and petted a beast as the modern. The cat, as my Spanish phrase-book teaches, is false to-day, and has never improved in heart or head; but this companion of man in his degradation, which always clings to him how low soever he plunges, seems also to arise with him, and in its sagacity, fidelity, and courage almost gives warrant of its possible immortality. Since Mr. Emerson allows that only about one man is born in five hundred years who is worthy of immortality, perhaps that rare example of the possibilities of our race may find as his chosen companion the alike fortunate representative of the canine race, and of that dog and that man the distich may prove true:

> "Admitted to that equal sky,
> His faithful dog will bear him company."

The convent gate stands open, and we gladly enter the deserted Desierto. A stream of coldest water leaps out of the face of the high terrace before the entrance, and gives us that best of drinks, which man's perverted appetite is so constantly rejecting for muddy and heavy beers and ales, and sour, sharp wines, and hot brandies and whiskies. It is one of the greatest proofs of his depravity, this plunging into false and fatal beverages. How great the work to be done in this country in rescuing poor and rich from these drunken abominations! And not this country only.

The buildings covered not less than ten acres. There were three large open courts, or cloisters, surrounded with arcades, a half-dozen long aisles, narrow and low-arched, out of which the cells of the monks open, and other apartments. Each cell had a private court of its own, open to the sky, but closed by high walls from all outward observation.

There were a multitude of smaller courts, three or four chapels or oratories, besides the church, and two large inclosures of several acres, which were possibly its gardens and possibly a portion of its approaches. The chief church was used for several years as a glass factory, and a huge furnace built under the dome and blackened walls still attest its change of use. It reminded one of the hero of "Put Yourself in his Place," who used an abandoned church as his furnace for the making of his tools, and thus made the ghosts useful in protecting his rights against opposing trades-unions and his high Tory uncle. So even the fertile genius of Charles Reade finds his fiction lagging behind this fact; and thus there is nothing new, not only under the sun, but even in the realm of the imagination. It did seem a little out of place, this glass-furnace where the altar stood; but the idolatry of the mass deserved perhaps this desecration, as Palestine had to be trodden under foot of the Gentiles because its chosen people had themselves trodden under foot the Son of God, an identity of words which the Holy Spirit expressly uses, with that verbal exactness which He always employs, in order to set forth the righteousness of that banishment and punishment which has continued now over eighteen centuries.

The mass is still an idolatry, worse than any the Jews fell into: and this desecration is but a type of many that have preceded it, and more that shall follow, until the true worship shall not be a repetition of an accomplished and, therefore, now idolatrous sacrifice, but a setting home of this sacrifice divine, with faith and prayer and earnest exhortation and conclusive reasoning, to the hearts and lives of the hearer and believer.

Outside this church is a spacious *patio*, or court, once surrounded by broad arches and shaded walks, only an arch or two of which remain. Go to the outer edge of it and wind down a narrow stairway, and you enter an under-ground series of cloisters, the size of the arched wall above—a dark, low, fearful range of dungeons, which not a ray could penetrate. Out of it opens at one corner a chapel of flagellation, perhaps of inquisitorial judgment, for tradition hath it that this convent was for many years the seat of the Inquisition, and that it was removed hence to the Dominican convent in the city. But this is denied by others, who declare that the Carmelites, by whom it was built, never had charge of the Inquisition; and that this, therefore, could not have had any thing to do with those persecutions. It is replied, on the other hand, that when the Carmelites abandoned this spot for one more retired, at a greater distance from the city, the Dominicans occupied it, and perverted it to their cruel purpose. I hope not, for I should hate to think so fair and so secluded a retreat could have been made hideous with that horror. Yet these doleful arches look as if made for such purposes, and one shudders as he creeps through them, and fancies he sees his Christian brethren, two hundred years ago, chained to these walls and sitting in thick darkness, on their way to the rack and the fagot and glory.

We emerge gladly, and take to the outer garden, where an oratory, inclosed on three sides and open to the western sun, gives a charming view of the grand mountains and grander forests. It has such echoing qualities that one whispering in a corner, with his face close to the wall, is distinctly and loudly heard by one in the diagonal corner, though no others in the room can hear even the sound of the whisper. Thus two gentlemen at opposite corners and two ladies talked each to each, and no one heard a sound except that whispered by their own opposite. It has singing qualities as well, and as the quartette of voices joined in national and religious melodies, one could but exclaim, with a slight variation,

"O listen! for the vale profound
Is overflowing with the sound!"

It seemed as if this bowl of stone bowled out the melody (do not read that bawled), and echoed in every rocky fibre to the exultant harmony. With what gusto did it sing the John Brown song (it seemed as though that had never been sung before), and "The Star-spangled Banner," and "Blow ye the Trumpet, blow!" and tenderer airs, such as "Tenting on the Old Camp-ground," and "A Charge to keep I have." They all melted together, and we agreed that when the coming camp-meeting is held in these old woods, this chapel in the garden will be a choice resort for the happy minstrels of those happy convocations.

The choicest walk, after all, is by moonlight. It is familiar to say,
> "If you would see Melrose aright,
> Go visit it by pale moonlight."

This far larger and costlier abbey, and situated more romantically, deserves like visitation. The flood of silver raining from that mine in the sky—an appropriate figure for this silver country—poured over all the *patios* and *azaleas*, or flat roofs, on the porcelain-tiled domes, into the gardens, everywhere but into the still roofed corridors and shut cells. They looked all the blacker and more fearful for the contrast. We climb to the belfry, and let the sound of our own music creep into our ears, while we also send out over the valleys and woodlands a cheerful summons to the robber serenaders, that may make us sing another song before morning. We sit on the flat roofs, with their slightly raised battlements, and continue our talk and song till the hour grows late, and the air slightly chill, for this is nine thousand feet above New York, and the midnight February air is not quite as warm as her midnight air of August.

All this vivacity was assumed. We may as well own it: we were really scared. The gentleman who conducted us, of undoubted personal courage, felt some fears for the ladies in his care. Of the two men with him, one made no pretense as a marksman, and had not even put a revolver in his belt. We prepare for the night by barring heavily the outer door of the ruin and inner doors of our apartments, as well as the shutters to their glassless windows. A fire is burning on the unused hearth, whose light is companionable and comforting. The ladies lie undressed on a couch before the fire, and the gentlemen occasionally on mattresses; for the chieftain is out most of the night patroling the walks, and his associates frequently creep around behind him. Every sound is caught by exceedingly erect ears, and many never made are distinctly heard, the spirit within hearing in the outward ear:

> "The airy tongues that syllable men's names,
> On sands, and shores, and desert wildernesses."

This desert wilderness is profuse in such vocalizations. A couple of charcoal-burners, perhaps from the mountains, grazed our gate, and came near being grazed by our balls. A whispering breeze in the tree-tops seemed to be the low orders of the assailing forces. A horse, if such there be, wandering loose on these hill-sides, if not a ghostly horse, sounded like the tramp of steeds rushing down upon us. The very breathing of the dog, who murmured in his sleep, was taken as an omen of alarm. So, with fits of feeble slumber and interludes of long waking, with wanderings about the ruins by moonlight, stealthily seeking a stealthy foe, we managed to get through the night; and the morning finds us, oh, so courageous! Who's afraid? Who cares for the beggars of Santa Rosa, or Guajimalpa, and other unpronounceable towns about us? Let them come by the legion. Our four revolvers and one carbine are equal to them all.

Yet we had reason to fear, for the master of the first village below had warned us of the danger, and the *administrador* of the place declared it not improbable that we should be visited. These villages harbor hordes of robbers, and we were well studied by their sidewalk committees as we passed through them. The two men who passed our gate at ten of the night, and even tried it, were perhaps a part of a gang, rather than charcoal-burners, who, seeing through two eyelet-holes one of the party with his carbine, gave such a report as dissuaded others from returning with them to receive our hospitality. Others reported, after we got back, that the country round considered the deed most perilous, and wondered at our escape. Perhaps our audacity or indifference was, after all, our safety. Undoubtedly, we did risk something in coming hither, and once and again half regretted our temerity. But it paid.

We take another climb in the morning to another summit— a two-hours-and-thirty-minutes' tramp, very different from the two-thirty of the racer. But the result was different; for we gained health and appetite, and a glorious prospect in our two-thirty toil up the face of the mountain. Before us and far beneath lay the high, uplifted plains of Anahuac, with the city on its breast, a dazzling diamond. The two snow-peaks blazed more brightly than the city they inclose; and all the valley, its lakes, meadows, and mountains, cities and hamlets, burned in the torrid flame. A slight smoke, the first I have seen, left some of the remoter ranges less distinct. Yet the Sierra of Real del Monte, eighty miles away, was not afar off, and more distant ranges girt the horizon. Below us the cleared knolls were patched off into pastures by hedges of maguey, whose dark, broad leaves, even at this height, were visibly glossy and green.

It was less *recherche* than the one the night previous. The convent was not the centre of the scene, nor the woods the circumference. They were put one side, as the city had been in that picture. I prefer the seclusiveness of the first; and, if I were rich, would give an order quickly to some of these deft artists, of whom Mexico has many, to put that beauty on the canvas. The Falls of Atoyac, on the mountain rim of the Sierra Caliente, and the Convent of El Desierto are the true perfections of loveliness so far beheld in this country; and it is hard to say which of the two is chief. This has the superiority in the mingling with its woods and ravines, man and history and the Mexic plain; that, in its dancing water-fall, plunging into a green basin, whose walls of tropical luxuriance rise two thousand feet above the white-sprayed bottom. Who will give me both? The greedy spirit cries, who? And echo

"The green silence doth displace"

with a mocking "who?"

Desierto has never had its desert in fame, though not without it.

It was a great resort in the middle of the seventeenth century, within fifty years after the first stone was laid. One Thomas Page, an English ecclesiastic, visiting it then, says: "The orchards and gardens were full of fruits and flowers, which may take two miles to compass; and here among the rocks are many springs of water which, with the shade of the plantain (or banana) and other trees, are most cool and pleasant to the hermits. They have also the sweet smell of the rose and the jasmine, which is a little flower, but the sweetest of all others; and there is not any flower to be found that is rare and exquisite in that country which is not in that wilderness, to delight the senses of those mortified hermits."

The rose-bush and the jasmine remain yet, the path through the garden being lined with the former, growing as tall as your head, and the latter clinging to the crevices of the walls and along the ruined battlements, as fragrant and as pretty in its pink and checkered blossoms as it was more than two hundred years ago. The garden is now neglected, but could easily yield all tropical luxuries in this frostless air. No wonder the place became a great attraction, and Desierto was the fashion for Mexics. "It is wonderful," says Priest Thomas, "to see the strange devices of fountains of water which are about the gardens; but much more wonderful to see the resort thither of coaches, and gallants and ladies, and citizens from Mexico, to walk and make merry in those desert pleasures, and to see those hypocrites, whom they look upon as living saints, and so think nothing too good for them to cherish them in their desert conflicts with Satan." Even so early had the fruit of sainthood begun to ripe and rot. Like Martha's Vineyard, it had ceased to be so much a spiritual as a luxurious resort. Will the camp-meeting to come here fall into like condemnation?

He says these visitors brought presents, and the image of our Lady of Carmel had treasures of diamonds, pearls, golden chains, and crowns, and gowns of cloth of gold and silver. "Before this picture did hang in my time twenty lamps of silver, the poorest of them being worth a hundred pounds." Quaintly and profitably he adds, "Truly, Satan hath given them what he offered unto Christ in the desert. All the dainties and all the riches of America hath he given unto them in that desert because they daily fall down and worship him." Is it so yet? Doth wilderness temptation supplant wilderness faith? Then will like desolations follow that have followed here, and in all the famous abbeys of the world, even the wasting of their treasures and the ruin of their palaces. Those twenty lamps, of ten thousand dollars' value and upward, where now? And the treasures, and gifts, and luxuries, and soliciting of prayers and masses, where are they?

The monks became aware of the perils this popularity was bringing, and withdrew to a remoter seclusion, farther up the mountain. Even there their mission failed, and the head of this convent was one of the first of those who rejected Romanism; though he has since returned to his old vows, not, I trust, to abide therein.

As we wander about these vacant cells and close-walled paths we fall into sympathy with their vanished life, and repeat with too much inward approval Southey's lines :

> "I envy them, those monks of old,
> The books they read, the beads they told,
> To earthly feelings dead and cold,
> And all humanity."

Yet there was not much of mortification or of reading, as we have seen. Little as there was, however, it probably surpassed that of the surrounding people. They kept alive what little literature did exist, and performed most of the penances that were inflicted. So we come back to this present, and say :

> "Yet still, for all their faith could see,
> I would not these cowled churchmen be."

Or, with piety and poetry surpassing Emerson, should we say, with Wesley :

> "Not in the tombs we pine to dwell,
> Not in the dark monastic cell,

> By vows and grates confined ;
> Freely to all ourselves we give,
> Constrained by Jesus's love to live
> The servants of mankind."

It is not in this hidden and idle manner that one must serve his generation ; but in earnest efforts to bring all souls out of sin, ignorance, evil habit, and all degradation. These monks of Mount Carmel fared sumptuously or sparingly ; but the peon still bowed his head to his burden, and the Spaniard still robbed and murdered. Better far less introspection and more outward action. Thus only will the world come nearer Christ and heaven.

We left regretfully the ancient pile and its more ancient surroundings. At half-past three that torrid winter afternoon our last picnic meal was shared by no less than four dogs, who ate the crumbs under the table, and even the meats off of it. They were worth eating, as I can testify. An English gentleman purveyed and a good English cook prepared the store which thus evanished at last from under the table.

We rode through the cool, rich forest, and out into the blaze, which burned our backs and necks as if it came through a burning-glass. There were the same burdened mules and men, donkeys and boys, the same lounging soldiers, the same sad-eyed women ; one group alone merry with laughter, as they chased a rat among their ragged huts. The sun drove the long shadows over the plains, disappeared in a crater of fire, that shot up flames from its black bowl, while Iztaccihuatl and Popocatepetl glowed rosily long after valley and hill-top were in shadow and slumber. The moon arose, and our spirits with her, for it grew perilous even on the highway as it grew dark, and we paced chattingly along the Empress Road from Chapultepec, taking a moonlight ride, that rarest and riskiest of pleasure jaunts in Mexico. It is too bad that to the very centre of the city there is no protection against robbery. We escaped, and entered our courts in four hours after we left that of the convent, tired and delighted with the ride, the fright, the tramp, the ruin, the whole of El Desierto.

X.

A RIDE ABOUT TOWN.

The Horse and its Rider.—Paseos.—Empress's Drive.—A Relic of Waterloo.—The Tree of Montezuma.—The Woods.—View of Chapultepec.—Baths of Montezuma.—Tacubaya Gardens.—The Penyan.—Canal.—Floating Gardens.—Gautemozin.—The Café.

THIS country is made for the horse, and the horse for the country. He paces and canters deliciously, and the air and the clime fit perfectly to his gait. Horseback in England and the States is a luxury pursued under difficulties. The first difficulty is in the horse, which is seldom trained to such service; and the second and worse one is in the weather, which is not sufficiently uniform to make the luxury a permanency. Here every morning is perfect, and about every horse. The saddle, too, is made for riding; far superior to the English saddle, it holds you on, and does not make you hold yourself on. So if you come to Mexico, take to the horse. Only gentlemen, however, indulge in this pastime, and very handsomely they ride: straight legs, laced with silver buttons, broad hat of white felt, with a wide silver band expanded into a huge snake-like swell and fold; their horses often gayly caparisoned, and delighting evidently in their lordly service. There is no more characteristic or agreeable sight in Mexico than these riders; far more agreeable than it is when witnessed a few miles out of town, more or less, and the graceful horseman politely requests of you the loan of your watch, wallet, horse—if you have one—and sometimes all your outer apparel. That is a sight not unfrequently seen, all but the last, close to the city gates. Two of these city riders were relieved by others of these city riders of horses and purses, our last Sabbath night, on the crowded and fashionable drive of the town, not a mile from the Alameda.

But it is safe to take these rides in the morning ; and American ladies, with the bravery of their blood, are willing to take them also. The prettiest ride is to Chapultepec. At six in the morning is the hour. A cup of coffee, hot and hot, and a sweet cracker are the inward supports against the jouncing and rocking. The Alameda is pranced past, scowling at us from its deep thickets, its very smiles changed to frowns under the possibilities of its contents, for robbers and revolvers may suddenly appear from out its greennesses.

The paseos open at its upper end, broad, straight, and handsome. Two or three of these carriage roads come together here about a statue of a Charles of Spain, the only royal effigy allowed to remain, probably the only one that ever entered the land. The decayed bull-fight arena stands opposite the monument, itself a relic, like the effigy, of by-gone institutions—by-gone in the city, but still extant, if not flourishing, in the rural capitals. Two of these avenues go to the Castle of Chapultepec. The one that leads directly to its gates was built by Maximilian, under his wife's orders, and is now called the "Empress's Drive," but for many a year it was known as "the Mad-woman's Drive." It is straight as an arrow from an Aztec bow, lined with young trees, and besprinkled half the way to the castle. It is the favorite thoroughfare for coach and horseman, though these dare not usually go over half its length. That is why it is wet down no farther. To pass that bound is to become possibly the prey of robbers, so bold are these gentlemen of the road.

We canter carelessly on, mindless of robbers in the morning calm. Do you see that little old man who trots easily along? He was the author of the fortunes of the Rothschilds. He was at Waterloo in their employ the day of the battle, took boat before the official messengers, and bore the tidings of the fall of Napoleon to London, to his masters. They instantly bought heavily in European government stocks, and made immense fortunes by their speedy rise. It is odd to meet this representative of the first and most successful of modern private expresses trotting his nag, in his su-per-eightieth year, on this drive, made by a creature of a third Napoleon from him whom he supposed on that day to be, in person and in family, utterly and forever overthrown; and that creature of his, too, a daughter of a king that succeeded that fallen emperor, and husband of an archduke, the nephew or grand-nephew of his own empress, Maria Theresa. Certainly history, even to-day, has curious combinations. You would never have thought that such a nugget could have been picked up on this far-off road. The hill and buildings rise majestically before you, more ancient than any other like fortress and palace in the world. It was a seat of power before the Spaniards entered the land. It is a solitary hill, apart from all others, thrust out into the plain like a nose upon the face of nature. It is a huge rock, whereon the waves of war have beat for a thousand if not for two thousand years,

"Tempest-buffeted, glory-crowned."

The gate is reached. A high wooden slat-fence keeps out the peon, but does not keep in the view. Soldiers as sentinels stand at its gates. The road winds through groves of ancient woods of Yosemite style in nature and in size. Not far from the entrance rises and spreads the gigantic tree known by the name of the Tree of Montezuma. It probably oft refreshed him before he dreamed of the terrible invasion of the white-face and the loss of his kingdom, and perhaps witnessed his bewilderment after that dread event. It is, however, silent on these scenes, unless these whispering leaves are trying to tell the story.

Farther on we enter a large grove of these large trees, a remnant of the vast forests of such that once overshadowed the land. Here picnics are held by city people, who forget the past in their momentarily happy present.

The road winds up the hill, past two Aztec idols hidden in the thick-leaved bushes, up the bare, steep sides which Scott's men bloodily mounted, and ends in a garden near the top. Here the passion-flower hangs along the walls, and a multitude of less hot-blooded kindred blossom by the pathways. Birds as brilliant as

THE TREE OF MONTEZUMA.

the flowers line the walls, and one without beauty of plumage conquers all with his wonderful beauty of song. It is the old law of compensation: "*Non omnia omnes possumus*"—"Every body can not do every thing."

The suite of rooms that compose the castle are large, and command a magnificent prospect. The city lies below, amidst green groves and gardens, with shining drive-ways and spacious fields between. The hills tower grandly beyond. It is a spectacle worthy of a king or emperor, or president—the worthiest of them all. No such panorama has any other palace in the world. Windsor, the next most beautiful, is tame to this. Schönbrunn, Potsdam, Fontainebleau, and all, are flat and cheap to this rare combination. But, then, one is apt to live longer in those palaces, and to die a more natural death, if one death is more natural than another, and that makes their occupants content with humbler luxuries. From Montezuma to Maximilian, the occupants of this hill palace have many of them made a violent exit from their troublous honors. Juarez dared not stay here after night-fall without a large body-guard; and it is abandoned to occasional state breakfasts, the heart of the city being judged a safer residence. Maximilian enjoyed the retreat, and filled the palace with his own pictures and the imperial symbols, the only remnants of which are a few pitchers and basins with his monogram upon them. This is pretty near the estate to which the first and imperial Cæsar sunk. If his clay was utilized to a chink filling, the crown of Maximilian turns into this clay of a wash-basin.

A dining-hall in the rear of the front rooms, on the backbone of the hill—hog's back it might be called for sharpness and roughness—opens pleasantly upon both northern and southern views. Here Juarez gave Seward a breakfast, the last public entertainment in this hall, and one worthy to be made, the saved fêting his savior; for had it not been for Mr. Seward's army of sixty thousand men at the Rio Grande, under General Sherman, and his letter to M. Drouhn L'Huys, requesting his master to gratify the President of the United States by withdrawing his troops from Mexico, Juarez would have still been at Washington, if alive. Both chiefs died in a few months after that breakfast; died at scarcely a moment's warning. So all that are to come to greatness here must turn to dust, as all have turned. Not much to choose between the Spanish blooded prince slain by an Aztec, and the Aztec slain by a Spaniard. Ecclesiastes is profitable reading at Chapultepec. "*Vanitas vanitatum, omnia vanitas.*" Its woods are old, its rocks, its landscape, its mountains.

> "Stars abide—
> Shine down in the old sea:
> Old are the shores:
> But where are the old men?
> I who have seen much,
> Such have I never seen,"

says the Earth-song, in Emerson. But Emerson fails to see why the earth sees them not, why the conscious lord of creation is its weakest victim. The earth has seen such. A thousand years was once their day. But only a day at that. Only a babe was Methusala to the earth, and the sea, and the stars. Ah, sin, sin, what hast thou done!

You can see from the southern windows the Molino del Rey, where the bloodiest of the battles of General Scott was waged. It is a white mill, not two miles off, on a spur of the mountains, and looking innocent of the fierce fighting which it had drawn around its thick walls and high hill-side. The Mexicans have erected a handsome monument there to their own valor, in withstanding with a whole cityful of two hundred thousand the shock of a little handful of a dozen thousand. It withstood for a season only, for they soon yielded and made their retreat good to this hill, whither the Americans followed, and whence they with steadfast step pursued them to the city and the President's palace. You can see the whole route of the troops, from their debouching between the snow mountains yonder, to their battles of Contreras, San Antonio, and Cherubusco, below the city round to Molino del Rey above it, and so hither, and into town.

But let us descend, for the sun is getting up, and we must be off. Just before we reach the gate-way we see a pool, cut into the ground, partly filled with water. It is well walled, with steps descending into it, and large enough for a comfortable bath. This is called the Bath of Montezuma, and was probably used by him; but it was only a receptacle. The fountain whence it sprung is just out of the present grounds, and is the private property of Señor Escandron, who makes many a penny out of its waters. We pass out the gate, ride under shading willows by the water-courses, enter the gardens of the bath, and the inclosure of the spring. Here is a pool fifty feet square and forty feet deep. The water is so clear that you can see it breaking out of the rock-bed, a tiny hill-side and hollow amidst the ferns and grasses that cover that natural floor with a perpetual carpet. Here to plunge you will find delightful in this rising heat of a January sun. An adjoining square the water flows into, whose floor is paved with tiles, and whose depth is not above your neck. So, if you are timid, you can splash in the artificial pool. A like bath for ladies is near by, and a saunter in the garden follows the refreshment.

THE BATHS OF MONTEZUMA.

If intent on a ride farther in this direction, we can keep on to Tacubaya, two miles farther out. There are found some superb gardens, the private grounds of the gentlemen of the city. Groves, ravines, rivulets, lakelets, mounds of flowers, tall Australian gum-trees, and a multitude of sorts we can admire but not name ; views of the snow range, cooling eye and picture ; a sumptuous house, with its broad courts open to visitors, encircled with flowers, sedans, and pictures ; even a chapel for family worship ; every conceivable thing, but—safety. The value of these owners is too high in the kidnaping market for them to trust themselves so far from town overnight. So the place is deserted except for fêtes, when a body of troops is detached for their protection. A little less glory and a little less danger would be desirable.

Another favorite drive is southward. The exit is less agreeable, but once out of town the trip is more natural and more delightful. We pass on our horses, no other mode is appropriate, hardly any other possible, by the great square, southward. One route leads us to the Penyan, a hill overlooking the lake, full of caves and of robbers, whose horrid lair is surpassed by their more horrid aspect. It does not seem possible that human beings can fall so low. The Indians of the plains are hardly as fierce and degraded as these children, perhaps, of Montezuma and Cortez. There is but little comfort in pausing among them; for you must give baksheesh as surely as if at the Pyramids, and you may not get off with what you are willing to give. The views hardly repay the risk. So let us turn to a more agreeable company and scenery.

Leave the city by the south-western gate. You will have hard work to find it. The straightness of the streets gets so narrow and short that it has all the effect of crookedness, as a straight line cut into an infinite number of short straight lines may become a circle. So these bits and threads of lanes have all the bewilderment of Cologne, the head of crooked towns. The streets are as dirty and the huts as poor as it is possible for either to be, and we gladly reach the gate and touch the open fields. Level and low lies the land. The road is hard, though pulpy.

The canal is soon struck. This is the feeder of the city. Along its watery way for five hundred years, perhaps more, have the people and the produce of the region come to town. It is the oldest canal in the world, unless China ranks it, which is doubtful. It is not a canal for horses; the boats are pushed along by the boatmen.

Garden "truck" is the chief freight, though green lucern grasses, for the horses of the town, frequently load heavily the little craft. Pleasure and carriage boats ply the waters, long, narrow, covered with awnings, and well patronized by the people on the line.

These canals were just as busy when Cortez first came over yonder pass as to-day. He saw and noted their traffic when he

THE CANAL.

marched along their side, the invited guest of Montezuma, to the doomed city. How many ages they had then been employed he knew not; no one knows.

Along their sides spring up villages, as the Erie Canal has made towns, great and small, beside its banks. Some of these villages rise to the dignity of towns; others are mere halting-places for the boats.

But what made the canal? Who and when, may be beyond our reach. What did it is more apprehensible. It was the floating island. That curiosity of this country is a veritable fact. As soon almost as you leave the wall, you perceive these novel lands. The ridgeway of the canal is wide enough for several horses. On one side is the long ditch, on the other many short ones, cut straight, not more than a rod or two apart, filled with water, and inclosing plats of ground of about a quarter of an acre. The ditch, cut square about these plats, allows the proprietor, lessee, or laborer to get easily around his lot in his bit of a dory, or scow, from six to twelve feet long, and two wide.

The ground is thus patchworked for miles. At times the spaces are larger; but that is their uniform character, at least near the city. Nearer the mountains they get into almost natural formations, and grow shrubs and even trees on their spongy foundations. This soil is largely made. The soft, saturated earth is superplaced with layers of muck and sand and other soils. These sink gradually by wash and by weather, and other soils are placed upon them. So they are kept up and made fit for culture, and grow deeper with every deposit.

They hardly float, but they rock and yield to a footstep. Farther out they are said to fluctuate somewhat, yet there they never float as a boat, but at the most wave a little to and fro with the moving stream. These gardens are cultivated the year round. "The plowman overtakes the reaper, and the treader of grapes him that soweth seed." It is perpetual seed-time and harvest.

We ride by the once famous hill, where the sacred fire was kindled once every half-century, a black-purple peak, perhaps three hundred feet above the marsh. All the fires in all the land were extinguished, and out of flint and steel, from the bleeding heart of the human sacrifice, the new flame was here kindled, and sent throughout the land. On return we enter by the paseo, where the

FLOATING GARDENS.

bust of Guatemozin stands, on a pedestal in the centre of a square, with commendatory words to his valor, as the last of the Aztecs. It is another proof of how the sons build the sepulchres of those whom the fathers slew. Why a statue of graceful, gentle Montezuma has never been erected, nay stranger yet, why one of Cortez has never been carved, is each a mystery, or would be in any other land than this. Guatemozin is fortunate above his conqueror; for not a bust even bears his features to posterity. But he is not the last of the Aztecs. They are rising again to power. The last President was a pure blood; many of the present leaders are.

Our rides have wearied the horses, if not you. Let us go back to the Commodia, give them up to the mozos, and ourselves to a delightful breakfast at this choicest of cafés. You will find coffee and rolls, fried and sliced potatoes, and ice-water, and beefsteak, equal to the best in the Palais Royal. Here we can sit and talk of the past and future of the fair and almost fairy-land, strengthened outwardly with bath and ride, and inwardly with this delicious berry and its attendants. Nowhere can you get such coffee as here. A small black tin pot of blackest and hottest coffee in one hand, a like small black tin pot of whitest and hottest milk in the other. Pour. If a native, you will not grunt "enough" till the tumbler (for that they use) is well filled. If a foreigner, a third of a glass satisfies from the coffee-pot, and the milk leaves it then stronger than you dare to drink it at home. This berry is native, and should replace with us the coarse Rio and costly Java, to the latter even of which it is superior.

XI.

A GARDEN IN EDEN.

A Temptation.—Up the Mountains.—The Cross of Cortez.—Sight of the Town and Valley.—The downward Plunge.—A Lounge.—Church of Cortez.—The Enchanted Garden.—Idolatry.—The Market-place.—The Almanac against Protestantism.—Palace of Cortez.—The Indian Garden of Maximilian.—A Sugar Hacienda.—The latter End.—All Zones.

In Eden was a garden. Eden itself was paradise, but the paradise had an inner paradise to which the outer delights were the same as brass and iron to the gold and silver in the age of Solomon. So Mexico may be an Eden, but there is a garden eastward and southward in this Eden that makes its other beauties tame.

My stay was drawing to a close, and a temptation to unite a little pleasure with business was too much for my feeble will to resist. So far I had made only one excursion of which the Church was not the sole end and aim—that was the two days and a night to the Convent of El Desierto, and even there I could not resist the conceiving, if not the planning, of a camp-ground in its ancient and magnificent woods.

But a cave of huge dimensions, second only to the Mammoth of Kentucky, if second to that, is reported to be three days to the south, less than two days beyond Cuernervaca. A party of ladies and gentlemen arranged to visit the cave. I was invited to join them. I hardly saw how I could take four days for recreation. In addition to the two already taken out of the sixty spent here, this would make a week's vacation—altogether too much time to throw away in this luxuriating clime. But if we were going back to some Ante-romanistic usages as well as faith, we might utilize the cave for hermit purposes, as the Desierto grounds are to be utilized, I hope, for camp-meetings; but we can hardly get Methodists to immure themselves in celibacy and huts, even in Mexico. So it is not possible to make that a *negocio*, as they say here ; a "biz," as the rougher Yankee of the West puts it.

I go to Cuernervaca because there business lies ; but the cave, I fear I must say, through a glimmer as to the possibility of reaching it, allures me on.

The city I seek lies to the south, over the mountains, between Popocatepetl and Ajusco, the third peak of the valley, and occasionally specked with snow. The morning is gray and misty, and if in the States would insure rain. Here it is an anomaly that will perhaps yield a shower, but more probably be burned up by the torrid sun on his way over Iztaccihuatl.

We ride through a long avenue, well lined with trees for several miles, a finer drive out of the city than New York or Brooklyn can boast, yet only one of half a dozen equally delightful and equally unsafe ; for cavalry patrol these roads away up to the city's gates to protect the traveler from the robber, the foreigner from the native.

It is fifteen miles before the spurs of the mountains are struck. A charming landscape it is, and a morning of exhilaration, despite the threatening clouds—nay, because of them. What lovely haciendas appear on the roadside, with trees sprinkled over them, brooks running through them, green beds where the sickle is busy cutting down green food for the market, broad plains, green and brown ; surely here is paradise before we start for Eden ! Yet these splendid properties can be bought for a song. Who wants to found a Christian college near the city? Now is your chance. For thirty to fifty thousand dollars you can buy immense estates with stone buildings, including often the chapel, all ready for occupation.

Mexacalcingo and other "cingoes" lie off to the left in moist meadows and lakes, with trees rising, like the earth itself, being out of the water and in the water, and islands floating, or unsteady to the tread. They float up and down only. Amidst these amphibious luxuries the people dwell in a Venice of perpetual greenness.

The road turns up the hills, and becomes very rough and steep. A long, sharp, strong pull of a mile brings us to San Mateo—St. Matthew—a village of bamboo houses, standing in black, fat sand, and among tall and very green and very beautiful ash-trees. It is as lovely and as dirty and as dangerous as you wish or do not wish. Robbers are thick, but we are safe, for the guard is our defense.

On we climb, through a frigid vegetation and temperature, as I found it on my return—"a steady pull at the collar," as Murray puts it in his "Swiss Guide"—for a dozen miles. Behind us glowed the Mexic valley, green and glossy, where lake and tree met together. It is a magnificent landscape, and naturally set Cortez violently in love with it, as it had the Aztec and the Toltec before him. One does not tire in admiring its wonderful combination of snow range and purple mountains, of broad lake and evergreen foliage, of pretty town and grand city. The lakes here are an important part of the landscape, if landscape it may be called which they make up. Tezcoco, the largest, seems to fill all the outer section of the valley. The lesser ones near at hand are besprinkled with trees and towers, green and white, mingling prettily with their level lustre.

The summit is reached at La Guardia, a small collection of huts, where a breakfast that I ate not was paid for. Its contents I do not presume to describe. It takes time to learn to like cod-fish, and beans, and sauerkraut, and tomatoes, and corn-bread, and all local luxuries; why not, also, to learn to like tortillas and chili, a hot and not a cold piquanté, and other dishes I do not dare to spell any more than to taste?

Breakfast over, we cross the summit through black and barren scoriæ, the tossings, evidently, of craters, and ere long sight a red stone cross upon a round gray pedestal, two or three feet high, called the Cross of the Marquis. This, it is said, is the boundary mark of the possessions of Cortez, who was created Marquis of the Valley of Ojaca, and placed this cross as the beginning of his possessions.

Woods now appear, pine chiefly, not large, sprinkled over much space, and suggestive of a cold climate. We are over ten thousand feet above the sea; surely it has a right to be cold. For several miles we gradually slope downward, until suddenly the valley we seek opens at our feet, ablaze with the hottest beams. Clouds cover us, and make the sunny hollow of Cuernervaca look the warmer.

It is a bowl, at this height seemingly not ten miles from rim to rim, yet probably fifty would not pace its base. The bottom is not level, even at this height, but embossed, as it were, in many forms and colors. That curved knot, looking not unlike the cow's horn which its name signifies, lying not far from this side of the embracing hills, is Cuernervaca. A belt of emerald surrounds it, especially deep in color and in extent on its farther or lower side. A little farther on you see spots of a light and very brilliant green. They are patches here, but miles there, of the sugar-cane, portions of the sugar haciendas, the chief produce of the valley. One rarely sees such a vivid green. "Living green" indeed these fields stand dressed in, like those beyond the swelling flood and the rocky rampart of death.

The valley is small as compared with the Mexican, but not small of itself. It is hemmed in by mountains, the tall Popocatepetl forming its north-eastern tower. This looks uncommonly grand in contrast with the fiery beauty which it coolingly overshadows and protects, like a calm and loving father bending over his beautiful and passionate daughter.

We scamper down a horrible road; through an Indian town named Huachilaqui; down a steeper and more horrible road, amidst boulders tossed up from the never-mended pavement; jumping from rock to rock, almost, in our mad plunging; the ladies, perched above the driver, scared and delighted with the leaping coach and the glorious landscape. For two hours we thus go headlong, until the hollow is struck, and we race merrily on, still slightly descending, and run down the rattling pavements of the clean town, every door and window of which seems occupied, to note the welcome arrival of the stage, which only once in two days is visible to the naked eye, and which is the only vehicle I have seen in all the town—a rarity, therefore, of a double value, in its contents and in itself. They gaze at the top seat, whose occupants are so busy, bobbing their heads to escape the lamps hanging on ropes across the middle of the street, that they can not gaze back in return.

The scamper ends in flying through a portal and coming to a sharp halt in the court of the Hotel Diligencias, as all the best hotels are called in this country.

To give you a taste of tropical perfection, I shall have to make a journal of my two days' stay in Cuernervaca. I hardly expected to stay as many waking hours. The cave, forty miles away, I could but dimly see by faith, and did not see at all by sight. One of the party was sick, and delayed his coming. We waited for him, but I did not go with them after his arrival. My vacation was no vacation. I made an inspection of the town for business, but also had some time to spare for enjoying its less official aspects.

Do you remember Poe's lines "to Ellen?" If not, get it, and read in it the description of this tiny city and its not tiny surroundings:

>"A thousand
Roses that grew in an enchanted garden,
Where no wind dared to stir except on tiptoe."

You have, of course, read William Morris's "Earthly Paradise?" It is cold in its warmest colorings to this natural and actual paradise. It is just the right length, too, for this lassitudinarian climate and people. Its oversweet prolixity exactly fits a land where "dulces," which are sweetmeats, preserves, and pastry all in one, are of very many varieties, and the tart and lemon-juice never acetate their sweetness; where even the lemons themselves lose their acidity, and are sweet to tastelessness, and lemonade is only half-sweetened ice-water. Tennyson's "Lotos-Eaters" also is a sample of the clime, except that he puts too much vigor into the thought, a blunder of which Morris is never guilty, thought being as far from his mind as from a Cuernervaca belle's or mule's.

Come with me on a saunter. It can be nothing else. The busy trot of New York or whirl of Chicago would degenerate into a "loaf" here.

First, let us go to that which is the most ancient, the Church. It is well to give our firstlings of a walk and a talk to the Lord as well as of all other things. Cortez, wicked as he was, was very careful to make these oblations. Oblations concerning which often, I fear, the Lord said, "My soul hateth." It is one of the most ancient on this continent, though very juvenile as compared with many in the older, but not Old, World. A large open square has three not large chapels at three of its corners. The southernmost is that erected by the conqueror. It has Maximilian's arms over the door-way, which Juarez sought to remove; but the citizens forbade his officers. They had a kindly heart for the fallen emperor. It has nothing especially attractive about it except a flying buttress and one or two high arches.

Just above it is the enchanted garden, rich in tropical fruits and flowers. It was built, that is, its walls, walks, fountains, steps, and other costly arrangements, by Laborde; not its present fruits and flowers, which are its chief attractions. Laborde was one of the discoverers of silver, who amassed wonderful fortunes. It was afterward a resort for Carlotta and Maximilian, and, though in decay, is still full of rare luxuries of vistas and trees and bowers and flowers. The roses run up on tall mangoes, and hang in white and wild luxuriance from their lofty branches; lilies with delicate and drooping leaves, the most delicate I ever saw, bow their graceful heads in fragrant silence. The mango's branches and leaves are so compact and dark that it makes a shade and a coolness like a lofty roof. The time of its fruit is not yet, so one can not repeat as quite *apropos* to this hour Hood's subtle and *pun*gent sarcasm on Constantinople as the place

> "Where woman goes to market as the man goes."

It is said to be as delightful to the taste as the Circassian marketings of the Stamboul are to the sight.

Bananas, cocoa and other palms, oranges, coffee, and all manner of precious fruit, abound; while the vistas along the broken arches, half-empty pools, and flowering trees, to the black mountains near at hand, are as beautiful as desolate. Like its once profusely wealthy builder and its profusely pompous occupants, it has itself become a ruin. How much better to have used this wealth in founding of hospitals and schools, that would have remained a perpetual illumination and elevation of this still degraded population! Will the overflowing wealth of America to-day be any more wisely spent?

Nowhere have I seen idolatry more rampant, or the Church authorities more faithfully upholding it, than here. On the walls of one of the chapels in the Cortez church-yard are proclamations by the Archbishop of Mexico and Bishop of Puebla offering eighty days and more of indulgence for a certain number of repetitions of the Lord's Prayer, Ave Marias, and the sweet numbers of Jesus, before pictures in that chapel of St. John, and that of the Magdalen, and the Virgin. These were all printed and put up as a permanent institution. I saw none earning the indulgence. Perhaps they had a number of days yet left from previous exercises, and did not need to go through any labor of prayer at present; as the Neapolitan lazzaroni refused to carry a valise because he had no need of money, since he had had his breakfast and the time of dinner was not yet. In fact, I saw hardly any worship of any sort in this city. It seemed as if the Church at all hours was, like the climate and the town, fast asleep. It can wake up like these mountains about us in blood and fire and vapor of smoke. It is reported to be already thus reviving. I heard a rumor, on the first day of my arrival here, that there had been a riot at Oajutla (pronounced Wahootla), forty miles from here, and that forty Christians had been killed. This rumor is not confirmed, but it shows something of the state of the atmosphere, and possible earthquakes and eruptions, that such rumors could get current.

But let us get away from the torpid present, and the perhaps volcanic future, into a once powerful past. Leave the gardens and churches on the highest ridge of the town, the backbone of the back, along which it lies. We pass down a clean and narrow street; the narrower the better here, for the narrower the cooler. A few rods and we come to the market-place, the prettiest, and one of the largest, I have seen in Mexico. It is surrounded by a pillared arcade broad enough for many hucksters to sit in the cool breeze and do their petty traffic. Walk around this shaded quadrangle, not halting long in the meat department, for those raw and bloody strips that dangle by the yard are not especially attractive to sight or smell. The fruit department makes it up, however. The women sit on the ground or on a mat, their stalls being on the ground likewise. Here are oranges, water-melons, peaches, bananas, and unnumbered fruits whose names you know not, nor their natures. They are pleasant to the taste, most of them too pleasant. Beans of many sorts and colors, mats, hats, maize, toys, and knickknacks, fill up the space with wares, and make it busy all the morning with buyers and sellers.

Here, too, I bought an almanac which shows the danger there is of a Romanist eruption. It was a common little duodecimo, entitled "Calendario de Mariano Galvan Rivera, para el ano de 1873." It is the popular "Old Farmers' Almanac" of the people. Over a hundred thousand are said to be circulated. The months are filled with Church annals, and the whole is more of a Church annual than the almanac of any American church. In the middle is injected twelve pages of fine type, giving what it calls "Origen del Protestantismo." The most of it deals in harangues against the old Reformers, Luther and Calvin, and in praises of the Jesuits. But it carefully shows that it is meant for modern purposes by its introductory passages, wherein are these paragraphs:

"The political dissensions which so lamentably separate Mexicans from each other, even in the bosom of the family, were not enough for the misery of our poor Mexico. There was still wanting the far more lamentable religious schism, to which origin was given by the toleration of forms of religion which were not in the country, both whose principles and whose very names were quite unknown among our people.* Hence, to give effect to the law of toleration, it was necessary either to invent new forms of religion, which was not easy, or else to import them from abroad. The second expedient was the simpler, because by the dollars (hard cash) of the missionaries, with its wonted efficacy and persuasion, innumerable adepts were to be procured; these missionaries being not a little aided by the ignorance especially of the people concerning the origin, principles, methods, and objects of the sects dissenting from the Catholic Church.

"As our almanac is an essentially popular publication, we think that in no place would an article be more appropriate which aims to make known the fathers of the distinct sects comprehended under the common name of Protestants. Indeed, let us copy from a Compendium of Universal History by a friend, still unpublished for immaterial reasons, the part which relates to the origin of the Protestant Reform. From this will appear the corrupt manners, the excessive pride of the Reformers, and the vile motives which impelled them to separate from the Church in which they were born, and to attack doctrines which they had believed from parental instruction when young, and through personal conviction when grown up. We shall see, like Tertullian, the confirmation of the proscription of Catholic doctrine against the innovators of all times, since it alone has sprung from the apostolic fountain, and runs limpid, unpolluted with corrupt and foreign elements, down to our days, precipitating foreign ideas into the impure gutters of heresy, and vigilantly guarded by two hundred and sixty popes in uninterrupted succession from Saint Peter: a phenomenon which has given it a character of truth and divinity in eyes less thoughtful or more prejudiced against it."

---

* The following was appended to the original: "Only our illustrious neighbors, the Yankees, have this faculty, be it said, unless we except the new sect of the Mormons, so that we are in fear and trembling lest our friends who have done us so much good should bestow it on us, and with them should come polygamy, community of goods, and other happy gifts which afflict our friends just mentioned; and, moreover, they are not very scrupulous, as we say."

How cunning is this putting of the case against "our illustrious neighbors, the Yankees." It shows the fear of the papacy and the power of the new movement, that such falsehoods as these are so diligently and widely circulated. It shows, too, where the persecutions arise, and who foster them. A priest undoubtedly wrote this perversion of history. The archbishop approves its circulation. They will create confusion and bloody work, but will not stop the new revival.

Opposite this fine plaza, on the opposite ridge of the backbone from the Empress's Garden, stands the palace of Cortez.

It is now a court and a prison. It was somewhat of both when he lived here, for he was a sort of prisoner, banished from the city of Mexico, and living as near it as he dare, under a surveillance, doubtless, all the time, of the emperor, for he was too great to be trusted with power and place.

When he was besieging the capital he made a raid on this town. The deep ravine which incloses it on either side was crossed at the eastern or lower side by a tree being thrown across the chasm, and thus making a bridge for his soldiers.

He was forbidden by the empress, as regent, from coming within ten miles of the city, because, as it is said, he gave his new wife four magnificent carved emeralds instead of giving them to the empress. So much for being more of a lover than a courtier. But he evidently gave them to his lady expecting to get them again, which he did. But he had better lost his gems than his capital.

He made this city his capital, and tried and hoped to make it the capital of the country. He built a large palace on the edge of the ravine we first crossed, that in its decay is a noble structure. It towers above the ravine for seventy feet or more, and covers with its courts several acres. The view from its *azatea*, or roof, is exceedingly charming. The snow mountains seem almost at the gate. The fields stretch toward them for a few miles in easy slopes. Then ragged black peaks of every contortion—a saw of iron—range along beneath the calm summits. They look like columns of lava, black, ragged, tall, and huge. The fields stretch off westward and southward in green and brown and gold, and all around stand the comforting and strengthening hills.

But just adjoining is the fairest scene of all. Right under the castle to the south-west, in a ravine and on its inclosing banks and upper rims, lies a paradise of perfect green. It is half a mile to a mile long and wide. The trees are lustrous as velvet, and every tropical delight of herbage greets us from these clinging gardens. They were a part, probably, of the grounds of the castle. Here sat Cortez and enjoyed their fragrant breath, unless, like his successors, he preferred to enjoy that of his cigar. Here he plotted to return to power; annoyed those who ruled after him and over him; got up expeditions to Honduras and California at immense loss of life, money, and almost fame, including among his losses that of the four grand emeralds, the holding on to which too closely caused his first and chiefest loss: that of the city he conquered and the government he craved. The emeralds were lost in the Mediterranean, on an expedition to Africa with Gonzalez. If any body doubts it, let him go and pick them up. In his case, as in so many others, it was proved that

"Quiet to quick bosoms is a hell."

This exquisite valley, this lordly castle that has such "a pleasant seat," the thirty cities that paid tribute to him, the wife and children that revered him, the fame he had won and never lost, all these were nothing to "the hungry heart" that set him a-wandering even to his grave.

Let us get into these delectable bowers at the foot of the palace, where they rest and toil contented to this day, the self same sort that rested and toiled contented in his day.

The debate as to the superiority of nature or art would never arise if you walked through the Empress's Garden, and then through that of the Indos. These lanes are as beautiful as England's, and that is giving them the highest praise. More beautiful in all save the dwellings of the people, and not much less so in that particular, for neither land lifts its peasant to his proper seat. Trees of every known and unknown sort line the roadway.

How would you "get on" if, inquiring of a gardener the name of a certain tree, he should generously and abundantly reply: "Esta es la zapote amarylla, esta zapote chico, esta el mango, esta la mamme, esta huave," and, pointing to the most beautiful of all, "esta coculi sutchel?" You would delight in recovering your English and your senses by saying "That is the ash." And as handsome as any is the ash, grand and green above its fellow of the North. Yet these trees are worth praising, and the flowers, especially that of the odd name, "cocoli sutchel." It is a bouquet of fragrance and beauty unsurpassed. It grows at the end of tall, gnarled, homely boughs and trunk, a dozen separate flowers, each as large as the largest pinks, but of few petals. Red and white, it crowns this homely tree, a perfect vegetable beauty and beast.

Magnificent roses blossom by the wayside, blush, crimson, white, as sweet-smelling as their best brothers next June in New York, and finer of tint and body than any you will meet there and then. Oleanders hang out their blazon, and huge white lilies depend parasitically from appropriated boughs. The orange bears its three-fold burden of flower, and green, and yellow fruit. One bunch of eight big yellow boys on a single stem is bought for four cents, and sent with the regards of the wife of the consul-general to the wife of Dr. Butler—a present, like all the best gifts, valued much above its cost.

Brooklets trickle by the roadside, and banana groves stand thick and tall as Illinois corn, thicker, if not taller, with bunches of fruit, and purple flower-buds big as pine-apples, and like them in shape.

Two children are playing bull-fight in the street, the boy on horseback, astride a stick, varying that Yankee-boy pleasure with throwing a lasso around the neck of a younger brother, who follows him around, bellowing and bullying. They laugh in wild glee over the childish imitation.

A school in these bowers keeps up the noisy rattle of studying aloud, the tinkling bell not suppressing but encouraging the tumult. It was amusing, in one of these schools, to see how some boys showed their assiduity in study, on the presence of these strange visitors, by a great increase of their volubility. Schools are everywhere, and these poor people can read and write very well, but have not any thing to read, and no occasion to write.

They are catching *zapote* from a tall tree, and I learn how to gather nice apples and peaches without a basket, or without hurting them. A boy far up in the tree picks the fruit, and cries out, "Vaminos" (here we go). A man below holds his blanket, or *serape*, and catches the apple-shaped *zapote*, and rolls it easily upon the ground. The cry, the catch, the roll are instantaneous. It will be well to copy this in other orchards.

The emperor had a garden here also, given him by the Indians, with their centavos, tlaquas, or cent-and-a-half pieces, and cuartillias (I spell these phonographically), or three-cent bits. A cottage was nearly finished, but never occupied, the veranda opening on a bath. It was a spot of luxurious idleness. He liked to come here and hide from the cares of state. In a little school-room near the church, in the farther of the two school districts, he gave a ball to the natives. They hold his memory dear; the only place in Mexico that it is thus esteemed. His garden is fast becoming a desolation, and ere many years his brick, open, unfinished cottage will be buried under this abounding life.

A sugar hacienda completed our Cuernervaca experiences. It is four miles from town. Horses carry us easily hither over a road impassable to carriages. High walls and strong inclose the court-yard of the hacienda. Indian workmen have their cane-huts just outside. Inside the wife of the administrador welcomes us gracefully, and offers coffee, chocolate, cognac, and cold water. We accept the last and best. She takes us round the works.

The first apartment is devoted to grinding the cane, which is crushed between heavy rollers, the husk passing out, literally squeezed to death, the juice running a steady stream, of the volume seen in an open water-spout in a steady rain, along channels or troughs to vats in the next compartment. Then it passes into boilers about ten feet deep, four feet of copper, two of brick, and four of wood. The copper only holds the liquid; the upper part, opening widely, is for the froth and scum, good and evil, to disport in. The boilers under fire are filled to the brim with this bubbling, which is constantly skimmed by workmen, with flat skimmers half a yard across. They deposit their refuse in a trough running along the front of the boilers, and this flows into other receptacles, to be distilled into the rum of the country. So the bane becomes more baneful by the banefulness of man.

The sirup is taken to other boilers, where it is condensed yet more, and is ladled into large earthen jars two feet long, of conical shape, with a hole in the bottom. These jars are set on earthen pots after a certain crystallization is attained, and the hole opened to let the uncrystallized centre drip away. They are covered with a blue clay, or marl, which is prepared carefully in a semi-liquid form; too liquid, it would permeate the sugar; too dry, not affect it. This black mud absorbs the yellow color, and makes the mulatto white, not the usual result of mixing black and yellow together. The white is a little dingy, and Mexican sugar is not as white as the American, they not using sufficiently powerful absorbents.

These loaves of sugar, the shape and size of the jars, weigh an aroba, or twenty-five pounds. Each donkey or mule has twelve of these put on his back, three hundred-weight, and marches off to Mexico with his burden. You meet hundreds of mules thus loaded. When a civil engineer said to an administrador of a hacienda that railroads would cheapen freight, he replied he got his freighting for less than nothing now. "How so?" "My mules I raise, and their feed costs nothing. I give the driver two reals a day, and he buys his necessities at my store, on which I make a profit of a real above what I pay him. How is the railroad to help me?"

But it will help the two-real laborer, and give him more money and better chance for its investment.

The corn-husks are dragged into the court, spread, dried, and used for fuel the next day. The fuel ready for to-morrow's burning was twenty feet high and wide, and two hundred feet long, the refuse of a single day. The clay, after serving as an absorbent, is

SAW-MILL.

used for compost, the field being enriched with its own sweetness, and the husk boiling its own juices. A chapel is connected with the hacienda, and will be a good place for a Protestant meeting one of these days.

This hacienda belonged, it is said, to Cortez, and is now owned by the Duke de Monteleone, who is said to be his descendant. It yields thirty thousand arobas, or seven hundred and fifty thousand pounds annually, worth ten cents a pound on the premises, or seventy-five thousand dollars a year. The workmen ought to have over twenty-five cents a day. Some of them, it is said, get fifty to seventy-five cents. But of this there is doubt. The only thing that is cheap here is man.

Our lady guide is thanked much for her valuable guidance, and we canter home amidst a glowing sunset. The mountains are cones of gorgeous color, and the clouds are redolent of flame.

The dear, delightful Indian paradise of fruit and blossom is traversed, none the less agreeable in this setting.

But another setting is here, of life, as of the sun. The two little bells of the little church are chattering quaintly, a half-way between a toll and a ring. A company of white-dressed peasants are busily shoveling earth in the yard. Women, in blue and brown and black, are in the rear of these working-men, lamenting loudly. "What is it?" we ask our guide. "A funeral!" is his short and sad reply. The bells clang and moan rapidly, the women moan, and the men, as sad as either, sternly obey that unwelcome order of nature, and bury their dead out of their sight.

It was a painful conclusion of a gala day. What does all this overflowing of life in tree and plant avail, if death is here? What this luxurious, idle ecstasy of being, if it ends thus? Ah, well, there's a better side even here. This despised peon is made majestic by "long-stretching death." He is now the equal of the duke and marquis that have lorded it over him so long and so haughtily. Oh, how one wished for power to speak to these brethren in a common sin and common grave, of a common deliverance from both sin and the grave! Out of their own ranks the preachers are coming that shall speak the comforting experience, "Mourn not as others which have no hope."

I found a proof of this that very evening in visiting the saloon where a congregation is gathered through the labors of Dr. Riley. About forty attend worship. It is growing gradually, and will, I trust, ere long be a power in all this region.

At four in the morning we leave this garden-spot. Rattling upward, we soon enter a colder clime. Still up and still colder, so that blanket shawls and shivers are our portion. And the noon rest is employed in sunning one's self on the south side of the house, among the pigs and poultry, who always know the best place for comfort.

An hour later and the descent into the Mexic valley relieves us of shawls and *zerapes*, and in two hours we are sweltering in summer heat; so easily do extremes meet in this extreme country.

We look down on the sea of glass, mingled with fire, which blazes over half the valley; the sea of glass, mingled with green, which covers more beautifully the other portions. The majestic snow-peaks shine forth their clearest and brightest. A Mexican saw-mill, off the road, but near the city, affords a quaint sight. The Spaniards stripped the plains and nearer mountains of wood, and so there is no need to-day of a more expensive mill than the old-fashioned handsaw pulled lazily along an occasional log. Our steam saw-mill rapacity will soon effect a like result in our own land. Popocatepetl looks quietly down on the quiet sawyer.

PLANTING CORN.

Down we hasten to the level plains and straight roads; past Cherubusco, a flat field with a big church, around which the battle raged; past the beautiful hacienda of San Juan de Dios (how pious are these names!), where men are planting corn in long rows, dressed all in white as snowy as the White Woman above them, a quaint procession—" there are forty hoeing like one "—over the long, shaded, half-well-roaded paseos, into busy burning Mexico. The city shows off best on this entrance, stretching wide and churchly along the open space. We have had all extremes in half a dozen hours. Our Garden in Eden is behind us. Our northern and better paradise before. Let us go.

XII.

LAST WALK IN MEXICO.

The Market-place.—The Murder-place.—Mexic Art and Music.—Aquarius.—Ruins, and how they were made.—A Funeral.—San Fernando Cemetery.—The English and American also.—Vaminos.

THE time draws near to leave this pleasant seat. The object of coming is so nearly completed that it can be safely intrusted to other hands. The beautiful cloisters of San Francisco, for which negotiations have been going forward for two months, are so nearly ours that the risks of losing them are reduced to a minimum. The four parties holding claims upon them are all disposed of but one, the lessee, and the church has to take the risk of him, and for two months holds the titles of a theatre. But the wet season exhausts his vitality, and he follows his fellows, and leaves the property for its proper occupants. Dr. Butler, the superintendent, arrives, and the route homeward begins to open.

Walks must be frequent now, if we would see all the town, and even then, as in all towns, much will be left unseen.

Let us go to the market-place.* This is usually the heart of the town. Here it is no exception. It comes close up to the palace and the plaza, being at the south-west end of the latter. It is made by the ending of the canal system in the very heart of the city. The canal makes the vegetable market, and *that* makes all the rest. It is the busiest hive of a market-place I ever saw. No European plaza, except on fair-days, no Baltimore street centre of a morning, or Cincinnati of a night, equals the crowd and chatter and push of this lively spot at almost every hour of the day. The boats' prows stuck in among the shops and stalls add to the excitement. Sunday morning is their fair, and such a crush and hubbub

---

* See illustration, p. 112.

are then encountered here as would forever cure the most radical anti-Sabbatarian of his desire to show his independence of the Scriptures by a desecration of the sacred day.

As one has to go through it on his way to one of our churches, he gets a glimpse of its desecration in spite of himself. Each vocation has its allotted place. One narrow avenue is filled with coffin-makers, driving a brisk trade with their black boards, for black is the color of your "wooden jacket" in Mexico. A dozen shops and several dozen workmen make this dismal trade hilarious.

SCENE IN MARKET.

Another long alley is appropriated to the eating business, and great stew-pans over handfuls of coals keep hot the flesh-soups and bones; while on the ground around sit groups of eaters, dipping their bread in the sop or sipping chocolate or coffee, each of which beverages they know how to compound excellently well.

Across the town we find another plaza, less noisy daily, but which has seen greater crowds and heard greater noises than even this noisiest and densest of markets. Pass down the Street of the Silversmiths to the Church of the Profesa, from whose top and whose street-corner we first contemplated the city. It is a majestic, cooling edifice. Its high roof and darkened light makes it one of the pleasantest of temples. Leave that and go straight across to the eastern side of the town. Behind the cathedral, half a mile away, you will see a long narrow square. On one side now is the custom-house; at its lower end is a church, with its high fence. Before it are big wagons, with their triple set of mules resting by their side, and their dark muleteers lying beneath the wagons.

In the centre of this square not many years ago stood an iron post. A dead wall on the side opposite the custom-house shows many a break in its surface, the size of a finger-end or larger. If, now, I were Victor Hugo, I should strike an attitude, and begin to make up the surprises. What mean these preparatory strokes? That now tame-looking building, which the government officials occupy, was once the Convent of Santo Domingo: that church fronting us was the temple of that name.

Still no light? he would say, in a line by itself.

The order of Saint Dominic had the Inquisition in charge. Ah yes! now it begins to glimmer. That mass of buildings was the dungeon of the church. There its victims were confined, tried, racked, and killed, save such as were reserved for the extremest punishment of fire. That church was where its priests and prelates performed their stately services. That iron pillar in the centre of the place, where the mule-wagons are, was where the burnings took place, for the repression of heresy. Mr. Black, long consul-general, a venerable gentleman of seventy, told me he saw the pillar when he first came here some fifty years ago, and its use for such purpose was never then denied. The Inquisition was then in full power, and had its authority been questioned, or that of the Church, its fires would have been relighted in this place.

A few years since, in digging away some of these buildings to open and widen the streets, a prison was discovered in which four skeletons were found as they had been left to starve by their sacred superiors of the convent and the true faith. Before they fell into dust their photograph was taken. It is a dreadful grave-stone of a dead system—dead, not because of its own desire to die, not because its managers had outgrown it, and voluntarily abandoned it, but because a power had grown up around and above it that compelled its abolition. It would break forth to-day had its Church her former power. It only awaits growth and opportunity to reproduce the starved inmates of an inwalled cell and the stake of fire. Such opportunity only Christianity can prevent.*

The fagot and the dungeon are gone, but the purpose remains. The power alone is wanting. No one would sooner light these fires over all the earth than the Infallible God now mumbling in the Vatican, or his chief-priests in Mexico. The murder of Stevens, the name and fate of the protomartyr, was caused and is approved by the Church. A priest demanded it. No bishop or archbishop has disapproved it. No government, city, state, or national, dares punish the murderers. They are as safe as were those of the first Stephen from the Caiaphas and Herod of that day. Truly can we say of Christianity what Madame Roland said of liberty. "Oh, Christianity! what crimes are committed in thy name!"

But what are those spots on the wall?

They are where the balls, fired at criminals and revolutionists who were done to the death on this square, missed the victims and struck the wall behind them. It is the government place of execution to this day. The shrive is short between conviction and death. A few hours and the criminal or innocent one, if condemned, is marched hither, set up against the wall, and shot out of the body. All crimes have one punishment. Murder, robbery, kidnaping, horse-stealing, treason, revolution, almost petty larceny, receives swift verdict and execution. The place is ghostly in the bustle of midday. Let us away to more cheerful sights.

One thing surprised me above all others in Mexico: its attainment and progress in art.

Come down below the plaza, by the eastern side of the palace

---

* See illustrations, pages 186, 188.

and the post-office, and you see a large building devoted to art. The galleries are longer and fuller than any others on this continent. New York, Philadelphia, and Boston are far below Mexico in these treasures. They occupy some eight or ten long rooms, and are of every age from the time of the conquest until now. Not a few of them are of much merit. They even claim Murillos among the spoils of the convents that have been transferred hither.

Modern art is not wanting, nor inferior. Seldom can you see on European walls more vigorous paintings than those of Noah and his family receiving the dove. It is a remarkable set of figures, every one a study, every one a life. Columbus contemplating the sea is a superb piece of work. Dante and Virgil looking into hell is awfully vivid. Mr. Seward expressed a desire for a copy of this masterly work. Several Ishmaels and Hagars are on the walls. It seems a favorite theme. Best of all, for drawing and effective handling of colors, is the Dead Monk. Rembrandt rarely exceeded it. A group of monks hang over a dead brother. Their gray cowls and robes, their scared and skeleton faces, their lights dimly glowing from the tapers in their hands, which are the only illumination of the room, and the dead prone in the midst the only calm one; these make a ghastly picture of great power and tenderness.

The galleries of sculpture are less advanced. Most of the groups are in plaster, money being wanted to put them into stone.

What is better than the galleries is the school of art. You see in several rooms, as you pass through and along the corridors, quite a string of youths, bending over their drawing-books and canvas. They are fine-looking lads of all shades and blood: Spanish, Aztec, and all between. They have as instructors the best artists of the city, and they are worthy of the time and cost lavished upon them. When shall our America give her lads equal opportunity? The best artists of our chief cities would be glad to render such service, and many a noble youth would be glad to have it rendered. What school board will be the first to open a real school of art? When that is done, we shall find our starveling galleries growing to fair and full proportions, and our larger and smaller cities alike enjoying real genius, expressed in real forms of art.

That there is a desire for this, the feeble attempts of girls' boarding-schools and the sometimes successful struggles of young men, bear abundant evidence. Could these girls have competent teachers, and these boys fair educational opportunities, there would be as grand an accession to our artistic force, as our musical conservatories, under the best professors of that art, have added to our musical culture. By as much as a permanent picture surpasses a burst of song, by so much will the school of painting excel that of music. Who will start a conservatory of art?

The Aztec does not neglect music. If you will come to the plaza on one of these superb moonlight nights, when it seems as if the purity of the atmosphere brought you nigh the silver orb (perhaps it is the silvery soil that does it), and the air is full of tremulous lustre. The brown Indian band take their stand on the raised round centre of the square. There is not a white, hardly a mixed blood among them. Pure Aztecs these. They begin. Did you ever hear more delicate notes, more softly rendered? The combinations are equally rich. They are not mere melody, but masterly intervolutions of harmony. Their touch is soft, and swift, and strong. They catch the soul of the music, and bring it palpitating before you. The moon seems to shed a directer ray. No Venetian night on the Plaza of San Marco ever excels these torrid-temperate perfections of moonlight and melody. The pieces are not familiar, and, I reckon, are original. If they are, then the two-fold gift of utterance and composition is theirs. The band would have won loudest applause if it had appeared at the Jubilee. Let Gilmore remember them in his Centennial Reunion, when all the world shall gather in Philadelphia, and he shall bring forth his bands and choruses for their delight. The Aztec band of Mexico will make French and German, English and Yankee, look to their laurels.

The schools of the city are in some respects superior to those of America. A large number of these are kept up by the Freemasons. One of these I visited, in an old convent, which was granted it by the State. The scholars were taught French from cards hung round the room, and primers, and *petite* story-books. Our schools could and should make the youngest children conversant with this and the German language. It is far better to learn a language, which a child can easily learn to speak and read, than to study grammar, which an adult rarely knows, and which it is impossible for a child to understand.

Here, too, all the girls study book-keeping. Their penmanship is exquisite, and they will thus get openings to fields of labor hitherto denied them. They also are taught needle-work, and so made useful for the old as well as the new. Over three thousand pupils are studying English in the public and private schools. That is a sign of the influence of our language. The French has fallen out of favor since their invasion of the country. Our invasion seems to have made our tongue the more popular. It is probably because of the diffusion of this language, and the consciousness of its growing superiority as a world-tongue, and especially because of its utility as a neighbor-tongue, that it has such pre-eminence in these public schools.

The city has a school of mines, with abundant specimens of the wonderful treasures of the country. It has also marble works, where you see the rare marbles of the land, translucent, transparent almost, full of as rich variations as a polished mahogany knot; a future article of great commercial value.

As we are walking, you notice that man with a double burden, a strap going over his head in such a way that he carries a big jar before him and a bigger vase behind. He is the water-carrier—the institution of the city next to the lottery-ticket vender. The aqueducts flow into cisterns, like that of Vera Cruz, situated in the courts of houses; not every house, but as frequently as hydrants in our cities. These aquarii take the water from these reservoirs and carry it from door to door. A cuartillia a day, or a few tlaquas, will supply a family its daily need. His business is steady. Desierto comes thus to town, and its purveyors carry it to every door.

One thing strikes us in all this walk over the city —the multiplicity of ruins. It is as full of ruins as Rome or Jerusalem. Great dust-heaps of vanished populations are on the northern borders. Cleft walls high and thick are all through the main thoroughfares. This is a feature of Mexico which did not exist twenty years ago. Then there were no ruins, except those of liberty and religion. The fall of the Church as a political governing power cut open the streets and laid low the convents. Comonfort initiated this work.

A WATER-CARRIER.

The American war had left the Bible and the light of Protestant Christianity to leaven the hard lump of antique superstition. It showed its leavening influence first in the opening of streets. At that time a large number of monasteries existed in the city. They covered from five to twenty acres. Of course they crossed the main thoroughfares everywhere, and interfered badly with the city's progress. They possessed gardens, parks, deep arcades around marble-pillared patios, dormitories, libraries, chapels, and magnificent churches. Their very halls of flagellation were richly bedight.

The convents St. Augustine, St. Dominic, and many others, were first emptied of their occupants. Friars and nuns were objects of ridicule. And then, if new streets were needed, the buildings were cut in twain. The chief of these was the Convent of San Francisco. It was the oldest and richest. None covered so large a space, or was so variedly and richly endowed. It was founded by a natural son of Charles V., and held for centuries the chief place in the regards of the citizens. It crossed the street parallel with the main thoroughfare. Comonfort desired to cut his way through it. The archbishop refused. It was sacred soil. We all know how tenacious some in our own land have been of sacred soil. That was sacredly sacred. The State demanded passage. The Church refused. The State prepared to force it. The Church prepared to poison or stiletto the State. Each chief chose his appropriate weapons. But one day, before the Church had arranged to stop the State by stopping the breath of its chief, Comonfort cut his way through, and called the street "Calle de Independenzia" (the Street of Independence).

The convent was cut in twain, like the vail of the Temple, from the top to the bottom. The old dispensation closed, the new began. Ten years passed, and all convents, and even churches, passed into the power of the State, and the city was full of ruins of a system and of its dwelling-places.

Part of this convent is occupied by the Church of Jesus, the first Protestant chapel in Mexico. The church is to be occupied by the same society. The cloisters have come into possession of the Methodist Episcopal Church, and have been fitted up for a chapel. The deep arcades are shut out by hangings, and the area alone is appropriated to church uses. The exquisite pillars of polished stone are more beautiful than the spiral columns of the cloisters of San Juan de Lateran at Rome. It is said to be a remnant of Montezuma's palace. Its delicacy and richness seem more European than Aztec. It is a worthy temple for the better faith.

Our long and varied walk must come to an end. Where can it end more appropriately than where all walks end—at the grave? Do you see that procession? Strangely enough, the hearse follows the coffin. The body is borne on the shoulders of men. Why is this? It is a *"custom de la pais,"* as they say here, a custom of the country. To show their regard for the departed, they take the body on their own shoulders forth to burial. It is a very plaintive and pretty custom.

One death I witnessed. Mr. Heaven, an Englishman long in the country, with a native wife, was gasping his last as I called with Dr. Cooper to see him. He remembered then his home faith. Asking him if his feet were on the Rock of Ages, he replied, "Yes! Not on the rock of Peter."

The next day we took him to the English cemetery. The sun shone bright and warm; the fields looked green and glad; geraniums in abundance reddened the parks with their blossoms. The trees were leafy as in June; every thing was alive but this man, who is of the head of every thing.

No female member of the family appeared at the house or the grave. Four servants of the undertaker carried out his body, followed by three ministers and one Methodist layman. Carriages took the gentlemen friends to the cemetery, and there a large crowd listened to the impressive service, most of whom probably had never before heard Scriptures read or prayers offered in their own language. May the seed sown at that grave's mouth bring forth abundantly for the regeneration of this land!

Among those present was the first man who ever read the Protestant burial-service over a dead body in this land: Mr. Black, the venerable ex-consul. He said that in 1824 an American, a shoemaker, was sitting in his shop-door on the plaza before the Cathedral. The procession of the Host passed by: the carrying of the altar, crucifix, and holy water to a dying man. He arose and knelt in his chair. A Mexican, passing by, knelt in his door-way, and ordered the American to get down on the floor on his knees. This was curtly refused. The Mexican instantly drew his sword and thrust it through the heart of the American.

There was intense excitement. Mr. Black, then a young traveler visiting the land, determined he should have a Christian burial. He got a Prayer-book, and accompanied the body to the grave, which was allowed to be dug in the gardens of Chapultepec. Stones were hurled at the procession, and one grazed across his chest as he was reading the service. They dug up his body and rifled it, and left it stripped on the ground. It was reburied, and remained so, perhaps because the ritual was not read over it a second time. That was the first time the Protestant service was ever employed in this city at a burial; this morning was the latest.

Great have been the changes in this country since that hour. The uplifted hats of all that stood in the street or passed by when the body was being brought out, and of many whom the procession passed, showed how great the change of feeling toward their brethren of other communions. May each land and all churches of Jesus Christ more and more fulfill the Divine pleasure, so that of all people it may be truly said, "Whether living or dying, we are the Lord's!"

The chief national grave-yard is in the grounds of the San Fernando Church. This church is on the Street of San Cosme, not far from the Alameda. The tombs of dead presidents, many, are here. Quite stately affairs some of them, standing in the open space, while the walls about the inclosure are filled with cells that are occupied only five short years by the dead inhabitant. Unless "*Propriedad*" is written over it, the slumberer is disturbed, if not awakened, at the end of that little time, taken out, turned to dustier dust by the sexton in a neighboring court, or patio, and either thrust (what is left of him) into a grave at last, or laid up on a shelf. Sometimes his skull and other bones are set off with flowers and other ghastly adornings.

It is money that makes this dire necessity. The Church gets fifty dollars for a five years' lease, and several hundreds for a permanent location. Next to the utter absence of all Christian faith on these square slabs, is this horrid unchristian unburial. In a country where acres unbounded are fit only for the sexton's spade, and where churches and ceremonies abound, such parsimony and infidelity are inexcusable. Among the permanently buried of the patio are some half-dozen presidents, and generals, and cabinet officers, and grandees many.

Guerro is here, the first revolutionist, who, failing to get votes enough, took to arms, and was shot, as he deserved. A brave, liberal, progressive man, who failed to see that submitting to a wrong ruler was the best way to get a right one.

Miramon is here, who was shot with Maximilian, and whom the emperor compelled to take the post of honor, the centre of the group, on that sad day. Juarez, who shot him, lies not far away, each as quiet now, as fierce and hostile then. Saragossa, the popular general who drove the French from Puebla, is here, only a year elapsing after that victory before death conquered him. Comonfort, who began the revolution against the Church, is in the centre, one of the ablest presidents the country has ever had. The brother of the present President, a powerful leader himself of the State, is here. My Old Mortality guide through this realm was the American minister, who had known many of them, as almost all had been placed here in the last few years. Most of these leaders died in their boots, died with their feet warm, as the witty Isaac O. Barnes said John Rogers did. It matters not how. Enough that they died. Finis is finis.

How mocking is life in such a place! How easy, it would seem, it must be to have all ambition and life-greed of every sort

"Cooled, like lust, in the chill of the grave."

Yet we walk out from this dusty assemblage of the leaders of this nation, and in an instant are among the hot and hasting crowds of the public thoroughfare; horse rail-cars are flying by; they fly, and do not creep here, as in all the United States; the only thing that does creep there, except snakes and babies. Coaches and horsemen, and water-carriers and other carters, whose shoulders and foreheads are loaded with huge weights, every body and thing, seems as if it would never die. Both are right. Live while you live, and yet live so as to be ready for this sure summons.

If we still walk on up the San Cosme road, we shall come, after a mile or more, to where the aqueduct suddenly wheels westward, and turns its face toward Chapultepec. Opposite this turn you see the shaded gate-way of the English cemetery. The American adjoins. Each is neatly kept; but the English had a prettier array of shrubs and trees and flowers, because they took more pains, or because they have more, and more wealthy, residents here, or because they have a more cultured taste for landscape adorning. An improvement has since been made, under the direction of our consul-general, in the American grounds, which now vie with, if they do not surpass, those of their elder brothers. They are getting sadly populous, but still remain undisturbed, a grave rebuke to the loose Latin notions concerning the dead, whose temporary permission to occupy their niches in the wall is a sad proof of the powerlessness of their faith. Their cold mottoes are sadder, for a glimpse or glow of faith, such as makes the underground catacombs light, rarely finds a place on their transient slab. Our higher faith strikes a higher note even here, and the grave of Protestantism is a proof of its superiority.

Inside the American is a monument to our soldiers who fell before Mexico. It is somewhat touched with time, and needs a little attention on the part of our officials or visitors.

We must give up our pleasant walks and rides about this pleasant capital. It is a long respite to ceaseless wanderings, this two months in one place. This room is almost home-like, and the lively little landlady, almost one's mother. True, not a few long excursions have been made in important directions; two last week, four days in one, and a day and a half the other. But the flight back has made this spot only the more like home. It must be left, hotel, streets, city, environs, friends not a few, and foes none at all.

Being told that poison, assassination, kidnaping, robbery, every thing baleful was my certain portion if I set foot in this city, under my own name or in any incognito, I must bear testimony to the contrary experience every time.

In a hotel owned or managed by a priest, I have had the best of treatment. Remember the Hotel Gillow, ye who turn your feet hither.

Daily dining with an earnest Romanist and distinguished officer in the United States Army, I have met him only in pleasant conflict on religious questions, and have had many proofs of his gen-

SOLDIERS' MONUMENT IN THE AMERICAN CEMETERY.

erosity and gentlemanliness. At the table of the American minister I have met as devoted a Romanist (who boasts of being a papist) as ever bowed the knee to the Virgin of Guadalupe, or believed in that miraculous folly; yet there was little of the inquisition in that inquisitress.

We could feel as safe in these devout hands as in those of their own brethren. There will no doubt be trouble and conflict in the outer settlements, but the only danger at the capital is too warm a welcome. Hannibal fell at Cannæ, under the luxuries of Roman hospitality. The Church should beware lest like Roman hospitality here destroy the courage to renew this land in holiness.

For that it needs such renewal, there is proof on every hand. The people are religious, but not in the true faith, nor with the true life. General education, enterprise, the uplifting of the toiling masses—these are absent. Especially is experimental faith, the personal, joyous experience of believers, gone. Nay, it never came. The Church needs renovation. A monopoly of religion is as dangerous as a monopoly of inferior businesses—the more dangerous; infinitely more. The Roman Catholic Church has suffered from monopoly. It is bestirring itself as never before, because of the invasion of other churches. It knows the talk about its being the exclusive Church is all humbug; that the other ecclesiastical expression of Christianity is as truly divine as any it claims from a Peter that never was at Rome, and a Church that has been historically the most imperfect of any that has existed.

We are needed. We are welcomed by the people, and shall yet be by the priests. All American churches are needed. The idea that it is sectarian for these churches to come here in their own proper form, is another folly more foolish than the Romanist counterpart, because more inconsistent with the history of these churches. Come in your own clothes, not dressed as Joseph or a harlequin. Come as Presbyterians, Episcopalians, Methodists, Baptists, and Congregationalists; the five fingers (for the thumb is a finger) that make up the right hand that Christ stretches out for the salvation of the world. Let not the hand be doubled up against itself, nor even against that left hand of superstition and irrational rationalism which so often unites to smite the Lord's right hand. Use your own forces in your own way, and God will give the increase.

That such increase is certain, I have no doubt. My stay here has convinced me that this is a very open field; that many are waiting our coming; that if the Church takes possession of it boldly and liberally, she will have instant and large reward. May her faith and works be adequate to the signs of the Lord's will and pleasure. Let her not smite the ground timidly, and only thrice; but in such abundance of prayers and means as shall show how strong is her faith, how ardent her love for her Saviour and her brethren. He that soweth sparingly, shall also reap sparingly; but he that soweth bountifully, shall reap also bountifully. Let her so sow that her harvest may be plenteous of saved souls and a saved land.

In this calm, sweet summer night I bid a Mexican *adios*, an English good-bye—God be with you—to this fair city, beautiful for situation, and which may yet be the joy of the whole earth. To my host, my friends, my brethren, adieu. To-morrow for the North, and a twenty days' long, long ride on a tempestuous diligence. *Vaminos!*

BOOK III.

FROM MEXICO TO MATAMORAS.

I.

TO QUERETARO.

The Start.—First and last Church in the City.—The Game-cocks.—First Scare.—Guatitlan again.—Barrenness.—Gambling and Tortilla-making.—Descent to Tula.—A Bit of English Landscape.—Tula.—Hunt for a Statue.—A silver Heavens and Earth.—Juelites.—Mountains and a mounting Sun.—Vista Hermosa.—Napola.—A stone Town.—An Interior.—The Stables.—Sombrero Walls.—Eagle Tavern.—Playing with the Children.—Gamboling *versus* Gambling.—Cazadero, the Bull Prairie.—Hacienda of Palmillas.—Blacksmith Idolatry.—Misterio de la Santissima Trinidad.—'Tother Side up.—Descent into the Valley of San Juan.—Lone yellow Cone.—Longfellow and Homer.—Elysium after much Turmoil.—A Dissertation on Beggars.—A Market Umbrella.—In Perils among Robbers.—The beautiful Valley of San Juan.—Colorado.—A Turner Sunset.—Sight of Queretaro.—The Aqueduct.—The Bed.

Do you want a trip of twenty days and twelve hundred miles in a stage-coach, through charming scenery, the ride made piquant with possible kidnapings, robbings, slaughters, and such like pleasantries? Then come to the office of the Diligence Company, in the Street of Independence, back of the Hotel Iturbide, and get your billet and place. The ticket will cost you ninety-nine dollars. You can deposit another hundred or two if you wish, and receive a bill of credit, on which you can draw every night, where the coach stops, of an administrador, or agent, of the company. This avoids the necessity of carrying much silver about you, and so of tempting overmuch the rapacity of the robbers among whom your journey lies. A few dollars it is desirable to carry with you in order to satisfy them partially for their trouble in stopping and searching you, and to prevent their giving you their pistol because of your refusal to give them your pistoles. If they should rob you of your bill of credit, you can telegraph back the fact, prevent its further use, and get a new one covering the amount then undrawn.

Armed with the ticket and the bill of credit, and with no other weapons, I take my seat in the coach. It is number one, the best back seat. I am the only through passenger from the city to the northernmost port. Three friends were there to see me off. One, a Mexican, parted with me in true compadre style, hugging and kissing, which were as compadrially returned. Three months had made a cold Yankee into quite a warm Mexican. It is a delicious morning in March; but as all mornings here are delicious, the remark is superfluous. The March wind is a June zephyr, and "December's as pleasant as May." The sun is not quite up, but the sky is gray with his sub-horizon radiance. The streets are silent and empty but for the rattle of the coach, which makes all the more noise seemingly because of the surrounding stillness.

We pass the first church built by Cortez.* It is well in the fields to-day, and only frequented by a few poor neighbors. Close by it is the penitentiary, and here military and other executions frequently occur. Death is the regular punishment. A captain, a day or two before, insulted his superior, was marched out here of a morning, and shot. Three men robbed a carriage on the paseo, and, as soon as captured and condemned, were shot. Four kidnapers of a gentleman in the city were treated with like summary justice. The action of General Burriel is after the fashion of the race: drum-head court-martial and instant execution.

The church is surrounded by heaps of ruined huts, the adobe brick dissolving into its original dust. Mexico looks like Rome, half a ruin, both in its central streets, where convent ruins abound, and in these dust heaps, black and homeless, that fill up its eastern sections. We pass the gate and emerge on a hard pike, which leads to Tolu, about sixty miles away. We traverse broad haciendas belonging to Mexican gentlemen, devoted chiefly to the culture of the maguey.

The first village is like most we pass—a string of whitewashed huts flush with the roadway, no sidewalk coming between the door and the rider. This one, unlike the others, is largely occupied with

---

* See illustration, page 195.

game-cocks. A breeder of them is giving his brood the early morning air. They stand on a raised seat running along the front of his cabin, prevented from general perambulation by a fastening to the foot. The trainer is teaching the young ones how to fight, holding a gray one up to a black beauty, and making each strike the other artistically. They are splendid birds, putting to shame the Shanghais and other gentry of bloodless and fightless fame. But even if of a fighting race, they have to be taught to bite and devour each other, and patiently taught. So brave nations drill their braver soldiers to fight, and then declare their natural animosity causes war.

My first scare occurs just out of this gamy town. A company of horsemen come riding down on us from a rocky hill-slope up which our half-sick mules must slowly pull, for the epizootic is in the land, and I take this thousand-mile ride and risk with that accompaniment. The gay-caparisoned riders, as they appear wrapped in their red and blue zerapes, are sufficiently brigandish to stir the fever in the timid blood. No weapon was mine save my mother-wit, and that was an exceeding dull weapon, and would be very clumsily used in the unknown tongue. So I wait patiently the coming of the foe. On they drive, nearer and nearer to us, on us, past us. "Adios" is the only shot they fire. They are muleteers from Chihuahua and Durango, going to town, a long three weeks' trip, to dispose of a few sorry mules. Time is of no value here. Two months and twenty dollars profit are good equivalents. Thus ends our every fright the whole journey through.

The Valley of Guatitlan is entered—a broad, pleasant country, well cultured, and inclosed with bare brown hills. At Lecheria, or Milk-place, we change one set of eight sick mules for another.

Guatitlan is galloped through, or would have been had the mules been well. The San Pedro hotel looks as familiar and uninviting as ever. I shiver as I think of that den where, like Bunyan's Pilgrim, I laid me down, but, unlike him, did not get a good sleep or dream. The town is large. Protestant service has been held here, and will be again.

Tecepitlan appears on the left, embosomed in trees, at the base of hills—a city of priests, all Church property, till the day of vengeance came: now a city of poverty and fanaticism. Cyotepec, a pretty village, is passed; and ten miles from Guatitlan we stop to breakfast at Huahuatoca, a sleepy little town, but with a good table. I can not promise for the correctness of this spelling. It is phonetic, and that should be the only way to spell.

CACTUS, AND WOMAN KNEADING TORTILLAS.

Now comes barrenness of barrenness. For ten leagues, or nearly thirty miles, all is a wilderness. Rocks lie loose over the earth, which is baked, and hard, and worthless. Half-way, we change horses at a hacienda.

I watch the men gamble for cents, and the women make tortillas. The former bet on two who pitch, putting up eight or ten centavos on the throw. The latter are more sensible in their vocation. They do not grind the maize, but soften it by potash, pulp it, and then prepare it for cooking. A smooth stone, inclined downward, two feet long, is the table. Behind it, on the ground, kneels the lady of the house. She rolls out the soft dough with a stone roller, takes up some of it, pats it and repats it over and over, and lays it on a brazier — a large, slightly-hollowed dish, over a small fire kept up by dried maguey leaves. The cakes look nice in the making, and do not taste bad.

The rest of the ride is through softer scenery — rough along the roadside, but opening into broad fields and hollows of rich earth and culture. Zumpango and its lake lie over to the right or north, a little, nice town, and a handsome water. To the left you see a deep vale, crowded with trees. The stage turns toward it almost by instinct. We wind down, and enter among green fields and trees, all out in their new spring attire. A square in a preliminary village, called Santa Maria, is especially charming. On we drive amidst these tender and brilliant fields and foliage, the barley a foot high, the grass velvety, and ash and oak superb in volume and color. The river Tula is crossed, English in its quiet, shallowness, and munificence of trees; and we put our sick mules to the jump, and run through the plaza of Tula. This is a town not less than a thousand years old. It was settled by the Toltecs in the eighth century. Stone pillars still attest their presence and power. It was too late to visit them; but one called Malinche was pointed out to me in a hill-side overhanging the green hollow. I tried to get a boy to go with me, but failed; so I started alone.

The country always whips the town when brought into fair competition. As I strolled through these rural lanes, with their fresh fields and pastures, even their trees all in their best attire, I thought "Mexico is cheap to this." I crossed a bridge which had little openings on each side, with iron railings, to let you look down into the stream. What bridge in America is equally excellent? Not one of our costly spans has a place for rest and observation. Will the East River be thus favored? If it is, few spots for rest and observation will be more popular.

I climbed the hill where the white face of the Toltec Malinche had been marked out to me. I could not find it. A ghost of the ages it represents, like all other ghosts, it flies on near approach. The sun went down, the moon came up, each brilliant in its work and way. But Malinche hid her white face before the white face of the moon among the tall cacti of the hills, and I came back disappointed to my hotel. Several huge gray shafts in its patio carved over (specimens of the pinea I found not) solaced me for my loss.

At two o'clock in the morning I was awakened by the mozo, as the house or body servant is called, of the Casa de Diligencias. The moon was up, and the sky, like the earth under it, was full of silver. A cup of excellent coffee and a fresh sweet roll, and I am safely stowed away in the coach. Fortunately, the whole back seat is mine, so that I can take my ease, if any ease can be taken in this peripatetic inn. The mules leap out of the court-yard and whirl away, crazy as the Pegasus of a new-fledged poet.

The cold is sharp, and the road rough, rougher, roughest. But sleep is too much for any road, and, lying on a pillow of coats, with a shawl for a blanket, I am tossed unconsciously for three solid hours; unconscious save for the cold that bites the toes, and which a redistribution of the shawl causes to retreat. The sun is up, and a hill-top station (also up), for changing the mules, gets me up. I get out, stretch legs, and renew coffee. It is called Juelites (pronounced Wheyletes), the name of an herb the Indians eat, which is worse of smell than garlic. These half-dozen "huts of stone" are such as Dr. Holmes would not be content with, I fear, despite his declaration to the contrary. There is existence here, and that only. Yet a school is held here, and some day the newspaper and the true Church will follow, and the hut of barbarism give way to the cottage of civilization, which has not been the case these three hundred and fifty years, in which a spurious Christianity has subdued, not elevated, this people.

The land slopes softly and prettily. The fields are frosty, the first I have seen, with one exception, all this winter; each was a light September frost. They are good for grazing, and their hollows ample for grain. There is no need of poverty and degradation so unspeakable. The hills, black, blue, and purple, and, when the sun lights them, golden-brown, as everywhere in Mexico, "brown in the shadow, golden in the sun," like Willis's beloved's tresses, form a grand background, the rising sun being in this case a grander background to the hills.

Our mules fly as fast as the fearful road and a partial epizootic will let them, to the stone-house village of Napola. Before we reach it, we note the superb roll of the land. It sweeps away in majestic breadth, black with the plow, or awaiting in yellow dryness the near approaching rains that shall set every germ alive. A hacienda in the heart of this grand landscape is rightly called "Vista Hermosa" (view beautiful). I had never seen one prettier. Nor did it lose its beauty because a tiny lake lay at the bottom of the valley, flashing in the morning rays. Some upper Minnesota views were not unlike it, only those lacked the mountains, a lack indeed.

The town disenchants you. Man is far below nature. It was burned twice by the French in their marches to and fro in the land, either because it did not give good enough pulqui or not enough of it, for their thirsty needs, or because it harbored republicans and patriots, and political Protestants, who resisted a triumphing foreign Church and army and tongue. "America for Americans," native or adopted, the motto of these United States, as well as those of the North, brought wrath upon Napola. It seems determined not to be caught that way again; for it rebuilt its town of stone. Not a stick in it that I could see, except the few that formed the doors. The stones are laid neatly, and even ornamentally in some cases, and then plastered over, so as to give a uniform whiteness when finished; for this city, unlike some in the West, and many in this country, can not be said to be finished. It has been finished twice in another way, and that gives it a chance to be a-growing again. Its name signifies cactus, and this hardy and useful tree is growing in orchards among its rocks. So it grows everywhere, and is well called the national tree.

Some of the stone cabins are of respectable height and size; but quite a number are of a type too common in the land. Look in at this door, or hole in the wall, for door I saw not. It is four or five feet by two. The room is six feet by eight, short. The floor is of stone, well swept and clean. Against the back wall kneels a comely-looking, youngish housewife, of twenty or thereabouts, over a sloping stone, on which she is kneading her tortilla dough.

It is rolled out by a stone roller about the size and shape of the kneading-pin the women of the North employ. A pile unfinished lies at the upper end of the stone; the roller flattens and curls the lower portion into thin rolls, which drop off into a small bread-trough at the foot of the stone. This afterward she takes and pats in her hands several times, and lays it on the slightly hollowed frying-pan that stands near, in the corner of this room. It is a pleasant sight and sound, the slapping the dough and frying the cakes.

This is their only work almost, except that of washing, which is very similar, being also done over a smooth sloping stone, by the side of running water, with profusion of slapping, soaping, and rinsing, but with no boiling, except of the washer-women in the hot sun. They vary making tortillas and washing with combing their long black hair, and cleaning it of its contents, and with affectionate attentions of like sort to their friends and family. Besides the tortilla-trough and stone and pan, there are in this room half a dozen earthen pots and vessels of various sizes for culinary purposes. I hardly saw aught else. No chair, no table, no book, no paper, no bed—strangest of all, no looking-glass. Six feet by eight of space, walled in on every side, with only this hole for entrance, and the young matron as cheerful as if she were the wife of Lerdo.

You get an idea here also of the stables of the land. The burning of this town has compelled the erection of new stables. There is one thing always sure of good treatment in Mexico: the horse. House and wife and children may go uncared for, but not the horse. Look at this stable of the Diligence Company. Almost four hundred feet square is it. Along one side stables are built over three hundred feet long. The face of the stable, where the stall is, is a dead wall against the street. The court side is built up four feet of stone and plaster. Every few feet round pillars, eighteen inches through, rise from this wall to support the roof, which depends courtward, leaving the stall higher at the horse's head, and thus giving him air. The space between the stone wall and the top of the pillars which support the roof is left open, thus securing constant ventilation. The horses are not stalled in here as in their boxes in the North, and as men are in oyster saloons. All the space is open from end to end. There is ample room behind them and around them, and air as good as a pasture affords. It seems to me a great improvement on our narrow-boarded stalls, without liberty and without air. The mules and horses are so tethered that they can not disturb each other, and yet the whole stable and court is as sweet and wholesome as an orchard. Here, too, we note another peculiarity in the building of the stone walls. They make a science of this here, for stone is an incumbrance of the land as much as in New England, or as trees are in Wisconsin. They put them into fences which beat New England's "all hollow." They make these walls very high—six to eight feet, and very broad—three to five. They put the small stones at the bottom, and not less than four feet up. Then they put on the big rocks. These big stones overlap the base with their rough edges, and make the wall look like a trim lad with a huge, tall, ragged sombrero. The lower half is very compact and comely; the upper very rough, yet strong. This is probably a protection, for the rough tall top stones are not so easily surmounted or dismounted. Where these are not sufficiently defensive, thorns are thrust into the upper tier to keep the robbing boys and men from the inclosed gardens. Sometimes they build the walls lower and of Yankee fashion, and once I saw them reduced to our narrow meanness of a single row of stones; but that wall was nearly all down, and soon disappeared, leaving the field open to every beast and boy. The only walls that were walls were the handsome structures built after the sombrero pattern.

The landscape lies rich and warm all the next posta to Venta

Aguilar (or Eagle Tavern), which is only a stage-house, and no village. Here I vary the monotony of waiting for the change of mules with helping three little girls, from three to five years old, make tortillas. They are pretty, laughing imps, brown of face, black of eye and hair, and would be called handsome by any mother or aunt of them, and will be by some not thus related not ten years hence.

They had a small piece of wood for the hearth, a little ground straw for the fuel, two or three black flakes of mud for the cakes, and a bit of earthenware for the frying-pan. The youngest and brightest of the three told me very chattingly what she wished to do. So, after all was in place, I astonished her by lighting a match and proceeding to kindle her fire. This was making the ideal into the actual a little too rapidly, and they declined the offered blaze. The mother came in from the next hut, and laughed with the children to see such a new friend of the family. Having been ordered by the doctor, a few years since, when prostrated with overwork, to play with the children, I am not quite weaned from that pleasurable medicine yet. But I will venture a guess that the mother and her tottlings of the Venta Aguilar will come to hear me preach when my Spanish is perfected, and I return to hold service at this solitary inn.

The soldiers who were busy gambling for coppers in the stable-yard, I fear will not so readily attend that service, for I made no impression on their minds while spending a moment watching their game. Two pitchers of cents followed the usual fashion of that game. Others sitting around put up their coppers on the throw. They got excited, and could easily have changed their laughs to blows. I prefer the gamboling of the little girls and their baby housekeeping.

From Venta Aguilar we have a delightful ride of six leagues, over as fine a prairie as ever gladdened the eyes of an Illinois farmer, finer, in fact, because encircled with grand hills. It is such a luxury, after our rocky roads and hideous joltings, to get on a plush carpet, and roll like a lad in the first spring grass on southern slopes. The air is warm and breezy. The fields lie twenty miles from hill to hill across our bows, and twelve from stem to stern. They are used for grazing, and were for a long while the favorite place for raising bulls for the bull-fights. These having been suppressed, the bull-raising has gone with them, and the splendid pastures are devoted to more honorable and peaceful grazing and tillage. I shall long remember with refreshing delight that posta, as the run of our team is called, across the airy plains of Cazadero.

We drive through the puerta of Palmillas, or gate of a gentleman of that name, and alight for breakfast at a high, cool, pleasant hacienda, where we get a warm and edible meal of the usual course: soup, three meats, salad, beans, dulce (or sweetmeats), and coffee, for one dollar. It is worth the money to us, though it cost the landlord hardly a quarter of that sum.

A blacksmith shop near the gate beguiled me of a few moments, and taught me a few lessons. An Indian boy was fusing some bits of iron in the usual fashion of his tribe. On the wall of the smithy hung a picture of the Virgin of Gaudalupe, and also one entitled "Misterio de la Santissima Trinidad," which was itself a sermon. The Father Almighty was depicted as a venerable man with gray beard, long locks, gown, and a triple crown on his head—the mitre of the pope. The Dove sat on his breast; and between his knees, with his arms over each begowned leg, on the ground half kneeling, half squatting, sat the Second Person in the Trinity, nearly naked, his wounded side exposed, his sad face crowned with a circlet of thorns. This cheap print is sold by the priests to devout lads like this; for a necklace of beads and charm attached beneath his open shirt showed that he was an honest devotee. I left that little smithy with a deeper ardor to give to this lad and his people a better Gospel than this idolatrous one.

> "Eterne alternation
> Now follows, now flies;
> And after pain pleasure,
> After pleasure pain lies."

This law exists even in postas. The last was so luxurious, I properly dreaded the one to come. I did not dread it too much. It was dreadful beyond description. We met it almost the instant we left the gate of Señor Palmillas. It was our descent into the Valley of San Juan. For six miles we plunged hither and thither over the rocky slabs and boulders and the gullies around them. The soil is worn away by the rain and the coach, and no attempts are made to build up an even pathway. It would not be difficult to make a pleasant drive-way down the hill; but *mañana* (to-morrow), and *no denario* (money), combine to make every hill-road I have seen in Mexico a torture to man and mule. The roads not ten miles from the capital that descend the hills into the city, and are frequented with teams and travel, are in the same condition. The landscape tries to soften the travel. It comes as a poultice to our bruised limbs. In the midst of the upheavals from beneath, we catch glimpses of a valley that shall soothe us for our tossings.

It is green with trees and fields, and stretches out along the base of the embracing mountains for a score miles and more. A mountain of a peculiar type comes into the landscape. It is off to our right, a cone of yellow rock with sub-cones truncated half up its sides. Alone it stands, not being connected with the ranges of ordinary volcanic hills that everywhere meet the eye in all these uplands. It seems a creation of another sort. Its color, shape, and solitariness are all its own. It stands back of the regular rim of the valleys, and looks at us through the openings between the hills. It may be fifty miles away, probably more. It is worth visiting, and were I here long enough I would make an excursion to the Lone Yellow Cone beyond the prairie of Cazadero and the hills of San Juan.

The road gets over its madness, or we over the road, and we scamper down, not easily, into the beautiful valley, reminding one of that finest line, rhythmically speaking, in all "Evangeline," which has many hexameters as musical as Homer's, as the world will find out when Longfellow is dead. How presumptuous of Bryant to put the hot and mellifluous "Iliad" into his cold blank (very) verse, when Longfellow was alive, who could do it into English hexameters as honeyed and galloping as its own Greek! Why will he not give his next ten years to this Conquest of Troy? But I have got a long way from my quotation in my dissertation. It may seem tame to give it now. Yet here it is:

"Into the Sweet-water valley precipitate leaps the Nebraska."

Our Indian words are as good as the Greek, and Longfellow has handled them as deftly. So we were precipitated into the beautiful Valley of San Juan, and flew through the streets of a large town of that name, halting short at the hotel in the plaza, and there resting.

A dissertation on beggars may as well come in here as anywhere. Beggars are an institution in Mexico, the most developed of almost any one of her institutions. They are especially so in the outer settlements, but few of them being seen in the city, where the police represses them. They have graced every station on our route. The most finished specimens of this class I have seen were at Cuernervaca. As I was leaving my dining-room, a gentleman met me at the door, dressed in a faded but cleanly suit, not unlike a retired clerk, or a superannuated preacher. He spoke low and courteous. I listened, but could not understand, and turned to a companion, and asked him what this gentleman wished. He listened a moment. "Only a beggar!" was his translation. I was shocked, or would have been, but that in my solicitations for help of feeble churches and Christian causes, I had been myself often called by that contemptuous name. So I put this gentleman among the clergy, and gave him what we get on such occasions—a smile, but no shilling.

Returning from a walk amidst the gardens of that delicious spot, a smiling lady of seventy or seventeen—her smile was of the latter age, certainly—met us, and beamed on us; asked us if we had been in the flower gardens (our hands full of bouquets showed that); inquired if we stopped at the Hotel Diligencias; and then prettily put her hands to her frock, as a courtesying girl would do, and sighed and smiled forth her soul for a sixpence. We were taken aback by the sudden unmasking of her battery, and staggered forth a broken promise, broken in language then, and in fact afterward, that when we returned we would grant her favor. But we did not return.

The beggars on this route have many arts. They whine and they smile. Blind men play the guitar and violin prettily; and one of them would not desist, though bribed with a medio, saying, with true Mexican independence, that "I play for the pleasure of it! Money! that is a mere trifling consideration." Old men and old women abound. The former whine, the latter grin. A jolly type of this last came at us in San Juan, and fairly beguiled our pocket of a penny by her bland mutterings and beaming eyes.

MEXICAN BEGGAR.

Two ways I have learned of treating these visitors. One is to say in broken Spanish, "I don't understand you. If you will speak in English, I will give you a medio." This Irish bull answers the purpose of getting up a laugh at their expense, and of nonplusing their wits for a moment. They are not ready for the proposition. Another is to give them a piece of bread or a banana. They reverse every thing here; and if you give them bread when they ask for a stone, or metal, which is stone actually, they are not pleased with your action any more than your children would be in the opposite process. So, standing among these beggars of St. John, and buying bananas and oranges, I courteously offer each of them one. They declined the offer, all but the one laughing old woman, and a make-believe crying girl. These accepted the less in hopes of getting the greater.

The market-place of this town was in the centre of the street, and each dealer had over him or her an umbrella eight feet high, consisting of a rude pole with a ruder canvas, six to eight feet square, spread across its top. It served as a narrow covering for themselves and their fruit, though its "looped and windowed raggedness" afforded about as much sun as shade.*

We are near the haunts of robbers. As we leave San Juan and climb the hill on the opposite side, they will surely assail us, it is said, with clubs and stones. Farther on, at Colorado, they are more sure to attack us with revolvers and Winchester rifles, which they lately stole, half-armed, from full-armed gentlemen in a stage. So we nerve ourselves for the coming possibility. One gets out three ounces, each of sixteen dollars' value, wraps them in a paper, and shows a cleft in the coach-door, where the window drops down, into which he proposes to drop them. Another, a French Jew and jeweler, has a box of precious stones with him. He is especially afraid of the stones and the metal not so precious as his own, and nervously describes the hoot and shout. A third is a clerk, with the only gold watch in the crowd. All these are armed with revolvers. One of the group has no revolver, and no gold ounces nor watches. He finds the Petrine admonition valuable here, as elsewhere, against the putting on of gold or costly apparel, and so leaves his watch in Mexico, while, as for weapons, he must rely on woman's and a minister's weapon—the tongue.

We take in another man at St. John, and rush madly out of town, and up the moderately high and immoderately hard hill. The men of the sticks and stones do not appear. The robber, as he has always been, thus far in my history, *non est*. We are in

---

* See illustration, p. 249.

jeopardy every hour. But the jeopardy is no worse than it was in England a century ago, when Dick Turpin reigned, and John Wesley traveled. Methodism will help do for this country yet what she helped mightily to do for England; make it safe everywhere. There are three prayers a day all over the land by all the people, and life is not safe three miles from any town. Yet it should be also said that most of the people are not robbers in act or sympathy. They are toiling, law-abiding, obedient, respectful. I have seen no Indian that looked ugly or dangerous. They treat you with great respect, take off their hats as you pass them on the road, and say, *Bueno dios, señor*, or *Adios, señor*, in the most courteous manner. The robbers are of their complexion, but not of their nature. These are getting less and less. They were created by poverty and politics, and with the cessation of pronunciamentos and the coming in of railroads they will die.

The Valley of San Juan is one of the loveliest I have ever seen. Irrigated by the rivers that come from the hills in the edge of Tierras Calientes, it glows in green as perfect as Cortez's emeralds. For more than twenty miles its enchantments lie under the eye. Trees are sprinkled over it; haciendas glitter here and there, white ships anchored in a green sea. There was one field of wheat which was not less than a hundred acres of level and rich color. I would say two hundred acres did I not wish to keep within bounds. This was a bit only of the big farm. Two of these haciendas belong to one man. They contain severally twelve square leagues, or over thirty square miles, and twenty-two square leagues, or about sixty square miles. They are called Ajuchitlan cito and Ajuchitlan grande, or small and great Ajuchitlan. Rodriquez y Helquera is the fortunate, or unfortunate, possessor of these vast tracts—well on to half the valley, and which ownership makes the people poor and robbers.

We pass two miserable villages, Arroyasecca and Sauz, fringing the magnificent fields with the rags of humanity, and stop at Colorado, the chief robber haunt, whose scowling gentry are sitting round a beer-table, or its Mexican equivalent, a pulqui stand. No place or people sink so low or soar so high as to get out of the reach of alcohol. We do not admire their looks or their bamboo like homes. Both are as bad as bad can be. It is hardly possible to make these men better till their condition is bettered. Grace is needed here, and then will come law, protection, progress. These horrid huts must first have family prayers, and then they will have goodly apparel, books, comfort, small farms of their own out of these broad farms, and true prosperity. Pray the Lord of the harvest to send forth laborers into this harvest.

This is the favorite robber haunt along the road. Stages are frequently overhauled between here and Queretaro. Only yesterday was there such a visit to the coach. Though government troops in large numbers are lazily lounging in that city, and though a few score of riders could clean out the whole pest, yet they are undisturbed, and the travelers are left to the cruelty of their tender mercies.

As we enter their paveless street, they eye us from under the coats of dirt upon their faces, and evidently reckon on some game in that stage for their rifles. When the mules are changed, the driver rushes from the stables with the usual whirl and mad display with which he enters and leaves the towns. But in this case it is evident that his scare adds wings to his speed. We fly through the village and in among the stunted oaks of a moderate hill-slope, up the rough road, hardly abating our speed, for such oaks are splendid for ambuscade, and we scarcely walk our tired mules until we emerge from the last low thicket that overhangs the valley and the city of Queretaro. The meadows of St. John are gone with their beauty, not unlike that of the St. John at Cambridge, England. The sun is setting in our eyes, sending a blaze like that of a furnace into the clouds he is looking down upon. What would not Turner have given to have seen that copper-smelting glow? No tint of canvas could approach it.

Far down the steep incline lies the city. One seldom sees a lovelier sight than this. We run down, over rocks and boulders, the terrible road knocking the passengers, if not the coach, to pieces. The city ever allures us on. Its towers and domes glisten in the dying light, half hidden among abundant foliage. Damascus never looked lovelier. Though I never saw that earthly Eden, I fancied I saw it in this sunset view. The hollow of the hills looks small from this height, and the city seems embossed on the bottom of a bowl of radiant green. It looks large and majestic from this hill-top. It is perfectly in the grasp of the eye. A farther descent brings the aqueduct to view, the stateliest Roman that is extant in America, and there is no grander in Italy, nor one so grand. It strides across the hollow, forty feet high, with massive pillars and broad arches. We rush beneath it, fly round and round dirty, mud-faced streets, into the thick of the town, and halt suddenly at the Hotel of the Diligence. The day's ride of over one hundred miles is done, and gladly the couch is sought and found.

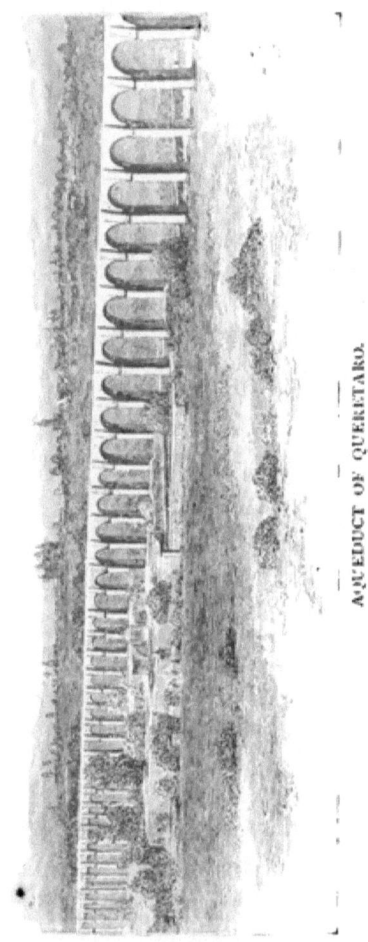

AQUEDUCT OF QUERETARO.

II.

QUERETARO.

Into the Town.—Maximilian's Retreat.—Capture and Execution.—Hill of Bells. —Factories and Gardens.—Hot-weather Bath.—A Home.—Alameda.—Sunday, sacred and secular.—A very Christian name.—Crowded Market, and empty Churches.—Chatting in Church.—Priestly Procession.—Among the Churches.—Hideous Images.—Handsome Gardens.

As I came rattling down the steep place into this fair city with the setting of the sun, I could only think of another sun that set here, and whose sad brilliance shot a lurid flame across the orb of the world. Here Maximilian met his fate.

This was the last landscape he ever saw; such a sunset on these same hills the last he ever looked upon. It brought a shadow over the picture, a shadow not of time, but of man. These are the fields and hills which

> "Do take a sober coloring from an eye
> That hath kept watch o'er man's mortality."

Maximilian and Montezuma, three hundred and fifty years apart in their history, are blended in a historic unity. They had much in common. Men of refined rather than of strong nature, loving art rather than arts, put in command of a turbulent people at a crisis in its history, with an instinct of honor rather than of government, they each fell into hands more powerful than themselves, and perished with regret, and yet with dire military necessity.

Maximilian retreated to Queretaro, after the French left the country, a step of exceeding unwisdom; for Mexico the city is Mexico the State, and the possession of that is nine points in the possession of all the country. He fled to this city probably because it was a clerical town, and one of his most ardent supporters, while the political capital might prove treacherous.

The Republicans surrounded it. Batteries were planted on the hill down which the diligence plunges; on a headland next to it, across a broad and deep cañon; and the third on Sierra de los Campanas, or Hill of the Bells, a knob of not much height, rising out of the meadows to the north-west of the town. He was in the Church of the Cross, with huge gardens attached, surrounded by a high wall, making a fortress of especial strength. One of his generals betrayed that fortress of a church, and he was captured. Tried by court-martial, he is condemned for publishing a cruel edict, two years before, which outlawed all Republicans, and caused the murder of many. He is ordered to be shot, with two associates, Miramon, ex-President of the republic, and Tomas Majia, a general. They are marched out to the Hill of the Bells, and in front of its fort, high up the hill-side, the three men fall by the bullets of the government. With them fell the Church power in Mexico. It was her last battle. For twenty years she had plotted, and raised rebellions, and introduced a foreign prince and a foreign army. Miramon was her Mexican leader, Pius IX. her European.

A favorite picture on the parlor walls of devout Romanists here is Maximilian and Carlotta visiting the pope. He sits on a daïs, holding converse with them about Mexico. They were blessed by him, and urged on their dim and perilous way. He was the real centre of the imperial movement; Napoleon was only his military director. All of it was Romanism, and Romanism only.

When America finished her war, Mr. Seward put sixty thousand men on the Mexican frontier, and sent a polite note to the French minister suggesting that the French troops be recalled from this continent. Napoleon saw that his stay in Mexico was at an end, and gracefully withdrew his troops. Maximilian should have gone with him. But he fancied he could win alone. He trusted the Church party. They were weak and weaker every day. Juarez, inspired by the United States, moved on him and drove him hither, captured, condemned, shot him.

Church of the Cross.   Hill of Bells.

QUERETARO.

The hill where he was killed is only a mile from the town. It is about a hundred feet high—a Bunker Hill in size, height, and history; for here Mexico achieved, in her way, her independence. He was placed a little below the summit, facing the east, looking toward Miramar and his mother's house. A sketch, made at the time, gives the sad scene. The three men stand apart from each other, and guards of soldiers are on either side. Easy and graceful in their attitudes, calm of feature, they await the shot that sends them to another world; let us hope a world where there is no war, nor wickedness, nor woe.

The spot where he fell is marked by a heap of stones, cast up without order by living hands. Many of these stones are marked with a cross. Some of them have three crosses on them, some five —the most sacred sign—emblematic of the five wounds of Christ.

This is the tribute of his party and Church, and could not have been done in many cities of the country. It shows how badly the cross is blasphemed, and justifies our Puritan fathers for abolishing its use altogether. It came to signify spiritual tyranny and superstition, and was rightly rejected. So these rude scratches are evidence of hostility to republican and tolerant ideas, of bitterest hostility to true Christianity. It may yet burst forth, not in crosses alone, but in crucifixion also.

The view from this Hill of the Bells is uncommonly fine. The valley lies about you, full of verdure. Never did any valley look lovelier. Hundreds of acres of wheat and barley and lucern, greenest of the green, seem in a race for superiority in color, while the trees are not behind in beauty. Flowers of richest hue glow in the gardens, and the city stands forth, with its glittering towers and domes, a spectacle long to be remembered. It would be hard to find the equal in beauty of this combination of high, bold cliffs, ranges of hills, velvet meadows, and stately churches.

The river makes the town. But for that, this valley would be as dry and yellow as that of Mexico. As it is, one can not see within the circuit of the spurs of the hills a barren spot. If but George L. Brown were only here to put this scene on his burning canvas, how many would haste to see the picture, if not the reality. I know not where is a richer bouquet. Other valleys are grander; this is complete. As if to keep the memory green of the great conflict crowned on this spot, some ancient nopals just below the crest still show the holes in their leaves made by the bullets of the besiegers. It is a monument that will not soon die, for nothing seems to live more leisurely than the cactus, and it well adorns the lustrous picture with its rude and strong appropriateness.

The whole scene is placid and lovely as a sleeping babe. How different when blood and fire and vapor of smoke filled all the hollow!

"Death rode upon the sulphury siroc,
Red battle stamped his foot, and nations felt the shock."

This inland town and this tiny hill made sorrow and trembling in the Tuileries and Schönbrunn. Consternation awoke in all courts as the stern decree was executed that announced to all the world that European monarchs must "hands off" to all American nationalities, and ere long to all American soil.

The city, like all in Mexico and everywhere else, has much that will not bear close examination. Its edges are not sweet, any more than those of London or New York. It has but few choice streets, and fewer choice houses. The most are depressingly degrading. Poverty has wrought its perfect work, and the last cent is both often and rarely seen by the pauperized people. Beggars abound, and thrust their offensive whinings into your unwilling ears. The plaza is a pretty garden of tropical delights, more bountiful than that of Mexico, for the land lies lower and warmer.

Other products abound. Under the portal of this plaza, among the shops, I saw a lad generously searching the long, thick, grizzled back hair of his mother as faithfully and as successfully as such mothers in other lands search such sons. It was a good evidence of filial affection.

A factory here deserves notice. It is two miles from the city, in a deep, hot cañon, and is big enough to attract attention, even in England or New England. On its looms it employs fifteen hundred hands. Mr. Sawyer, a New Hampshire cotton-spinner, superintends several rooms. He took me over the whole of it. I know little of cotton-spinning, though I have been taken through many mills. I saw this had the familiar whirr and fuzz of such mills. Rooms as long as those of Lowell were driving their looms. The main building is but three stories high, and most of them only two. The cloth manufactured is of poor quality, not worth over six cents in the States. Here it sells for eighteen and three-quarter cents : a real and a medio.

A COTTON FACTORY, QUERETARO.

The most striking peculiarity about these mills is the garden in front of them. This garden is full of orange-trees laden with the ripe fruit, with peach-trees in blossom, figs, pomegranates, trees bearing crimson flowers called the "noche buena," or the Christmas flower, as it is much used for that holiday. Roses, geraniums, fuchsias, and many unknown to the cold North are blooming in this factory yard.

More striking is the old mill in this vivid contrast. It stands back from the street, near the water-course. It is inclosed on three sides with a high iron fence, light, graceful, and tipped with gilded points and balls. Inside is a spacious garden, with walks and founts and foliage and flowers. Several gardeners daily care for the nourishment and pruning of these thirsty and wanton luxuries. Benches are scattered around. Thickets of green and natural houses are daintily grown together. Every thing is after the best type of a lordly pleasure-garden, and yet it fronts a factory where whirring spindles and looms are its constant music. Flutes and soft recorders would seem more fitting.

How would our factories be improved with a slight approach to this beauty! Perhaps they prefer to give their hands more than thirty-one cents a day, and to work them less than fifteen hours, than to adorn the grounds so richly. That is what these workmen and work-women get and do. For two reals and a medio they work from six in the morning to nine and a half at night; some from five to that late hour, with a recess of one hour and a half. All the workmen pay a real a week for the doctor, whether they want him or not, and take one-third of their pay out of the company's store; so their fifteen reals, or one dollar and seventy-five cents a week, becomes fourteen, and ten of these, or one dollar and a quarter, is all their cash in hand for ninety hours' steady work, at half-past nine on Saturday night. No wonder the huts they occupy, my lord, the owner of the mills, would not put his favorite dog into. He even keeps a judge, before whom he requires all their grievances to be brought, and over the door of his office is printed "The only Judge." This signified that none should seek relief at any other court except at his peril. The owner of these mills is successful and unsuccessful, making and losing many a fortune. He is a young man who inherited the establishment, and who has the odd fancy of going daily to town in a red stage-coach with four horses, which he drives, preferring this startling mode to riding horseback or in an ordinary vehicle. I saw him thus flaunt out. His mills do not pay, despite the elegance of the gardens, the poorness and price of the goods, and the cheapness of the labor. He is constantly and overwhelmingly in debt. So the Yankee mill-owner may conclude it is wiser to make his mills less romantic and his profits more sure. If he also will work his people less and pay them more, his lack of taste may be condoned. Still, if to all excellences he adds these factory gardens of Queretaro, he will find his mill the more attractive, and make of duty a delight.

The valley runs up into the hills, filled with groves of fragrance, fig, orange, cactus, agua (a vegetable butter-apple, used as sauce for the tortillas), zapotes, and other nameless fruits. At its head a bath attracts many visitors, placed among groves of incense. The very air is burdened with spicy odors.

The aqueduct that stalks so majestically across the short campagna has its fountain-head near these baths. It runs along the mountain-sides for three miles, and then marches across the valley to the town. It makes a superb feature in the landscape; and is the only real Roman relic, save what the church affords, on the continent. It is ante-Roman, older than the Cæsars, old as Rameses and Solomon.

The alameda here is the pleasantest I have seen in all the country. It is a little one side of the town, and has a country look such as Boston Common used to have, and Druid Hill now has. It is about fifty acres square, has a drive around it, and long, straight diagonals going from a central circle to the corners. High, grand, green ash-trees make its chief shade. Grass, well sprinkled with dandelions, lies open to the free play of children, and wanderings of their elders. The familiar tree and flower made the spot more Northernish and home-like than any of its fellows. It was a delicious spot to sit and muse, and grow mellow with homesick longings. London parks, the only country fields in the heart of a great city, are not more homely and homeful. One forgets his strange surroundings, hostile even though they be, in this

"Society where none intrudes,"

for beggar, nor priest, nor lordling frequent the spot. There is no wealth to come, and the others go not where wealth is not. When you come to Queretaro, be sure to take a long lounge through its alameda.

The Sunday begins, like all other days here, religiously and secularly. The trumpets of the garrison ring out the first reveille, and the bells of the churches ring out almost immediately their *oracion*, or call to prayer. By five the tintinnabulations play on the tympanum, like a Fourth of July at home, and "sleep no more" is a decree that has to be obeyed. It was a pleasanter sound, certainly, than the music of pleasure bands and factory bells, and I almost forgot myself for a moment, and fancied I was going to have a goodly service on this sacred day. This impression was deepened by an incident which occurred while I was taking my *desayuno*, or first breakfast, which consists of only a cup of coffee and a small roll. I ask the waiter what his name is. "Trinidad, señor," he replies, respectfully. Shocked at the answer, I repeat it. "Trinidad?" "Si, señor." "La Santissima Trinidad?" "La Santissima Trinidad, señor." So I was talking with the Most Holy Trinity in the form of a poor Aztec boy. I never supposed their baptismal names had reached that pitch of profanity. "Jesus" is as common as John at home; more so: but "La Santissima Trinidad!"

I asked this wonderfully named youth if he went to church. "Yes." "Every day?" "Every eighth day." "What day?" "Sunday." "At what hour?" "Between five and six." So that bell-ringing had taken him to church. I asked him if he could read. "Yes." "Have you a Bible?" "No." "Would you like one?" "Yes." All I had was a Spanish Testament, and that went to La Santissima Trinidad at the risk of disclosing my business, and bringing the kidnapers about my ears. How strange to call a child by the most holy name of God Himself. The priest that baptized such a babe needs himself to be renewed in the spirit of his mind, and the Church that admits it certainly should be reformed.

This utter insensibility to all distinctions as to sacred and divine things was strikingly shown at a dinner-table in Cuernervaca. A company of Americans and English, all Protestant in their training, had a leading Mexican of the section at meat with them. A water-melon was brought on. He cut off the end, and pouring a bottle of wine into it, said, "This is the blood of Christ. This" (feeling of the melon) "is the body; and the two, coming together, make a soul." He said this blandly, and as though he were getting off a good religious thought. Even the freethinking members of that party shrank from that unconscious profanity. So thoroughly are this people saturated with form and void of power, under the education of mere form, in which they have for so many generations been trained.

I went out, after my coffee, to church; for though I have little faith in Romanism, I feel that it is better to go to the house of God, strangely perverted though it be, than to idle the day away in outward non-observances. One can himself pray aright, if the others pray awry. The plaza before the cathedral was crowded with trades-people. Bazars had been formed by temporary shanties, and the streets adjoining were lined on both sidewalks; the stores were in full blast. Never a day more busy. The divine names given by the priests do not prevent the desecration of the divine day. It would be easy to stop all this. But the Sabbath, and the Bible, and the very titles of our God and Saviour are alike cast out and trodden underfoot. Is it any wonder God has cast them out? Over all this land nothing is writ so plain as the annihilation of ecclesiastical power and wealth. Every church they hold, not as their own, but as a loan of the government, while convents, immense in extent and costliness, are everywhere deserted and in ruins. This city is full of them, not yet driven through by the plowshare of the street commissioner; for there is not money enough to level them, and make them into highways. Yet they are all the more desolate from their utter emptiness and silent crumbling into dust. One of these plazas, and the most beautiful, was made from the garden of a convent belonging to the cathedral, and along one side of it, coming up to that church and covering not less than ten acres, is a heap of ruins, in the very heart of the city. You wander under lofty arches, and into courts without a window, door, or dweller—a ruin as complete as Melrose Abbey or the Coliseum. Such is it in many places in this yet intensely papal town. Let the true and living Church come and build up these waste places, and fill these empty courts with heavenly songs and teachings and testimonies.

"Hasten, Lord, the glorious day."

I entered the cathedral at about half-past eight. Mass had already commenced, though only a few were present. They kept coming in and dropping on their knees. There are only one or two benches, so the floor is the sitting-place. Two ladies, dressed in blue silk, with all the fashionable flounces and over-skirts and trails, floated by me, one kneeling at the foot of the altar, where she could sit also, when she desired; the other seating herself on the bench where I sat. They wore black lace veils, and no bonnets. I have never seen a bonnet in a church here. As others came in of their friends, there were nods and smiles of mutual recognition; and when some of them knelt at the side of those on the floor, conversation ensued, the service constantly going on. So I saw that kneeling in a papal church did not any more necessitate devotion than sitting in other churches.

After much singing by the boys, and other incidents of the mass, a procession is formed, and a silken canopy, wrought with gold, is borne by six Indians, who, I note, are never priests—only Gibeonites. I have not seen a full-blooded Indian in high Church orders. They rule in the State, but not in the Church. Yet I hear they are found in some parts of Mexico. Before this canopy marches one with a silver crucifix. Under it a very old man carries a silver star or sun, on which the crucifix stands, seemingly a very sacred affair. Hard-looking officials accompany this venerable bearer. They stop opposite my bench at an altar, and bow and kiss the silver sun, move on to the high altar, and place it in the centre. It is as powerless and useless as the opera operations of some more intelligent, if not more Christian congregations. It was nothing to the crowd that witnessed it, or the men that performed it.

A sermon was preached at this stage, which, as I could not understand, I did not dislike ; nor did I dislike the manner and appearance of the preacher, who seemed earnest and devotional ; and I especially liked the breaking off half way in his discourse and engaging in prayer, in which all the congregation joined. I should have liked it better had I not seen the same thing twice before, and therefore judged it formal, and not of the heart. Yet I do not condemn a good practice because of possible formality, and would not object to seeing a like invocation by preacher and people at the beginning, middle, and end of our sermons.

After attending this service I visited the churches. Few of them are in a good condition. None have a fresh and animating air. All overflow with images. Never did a nation so give itself up to image-worship. Hundreds of little white images hang near the shrine or doors, probably to be sold for household gods. The Virgin Mary is dressed in every sort of garb and color, sometimes with crinoline, yards across. In the Church of Santo Domingo, in Puebla, her robes stand out with an enormous spread. Blue, purple, yellow, lace, gold and silver ornaments—every array is she set forth in. Once I admired the simplicity of her apparel. At the Church of San Felipe, over the top of the high altar, she stood in perfect white marble, or hard and shining plaster, hooded, almost, as to her face, holding in one hand a candlestick, and in the other a crucifix. It was too simple and severe for the tawdry taste displayed usually behind these glass fronts.

A crucifix below, on a side altar, made amends for that simplicity. Christ was on his hands and knees. His whole backbone seemed laid open by the lash, and blood was flowing from every rib and cord over his sides. It was horribly hideous and false, as were the two courtesanish-looking faces of fair, fat, forty, and finely-dressed women that were made into angels, and hovered dolorously, but not sympathetically, above him.

The Church of the Cross, where Maximilian lived, and which he fortified, and where he was captured, is one of the chief churches, with some ornament, but especially noticeable for a graceful tomb, a shrouded female with a long wand, leaning over a tablet, on which the name of the dead is graven.

Santa Clara, where my astonishingly-named *mozo* goes, is the most ornate structure. Such a profusion of gilding I have seen nowhere else. Five altars from floor to ceiling are covered with figures and carved work, all thick with gold, while the arches around and above the door-way are, if possible, even more overlaid. It is astonishing what an outlay of precious leaf has been made on these shrines. This church was crowded at vespers to the pavement without, where many sat, joining with the voices that took up the refrain from within. These were all the poorest of the poor. Rags and beggary and utter penury knelt on the floor or sat on the benches of this gilded chapel that cost more than any church, probably, in the United States. When shall we equal them by our equality?

The Church of the Virgin of Gaudalupe was almost equally adorned with gold, but had only a few worshipers. Its convent has become a hospital, and exquisite flowers fill its courts with beauty of odor and of sight. Its front is of the Moorish type, more so than any in the capital or Puebla, and its graceful minaret and very quaint buttresses, flying out from the wall like a scroll, are proofs of the influence Grenada had over Madrid.

The churches and priests are the chief characteristic of Queretaro. No wonder it is such a church-town. It is more completely filled with these structures than any city I have seen—than any, probably, in the land, except Guadilajara. Puebla has far less, proportionately to its inhabitants, and far inferior ones, excepting its cathedral, which here is cheap and poor. One I strolled into (I forget its name) had five altars, with ornaments carried to the roof, most elaborately and profusely carved and gilded. Statues, globes, hearts, and even the coils of the entrails, are perched on every possible spot, and covered thick with gilt. The door-way to the sacristy was remarkably adorned in this fashion. Only those of Santo Domingo chapel, in Puebla, were equally brilliant at the time of their execution. They make none such nowadays. Gold is too dear, and the Church too poor for this luxury. It looks faded also, and, like its service and power, is out of joint with the present.

Priests abound. I have not seen as many, in all my stay in Mexico, as in this single day. Some of these big convents are as yet unopened, and the day of their sovereignty has not yet closed. It will be perilous, perhaps, to establish the true worship here, though there are some who look and long for its appearing. I heard of one such, a Mexican workman of influence and position. I understand there are others who are ready to cast away their beggars' robes of idolatry and formalism and arise and come to Jesus. May many and all soon come!

We close our visitations, convinced that much prayer and faithful labor must be put up and put forth before this people will be weaned from their idols and their Sabbath-breakings, and brought to the feet of Christ. And that prayer is going up, and that labor is going forth, and Queretaro shall be a city holy unto the Lord, with sanctuaries filled with grateful, joyful, holy, intelligent, prosperous worshipers. No rags, no beggary, no Sabbath-breaking, no superstition.

III.

TO GUANAJUATO.

A bad Beginning.—A level Sea.—Celaya.—A Cactus Tent.—Salamanca.—Irapuato.—Entrance to Guanajuato.—Gleaning Silver.—The Hide-and-go-seek City.—A Revelation.

I HAVE had two real panics since my arrival in this country, both short and severe. The first was the night of my reaching Mexico; the last, the night of my leaving Queretaro. Both were groundless; but so was Mr. Parrish's scare in North Salem, almost two hundred years ago, about witches, if he was scared at all, which is doubtful, there being good reasons for believing he was simply carried away by revenge in a church quarrel. That scare has given the enemies of Massachusetts a good stick to beat her with from that day to this, and faithfully has it been used.

My first scare was caused by the horrors on which I was fed from New York to the capital. I was told that I must go under a feigned name, or I would be poisoned, stilettoed, kidnaped, robbed. This is an anticlimax, but a true one to some souls, loss of money being to them the greatest loss. I found on my arrival at Mexico that one minister, not being well, thought that he was poisoned by the Jesuits, and was urged to have a private room and an American or English cook. I took a room in a hotel rented by a Jesuit priest, his father owning it, and went to bed. The room was very large, the bed very small. The farthing candle did not throw its beams very far, and only made darkness visible. Lonely, weary, heart-sick, homesick, I was in a good state for the panic to strike; and it struck. For some minutes I rolled in the trough of the sea of fear. All its waves and its billows went over me. "Then called I on the name of the Lord; oh Lord, I beseech thee, deliver my soul." The work was His, not mine. The peril mine, the preservation His, and preservation far surpassed all peril. My favorite talisman, that had done excellent service often before, was again at hand, and I repeated,

> "Jesus protects! My fears be gone!
> What can the Rock of Ages move?
> Safe in His arms I lay me down,
> His everlasting arms of love."

I had no return of that panic in Mexico. Though out late and in out-of-the-way places, I took my possibly poisoned coffee as cheerfully as Socrates his really poisoned drink, and came and went indifferent to fear. Though in consciousness of peril, there was no panic, nor thought of panic.

It came upon me again at Queretaro, and as foolishly. I had been even more earnestly warned against making this tour. I had most unwisely allowed my letter of credit on the Diligencia company to be made out in my first name only, and my ticket to Matamoras likewise; and with a Spanish ending, Señor Gilberto, which, under the novel pronunciation of "Hilberto," was sufficiently concealing. This was done without my knowledge or consent by a too careful friend, but I allowed it to pass. It did not increase my courage. A disguise, however thin, makes the wearer weak.

At the head of the breakfast-table sat a fine-dressed gentleman, whose dulces and Champagne, freely proffered, made him autocrat thereof. I was told afterward that his style was above his known means of support, that he was watched by the police, and that he was suspected of being in league with robbers, giving them information of any rich placers his position, as a boarder in the stage-house, might enable him to detect. I was to go at three in the morning, alone. Possibly the tea and coffee helped it along, but it came—the panic. I went to bed for a couple of hours, knowing better than "Probabilities" knows the coming weather, that there was to be a storm. The soldiers woke me at two, with some delicious soft notes. I rarely, if ever, heard any thing more mellow. But I only thought of the poor captain shot the day before I left

Mexico, for insulting his colonel, and fancied this bird-like sweetness was a knell.

I took the coach, my sole companion opposite. Three armed men had accompanied me to Queretaro. One, perhaps unarmed, goes with me out of it. I had been trusting in those arms, though I pretended not to be relying upon them. I had repeated to a splendidly armed and trained shooter that I was sufficiently armed; for

"Thrice is he arm'd that hath his quarrel just."

And when he was not satisfied with his favorite as an authority, I fell back on one higher and better, and said, with David: "The angel of the Lord encampeth round about them that fear Him, and delivereth them." Now here I am, without the language, or a rifle, or a companion, alone on the high seas of travel. I am tempted sore for a little; then comes my talisman again:

"Jesus protects! My fears be gone!"

And they went. I laid down on the rocking seat and slept. I awaked with the sun. My sole fellow-traveler left me at the second posta, Apiasco, a long adobe town.

I got out of my dignity and dust, and mounted behind the driver; no one is allowed to sit at his side. I exchanged verbal commodities, giving him English, of which I had plenty, for his Spanish, of which he had plenty. So we rode for a hundred miles; and the experience of riding alone and unarmed through the country was settled ere that morning sun grew hot. I forgot all about the gentleman who was to let his robber friends know that I was on the road—a conceit that only a panic could have created; for I was no fit game for their rifles. I felt as comfortable and secure with the driver and his unloaded rifle as with the best sharp-shooters of the country.

The country too, from Queretaro to Guanajuato, I had totally misapprehended. I had supposed, as the latter city was a mining town, the road to it must be far worse than any I had seen. I was condemning myself for my folly in going off my track home a hundred and fifty miles to see naught. It was as if one going to Albany from New York should have gone round by Springfield, except that this was all stage-riding, rough and tedious.

But duty called, and I obeyed. "*Per aspera ad astra*" I tried to make my motto, through hard places to the heavenly. But it turned out, as is so often the case when we fancy we have a big cross to take up, on taking it up, we find it no cross at all.

The road was smooth and level as oil. Only where it crossed a dry brook, or where the coachman took the paved centre instead of the soft sides, which he did occasionally, was there any approach to rockness. The day was splendid, cloudy, and coolish; the scenery was grand: a prairie a hundred miles long, and half that in width, with mountains ever inclosing the vision. The fields were almost all under cultivation. Irrigation gave them a green and gladsome look. The alfalfa, or lucern, was the greenest of the green. Wheat, barley, maize, and chilli were growing luxuriantly.

Celaya was our first large and pretty town, some forty miles from Queretaro. A landlord, very bland and child-like in his smile, told me the city had a hundred and twenty thousand inhabitants. "Twelve thousand," I suggested. "No, señor; one hundred and twenty thousand." I wrote down the figures, "12,000;" he corrected them to "120,000." Somebody blundered; for the driver said there were not over eight thousand. Another traveler says there are twenty-five thousand. Perhaps he meant Leon, for which I was aiming.

The market-place was full of flowers. They sell large bouquets of roses, tulips, and other flowers for a tlaqua (three-fourths of a cent). This is the only Indian name used in the currency, and was the bottom cent, an eighth of a real, until the centavos appeared, a tenth of a dime, and the new baby displaced the old one. Still the old dies hard, and every thing is sold by the tlaqua, and not the centavo.

In the middle of the prairie, where we changed horses, a woman had made a tent of a cactus, and was busy rolling, patting, and frying her tortillas, putting upon them a small spoonful of beans and a smaller spoonful of chilli, or pepper-sauce, folding them up for the driver and his *mozo*. This combination is not bad.

There were not unfrequently stands by the roadside under a cactus-bush, and sometimes dinners, and sometimes dwellers there. The two chief towns, Salamanca and Irapuato, are not far from Guanajuato. The first is pretty; the last, beautiful. I have seen none more so. It contains a population of twenty thousand. The houses are freshly and prettily washed; and it is lively withal. I sauntered through the plaza, talking and being talked to by beggars many. How lovely are these plazas, with all manner of lovely flowers! How unlovely their human weeds! How strange such beauty can be so beset! When shall our country villages see their greens and squares thus transformed? Will they then be equally deformed? I found this place had a local fame, and was the Northampton or Canandaigua on which a traveler might stumble, and fancy he had made a discovery, when lo! their beauties had long held a high place among their neighbors. So this city is a favorite the country round. It deserves to be. No preacher need be sorry if he is stationed at Irapuato. He will enjoy every minute of his triennium.

The road runs on, still smooth and velvety, amidst hollows and Peru-trees, and the mesquite. We pass the hacienda of asses (a large and popular one, of course), and come to the hills that evidently conclude the valley. Our prairie is gone. What you could not do in a day in Illinois, we have done in exactly that time. We turn to the mountains on our right hand. They encircle us close, coming round in front, having been for a hundred miles on both wings. There is no way, seemingly, through, or over, or into; and yet a city of fifty to sixty thousand inhabitants, the greatest silver town in the land, is right close to us, in among these bald, rocky bluffs. There must be a valley over there in which it lies embosomed. But where it can be, or how, are conundrums too hard for us. The plains are deserted, and we begin to wriggle in and out the spurs. We climb the hill slightly and softly, our good genius of the road still keeping off the stones. No valley the other side; only a ravine. We enter it, pass a mud village, pass men spooning water with a jerk upon an inclined plane of stone, covered with whitish mud. This is the last washing of the silver mud, and done, like gleaning, by the workmen out of hours, as their own private speculation.

CHURCH OF SAN DIEGO, GUANAJUATO.

Stone walls twenty and thirty feet high, and with a castellated look, inclose these reduction works. The hills grow closer together, as if to resist invasion. But the driver defies the hills, and dashes on, winding round, crossing and recrossing a shallow brook with no sign of a city, except now and then a gleam from a church high up the mountain-side, which increased the deception; for the city was not there; clinging now to the brook, now to the precipice, now to both together, narrowing and narrowing, like an old lady the toe of the stocking she is knitting.

Swinging round one of these blank and profitless points after another, we suddenly strike a small but beautiful green garden, full of loungers. Another sharp turn, and we are in the busiest street I have seen in Mexico: one side set with seats all occupied, the other with shops, chiefly of drink, and all the street alive with people. So we race through street after street, narrow, backed up against the hills, intensely crooked (as how could they otherwise be?), until another green plaza is passed, and we halt with a jerk, and a crunch as of steam-brakes, in the heart of the hole, at the Hotel Concordia.

It is the most Yankee town in Mexico. Indeed, few in Yankeedom are as Yankee. Dover and Lynn do not turn out as many gazers at the passing trains as these sidewalks and windows do to the rattling coach. Lowell is as full of street loungers; Manchester, perhaps; but no other.

I found Americans here, and was at home, both in the place and the language, from the start, and rejoiced at so delightful an ending to my unusually bad beginning. The road of which I had heard nothing, and which I had supposed so rough, was smooth as a Red River prairie. The robbers changed to chatty drivers and market-women, and the end was as home-like as the Merrimac or the Alleghany. So may every dark still turn to brighter day!

IV.

A SILVER AND A SACRED TOWN.

Native Costume.—Reboza and Zarepe.—The Sombrero.—A Reduction Hacienda.—The Church in Guanajuato.—Its Antipodes.—A clerical Acquaintance.—A mulish Mule.—" No quiere."—The Landscape.—Lettuce.—Calzada.—The Town and Country.—Fish of the Fence.—The Cactus and the Ass.—Compensation.—One-story City.—High Mass and higher Idolatry.—The God Mary.

Dust off, and clothes changed, let us go out and look at the city. The streets are full of people. This is a festa day, the day of St. Joseph, and nobody is at work. The folks are out in their best array of *reboza* and *zarepe*. The reboza is the mantle of the ladies, and their weakness; the zarepe that of the gentlemen, and one of their weaknesses. For sexes, like every thing else here, go by the contraries to what they do elsewhere, and men are much more dressy than women. The reboza is always quiet in color, black, blue, and brown being the prevailing tints. It is a thin-wove, light cotton mantle, some three yards long and three-quarters wide, which is worn over the head and shoulders in an easy and graceful manner. It is the only adornment they possess, apart from the pleasant faces that beam from within it, and which are as good-looking, that is, look as good, as their whiter sisters here or elsewhere.

The men are more set forth. They essay the zarepe. I do not find this word in my lexicon, but suppose that is the way to spell it. This is a thick shawl of many colors, sometimes striped in red, yellow, green, blue, and white; sometimes with light centre and embroidered edges. They muffle up their face, and wrap their shoulders in this gay shawl even in the hottest days. It is their pride. Some of them cost two or three hundred dollars, and they rise, with gold and silver lace embroidery, to the height of five hundred dollars and over. Not so the ladies' mantle. The highest-priced reboza I have seen was worth fifteen to twenty dollars, and was a plain light-blue, checked, not looking a whit better in color than a blue checked calico of a ten-cent valuation, but of course soft and fine. It has also an edging of stiffened netting, a quarter of a yard wide, which is a sign of its aristocratic rank.

The men are not content with their radiant zarepe. They essay the sombrero in silver and gold. Broad, light gray-and-white felts are faced with broad silver lace, and fantastically wrought. They have bands of silver swollen into a snake-like form around the bottom of the crown; also buttons and stars of silver. They are often very costly and ornate.

Then come their pantaloons of leather, if they are on horseback, with a row of silver or brass buttons, close packed from pocket to heel, on the seam of either leg. The extra-fashionable adorn this garment by fancy facings on back and legs, set in very prettily, and making that rude patch of our childhood and of many a manhood a really handsome ornament.

It is but proper to say that the ubiquitous European is changing these fashions, and that more soft hats and silk hats after the New York and Paris fashions are seen to-day on the plazas of all the chief cities than the magnificently gotten-up sombreros, while the zarepe is almost entirely remanded to the working-classes. Even the brimless hats, with their towering feathers and flowers and lace, are replacing modest lace veils and black shawls for church, and blue rebozas; and Mexico will soon, I fear, be undistinguishable in dress from New York.

The mines have created this city, and still enrich it. They are located in the hills behind and above the town. Humboldt reckoned that one-fifth of the silver of the world had come from one mine here, and the yield now is five millions a year. They are worked on shares—the laborer half, the owner half. These "diggings" are carried to the reduction haciendas, as grain is carried to a mill, and are either sold to the haciendados, or reduced by them for their toll. There are over fifty of such haciendas, some of them quite extensive. Mr. Parkman, of Ohio, has one of the oldest and largest. He is now somewhat feeble in years, and his sons carry on his business. His house, spacious and cool, overlooks his works. The miners and owners bring their ore here. It is distributed according to its apparent value, the best masses being reduced by themselves. The ore is beaten under huge hammers, ground by mules walking round a press, in which it is reduced to powder, placed in open vats, mixed with dissolving chemicals, salt, sulphurets, and powerful solvents, and trampled by horses to get the soil and solvents well mixed together. But the powerful chemicals soon injure their feet. Mr. Parkman, with his Yankee wit, provides a cheap and admirable substitute. It is simply a barrel moving along an axle. The axle stretches across the patio from the centre to the circumference. Horses outside pull it round. The barrel on the axle both revolves upon it and moves up and down it, reaching thereby all the composition, and commingling it more perfectly than horses' feet can do, yet with injury to none. It is a simple and seemingly effective remedy.

From this patio the substance is put through several waters, and the silver at last nearly extracted. It is then placed in furnaces, and by heating, the still adhering and undesired elements are driven out; and so, through fire and water, the well-sought silver is brought into a narrow compass. Even then it is ragged and unfit for working. It must be run into bars, and carried to the mint, and coined into solid dollars, halves, and quarters, for the delight and destruction of mankind. In Guanajuato they vary this form of its ultimate disposition with those more pleasing and artistic; and horses, horsemen, muleteers, carboneros, and other native peculiarities are cast in solid silver, and sold as curiosities at comparatively low rates. In fact, silver is about all that flourishes in Guanajuato. The people, like those of most mining towns, are reckless of money and morals.

The church is more than silver. How is it in Guanajuato? Not very hopeful. Like most mining towns, it is more free than religious. It has several Roman churches, some of which are rather handsome. But there is little power, even of this church, over the city. Making money too easy, it is feverish, gambling, dissipating, indifferent to the Church. There is room here for work of the right kind, much room. It would do no harm, but much good, if every Christian church had earnest missionaries among this half a hundred thousand population.

One thing does flourish, if the Church does not—the liquor saloons. Here, as everywhere the world over, the chief of devils is drink. But here, unlike the States, it assumes its true name. See that one on the chief street, rightly named, "El Delirio" (The Delirium); and this is "La Tentacion!!" with two admiration points—(The Temptation!!). Well named. I have seen one entitled "El Abysmo" (Hell). If our beer and whisky saloons were equally honest, some of their victims might be saved from temptation, delirium, and hell, which they now, under false pretenses, too surely bestow.

Let us wind out of Guanajuato, and see its antipodes. One need not go half round the world to find his opposite. He meets him often at the next door, nay, usually in himself. So we find the antipodes of Guanajuato fifteen leagues off. Leon is said to be the second city of the republic in size. It must be worth visiting. Five in the morning we are scampering through the streets of the city, in which the mules, like the Oregon, according to Mr. Bryant, hear no sound save their own dashings, and the city does not wish to hear even that. I am alone in the coach, and essay sleep, not very successfully, for I had unwisely been advised not to take my shawl, and more unwisely had followed that advice. The morning here is chill, though the day be hot. Since I could not sleep myself warm, I strove to sing myself thus, and to admire the sun rising over the Queretaro plain. But all of no avail. So, believing the best way to conquer any disagreeabilities is to face them, "and by opposing, end them," I concluded to take the whole dose of cold, fresh and full, on the top of the coach.

The first posta is at the brisk town of Silao, where I mount behind the driver, and find a seat on the same shelf occupied by a priest dressed in his robe, beads and all. It is the first sight of this sort I have seen in the country. He would not have dared to have done it in the city of Mexico. But they are less rigid here in respect to all interdicted matters. They allow bull-fights and priest's robes, neither of which can occur in the capital.

He seems clever, this priest, and is disposed to be conversational. By means of broken English and Spanish, helped on with some broken French and Latin, we contrive to get at each other's meaning quite fairly. He informs me that he is a priest of the new order of the Paulists, that he is conversant with Greek, Hebrew, Italian, and French, as well as Spanish; that he has never been at Rome, but expects to go next year. He inquires my profession. "A writer for the press," I innocently answer. It is well sometimes to have two strings to your bow. But I add, " I am a Methodist." I meant to tell half the ecclesiastical truth, if I shrunk from telling the whole. This reserve is not unwise; for Leon is the most fanatical of cities; and the knowledge that a Protestant minister was entering it, even as an observer, would have been reported to the bishop before I had been fifteen minutes in the town. What consequences might have followed, poor Stevens's fate suggests. It was only about two days' ride beyond Leon, in a less religious town, that he was massacred by order of the Church authorities. By this semi-reticence, too, I got out of my Paulist friend light that I should not otherwise have gained. He caught at the word "Methodist." "How many churches have you," he said, "in the States?" I tell him there are six leading churches: Baptist, Catholic, Congregational, Episcopal, Methodist, and Presbyterian. He asks the peculiarities of the five of which he is ignorant. They are given. "Any Lutherans?" "A few churches of that name, composed principally of Germans." "Any Calvinists?" "Many of that faith, but no church organization of that name." "Are not many *indifferentestas?*" I repeat that word, not catching its meaning. "Yes," he replies; "no religion, no faith, no confession, nothing?" "Yes, there are some who are not Christians, but most have some religious opinions they hold to, and many who are not members of Christian churches support and sympathize with them." Being asked what objects of interest were in Leon, "The theatre, the cathedral, and some haciendas," he answered. "Methodists never go to the theatre," I replied; a remark at which he winced a little, and perhaps I ought to have winced also; for it is rather a past truth, I fear, than a present one, though it ought to be true to-day as it was aforetime. He explained by saying that it was architecturally attractive.

A mule displayed his nature in an unusual degree. The epizootic had reduced the working force of the road, and new mules had to be brought on. One of these dirty cream-colored fellows was in the thills. He was not disposed to be conquered, even with seven obedient fellows to drag him along in the path of duty. He was not to be fooled by any such tricks, so he held steadily back while they trotted fast, and was dragged forward in spite of himself. The lash and the stones did not change his views of his duty to himself. He only held back the more. It was a novel sight to see him thus dragged along by his collar, his heels flying in violent resistance to his will.

At last, determined to end the contest by a *coup de grace*, down he flung himself on the ground. The seven brothers were on the full gallop, and would have dragged him to Leon. But he had cost too much to be used up that way. So the coach is stopped; the obstinate chap, after a deal of resistance, is got upon his feet; a rope is tied from his saddle under his tail, so as to make resistance less agreeable to himself; and off we start again. He begins soon, like Barbara Lewthwaite's pet lamb, to pull at the cord as bad as ever. He spurns the tail and saddle device, and after letting his legs oppose his will for a mile or two, down he goes again. He has learned the trick, and will play it till it wins. He is dragged fifty to a hundred feet on the flinty soil. It is of no use. He will not get up if he has got to go on. "*No quiere*," says the priest (he does not desire). This is the Spanish way of putting "he won't." Pretty evident is it that he does not desire to conform. So he is released, put into the hands of the *mozo*, and we are subdued, not he, and go into town with only six animals, while he walks in, free of harness and coach. He had to pay for his liberty, I doubt not, and a big price, too, in the flogging he got, and did not afterward very often lie down in the middle of his route.

Is the mule here called *mula* because of this force of will? And did the word come from *mulier?* The opprobrious epithet of the parent of the mule is never applied to the sex. "An ass" is an insult given only to man. *Mula* takes the other side in its termination, and in this instance forcibly illustrated the saying, "When she won't, she won't, and there's an end on it." *No quiere* settles many another attempt on the part of driving man to bring the other and higher creature into subjection.

The mountain ranges on each side are about ten miles apart. The plain is very level, and most of it very fertile and highly cultivated. The hills are full of silver, quicksilver, and other precious minerals, so my brother-priest informs me, but can not tell why they are so little mined. They are awaiting a people who can make them unveil their charms. "*No quiere*," they say to-day, and their human masters respect their wishes, showing thereby that they are not their masters. It will not be so always. Either these or others will subject these mountains to their sway, and compel their gorges to disgorge their treasures of ages.

The fields lie very lovely to the eye, outspreading in their everlasting verdure, fed perpetually by streams from the mountains; the beds and roadside glowing in tulips, roses, violets, and many a strange beauty none the less beautiful for her novelty. Wheat, alfalfa, barley, and corn are making glad the heart of man by their abundant growth. Haciendas claim immense territory on the left, but on the right the soil is cut up among little proprietors, or at least those who can lease and cultivate a few rods in comparative independence.

Leon draws near, spread out at the base of a range of hills that terminates the valley. The older Indians and the children note the priestly dress and take off their hats in reverence; but the young men, I note, are less respectful. At first I thought it was a politeness meant for me also, and returned the obeisance; but I soon found it was for the higher being by whose side I rode.

We cross a bridge and drive through the calzada — a finely shaded avenue, with drives either side, and a walk and benches in the middle. Along the benches loungers are sitting, and market-women are selling lettuce, which is the chief esculent, seemingly, here. It grows very large, and the outer leaves are torn off and thrown away. The inside ones are pressed together, and the tall, compact bunch of delicate white and green looks good enough to eat, and is as good as it looks. They sometimes put tulips and roses and other flowers in the top of these bunches, and thereby increase their attraction to the eye, but not to the palate.

A Sister of Charity here, as everywhere else, hideously dressed, has a bevy of school-girls on the calzada for recreation. The Roman Church has not lost all its wits yet. These fine-looking young ladies will cling to the nun and priest, and the young men will cling to them. Only a great outpouring of the Holy Ghost can open the eyes of this land by taking the veil from off their hearts.

The hot streets are run through in our usual Gilpin style, and we are reined up sharp at the door of the Hotel Diligencias.

I bid *adios* to my friend, the priest of the order of Paul, and go out to conquer the town. It is soon done. He told me the truth. Only the cathedral, the front of the theatre, and some haciendas. The last it is too hot to visit; the first is looked into, the second looked upon. I am in for a day here. There is no return stage till to-morrow at eleven. So I wander through the market-place, a dull spot, and soon exhausted; where brass coin is all their currency. Guanajuato touches nothing but silver. The plaza holds me longer. It has a very rich tropical garden, banana-trees, orange, and flowers of every hue. It has also around it broad shaded arcades lined with shops and stores. Nowhere have I seen so much of a display of dry goods. A whole side of the square is lined with these stores, and very fair in their attractions they are.

The cathedral is after the usual sort, and not especially ornate.

Its specialty is blasphemy. Dancing girls, with their skirts open to the knee, are placed over the altar as the angels of the sepulchre or something, and over all is the image of God the Father, a gray-bearded old man, with the triangle of gold, sign of the Trinity, over his head. No wonder the first spelling-book for children, with its alphabet and a-b, ab, condenses the Ten Commandments, and puts the first one thus: "Amaras a Dios sobre todas las cosas" (Thou shalt love God above all things). That is the whole of it. Not a hint about this idolatry, which the original expressly prohibits. The commands of Sinai are perverted to their own idolatries. I bought this little tract in the market-place. It is sold by hundreds of thousands, and that is the way the Church wrests the Scriptures, may it not be added, "to her own destruction?"

The tedium of the day was greatly relieved by a horseback ride with an English resident, Mr. George Gray. I found out him and his brother, both bachelors, one a clock-maker, one a machinist, sons of a mine-worker who came out some forty years ago. The clock vender said business was dull. "Yankees like a clock in the house; Mexicans, a saint," he said, half bitingly. But what use have they for clocks? Time is of no account with them.

His brother takes me to ride; that is, lends me a horse, and goes with me. We drive among the small proprietors, to the east and north of the town. The gardens are green with irrigation. They are full of esculents, with little patches of flowers among their honest lettuce and maize, like a pretty and not useless child among her industrious associates. It is difficult to raise wheat here. The land has to be flooded with water for a long time, and otherwise carefully nurtured, and then it produces but little. Better exchange its silver for Minnesota's wheat. Both will profit by the change.

Here are large fields laid down to chilli, a sort of pepper, almost the only condiment with their beans and cakes. Others are green, very, with alfalfa, or lucern, the favorite green food for mules and horses. It looks a little like clover, though seemingly richer and juicier. Many pastures are brown, awaiting the rain of heaven, and not that from the ground. Wells are busy. They are dug two and two, together or opposite. The swinging sweeps, which once existed generally in the North, here stand together or over against each other, and the boys are plying them all day long. Thus the fields are always producing, and Nature never rests, if man often does.

An old woman with a long stick having a knife on the end is cutting green buds from the prickly-pear (the nopal) that lines the roadside. "She is getting fish of the fence," said my friend. Not allowed to eat meat in Lent, they gather these buds, and cook them as a substitute. Hence this saying. The nopal is the fencing stuff of the country. It grows in orchards, grows along the wayside, wild and cultivated. It is as homely as the ass, of which it is the vegetable counterpart in universality, ugliness, and utility.

It has one redeeming feature, as has also that creature. Its blossoms are beautiful. Seldom does one see more exquisite and delicate tints than break out all over these horrid bushes, and seldom does one see so exquisite and delicate a leg and foot on beast or bird, or man himself, as concludes with a good ending the exceedingly bad beginning of the ass. It is straight, small, delicate, a natural Chinese beauty of ankle and hoof. The finest horse's leg and foot are coarse to it. So, if you will only look for it, you will find some redeeming trait in every creature of God. But this trait often makes the others more homely. Glance from a donkey's legs to his head and ears, and you are amazed at the terribleness of that opposite termination. You can not see how the two could possibly exist in the same creature. You even believe it to be a cursed degradation. It must be witchery. It can not be nature. So the nopal seems the uglier as you turn from its delicate blossoms to its leather lap-stone leaf and ungainly trunk, and general asinine vegetable humiliation.

But each serves quietly, says nothing, and waits patiently the hour when the fairy curse shall be removed, or that unfairy curse resting on all creation, the curse of sin, of Eden, and of man, and they shall have a complete symmetry after the exquisite fragments and indices that each now possesses.

We ride home among Indian huts, in a delicious sun-setting, under greenest of trees and among corresponding verdure. Along the banks of the almost waterless river, boys are flying kites, and women washing their few garments. A frock is on a bush, and a lady, in her reboza alone, is sitting in the stream, awaiting the drying of her tunic. The dogs and children are enjoying themselves, as much, perhaps, as if they were the children and dogs of the Prince of Wales or President Grant. Possibly more.

FUNERAL OF GOVERNOR MANUEL DOBLADO.

We pass down a long street of one-storied houses. They are all of that height. Not six in the city are two-storied. The widow of Governor Don Manuel Doblado occupies one of the former sort. He died in New York, and it is thought would have been president had he lived. Her house is spacious, and has every luxury, including that best of luxuries, its height. A very sumptuous funeral was granted him in Guanajuato, as he deserved.

Most of the houses are very poor, and the people look poorer than the houses. Many are empty, the houses, and people probably also. Hither come thousands from San Luis Potosi, Queretaro, Guadilajara, and other points, when revolutions roll; for the governor of this State will have peace if he has to fight for it. It is the State of Guanajuato, and that city gives the nerve that gives the peace.

The next morning I attended high mass. It was St. Joseph's day, and held in high remembrance. So the bishop is out in his full and faded costume. A large number receive the wafer. A red-jacketed boy, followed the priest who gave the wafer, presenting something like a love-feast ticket. Was it one? Have they revived that lost art of Methodism? When the bishop entered, the crowd, dreadfully ragged and poor as most of them were, kneeled down the whole length of the church, making a narrow lane each side of him, and he stretched out his hands for them to kiss as he moved up to the altar. How eagerly they clutched at them! I saw one old woman get the seal-ring to her lips. She looked as if she had touched heaven. I have seen others than uneducated papists overworship their minister, but never so believingly and devoutly as these.

The ceremony is after the usual spread-eagle sort. A great crowd kneel at the beginning, but they come and go, and the shifting performance moves forward before a more shifting congregation. This is the bishop who has since refused to obey the laws of the State enforcing toleration, and has called on his people to resist those laws. His ignorant followers could be easily worked up to persecution.* What would he have said had it been told him that among the spectators of his performances that morning was a minister of the anti-Roman Church, meditating on the coming establishment of his Church in this city, and the extinction of this ruin of souls and faith in that purer doctrine and life? Had he suspected so much, or had our priest of the coach-top dreamed it, there would have been small chance of that minister's having had

---

* See Appendix A.

much to do with that reformation. Would not that crowd have leaped on him, and sent him swift to Hades?

Around the uppermost balcony of the church are shields of green, with words in gold upon them. One whole side is appropriated to Mary directly; the rest possibly incidentally. Among her shields are those with these inscriptions: "Mater Creatoris," "Mater Salvatoris," "Virgo Potens," "Virgo Clemens" (Mother of the Creator, of the Saviour, Virgin Powerful, Merciful). The central and primal and ultimate idea of every motto is the Virgin. As if to refer all this to her, and give her at once divine honors, all the opposite side has such phrases as these: "Sedes Sapientiæ," "Causa Nostræ Lætitiæ," "Fœdaris Arca," "Janua Cœli," "Refugio Peccatorum," "Stella Matutina" (Seat of Wisdom, Cause of our Joy, Ark of Faith, Gate of Heaven, Refuge of Sinners, Morning Star).

These may refer to the Church herself, and not to Mary. But below, at an altar, she is called "Refugio Peccatorum," one of the very phrases found up here also. There is no hint that this is not intended. If so, then see how high a pitch of idolatry these priests and bishops have been guilty of, are guilty of to-day, in thus ascribing all the work of salvation to Mary. The people believe it is so, whether they have themselves a sense by which they can escape or not. The crowd have none. The Church is the Church of the Virgin; with her they rise or fall.

A little image of the Virgin and the Child was being carried to a village by a few of its men, to grace a feast there. We passed it on our way back. On their shoulders they bore it, in a white box closed on all sides but the front, set off with flowers. It was sheer idolatry. Leon's cathedral has its graven god and worshiped woman, and poor ragged wretches for an audience. When will it receive the true Gospel? Not without difficulty. They are very fanatical, these poor people. A German came here to preach, and they threatened him with a coat of tar and feathers, and he did not open his lips. They were the most reverential to the priests of any city I have been in. As I stood among the kneeling crowds of the cathedral, I noted more than one lowering countenance. Large numbers are at the earliest orisons and the latest vespers. The bells clang all day long. It is church, church, and nothing but church. There will be a big fight here before this Diana of Leon is dethroned. But it will come. These poor people inwardly sigh for a happy Christian experience. How happy they would be if they once experienced it! How they would throw off their rags and rejoice in a religion that lifted up soul and body! Pray for Leon, the city of superstition, that she may pre-eminently be the city of faith.

Gladly is the coach welcomed the next morning, and the ride is taken, hot and dusty, to Guanajuato.

V.

A HORSEBACK RIDE OVER THE SILVER MOUNTAINS.

Indian Dancing and Gambling.—A sleeping City.—Wood and Coal Carriers.—Mineral de la Luz.—A Mountain Nest.—Sometimes up, sometimes down.—Berrying and Burying.—The Apple-tree among the Trees of the Wood.—Off the Track.—A funereal Tread.—Lunch in the Air.—The Plunge.—A Napola Orchard.—Out on the Plains.—Valley of the Sancho.

I am so tired with fifty miles of horsebacking that I would gladly get to sleep, especially as I have to be up by three, and off again at four. But the sound of guitars and harps in the open court without our quarters, to which Indian girls are dancing, prevents that luxury. They must be very busy by the unceasing sounds that flow into my open window. It is an Indian festa purely, neither Spanish nor Romish seeming to interfere with it. It is probably as ancient as any Aztec event now in vogue. A half-dozen tents have a girl or two each, trained to great nimbleness of toes and heels, who skip double and quadruple measure and all sorts of shuffles to the quick time of the harp, singing, in Indian, a murmurous accompaniment to the steps. The lookers-on can participate with her for a real a round. Of course there are plenty of men of all ages ready to pay their "bit." So the old folks earn much money out of the feet of their daughters.

Walking round these booths, I was invited by one of these venerable fathers to enter his shed. I assented, not knowing whither I went, for I had not yet spelled out the purport of the festa. He gave me the seat of honor, fronting the outside crowd. I soon saw the incongruity of my position, but was withheld from disturbing the meeting. It was the first ball I had seen since I was sixteen, when I had sat through the night a looker-on, as now. I was soon relieved of my unwilling bondage to courtesy. I retreated to the rear of the gazing crowd in good order. In the midst of the whirl, at my feet lay two small dogs, a white and a black, nose to nose, fast asleep. Two children, also white and black, I saw at a Southern school festival, lying on a seat in like position, head to head, fast asleep. Each suggested peace and fraternity among both dogs and men, and no distinction on account of color.

The dancing-girl was modest in her goings, which Christian (?) dancers are not. She allowed her partners none of the immodest privileges of the waltz and polka, and kept her dignity both of carriage and conduct. The ballet troupes, cancan, and even the fashionable dancing of city balls are far less chaste. Civilization could get civilized at these festas.

Gambling was going on as busily as dancing. Groups sitting on the ground were rapidly losing their centavos to the cool heads that held the pool. Thus the earnings of the girls slipped through their fathers' fingers into the hands of the Aztec John Oakhursts, who probably, like him of California, were exceedingly honorable to those they robbed, and so might well be portrayed by the overturners of morality as the saints of their tribe.

This show saluted me on arriving at this hacienda, after a long, wearisome, but repaying ride. Let us get away from these poor creatures into the grand mountains, and draw from them the rest and strength the god-like creature man can not bestow.

It was hardly day-break when I mounted my horse, and rode through the silent streets of Guanajuato—silent only for the little season from midnight to sunrise; for no town of equal bustle have I seen in Mexico, and not many in the United States. Romantic in situation, and full of movement, it is one of the places one craves to see again.

We climb up the stone stairs, up and up, steep almost as the side of a house, looking down on the sleeping city with its fifty thousand souls. What is more lonely than a great city with all its people asleep? I have trembled with awe as that thought has struck me in a crowded population. All, as it were, dead! Every house has not only one, as did the Egyptian, but all dead. The rich are as poor as the poorest, perhaps poorer, in their dreams; the poor rich as the richest, perhaps the richer in their dreams. The whole life wiped out, and as though it had never been. Ah, if only that unconsciousness could come after death, which some so anxiously seek to detect in the Word of God, but detect it not—an everlasting sleep—it would be a relief to the sinner! But it is not the revealed will of God thus to give relief to the sinner. He must dwell in his own consciousness. He that is filthy shall be filthy still. The lustful, the revengeful, the miserly, he shall still be possessed of his own passions. The saintly wife sleeping by the sinful husband may know no difference in this unconscious state; but the first breath of the awakening morn reveals to each no more clearly their existence than it does their character. The saintly one is still saintly, the sinful, sinful. The first thought of one is a prayer, of the second, an oath. Before the lips are awakened the mind is, and the heart, and out of their abundance the mouth speaks. So will the slumber of the grave be broken.

Eternity is not a sleep of the righteous or of the wicked, nor is it the sleep of one and not of the other. They are alike in their consciousness, as at the beginning; alike in their free choice; alike in their corresponding liberty of action; alike in their inward constitution; alike forever in heaven, forever in hell.

A mile or more up, and we enter a little suburb, whose church, perched on a scarfed cliff, looks down the gorge into the city, and out far away into the valleys that open on Leon and Queretaro. How apt in location of their churches this Church ever is, apt for effect, not always for utility! Here they combine, and the centre of the hamlet is the key of the landscape.

Still up we go, meeting at this gray hour the descending laborers. Who is this coming forth to meet us, with his coffin on his back, or the coffin of some Goliath of the mountains? It towers a yard above his head, and goes down his back to within a foot of his heels. If my fears had not pretty nearly given out by lack of any success in the employment of them (every attempt having been a failure), I might have got up a little excitement over this apparition. As it is, I calmly await its coming. It proves to be a wood-carrier, and the coffin is a length of corded wood, lashed together in a symmetric and solid shape, and stretching out its eight or ten feet, two feet in width, a burden not easily to be borne, one is sure, though these men, old and young, seem to carry it lightly. They bend under it, and take a staff to stay their steps down the headlong descent. They, however, have erectness enough to recognize us, and give and get grateful "Adios." The charcoal burners follow the fagot bearers. There are degrees in every thing. A fagot is less than a straight stick, but above a chip and a knot. The latter go into coal, which goes down behind its aristocratic kinsman.

"Every thing's nothing except by position."

They are compactly and prettily arranged. Bound together with nets and with wisps of green grass, arranged along the level side, which is laid against the back, they look ornamental even, and make the charcoalist a florist. Why not? His stuff is diamonds in disguise. Why should not its arrangement be crystalline?

The rise of the sun and of the path set the city below, and the mountains above, and the plains beyond in clearer light. The town, romantic from every point, is not the least so from this hill-top looking down. It is waking up, too, and the sound comes up hither of the crushing mills grinding the rocks into powder, of the water washing the powder into mud, of the mules treading the mud into chemical mire, and of the furnaces evolving the chemicals, and burning the white metal out of its ancient, and as it perhaps had thought, eternal, companions. The street-cries, the rattling carts, the living man awakening from his death, and coming out of his grave the same that he went in—all these salute us with the breaking of the light over the mountains; at least so far as these sounds can reach the ever-ascending sense.

Not far to the west, on one of the peaks, lies a white cluster, called the Mineral de la Luz, or Luz alone, as these Yankeeized Mexicans cut it down. It is a famous mine, not now in its best working order, but its yield has been wonderful; and draining of superfluous water will doubtless restore it to its former pre-eminence of value akin to its pre-eminence of position.

All around us rise these peaks of brown and gray, tall, even though their base is far above the snow-line of the Alps, and of every variety of shape, sharp, round, crater-like, cleft and gashed by the creative knife (as proper a figure as the "creative chisel," which has long been a stock-tool of the paragraphists). They are all probably full of silver, as the vast subterranean chambers of the chief mine of Guanajuato clearly illustrate. But the expense of digging is costly. Mining is no luxurious idling, but steady and slow, with small gains. So these mountains await the men that are not to be put off by any coyness or resistance, but will compel them to yield up their treasures. It is not the kingdom of heaven only that suffereth violence, and which the violent take by force; it is every valuable kingdom, whether of wealth or wisdom, of place or power, of reform or religion.

The sun comes up as we go down into the first of the valleys beyond this ridge, so many of which we must descend into and ascend out of ere the long looked-for hacienda appears. Over to our left, perched on the side hill, high up among the clouds, is a pretty bit of a village, whose name I have forgotten, that is the home of the charcoal venders and wood-cutters, as pretty an eagle's nest as one often sees; at least, at the distance of the mile or so which we are from it. Perhaps, like other eagle's nests, it would hardly bear examination.

We take our last glimpse of the city beneath us, the hills hugging it and bending over it, like a mother, or a dozen of mothers, fondling a childling. The plains of Queretaro and Leon glisten in the morning slantings, and Luz, like that of old, sits at the top of the land, glowing like the silver at its bottom, responsive to the coming day.

When I was a lad, I remember hearing a good brother of limited variety of tones and themes engage in prayer. He almost always had in his petitions this verse, expressed in a peculiar rising and falling sing-song. If the printers will help me, I will try and put the very tones in type:

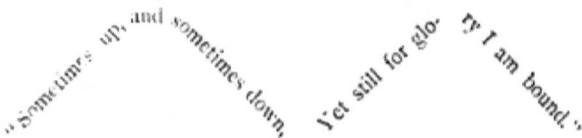

So, as we ascended and descended, I thought of the good brother's sing-song verse, and hoped that his successful accomplishment of his purpose, for he has long been in glory, might be not only exemplified in this minor effort, but in the major and maxima ones that absorb the whole life and being.

We had been going up, up, up; now we go down, down, downy. Far below the level of our original point of departure we plunge, sliding down on the close-set feet of the safe little Mexican horse, plunging through more than one degree of latitude.

The top gave us the high blue-berry bush just blossoming, a dear reminder of boyish tramps in Lynde's Woods, yet uncut, but every day in danger of the knife of the spoiler. May some good providence turn them to a use that shall perpetuate both their memories and their berries! A big town, well-nigh a city, is growing to them. If it would only appropriate them to a cemetery, how happy would one wanderer be to come and haunt them occasionally while living, and to sleep under them at the last, in age, even as he has slept under them often in happy days of a vanished childhood, awaiting the call of the clarion of the resurrection. Grand old trees, dear high blue-berry bushes, lowly huckleberry bushes, not the less lovely for your sweet humility.

> "The lark that soars the nearest heaven
> Builds on the ground his lowly nest."

So these humble bushes, where we sat and picked and laughed, and strove as to who should first fill his pail, and broke them in big armfuls, and took them to the shelter of the big trees for cooler stripping, how your black eyes now beam upon me, little luscious beads of light and life, through these long, long years! Ah, save, oh good fathers of my old home town, save us the Lynde's Woods, where we so often went a-berrying, for our own time-long burying. What a life-pleasure a boy bred in the country has over the city lad who only visits it on vacation! It is a joy and strength all his days; none the less so, if his after-life is passed among brick walls and stone pavements which give scarce a glimpse of either earth or heaven.

This high blue-berry bush on this high Mexic mountain has set me off on a high horse that is in danger of throwing me: for sentiment is the last thing any body allows in any body else but themselves. Balance is restored by the venerable nopal, better known as cactus, that stands stiff and changeless among these Northern reminders. No cactus is found by New England roadsides and country lanes. This is tropical and new. It is of yesterday to the land, but of to-day to the traveler. He can not shed imaginary tears over its earlier suggestions. The laurel is also here, beginning to put forth those pinky-white buddings that shall soon burst into complete blossomings. So the North country again appears, though this crown of poets and favorite of Apollo is a Greek rather than a Yankee.

The bottom of the hill brings us to a cluster of huts perched on the steep side of the opposite mountain. We pace along its base for some distance, enjoying the odor of its flowers, cultivated and wild, and especially the bloom and balm of its apple-trees. These are bursting into flower, not the broad, grand, full blossom of the North, where it really belongs, but still of the old blush and bloom. They are scattered all along the river's edge, where only wild trees besides are found: and, amidst the flowerless and odorless boughs of ash and birch and oak and nopal, one feels more than ever the force of that compliment and comparison which the love-lorn wife pays her husband, in the song of songs which is Solomon's, "As the apple-tree among the trees of the wood, so is my beloved among the sons." One sees the exquisite beauty of that compliment in these gorges of the Cordilleras, where the apple-tree stands among the trees of the wood, clad in its many-colored robe, fragrant with that odor that gives it the headship in sweetness over all the trees of the garden. It is not impossible that this is the very tree of which Eve partook, and that its Edenic supremacy is still not largely lost. Whether so or no, the loving wife was right in her comparison, and this wood proves true, in that respect, that song of monogamy by a polygamic transgressor, that song of the spiritual longings and lovings of the Church and her husband, the Christ: "As the apple-tree among the trees of the wood, so is my beloved among the sons."

We cross the brook we had sauntered near so long, and pull up a steep grade; in fact, get off and pull our horses up, it is so steep. The road becomes less and less a road, and my guide is bewildered. He has lost his path. It is the second time already, and we not a quarter of our journey done. Across the ravine he spies a wood-cutter, and speaks softly to him. It is remarkable how low a voice they use in making inquiries. His was not above a drawing-room pitch. Is it humility or good breeding? A little of both, probably. The wood-cutter answers alike softly, but distinctly; we drag our horses down again, recross the brook, which we should have ever kept on our left, and pull up a steeper pitch, pass our wood-cutting befriender, through another long and shaded and luscious ravine—how summery cool it was!—and out upon a rancho, the midway spot of the journey.

The men and women and babies stared respectfully, and said "Adios" prettily. The men take off their hats usually as they meet us, especially the elderly ones. The young ones, if not very young, are more independent.

The rancho leads us up on the tepitati (I spell by the ear), a volcanic rock that is hardly a rock. It seems soft, and sounds hollow. It whitens under the hoofs of horses, and glistens like marble dust in the hot glare. It abounds all over this land; you strike it on almost every road, a soil seemingly without possibility of culture, yet a substance used in lighter buildings. It is a long climb up its white face, along a white ridge, and up another like white ladder, to the crest of our road. The path is worn in its chalk-like surface, now in narrow grooves, scarce wide enough for the two legs of the steed to stand in, now over long slippery slides, now into stairs of unequal length, but of uniform smoothness, while the echo of the tread seems ever to make us shrink and heed that order of Emerson's,

"Set not thy foot on graves."
"The ground sounds hollow from below,"

is Watts's nervous putting of our mortal estate. It is not inapplicable here, on perhaps the highest point my feet have trod in all this exalted land. As these loftiest places of earth sound hollow, so do the loftiest stations of man. The ground beneath the feet of kings and potentates is not the echoless granite, but the reverberating tepitati. It is rotten, barren, glittering, resounding dust.

"Princes, this clay shall be your bed."

Nay, more: you are of the same clay. Let us take the lesson to heart which the topmost soil that we touch on the continent so sadly preaches.

Here we take a lunch of *pan y mantiquia*, bettter known to you as bread-and-butter, a piece of roast beef, and some German-made tarts that had, therefore, a tart in them, which Mexican dulces never have. Always choose well your table, if you can not your food. Where is a better place than this highest point in our pilgrimage? So we spread our lunch under a not-spreading cactus-tree. It makes me think of Elijah's juniper-tree, for it gives but little shade from a torrid sun, in a mountainous land. But it is something to eat a slice of meat and bread under a not-spreading cactus-tree. It will do to tell of, and it is told of. Then judgment gets the better of sentiment, and I adjourn my spreading limbs and spread bread to the large-leafed robli: so my guide told me to spell it. It is a sort of oak, with large leaves, some green, some brown. It gives shade, and the breeze gives coolness.

The view from this apex is grand. The hills, of all sorts of strange shapes, rise all about us, for miles and miles. Just below is a hollow that has a bit of a white chapel, a few brown huts, a green sweet sward, and a glimmering of water; how I wish for a drop of it to cool my parched tongue, and wish in vain! Shall I ever have a like powerless craving from the opposite of this summit? Christ forbid! yet if another feared lest, having preached to others, he himself should be a castaway, how much more I! The basin looked, among these hard, stern, rough mountains, like the "Luck of Roaring Camp" among its hard, stern, rough protectors; only these mountains never swore, nor drank, nor gambled, nor murdered, nor were in any respect unfit protectors to the babe they embosomed. Would that their human imitators were as human!

They assume strange shapes. One of them lifts itself out an encompassing plain, like a bowl bottom side up and the bottom broken off, so that you can look into its hollow from its ragged edge, down side up. Others bend themselves in huge concentric arcs that look like the same bowl, with one-half of its already beheaded, or bebottomed, portion cut away from it, exposing to view the inside of the remaining part—a hollow hemisphered, truncated cone. Others look after the fashion of hills elsewhere, only handsomer, very smooth domes and cones of glistening rock. Among them glided, like huge mottled snakes, pastures brown and gray with stones and winter herbage, waiting the rains that shall clothe these rocky fields in "a mist of greenness," the mottled snake turning to its greener kindred. So precious are the bits of soil in this almost soilless region that you can trace the boundary lines of these patches far up the sides of the mountains.

Far away to the north and east, the grand plains above Queretaro roll out, a scroll written over with industry and its rewards. It will be yet better written, when this age shall be a palimpsest for the one, near at hand, of equal rights, higher faith, universal culture, and social reform. How intense the solitude of these mountains; how profound their silence! It is a stillness that can be felt. Not a bird wings its way across the summits, or sends an echo along their sides; not an insect hums. No leaves

> "Clap their little hands in glee
> With one continuous sound."

Yet there is strength in all this calm. "He setteth fast the mountains," is the emblem of Divine omnipotence, "being girded with power." But these mountains are not always set fast. The "everlasting hills do bow." Here, not unfrequently, they tremble and bow. Is it "at the presence of the Lord, of the Lord of the whole earth?" Why not? Is not this as proper a solution of that physical problem as those less spiritual? "For He cometh, He cometh to judge the earth." Does any earth need His coming to judgment more? "He shall judge the people righteously." Even so. "Bend the heavens and come down."

> "Earth, tremble on, with all thy sons;"

and may His feet be on the mountains, publishing peace, and giving them, and all that they inhabit, everlasting righteousness and rest.

Our road soon descends again, more rapidly than it went up, though not more easily. It hangs half a thousand feet over a basin edged with a flowing river, skirts the rancho of Sancho (an alliteration not our own), with its tiny field of wheat and plat of gay flowers, and little peach-orchard, with flowers and half-grown fruit on adjoining trees. It is lovely in all save its dogs and their owners. How can nature be so grand and lovely, and man and woman so mean and unlovely?

> "Like vermin crawling on a lion's crest,"

said Tom Moore, bitterly and not untruly, of Americans more than a half century ago. It is not untrue of some of these Americans to-day. But Christianity is coming. It has never really got here yet, and we shall see these "vermin" pretty, cleanly, cultured men and women. The girl that gave us a cup of cold water, or as cold as her cabin afforded, and illuminated my mozo with her smile, as well as with her answers to his inquiries, shall not she and her kin, who bow and take off their sombreros and salute us so courteously over the wheat plat, yet arise from their hovels into comely homes, and be all beautiful in condition as in possibility?

It is a long following of a dry river-bed, crossing and recrossing its loose rocks many times under a sultry sun, before we strike a rattling brook of delightful water, and a hill-side that looked as if covered with an apple-orchard, and must certainly reveal a white house amidst its green foliage. It is a nopal, or cactus, orchard, and no white cottage glimmers among its leather lapstone-shaped leaves, but only the same adobe hut, the same half-naked women, three-fourths naked men, seven-eighths naked youths, and entirely naked children, all sitting on the bare ground in poverty and degradation extreme, yet as courteous and kindly as the princeliest soul in the princeliest palace.

We pass through this nopal-orchard, with its many-tinted blossoms and small egg-like fruit, and emerge on a wide plain. Our steps have turned a little too far to the south. A kindly-voiced native, neatly dressed in white, with a blue girdle about his loins, gives us directions, and our untired horses step away, *sobre passo*, or the "overstep," the favorite pace of long day traveling. Another rancho is traversed of like disgust and like courtesy; a high, hot, shadeless hill is mounted; a hotter cañon crossed; another long plain traversed; another rancho, with its organ-cactus walls, is entered and left; a long stretch of open upland paced over. The "cinquo leguas" (five leagues), gradually diminishes to "quatuor, tres, dos y medio" (two and a half) or "dos, mas y menos" (two, more or less), where it hangs a long while. At last an adobe cottage close to a waterless river-bed is reached, whose pretty maidenly girl says it is "una legua" (one league). For that information, as well as for her pretty ways and name (Arabella it was), and for the abundant and cooling water she gave us, we responded with *mille gracias* (a thousand thanks), the *débris* of our dinner, and a medio. Which of the three prized she the most, think you? A miss of fourteen would not hold the medio in chief esteem. That her mother prefers, and she the cakes and compliments. *Suum cuique.* Each gets her own, and all of us are satisfied.

The dry brook, with its superabounding rocks, is our highway for over a mile. A huge rock rising from its brink, is the last resting-place for horse and rider. It is of clay or soil of the country, and has embedded several strata of loose stones, as if formed by the deposits of freshets, and then left for the sun to bake into a solid pudding. The epizootic shows its green presence around the nostrils of the mozo's horse—a going and not a coming presence—which has notwithstanding walked and paced its nigh to fifty miles, patiently and pleasantly, and will rewalk it homeward on the morrow.

The high-road is soon struck, and the Valley of La Camada lies before us, like every valley of Mexico, a thing of beauty rare. The brown earth, soft and sown, awaits the coming rain that shall fill it with life. The silver-gray hills lie near us, seemingly, though a score of miles away, bare of all save sunlight. The river Sancho winds, broad and shaded, along the foreground ; broad in its plans and ultimate fulfillment, though now it is dwindled to a shorter span along the farther bank and under the willows thereof, while grass is springing up in its bed on this side, and the cattle are eating it. Trees and grasses make this central line a line of beauty which, were we less tired, would be lingered over longer. But this fifty miles by an unused rider has made back and brains give out, and the plaza of the hacienda is more fascinating than all fields, or brooks, or trees, or grasses, or cows, or any other creature. The Indian festa, with its chirruping guitars and twinkling feet, is alike unheeded. The court is entered, and the couch is sought, and on its restful bosom all the mountain climbings and anti-climbings, and all the scenes and musings thereto belonging, are as though they had never been.

VI.

TO AND IN SAN LUIS POTOSI.

Aztec Music.—Low-hung but high-hung Clouds.—Troops and Travelers.—A big, small Wagon.—Zeal of San Felipe.—Lutero below Voltaire.—Rough Places not Smooth.—Mesquite Woods.—Silver Hills.—Two Haciendas.—How they Irrigate.—Lassoing.—The Frescoes of Frisco.—Cleft Cliffs.—The Valley of San Luis Potosi.—Greetings and Letters.—The Church of Mary.—The coming Faith.—A costly and Christly Flag.—Joseph and Mary worshiped in vain for Rain.

How different the strains that fell upon the ear last night and those that are now addressing us; and both are musical! Then it was the dancing-girls' guitars and harps, making a twitter as of caroling swallows. Now it is a Government band that, on a broad and lighted plaza, discourses music that even Berliners would walk around to hear, especially if they could soon thereby reach a beer-stall. These Government bands are found in all the large towns, and are a great source of pleasure to the citizens. They play twice or thrice a week, and draw many loungers and listeners to their soirées. They are exceedingly refined in their touch. You never heard a clearer, softer note than that flute is now trilling; and the airs are gentle and recondite. How one forgets the long hard ride of more than eighty miles, the slow pulling along over heavy and rocky roads, as he listens to these rich strains!

> "Here will we sit, and let the sounds of music
> Creep in our ears; soft stillness and the night
> Become the touches of sweet harmony."

The country and the people are made for music. Remember that all these players are Indians, "brown as the ribbed sea-sand," and a good deal browner than any I ever saw—brown as the old red sandstone. Are they made from that antique dust? All these are admirable performers. I have never seen a white face among them. In Mexico and all the cities of the land they are of one hue. The passion of the people is for music. The upspringing Protestant churches are bursting forth in song. As this hard, dry soil breaks forth in flowers the instant it scents the water, so the water of life touches their parched and barren souls, and they flower into song. I heard a poor untrained clothes-cobbling sister and her daughter sing the "Gloria in Excelsis" as I never heard Trinity or the Tremont Street choir approach; so simple, so full of soul, so grand, so upswelling. They bring forth new songs day by day. Once visiting their house (the husband is a preacher), they sang me Juan Bron. I was surprised to find my old friend John Brown in this new shape. How it rung, especially the chorus, closing with "Al Cristo alevad!" (praise to Christ). They had set it to the praise of the Creator, Christ; for it is as easy for them to make poetry as it is to make tunes. Their gifts of improvisation are Italian. Our frequently no browner brother of the South is their only equal in this respect, but he has not that operatic quality, that delicate tone, which belongs to this people.

Then the climate helps the gift. It is just the air for song. It is never too hot nor too cold in the evening, the time for music. Every night they can revel in this relief. Their burdened bodies and souls can rise on these wings of song to a realm of rest and joy. But this band must not beguile us from our purpose. The rather let them accompany us on our story of the journey, making its rough places smooth with their melody.

It is a good trait of this staging that it begins in the fresh of the morning. You get a good start of the sun, and the hot centre of the day is given to breakfast and to rest. So I am up at a little after three, take two cups of delicious coffee and milk, and a single roll, and go in the strength of that beverage and bread till midday. One cup is the usual allowance, but, being tired, I treat myself to a second cup of hot milk with a suspicion of coffee therein. It is also odd that one feels little desire for more food or ere the ordinary hour for dinner arrives—so easily we can get accustomed to our condition.

Rain had fallen in the night, and clouds, as the morning broke, appeared, hugging the bases of the hills. They almost swept down on us with their wet wings. Had they been in action they would have done so. Low to us, they were high in the heavens, being two miles above Vera Cruz or London, a high point for raining clouds to hang.

They do not hide the landscape, which lies wide, and level, and rich, and cultivated, a grand plain, like so many of Mexico. Soldiers pass us, dressed in the white costume of the country; artillery-men follow, five cannon, drawn each by ten mules, and their attendant caissons; cavalry and commandery—quite a detachment of an army. Their faces and shoulders are wrapped in their bright zerapes, not so soldier-like as comfortable. Following them are a score and more of heavily laden wagons, each drawn by a like number of mules, and each having a goodly company of men, women, and babies on the top of the baggage, one woman sitting on the beam (I know not its farmer name) that passes from the wagon to the oxen's yoke, as I have seen many a farmer at home ride, but never before, his spouse.

MEXICAN MULETEER.

Following these are the other mule wagons of ordinary luggage, a baggage-wagon like that of the States, except that this is half as long and well-nigh twice as high. Perched up on tall wheels, and its maguey-cloth roof, covering wide flaunting bows, it seems a monstrous affair, till you get close to it, when you find all this enormous height and swell is only two wheels long—half the length you anticipated, and that its pretensions required. It is a little giant, and is not unlike many another swell who begins his career much bigger than he ends.

This multitude of teams shows the readiness of this country for the railroad, as the level land shows its fitness. There is no doubt that a road, well and wisely made, will be a paying investment from the start.

The city of San Felipe is our first stopping-place. It is a largish town of five thousand inhabitants, dirty and adobe in most of its streets and houses, gayly got up, with colored washes and fancy figurings in its plaza and neighborhood. The time for changing horses allows me to visit the church. It is about eight in the morning, and fifty to seventy-five persons are at worship, while a priest is delivering the consecrated wafer to an altar full of coming and going recipients. At the corner near the entrance is a painting on the walls of the church, with the face of a woman, but habited as a pope, with the triple crown on her head, and two angel boys offering her an open book, on which is written in Latin, "The Word was made flesh." Her right hand is waving authority to lightnings that are diving at the heads of four apostates, who are disappearing under their forked fires, while over them is written, "*Qui ecclesiam non audierint, sit tibi Sicut Ethnicus et Publicanus*"—Matt. xviii., 17 (Whoever will not hear the church, let him be unto thee as a heathen man and a publican). Now who do you suppose that verse and these lightnings were hurled at by that female pope of a church? Arreo, Voltaire, Rousseau, and Lutero. The last was the lowest, as if the quickest to sink into hell. That painting was fresh, and put up by some priest who scented what was in the air, and is getting the people ready to resist its coming. But Luther will be erased yet from those walls, and the triple crown from the head of the church; and those poor sisters, that are only allowed half the sacrament, shall enjoy the whole supper of the Lord in company with the disciples of this Lutero.

The road soon enters a divide, which is rough, though not high nor long. An attempt is made to have a smooth and handsome road, and this succeeds for a few rods, and shows what might be everywhere, were a little constant care kept up. It soon gets tired of being good, like a spoiled and wayward child, and cuts up badly, as such a child is apt to do after its fit of momentary excellence. It goes round the spurs of hills staggering fearfully, and makes us, who are two only, stagger as bad as the road and worse. There are two ways to arrange for traveling safely over rough regions: one is to make the road good, the other to make the coach strong. They prefer the latter course here, or rather the diligence company do that for the preservation of their custom and coaches. So you have no fears, how much soever you are knocked about, that the coach will be knocked to pieces. It is made to stand, and it will stand. Never a lesion have I seen in these hundreds of leagues of travel, and over intolerable ways. They tumble into holes, whirl and toss and heave among loose boulders, or rocks *in situ*, down hill and up, trembling sometimes like a ship struck by mighty waves, but never springing a leak, or shivering a timber, or loosening a brace. They reel out of the rocky gulfs, and are off on a gallop in an instant, if road permits.

These low but tortuous and tossing hill-sides open shortly on another valley more attractive to the eye than the one just left, in that this is full of foliage. As far as the eye can see, it is one mass of feathery green. But all is not gold that glitters, or silver, even in Mexico, and this fascinating woodland turns out to be cheap mesquite and cheaper nopal, or cactus, that are growing wild. It is an uncleared forest. Still, an uncleared forest is a novelty here as well as in most of the United States, and will soon be in all parts of both countries; so I like it perhaps none the less.

The mesquite is not unlike the Peru, and both resemble in some sort our willow, except that these grow everywhere, the dryest places suiting the Peru just as well as the moistest. It spreads like the apple and peach, though lighter of trunk than the former, and not so loose in the lay of its limbs as the latter. It bears a pod, which is sought as an esculent. These woods are encompassed with high bare hills, those on the left hand being not over a league from the roadway. They are of the type that lay behind La Camada, a gray and silver frame to that fair picture. The hills may not all be full of silver, but they all suggest it. They are all of the same blood as the silver mountains proper, and put on airs as become the kin of so rich a house. They are basaltic almost in their castellated forms, and look rather like a column of giant "graybacks" opening their serried ranks to let this column of green, and perhaps this coach and company also, march through.

Our change of mules is made in the heart of this forest. The turtle-dove (*palumbra triste*, they call it here) fills the air with his melancholy wail, a single note of the whip-poor-will's strain. Women are frying and men eating tortillas under a cactus by the wayside; the vista opens deep into the green forest, and every thing is quiet, soft, salubrious. One could almost make himself into a Robin Hood, and live his life in this secluded richness. How wonderfully human nature adapts itself to its condition! We go from mountain to sea, from cell to city, with a zest for each that seems insatiate. But only one offers its attractions at a time. We can not at once sail the sea and climb the mountain, unless it be a mountain wave. We are like the lad who wished every season might last forever, and was met with a record of his contradictory wishes at the end of the year.

They are not contradictory; for we are so fortunately as well as wonderfully made, that we like truly and with all our heart the conditions in which we are placed. Thus the Creator fits the clothing of the world to the shape of the soul. Whatever be that wardrobe, it seems a part of the spiritual being whom it incloses, and every place affords a sympathy with every fibre of that being.

> "Where it goeth all things are,
> And it goeth everywhere."

The two haciendas are called San Bartoleo and Goral. They are practically one. From six to eight thousand persons live on these vast estates; from four to five hundred men are employed in their cultivation. They and their families absorb the chief of the population. The rest, as in all the *pueblos*, or towns, find their little livelihood as they can, carrying burdens, driving mules, here a very little, and there still less.

The grand house at the hacienda of Goral is elaborate enough for a castle or a convent, the two biggest things in this country. Its high front wall is set off with square pink blocks of water-color, and it looks big enough for the entertainment of Queen Elizabeth and her retinue. The contrast between this palace and the clay-colored adobe huts about it is painful, though it is universal outside of the United States, but nowhere else more violent and extreme than here.

The fields lie wide and magnificent before it; but the fields are not for the tillers. For a real a day or thereabouts they work and starve; for nothing a day this gentleman idles and abounds. I think some of the most scared anti-agrarians would be almost as fanatical and wise as Wendell Philips, the wisest man as well as the most eloquent of his generation, could they but look on these Mexican pictures. How much better are the huge manufacturing corporations, and railroad monopolies, and land-grabbers of the United States? Take heed in time, and let Christianity have its perfect work, or antichristianity will have its.

Curious grain vaults are on its plaza, pyramids or cones built of mortar, thirty feet high, for the storing of the harvests. The reason for this shape I did not learn. They give a quaint air to the plaza. A school and two churches and a half-dozen begging old women help break up the monotony of scenery and silence of this grand farm-house. The lordly owner ought at least to take care of his own paupers, and not allow them to prey on the traveler.

The wild wood, after leaving this posta, soon gets inclosed in a wall on the right hand, too high for us in the coach to see whether it be still a forest, or has become a fruitful field. It is a part of two haciendas in name, and one in fact, that stretch all this posta and beyond, from four to five leagues, from ten to twelve miles. The wall is admirably built of stone well capped, or of adobe brick, its only fault being that it is too high for our heads. Glimpses occasionally show much culture, and a ride on the stage-top afterward exhibits a wide range of rich fields. All of it could be subdued easily. It only wants water. And that is obtained by the simple digging of wells. You can see them all over this land. They are usually of the old-fashioned Yankee sort, a pole balanced on a cross-bar, with a stone at one end and a bucket at the other. The drawers of water stand two and two, either side by side or front to front, so that they can stimulate each other in their work. Sometimes they arise to the aristocracy of a horse turning over a wheel around which buckets are fastened that catch the water below, and dip it up, and turn it into troughs and tanks. This for surface wells. Deep ones have still a different way of being operated. A large cowskin bucket hangs by a pulley over the well. The rope passes over this pulley and is passed round a big wheel, or barrel, six feet in diameter, a hundred feet away. The horse pulls the rope around this wheel and so hoists the water to the trough.

Still other modes are used, but the chief is the old beam and the double man-power. We can save all drought in the States by these and more simple and cheap appliances. The long dry seasons to which we are not unfrequently doomed can be remedied by these preparations. It is far better for the farmer to be thus busy than to sit and see his crops perish of thirst. They will not cost much to get ready, if they are not used, and will repay all their expense in a single year of drought.

The hacienda continues for two or three miles, blasted outside its walls, luxuriant within. It closes with a handsomely constructed corral, into which a company of horsemen are driving a herd of cattle. One of the younger fry, not having learned the futility of all attempts to escape, breaks away from the herd and scampers adown the field. Instantly three of the horsemen race after it. It is an unequal contest from the start. The little black "beastie" shows pluck. But they are too much for him, those three men and three horses. Forty feet off out flew the lasso, and caught him just where it aimed, around the horns. They can grip anywhere, it is said—hoof, ear, horn. An enthusiastic laudator of their skill, who said they could fasten their lasso where they wished, was asked if they could catch hold the tip of the tail. He has not answered yet. The heifer casts itself on the ground; but it is no use. Its fight is fought, and it has lost. It surrenders, and trots submissively into the corral.

The country still holds its wildness, whiteness, and greenness. For a dozen miles the road winds in and out among the mesquite-trees, a good pathway and exceedingly romantic. It enters then the pretty town of San Francisco.

No village so ornate in water-color frescoes have I seen in Mexico as this bit of a city. Irapuato is its only rival, and that is not so daintily touched up. The hand of a master is here. Look at that drinking-saloon on the south-west corner of the plaza. Never was an inner fresco of a Parisian parlor more beautiful. The straw-tinted wall is bordered at top and bottom with mode colors, representing cornices and pediments of variegated marble, rich and strong and delicate. La Plaza it is called: it deserves a better business. All round the square this passion rages. It has caught the church, which rejoices in its blue and white dress. All are more pronounced than the La Plaza, which has touched perfection's height in this cheap and pretty adornment. A statue in the square is an additional proof of the taste of the inhabitants.

Jesus Maria is the next dirty village, a good name for a Nazareth of a town.

Arroyas, the changing-place for the mules, has two or three huts, one of which without chimney was full of smoke of a tortilla-frying fire. At the other were a half-dozen ancient oranges, of which the lady sent me one by her little six-year-old boy, and which I as generously gave to the mozo, sending her back my card for lack of a more valuable commodity less than two reals, which I thought too much for such a compliment. You will find it, doubtless, on her card-rack when you pass through that station.

Now comes another hard pull over the uncovered rocks. Where the soil is on, the road is good; but where it is off, no attempts are made to replace it, and we stagger along on the bed rock which the one or two feet of loam has left in some summer shower for parts unknown. The hills lose none of their grandeur. In fact, they increase therein. Nowhere in the country have I seen a more magnificent colonnade than accompanied us, on our left, this last ten miles. It was close at hand, and we could see far into the depths of these cavernous cliffs. Here are truncated cones, with their craters lying open half-way down their sides, a hollow to which sun and cloud-shadow give yet greater effect. Other portions of the vast façades are rent in twain from the top to the bottom. Chasms, hundreds of feet deep and wide, wind inward, and present, from this distance, rare effects. What would not nearer views afford?

The road rocks its way along on the level earth at the foot of this cliff range, and begins to slightly ascend a more ridgy but not more rough path, and suddenly the Valley of San Luis Potosi breaks magnificently on the sight. How exceedingly fortunate is Mexico in the location of her cities! If great rivers elsewhere flow by great towns, as Nature is said to condescend to man, here, for lack of great rivers, she surrounds the chief towns with superb circles of field, lake, wood, and hills—always the last, and one or more of the other three. Mexico has lakes for her chief circlet, a necklace of pearls: Puebla and Queretaro and Leon, fields of greenest green and brownest brown; Guanajuato is bound about with mountains only and closely; and San Luis Potosi with forests, a necklace of emeralds. The woods fill all the hollow for twenty miles by fifty, as seen from this slight eminence. Two villages peep above them, at least their church towers do, all that usually have height or right to arise and shine. La Pila the nearest one is called. The other perches on a shelf beyond the woods and under the hill-sides. To the north, look, and amidst the foliage you see many a steeple and dome, with which the setting sun is playing. The trees hide every thing but those dancing lights on the church tops. Even in the chief cities every thing is lowly but the church. That is every thing. San Luis Potosi is that congregation of flashing minarets, the chief city of Central Mexico. All over the green valley are corresponding points of glittering gray and gold, telling where subordinate churches rule subordinate towns. Clouds that have hugged us close all day lift a little to let us drink in the beauty of the scene. They break clear away from before the face of the sun, and let him smile his parting *pax vobiscum*. It is a picture long to be remembered.

The fields are not all woods as you approach them. Those near us have them scattered over the plowed grounds, as elms stand in the heart of New England pastures, and maples in those of New York and Pennsylvania. The Peru or pepper tree grows to an elm and maple size and beauty in these rich spots, and sets off the fields as well as its statelier sisters. The effects of irrigation are seen in the barren and utterly worthless common, one side of the roadway, and the dark, loamy, fruitful soil on the other. It separates the sheep and the goats. Natures human so near are often as far apart in real condition: all for the want, or the possession, of grace. Not Athabesca's divide alone sends its streamlets to opposite seas and eternities; this dusty roadway is a like division between life and death. Every path of life reveals the same profound, perpetual departure, each from each, forever and forever.

The mules change their slow pull into a gallop, and go, lashed and leaping, through the streets to the plaza of the city. This northernmost of the central cities has but little in it that is attractive to a sight-seer, but much that will draw the heart of the Christian, much over which to grieve, much already over which to rejoice. It was good to meet on the hotel stairs the greeting of Rev. Mr. Thomson, the Presbyterian missionary, located here. He had been here six months, and this was the first opportunity he had had to take a brother by the hand; so our joy was mutual. Saturday was spent in that most delightful of tasks, the reading of the mail. It had followed me from Mexico, and I greeted the far-off faces of home and friends in this unexpected place. How doubly dear all such favors are when thus served up! It is possible that

> "The nightingale, if she should sing by day,
>   When every goose is cackling, would be thought
>   No better a musician than the wren."

But the wren is as sweet as the nightingale when heard in a faraway land, and no nightingale of professional art can equal the melody of the home bird, heard on a foreign shore.

So, also, these ministerial letters are full of refreshment. Why is it that ministers so seldom correspond? There is a world of richness in the mutual unbosoming of their souls. How passionate for Christ are these outgushings! How uplifting these aspirations and dedications! How the world melts, and three thousand miles is a cipher to the burning pulsings of electric souls! Write to your brother in Christ warmly, frankly, naïvely, wholly. The best letters are clerical. "Forty Years' Correspondence with Dr. Alexander" is the only American book of letters worthy to stand with Cowper's and Lamb's.

There is not much to see in San Luis. Its sixty thousand people are as monotonous as six. The cathedral is an improvement on the one in Mexico, in putting its choir behind its altar. It gives breadth and effect to the height and arches. Other churches many it has, some costly, and heavily laden with gilded altars. Chief among these is the church dedicated to Mary at the end of the paseo, or calzarda, a broad tree-lined walk of over a mile. This church has only ascriptions to Mary on its walls. "Madre del Creador," "Madre de la Divina Gracia," "Madre del Salvador," "Madre del Jesu Cristo," and many others. Some of these are on the high road to blasphemy, if they have not reached it. The Mother of the Divine Grace, the Mother of the Creator, are two vast strides in that direction. They are like those on the cathedral of Leon, though these fall short of the suggestive divine assumptions that Leon ascribes to her nature and power.

This city still maintains its bull-fights, and the amphitheatre is preserved, and used every Sunday night, except in Lent. The priest has to be busy then, said a good Mexican Christian, in absolving the bull-fighters. Near this favorite resort is the alameda, dry and treeless, and far inferior in beauty to Queretaro. For so large a city its attractions are exceedingly small.

But that which drew me hither was exceedingly great. Small it is in the estimation of the people, small probably in the opinion of the country at large, but it is by far the greatest thing in the city or the State. Let us go and look at this marvel of San Luis Potosi. You pass up the long and narrow street that goes out from the west side of the plaza, as I locate points of compass. It may be the other way, for all I know. You will see on the side of the house, on the corner of the plaza and this street, many scars, made by bullets and cannon-balls. They are reminiscences of the revolutions which are apt to rage fiercely in this city, and which always centre about the governor's palace, on the plaza close to this corner, at right angles to his house. The fight ran up and down this street, and around that corner. Go down the narrow lane a third of a mile, and you reach the first street crossing it. On the corner of that street was another battle fought, another revolution won, and one that is not to be lost, though it may have to be fought over several times before it is completely achieved. The Christian's battle, like the freeman's,

> "Once begun,
> Descending long from sire to son,
> Though often lost, is surely won."

In that corner building, a few weeks before I was there, a mob attempted to break up Christian worship. Señor Vivera, a live man he is, as his name signifies, has been preaching here for some time; of late under the direction and with the co-operation of the Presbyterians. That Sabbath there was an attempt made to mob him down. A gang, made drunk with pulqui, were pushed into the room by their confederates and leaders. His little daughter, only five years old, began to cry. He told her not to be afraid; that the same God and Saviour would take care of him that took care of the prophets and apostles when mobbed; that he did not fear their wrath. He appealed to them as to his conduct, for they had known him for many years. They filled the room, and insulted him. The police were sent for, and the mob left, but kept up a stoning of the windows. Three thousand were in the streets, full of threatenings and slaughter. He went through the midst of them to the governor's palace for protection, they hurling stones at him all the way. Afterward summoned to the court, he asked the brethren to pray for him, that he might be preserved from danger; and prayer did ascend for him fervently. The prosecution, as he supposed, was caused by the priests, who charged him with abusing them. This he denied, and proved himself innocent.

These riots have increased his congregation, many learning by them, for the first time, that any other church but the Roman existed in the city.

He was holding his meeting a little farther down the same street, his lessor having risen on the rent till he was driven out. He has a pleasant casa, and Sabbath morning a roomful gathered to hear the Word. Rev. Mr. Thomson assisted in the service, and Señor Vivera read a written discourse and prayed. He is a small, well-knit, resolute man, full of faith and zeal, well known and respected in the city, as I found on visiting with him many of the places of business.

He is fond yet of symbols, and has a flag in preparation for his Sunday-school that exhibits both his taste and the skill of these natives. It is of equal longitudinal sections of purple, white, and blue silk. A small cross of *lapis lazuli* tipped with gold tops off the flag-staff. On the white or central section is placed a symbol of the sacraments — a conch-shell, significant of baptism, with a wreath of wheat in gold embroidery and a cluster of grapes for the Lord's Supper. A crimson cross is to be wrought on the purple silk, and twelve silver stars on the blue, for the twelve apostles. This is wrought exquisitely in silk and gold, and surpasses any Sunday-school flag I have ever seen. It illustrates, perhaps, the education of this people, and they may need to be taught the vanity of all symbols. But there is stuff in him, doctrinal and practical, and I think he will be more and more a power in this city.

THE VIRGIN.

It needs him, for it is woefully given to idolatry. The image of the Virgin of the Ranchos, a league out of town, is visited by the image of Joseph, just before the rainy season begins, and he escorts her to town, where she stays as his guest until the rain falls, when she is escorted back again. This procession, it is said, causes the rain. It was worldly-wise to select that time for the visit. But it has failed lately, perhaps because of the presence of the Protestants. There has been scarcely any rain here for two years, despite these visits of the images and their worshipers. This failure may open their eyes to the folly of this idolatry.

We held English service at Mr. Thomson's house in the afternoon, which many Mexicans attended. He re-preached the English sermon over to them in Spanish. It was an exceedingly impressive occasion.

Here is the seed-germ of the new life that is to come to all this people. They are beginning to discern it. A priest said that very afternoon, at a funeral, that the Protestants would succeed, for they cultivated piety. May they cultivate it more and more, here and at home! That is the true trait of the Christian—cultivate piety. These brethren and sisters seem to enjoy religion. I was charmed with their simplicity and

JOSEPH.

heartiness. One, a poor shoe-maker, was dressed in his white cotton pants and overshirt, his whole wardrobe for all days. He repaired my boot, but would take no pay, nor could I force it upon him. He clung to me as a child to its parents. Others are faithfully seeking the light. Students are spending hours in searching the Scriptures. The dawn is breaking. The Sun of Righteousness appears. May His beams soon fall on all this darkened land!

VII.

OUT AT SEA.

Leaving Shore.—A hot Companion.—Parallel Mountains.—Parks and Divides.—Hacienda of Bocas.—Gingerbread Pigs.—A ragged Boy Apollo.—Marriageless Motherhood.—The Widow's Reply.—Sierra Prieto.—Mortevillos.—Reveling in the Halls of Montezuma.—Strife of Beggars.—Dusty Reflections.—Venada.—Chalcos.—The Worship of the dying Wafer.

To launch out from San Luis Potosi is like leaving the Irish shore for America, or Halifax for Europe. You feel that you have got fairly to sea. San Luis is the last of the group of central capitals, lying nearest the north, yet identified in its location and life with the cities lying not far below. Zacatecas, farther to the north, may claim like kindred, but not as close. The five towns of Queretaro, Guanajuato, Leon, Guadilajara, and San Luis Potosi are a sort of central league. To push above the latter, especially on the road to Monterey, is like swinging out into another country. It is four days to Saltillo, with no town of importance intervening; four days of reported peril from robbers and greater peril from the fears of robbers. If a sense of loneliness comes over one when he rounds Cape Clear and steers straight into the harsh Atlantic, even though he is facing, and moving toward, home, so may a like sense affect one as he turns his back on the real Mexico of population, history, and power, and moves northward and homeward from San Luis Potosi. Especially would this loneliness deepen if in his case he were a solitary traveler. It is like crossing the ocean with no fellow-passenger. That abyss is yet more abysmal. One is then apt to feel and to quote the dreary lines:

> "It is not grief that makes me moan;
> It is that I am all alone."

Such might have been my feelings as I entered the coach at four this morning; for although I found another passenger there, I was as far apart from him as Nimrod's leaders found themselves from each other, all of a sudden, on the plains of Shinar. And at the end of a single posta, we separated in body, as we had already been in tongue, and I was actually left in the Selkirk condition. I made a pillow of the coach side till morning, not letting solitude destroy slumber. The road was easy, and the sleep not much broken. At sunrise we change horses at a little cluster of huts, dignified with the stately Spanish name of La Estansuela. It is remarkable, this swell of names over nothing. The land is full of it in many other ways.

Here we commenced climbing the slight ridge that limits on this side the beautiful valley of San Luis. All the ridges so far are slight, but all exist. The divides are of various breadths, from two to five miles, are barren, dry, stony, but with irrigation from the surrounding hills could be turned into blossoming gardens. The cactus grows wild over them, and the maguey, showing the capacity of the soil, and its readiness to yield to suitable culture.

The sun breaks in upon us with a fierce glare, like a lion on his prey. He says, evidently, "You want a companion; I'll be a good deal more of one than you desire." There is anger in his eye, like the blistering risings of the heated term in the North. He is as good as his word. A hotter day I have not seen in Mexico or elsewhere.

The mountains range on either side of the road from three to five leagues distant, and never approach it much nearer. You are sure they will shut you in ahead, they look so near; but a sharper or a nearer view shows a gap perpetually opening, and through that gap you are constantly passing. It is indeed no gap, but the mere line of the uneven parallel. How far it may continue I have yet to learn. It has been with me so far ever since leaving Mexico, and especially uniform this side of Queretaro. In fact, it seems a trait of the land, the side journey of a hundred and fifty miles to Leon being a perpetual path between lofty ranges of hills, from ten to twenty miles apart. These divides open into lower parks, circular or oblong, of various sizes, some embracing a hundred square miles, some sixty, some forty, some ten. These parks are usually cultivated, especially in their lower levels, where they can most easily command the needful irrigation. They are beautiful, as seen from the low ridge that incloses them on the north and south, and when under culture are beautiful on closest inspection. Otherwise their parched and wild condition mars their countenance, on a nearer view.

The first divide north of the San Luis Valley on this road opens upon the hacienda of Bocas, or Mouths, as pretty a spot to the eye as one would wish to see. It is a bit of park, full of trees in full leaf, fields of wheat and barley intensely green, and contrasting wonderfully richly with the surrounding nakedness. The drawing up to this hacienda and halting do not improve its effect. The human aspect is not equal to the earthly. It is the more earthly. Boys and old women and men are busy at this early hour in begging for their daily bread. I invested a cuartillia (three cents) in ginger-snaps, cut into the shape of pigs, a favorite form of that gingerbread here, for which three cents I received eighteen of the gingerbread pigs aforesaid. Having been treated so liberally, I felt inclined to treat others liberally, and so dispensed my swinish favors to the boys and girls scattered around.

One boy was especially attractive; he wore his ragged zerape over his naked shoulders, a feat somebody was laughed at for saying Apollo did; but this brown boy Apollo did it. It was in tatters and small at the start, but he wore it as a king. A like ragged girdle was worn in an equally stately manner. He had his kite ready for flying, and was as perfect a model of boy as ever sat to an Italian artist. How Eastman, who painted the "Barefoot Boy," would have delighted to have this ragged, royal, three-fourths naked little scamp sit for his picture! 'Twas easy to give him a ginger-snap pig. I hoped to see him some day not as romantically clad or subclad, in some Christian school, and possibly pulpit. *Quien sabe!*

A hideous, homely dame was at the fountain, filling her pitcher.

A girl of fifteen was on one side; one of five on the other. I made friends with the mother by the gift of one of my pigs to the little one. I asked her about her husband. She had none. Was he dead? "No." Where was the father of these children? "In Monterey." How many children had she? "These two only." The same father? "Yes." That conversation revealed the Samaritan-woman condition of this people. Very few are married. It is said the fees of the priest are so high as to prevent it. He asks eight dollars a wedding. But as all marriages now are civil, and the price the State asks is not high, I think the charge against the clergy does not explain the real cause of this social degeneracy. It is in the blood. There was no seeming sense of shame in her answers, no modesty, or lack of it. Far prettier and more affecting was the answer of an old beggar-woman, later in the day, to my inquiry, Where is your husband? She pointed to the ground, and said nothing.

It was a strange feeling that I had as I sat thus by the well, and talked with this poor outcast woman, who is without any clear, convincing conscience, and has no hope except that Christ comes and talks with her and such as her through His ministers and Church. "Lift up your eyes," you can hear Him say, "and behold the field; for it is white already to harvest. Pray ye therefore the Lord of the harvest, that he will send forth laborers into His harvest."

This hacienda follows us for ten miles, skirting the mountains on the lower or eastern side, and looking rich exceedingly in orchards and fields. The road runs on the higher levels, burned to ashes with six months' rainlessness, but still growing the mesquite in large numbers, which give a pretty wild-wood, rural character to the road, as it winds in and out among the light-green feathery branches.

The mountains come nearer the road on the west, mountains full of silver, the mozo of the coach says; for I have climbed out of my lonely centre to the seat with the driver. The range is called the Sierra Prieto. At its base is a horrible cluster of huts, only four or five feet high in the ridge-pole, covered with thatch, and barbarous almost to the Ottawa condition of debasement. It swings forth the stately title of Mortevillos, which, if it meant "Deadville," would not be far from the truth. It is a painful answer to all this silver range, this terrible, debased humanity. It is a greater answer to the Church that professes to guide them. A cross over one or two of the huts shows the faith without works which so characterizes the most of the Roman Church in this and every country.

The valley, whose southern edge this ragged rancho fringes, is broad and handsome, but not as seemingly well cultivated as the one preceding; perhaps because the one owner there keeps up a more perfect establishment than the many owners here.

In its centre you see the white towers and domes of a church, and, driving to it, find yourself in the large and fresh-looking village of Montezuma.

In my college days I had heard much of reveling in the halls of the Montezumas. It was the time of the Mexican war, and that was a favorite phrase of that conflict. I had had no good opportunity to indulge in such reveling heretofore. There is only one place where it could even pretend to be in the halls of that emperor— Chapultepec, and that was built long after he died; and Lerdo gave no breakfast there while I was in Mexico, and had he done so I should not have been invited. But here comes, unexpectedly, the real article; for breakfast is to be served up here, and we shall indeed revel in the halls of Montezuma.

Do you wish to know in what the reveling consists? Enter the large square court-yard of the Meson del Refugio (House of Refuge). A door on one of its sides opens into a clean, cool room; the white cover and clean plates look attractive. Our bread is hot tortillas. Truly Montezumaish, for he never saw French rolls, and, curiously enough, this is the first place I have not seen those rolls in all the journey, and only once before in all the country. The cakes are light, warm, and edible, more so than corn-meal fritters in the States.

Next comes rice, also cooked better than in the States, cooked dry, and each kernel by itself, not mashed and moist. It is also spiced with cloves—the first time I ever saw it, and I hope not the last, for it greatly improved the dish.

The meat fell back from this high standard. Steaks, fried in fat and chilli; goats' flesh, in a gravy of chilli, a hot, thick, tomato-colored gravy. To neither of these did I incline. But the frejollis, or beans, were good, and the tea and coffee excellent. So I reveled, quite Spartan-like, in the hall of Montezuma, and all for four reals, or fifty cents. As I took my seat at the table, beggars came and took their stand at the door-way, first an old man, then an old woman. Very decrepit, but very obstinate, was the old lady. She was going to march immediately on the enemy's works; but the old man held her in. So she squatted at the door-way and talked with him, waiting my outgoing. She grabbed my legs with her skinny clutch. I surrendered, and gave her a cuartillia, on condition she would give the old man half. This she promised, but I fear failed to keep her word, for he came to me afterward and said she had not given him his share. He was not the first victim of misplaced confidence, especially of man in woman. How can beggars be charitable? Perhaps, however, she gave him his share, and he pretended she had not in order to get a duplicate from me. Who can trust who here?

There is a fine stone monument in the plaza to Montezuma, and some of the buildings are pretty. The fields about are green, and in the cool of the day there are a good many worse places than Montezuma.

I leave these beggars, who look old enough to be the very contemporaries of the unfortunate ruler, and get inside the coach, having all the three seats to myself. I stretch upon them all, and sleep as soundly as if on a bed, more soundly than on my too fully occupied bed last night at the San Luis Hotel. As I rolled softly along, I felt the superiority of this sort of travel over the tossing and sea-sick steamer, and was adapting Saxe to the occasion:

> "Bless us, this is pleasant,
> Riding in the stage."

Even when the dust and heat grew dense and potent, I found relief in that sublime line of Cowper, and changed this cloud into that grand vision:

> "For He whose cars the winds are, and the clouds
> The dust that waits upon His sultry march
> When sin hath moved Him, and His wrath is hot,
> Shall visit earth with mercy; shall descend
> Propitious in His chariot paved with love;
> And what His storms have blasted and defaced
> For man's revolt, shall with a smile repair."

May He descend in mercy soon upon this long-suffering people.

The same parks and hills and divides accompany us into the next cultured hollow, which incloses the flourishing town of Venada. Thence our last posta brings us to Chalcos, a mineral town of fifteen thousand inhabitants. Into its large square, centred with a fountain, we gallop, before five o'clock, and finish our first day at sea. How glad the sea-sick people on the Atlantic would be if they could get off, and get into unshaking beds every twelve hours. This gives even the stage a vast superiority over the ship. Twelve hours' run, twelve rest, carry us without great weariness forward to our port.

This is a flourishing silver mining town of small size. Yet a million of dollars a year are taken out of its mines. Four haciendas reduce the ore. The mines are owned by French gentlemen. Several pretty plazas adorn the town, which romantically lies on the slope of not steep hills.

As I was walking through the street just at dark with a native who was showing me the place, I saw the people kneeling, and heard the bell toll. Asking my man the meaning, "El Viatico," he replies—the Holy Wafer borne to the dying bed. The priest came, with a black umbrella over his head; boys with candles on either side, and a few persons walking with him. He held the wafer in his hand. Down went my guide upon his knees. After he had passed, I asked who it was that was dying. "Un grand hombre" (an old man). "Sick long?" "Only fifteen days." "Of what?" "Fever." So a poor soul is going to his account to-night in this town. How many elsewhere the wide earth over! Our first day may be our last. "Be ye also ready; for in such an hour as ye think not the Son of Man cometh." This was the first sight of the procession of the Holy Wafer I had seen. It would not have been allowed in the larger cities. Nor could I have witnessed it without kneeling myself a few years ago, except at the cost of my life.

The hot day has grown cool, a fresh breeze blows from the hills, and a good rest will prepare for our second day at sea.

VIII.

MID-OCEAN.

The "Rolling Forties."—Ceral Hard-tack.—Not so Hard.—Mexican Birds.—Smoking-girls.—Laguna Seca.—La Punta.—First Breakfast in an Adobe.—Hacienda of Precita.—The Spanish Bayonet.—Mattejuala.—Birnam Wood marching on Dunsinane.—The first and last Mosquito of Mexico.—Yankee Singing.—Worse threatened.

THE point in a journey where you strike the dead neutral centre between the coming and the going is almost always one of intense disagreeableness. Such the ocean wanderer finds the "rolling forties," in "the dead waste and middle of" that tiresome ferriage. I am in the like condition now. I doubt if many would take this trip could they see this room before they start; nor would many cross the ocean if they were treated to a foretaste of that ridge where the waves roll east and west, and the spirits sink like lead in the mighty waters.

The room is in the Casa Diligencias Generales, in the town of Ceral, which contains three thousand human inhabitants. Of course, being the stage-house, it is the best in the place; and it is the best room in the house; since I, being the only passenger, have my pick. Look at it. First look at that muddy water, a tumbler of which that dirty boy has just brought in. A Mississippi boatman could not taste it. It is worse than the Thames after Hood's "Bridge of Sighs" had spanned it.

"Drink of it, lave in it then, if you can."

It stands on a dressing-table that saw paint in spots a century ago, and has hardly seen soap since. Adjoining it is a like white-and-gray wash-stand, its legs inclining inward from the decrepitude of age. In the centre is a round table, on which this is being written, that is not quite so venerable. The red of its varnish still largely covers it, but it makes up in dust for what it lacks in years. A single chair is present, alike venerable, too venerable to be in service, like a worn-out preacher not well supported with Conference gifts. One fears all the time that it will break down in its present occupancy, as one fears a like breakdown in a like superannuate if he is put to work belonging to his prime. A like dilapidated bedstead stands in each of three of the corners of the room. All together do not seem strong enough to uphold their probable present occupants, let alone two hundred pounds more.

The floor is of cement, like a good cellar bottom, well covered with dust. The paper is torn off half up the walls, and is badly rent in the ceiling, which is of the same unsubstantial stuff, as is not unfrequently the case in this country. A door opening into another apartment has three of its six window-panes knocked out. Truly one might well sigh for some other lodge in this vast wilderness.

Yet every cloud has its silver lining. The "rolling forties" at least roll well. What are the good points about this *cuarti?* First, it is roomy—fifty feet at least long, and twenty wide. It will make a good chapel for us one of these days. Then it has a fine picture of the Virgin—of course it could hardly be of any body else here—a picture that an artist made, her sweet looks raised heavenward, a dove in one hand resting over her heart, an exquisite bouquet in the other lifted to the skies. I should like to carry it off, both for its beauty and for its lack of fitness to these disagreeable surroundings. Then it opens on a sunny court surrounded with flower-pots, but not many flowers, though roses and geraniums give it a home-like look, and feeble agave varieties show that we are in the tropics, but getting out of them. Birds line the walls, singing merrily their vespers. The chico is the favorite in number, if not in melody. This is not so very small as its name signifies. Perhaps cage-life has made it greater in size as well as song. It is gray and white, not unlike our ground chip-bird, though larger and prettier. The burrion is small, canary-like in size, dark-striped, with yellow streaked slightly in. Here is a blue canary, the first I ever saw—*canaril azul* the hostess calls it. It is as handsome as its yellow kindred, and, for a novelty, prettier. The cardinal bird concludes the circuit, radiant of plumage and crested with scarlet, a haughty representative of his name. So birds and flowers are some consolation, and may even incline us to apologize for the dust, for which the mistress is perhaps no more to blame than is Cincinnati for its coal grime, or Boston for its east winds, or New York for its mosquitoes. For the plains are dry, and the winds high.

Another good point about this place is its situation. Seldom has a better or bigger town an equal location. The mountains come close to it on the west. Superb black sierras they look, after this sunset hour, superb golden purple just before. They are, however, inwardly neither black nor golden, but full of silver. The one nearest, and that rises solitary and splendid out of a vast plain, is the Sierra Catorce, and it is said has yielded a million of dollars in two months. These mountains are offset by the plain which they limit close on this side, but lie low in the eastern horizon, being there thirty miles away.

Last and best, this has the good point that it is nearer home than any previous casa. The mid-ocean is agreeable, if for no other reason, because it is *mid*-ocean. So in this feature of our dismal house we rejoice, and will rejoice. When the lad said we started away at three, I said "Good ;" if he said "at twelve," I should have said, "better ;" if "now," "best." Let us while away the interregnum with recording the log of the day. It will make the night less tedious.

We left the town of Chalcos at our usual hour of four, four of us this time, for a rarity, being in the coach. At six we concluded our sleep, and looked each other in the face. My fellow-travelers were two young ladies, of seventeen to twenty, and their little Cinderella, a maid of twelve. They were going to Mattejuala, three postas off. The youngest of the two smoked several cigarettes before the day had fairly begun. She was a bright, laughing girl, who was only following, as they say here, *la costumbre de la pais* (the custom of the country). How is it worse for girls than boys? Men and women drink together. They can as properly indulge in this vice. Not far from sunrise we pass the beautiful hacienda of Laguna Seca (Dry Lake). It relieves the uncultured dreariness of the landscape with its finish and fineness of luxuriant green. The gate towers of stone are prettily capped and pointed in colored mortars. Its large plaza is swept clean. A pretty little pond, faced, walled, and encircled with trees, increases its attractiveness, and even the huts of the laborers are made into cottages. A dozen or more stand end to the street, neatly built and thatched. I was surprised at this, for it was the first attempt I had seen on any hacienda to make the home of the work-people attractive. It soon dies away; for only a few rods off is a cluster of as mean huts as any in the worst spots on the roadside. It would cost too much to fix all the homes of the people that way. These are specimens of what might be done and will yet be done; for all these dens are to be yet pleasant and comfortable homes.

Leaving this partly perfect spot, we soon get into the thick of the hills. The open pass which I had thought yesterday would accompany us all the way gives out, or we turn away from it. The spurs of the hills hug us, and we wind around and around them for several leagues. The soil is parched, cleft, barren, save of the perpetual cactus and mesquite. We get at last away from these too-close embraces, pass some plowed fields, and large thickets of the mesquite, and change mules at the poor station of Solis, a mere rancho. The scenery broadens, and in a few leagues we scamper through the quite good-sized village of La Vega de Gaudalupe.

A bit of a rancho of two or three huts, called La Punta, is our next stopping-place. It is our breakfasting-place also. It is a new experience to enter an adobe hut for breakfast, but traveling is intended for new experiences. So hunger drives me to the white table-cloth, the clean earth floor, and the bill of fare. A brisk and pleasant lady serves the table, assisted by a not so brisk or pleasant, but much older, man. The tortillas are warm, and the roasted chicken is as good as I have tasted in the country, far better than most I have tried to eat. Milk is wanting; they have not any. I protest and persevere until he brings me two tumblers of delicious milk, for which he wants a real extra, but is content with his half-dollar at the last. I asked her if he was her father. "No," she replied, laughing; "my husband. He is *mas grande*" (much older). They had twelve children. He said he went to church every Sunday with his wife and children to Mattejuala, twenty miles off, which I doubt. If any body wants good milk and good roast chicken at a rancho, let them call on Señor and Señora Tebucio, at La Punta.

The hills fall back from this point (probably called La Punta from that circumstance), and we descend gradually into a handsome plain, almost a circle, from six to ten miles wide. We skirt its eastern side, leaving all the plain to the vast fields of the hacienda of Precita. The hills close it in on every side, except a tiny opening on the north-east. This, as we come near, widens into a pass, called El Puerto del Terquaro (the Pass or Gate of Terquaro). This lets us down gradually, as by terraces and slopes, into the handsome plain of Mattejuala. In this plain the palma, or Spanish bayonet, as they call it in Colorado, assumes pre-eminence over all rivals, both for number and size. It had been coming into note more and more the last score of miles. Here it opens into forests, miles square. It assumes almost the majesty of oaks, and extends an ocean of verdure, refreshing to the eye, though not of especial value to any other sense. A score of miles along its quaint hedgerows and deep green effects brings us to Mattejuala, the largest town between San Luis Potosi and Saltillo. Here our cigaretting girls disembark, and hie round a corner to the broad-leaved gateway of a cool one-story house, where they probably still keep up their chattering and smoking. The town is large and lazy, not having life enough hardly on that lazy day to harness our mules, or even to see it done. They, however, have enough to fly away, and dive into the outer country of palms and mesquite like a mountain torrent. Idler fancies crept over them as soon as they got well out of the last adobe lane of the gray and glowing town, and they fell into a soberer pace. It was another stretch over the same wide, bayoneted plain, which looked as if myriads of soldiers in Lincoln green were standing firmly at their arms over the wide prairie, or as if Birnam Wood was getting ready to march on Dunsinane. It was a superb army, and suggested the prettiest of uniforms for a soldier's gala-day, if not for actual service.

The level drive brought us, ere fall of night, to this dingy dwelling-place of Ceral. I stroll in its dull plaza, and buy poor oranges and poorer bananas. The Hot Lands are leaving us. A mosquito buzzes about my ear, the first I had heard or seen in all the country. He seemed so lonely that it appeared a deed of charity to put him into the ghostly company, innumerable of his kindred, that the hand of man has slain.

An imaginative metaphysician said once, in a sermon "On Compensation," "The little insect you crush between your thumb and finger sails away on silvery wings to a loftier Empyrean;" and an irreverent listener commented, "Every time, then, you kill a mosquito you sting an angel." This was not of so high a faith as the little girl, who soliloquized to a fly, held between her thumb and finger, "Itty fy, you want to see Dod? You s'all see Dod;" and a crunching of her finger and thumb, and grinding of the fly between them, puts her promise, as far as she could do so, into effect. So far has this mosquito murder led us, and him, away from this dismal plaza.

Vespers were being held in a little church, and a melodeon, with a boy player and girl singers, gave this usually formal service a home-familiarity that was so far agreeable. May this attainment lead to higher graces of social worship.

The sun sinks behind the silver hills, changing them to amethyst and gold, and the dreary cell of Ceral is reluctantly re-entered. Dinner is as bad as the chambers; bed and board alike disgust. The meats are cooked horribly, and are of horrid materials. I follow Meg Merrilies's advice, "Gape, sinner, and swallow," and make out to worry a few mouthfuls down. The administrador of the Diligencia Company, to whom I complain of such accommodation and fare, replies, "Wait till you sleep in a rancho to-morrow night." So I anticipate worse horrors on the morrow. Shall I find them?

IX.

NEARING SHORE.

Preparations against a Rancho.—A golden Set.—Bonaventura.—A Rancho: what is it?—Companions.—Aztec or Chinese?—Desolation.—Tropic Thorns and Flowers.—An Oasis.—Hacienda of Solado, and its unexpected Hospitalities.—Freaks of the Spanish Bayonet.—Green velvet Mountains.—The true Protector.

ONE day's sail from land is not thought much of by the seatossed traveler. The stage-tossed may feel equally comforted. Though the stage is to be my companion more days than the one, still this oceanic stretch in its voyaging will come to a prosperous issue, God willing and working, to-morrow at the heat of the day, which is not noon, but three in the afternoon, in this burning sky.

I was warned last night, at my dismal quarters at Ceral, that this night would be far more miserable. So I fortified myself with big gingerbread swine—their ginger-snaps hereabouts take no other shape—with a French roll, a Bologna sausage that has done duty heretofore as a pistol, its tinfoil covering making it look like a shining silvered barrel, and all the more terrible, as it peeped from my breast-pocket, to the non-appearing robbers. So fearful was I that this would protect me, that it was hidden away in my valise, and is now to be agreeably eaten. That is more than turning swords into pruning-hooks, even pistols into meat. For dulces I had oranges, bananas, and pea-nuts. But the pea-nuts are not baked, and the bananas are hard and horrid, so that I have to fall back on the oranges, and sour they are.

The rancho food thus being provided for, the rest of its accompaniments are easily accepted. On a big log, resting on a white artificial mould thrown round a little pond of brackish water, I am looking at the setting sun and writing these rambling notes.

The rancho "has a pleasant seat." All around it tower magnificent mountains not far away, from two to five miles. They completely inclose it, except toward the south, where a green opening shows no end. Like the green sea, it lies on the horizon, only it is still, as that sea is not, and is touched at its sides with the hills of blue. The western ridges, where the sun is just descending, are black already with the shadow of night, the eastern glow richly in his rays. In blessings over the sleeping scene, a high and solitary peak just across this pond lifts its white castellated front like a venerable, bearded priest, and therefore not a Romanist, who is beardless as well as crownless. Off in that southern green ocean is a green cone, as perfect as a rounded pyramid—a Teneriffe covered with eternal spring.

To the north the hills, more distant, shine the brightest in the vanishing hues, while the sky above and along the northern side, and far around to the eastward, is still aflame. The valley itself thus superbly inclosed is a sea of green, all its white, bare, barren, disagreeable features being lost in this dying hour of the day, as all the bare, barren, disagreeable features of a life so often fade and disappear in its setting. As we drove up here, weary with the hot and long and dusty ride, and saw this white embankment and the white adobe of the rancho shining in the sun, with a half dozen tall green willows standing guard over them, I was glad to welcome it as my home for the night, and to bless its name, Bonaventura (good coming), as prophetic of this advent. And now, as this lovely flush overspreads all the heavens, like a bloom and a smile on the cheek of the dying beloved—I have seen such, have not you? —I feel yet more like blessing the good angel that has brought me thus far happily over the burning and the brilliant, yet dangerous land. How that rose deepens, and rims the north with fire! Where did you, where could you ever see a grander setting? How vastly ahead of the tumultuous and fatal sea! Ah! you say, your land is tumultuous and fatal also. Those brown fellows, do they not weigh you in their balance for so much gold? You are pistolless, and they know it. Perhaps they know too that you are a Methodist parson, and therefore their legitimate, nay, commanded, prey. "When you say peace and safety, then sudden destruction cometh." Well, it may be so, and so may it be on shipboard; but it may not also. They have treated me splendidly so far. I will believe and hope unto the end.

The scarlet is becoming crimson, and its darker edges purple, the sure sign of approaching dissolution.

The hundred horses that have just been up here drinking, and then out in the chaparral for a nip at the new grass, are wandering back to their corral, an inclosure of upstanding logs. We shall have to leave our log and outlook, the big willow standing in water just at my feet, the green landscape fast turning gray, and the solemn, affectionate, parental hills, not so solemn as that they are not happy-looking also, as all properly solemn persons are, and hie us to the inside of our rancho.

You have heard much about ranchos. Let me describe this one. It is a very small pueblo, or a tiny corner town, like the larger towns, except there is in it no Casa Grande, no brick or mortar dwellings, only adobe. But our rancho, like a new Western town, aspires to a future, and is laid out with more care than most of such villages. It has a square, or plaza, on this small prairie, three sides already surrounded with the huts that may give way sometime to houses of grander make and material. But here the law of the larger houses prevails. As a log-cabin is a Fifth Avenue house in its germ, so a true rancho is a Spanish castle or Mexican casa grande in its beginning. First logs, then wood, then marble; first mud, then mortar, then marble. This rancho is exactly after the type of Barron's and Escandron's great houses in Mexico; a common gate-way for horses, carriages, men, and dogs; in this case, pigs are added, a luxury not allowed in the city. A door opens to rooms on either side of the gate-way, porter's there, owner's here; then comes a large square court, with rooms opening into it. The rear side of this court is a stable, and another court behind the first admits you to the rest of the stables. The room where I write opens into the court on the left. After passing the porter's room into the court, turn to the left, first door; enter. There I sit at a table, with a tallow-dip upon it. Three single cots are in the room, and all occupied to-night; floor of hard earth, every thing comfortable. It is no worse, though less pretentious, than the hotel at Ceral. It is not so disagreeable. My fellow room-mates are a Mexican gentleman, and a German youth of nineteen, who left home to escape the draft, and is to make his residence in Durango. He took the precaution to arrange at Brownsville to become an American citizen at twenty-one. So Bismarck and Moltke have lost him for their battle of Dorking. The Germans do not like to "train" any more than the Americans or English; "'tis not their trade." They will have to abandon that purpose, and trust, as do their kin, to patriotism to defend what patriotism, more than military training, won.

This bright boy is afflicted, as most boys and men are here, with a tendency toward Cognac, and yet complains of the very ailments Cognac pre-eminently induces. When will the good cause of total abstinence preserve youth and men from this dire curse?

Let us run over the log of the day. Out and off at four, in a magnificent starlight, as clear and lustrous as a Northern coldest winter's night, and as warm as a Northern summer's. It chills a little in the riding, and a bonfire of corn-stalks at the first posta is not disagreeable. A peon has kindled the fire, and stands over it in his white cotton trowsers and shirt, with his zerape round his shoulders, his feet bare save of sandals and thongs. He is on a walk from Mattejuala, to work on a road for three reals (thirty-seven and a half cents) a day. Think of that, ye who are giving Irishmen three dollars, and sending to China for substitutes. Here are millions of industrious and ingenious gentlemen—I use that word in both senses—whom you can get for a dollar, and they will think themselves wealthy. Let our Samsons find China at their doors.

The apple and quince trees hang full of blossoms, in a garden attached to this rancho, and other flowers and growing grains give proof that the air here, if chill, is never cold.

A long, long posta of fourteen leagues (thirty-six miles) follows, over a wide plain, with scarce the sign of habitation. Five leagues out we meet a private coach and gentleman, the coach covered with cloth, a common usage here, to preserve it handsome for the city paseo; for this coach contains a Congressman, who is on his way to the city, and the session. Not another sign of life, save in bush and tree, and not much in them, till the twelfth league is reached. Some horses grazing in the bushes look wistfully at us, envying, doubtless, their brothers in the coach, as boys, with all their liberty, envy the burdened man, harnessed and dragging his weary load up hill and down hill till he drops it, or drops under it, dead. A rag on two high bushes marks a house for an Indian family, and relieves the monotony of desolation. The sun has risen with a burning heat. Yesterday we shivered in a shawl till near noon; to-day we swelter in the shade, and solicit and enjoy the breeze that blows through the coach, albeit much dust gets mixed up with it.

The vast prairies are thinly covered with shrubs of mesquite, and even the Spanish bayonet gives out, and dwindles to meagre proportions. A red-headed cactus, big-headed too, glows by the roadside, sharp, but not unlovely. This is the beginning of the chaparral region, whereof we heard so much in the days of General Taylor, and which Lowell so humorously sets forth in his "Bird of Freedom Sawin'." It is hard-looking stuff to march through, being short, and as sharp as a virago's temper.

How is it that these tropic plants are so apt to be prickly? Almost every bush and tree you meet from here to Mexico is of this repellent type. Is it that heat in the blood of nature is like heat in the blood of human nature, and produces the *noli-me-tangere* state of the Scotch thistle and Scotch terrier? These palms, this mesquite, the cactus, all are thorny, cross, and "let me alone."

"He talked about delishis froots, but then it was a wopper all,
The holl ont's mud and prickly-pear, with here an' there a chapperal."

Every reader of these pages has undoubtedly heard of oases in the desert. You did not hear of much else in the way of figures, if your juvenile composition life was passed where mine was. It was a cheap and favorite illustration of sentimental youth, who called every "goody" their mothers sent them, every holiday their teachers gave them, every love-sick emotion a fair face bred in them, oases in the desert of their lives.

Well, what they fancied I experienced in reality. I had tried every way to get over the long, lazy stretch of thirty-six hot and pulverized miles of dismal monotony. We drove past a line of wagons, four yoke of oxen to each, and the wagon itself, about two feet wide and six feet high, with palm-leaf matting sides and a peaked roof like a house, covered also with matting, the most curious wagon in the country so far. The wheels were bigger than the house upon them, and the eight oxen seemed intended to drag the wheels.

The wind blew the way we were going, and so we added their dust to our own, a proof that we do not always get out of other folks' dust by getting ahead of them. In fact, we not unfrequently get into it the more; for they blow after you that which they can not leave after for you.

After this weary eating of our own dust for so hot and long a spell, and even of that of those whom we had passed in the slow race, we came in sight of a stately hacienda. Its white walls glistened like a fortress. Its silver reduction chimneys towered, cannon-like, above its gates. Its broad, clean plaza, very broad and very clean, received us. The driver stopped in its centre, regardless of the hotel door, where he usually pulled up. I ask where breakfast is to be got. "Anywhere," he says, tossing his head quite indifferently. I push round to a gate-way, and ask a servant the same question. He points to a closed room. In it I see through the window a man writing. Not much sign of a breakfast there. I push my inquiries farther with like cold courtesy. At last, bewildered, I express my indignation at their neglect. A young man in a wide gray sombrero, pistol at side, white-appareled, says in good English, "You wish for a breakfast, sir?" "Yes, sir," is the reply;

"I am glad to find one man who can speak a Christian language." "Go in there, sir, and I will meet you soon." The servants are immediately and uncommonly attentive. I enter the court set forth with flowers and birds, peacock, clarine, and others of gay apparel, enter the cool dining-room, vacant, and take a seat at the first place, which happened to be the head of the table. Soon the courtly youth entered and sat down to eat. Three others did, and I found, instead of being at a hotel table, I was a guest of a gentleman, and occupying his seat. "So foolish was I and ignorant, I was as a beast before" him. I bethought myself of him who with shame had to take a lower seat.

But the young gentleman did not object, and so the seat was kept. I found he was educated near Alexandria, could talk English well, was full of interest in the railroad question, as every body seems to be here. This hacienda was his uncle's, whom I had met seven leagues back, on his way to Congress. It was a cattle-raising farm, had on it now about five thousand cattle and forty thousand sheep and goats. It contained thirty square leagues, over seventy square miles, had on it silver and gold mines, but little worked, though the English ex-consul of Mexico had lately organized a company for their development. The thick silver spoons of the table were from the mine; an eighth of an inch the spoon was across its edge. Had I not had the fear of the unjust fame of my once military commander before my eyes, I would have begged or bought one of those specimens of the product of this farm.

He said the grazing here was excellent most of the year; dry now on the plains, but sweet in the mountains. The cattle were worth ten dollars a head at the hacienda. They kept three hundred men employed, and supported fifteen hundred to two thousand people.

He gave me an excellent dinner, for which he refused any pay. He was pleased, he said, to see Americans, and to revive his English. It revived very easily. I commend to all passers on this road the hospitalities of Señor Gabriel Bustamante, of the hacienda of Solado.

The Spanish bayonet here comes to the front again, and puts on some of its queerest forms; and nothing can look queerer. Here is one with two legs coming together in its spiked head, like a boy's picture of a scared man, with his hair erect. Another has a single trunk and two arms stuck out, and a bushy head between, another infantile drawing. Two are ogling each other, their crooked backs crowned by projecting barrels of spikes that look like grinning faces; and here are two others, evidently back to back, frowning fiercely out of the same wrathful hair. A row of them, of every size, shape, and position of crookedness, looks like Falstaff's army, with tremendous fierceness in their weak though plumed heads. One was so perfect a statue, that I could not believe it to be any thing but a man till after passing it, and hardly then. Their grotesqueness is inimitable. Hood's queer pictures, and Thackeray's and Nast's and Cruikshank's, are all surpassed by the common doings of this palma. It is the harlequin of Nature, the clown and the court fool of her royal palace here.

The hills seemed to grow greener, and the fields also, perhaps because of the refreshment body and spirit had received, perhaps because I had learned that it was their intention to do so soon. Still they did increase in verdure. The hills especially began to put on velvet. It became them well, but no better than their previous nakedness. They were sculptured so admirably, that one feels as if they were statues, and needed no wardrobe.

> "The sinful painter drapes his goddess warm,
>   Because she still is naked, being dressed;
> The god-like sculptor will not so deform
>   Beauty, which limbs and flesh enough invest."

But that western side, so daintily robed in soft, short green, does not look any the worse for the apparel. Indeed it is an improvement, for it fills up the rough clefts and rounds out the contour to a perfect symmetry. You never saw and never will see out of Mexico such foldings of rock, draperies tight-fitting yet flowing, cavities that are dimples, and swellings that are the rounding out of youthful cheeks and forms. It did not seem possible that rocks could be so lady-like; soft, yet firm;

"So moving delicate, so full of life."

I gazed, and envied the coming circuit-riding brethren over this hacienda. We pass one of its ranchos, clean and comfortable compared with many below, the men gentlemanly and the women lady-like. They came and shook hands with the driver; a chatty mother offering him cold water, and all showing the American training of the young haciendado, and preparing the way for the chapel and the stationed preacher.

This posta of twelve long leagues is pulled across through heavy, dusty, level roads, but also through this munificent landscape of green and silver, and we come where we began, and where, at near the midnight hour, this writing is being finished, in the peaceful rancho of Bonaventura.

One more day and we see the city that concludes this ocean section, and we get to the end, practically, of Mexico. May the robbers keep still aloof, though my German lad sleeping over there says they are plenty and bad above, and tells a story of what they lately did, to put me in bodily fear, shooting a woman, and tying two men to a tree. He is armed, and thinks that is his protection. Shall I get out my tin-foil sausage, or beg a revolver? Nay. I sing my talisman:

"Jesus protects, my fears begone!
  What can the Rock of Ages move?
 Safe in His arms I lay me down,
  His everlasting arms of love!"

X.

INTO PORT.

Sunrise.—Villa de Gomez Firias.—A lost American found.—Flowering Palms.
—An unpleasant Reminder.—A charming Park.—Agua Nueva.—La Encantada.—La Angostura.—Battlemented Mountains.—Buena Vista.—The Battlefield.—The Result.—Why.—Saltillo.—Alameda.—Friends.

The four days' trip across the wilderness ocean is completed. The pleasant harbor is made; the perils by land are at an end. True, four days' staging yet remain, or ere the country is left, and the robbers, if such there be. And as a vessel has been wrecked in sight of its port, and coaches have been robbed within two miles of Mexico, there are plenty of chances yet to experience all that is threatened and feared. But the chief perils are past, and the chief weariness; and it is to be hoped none that follow will exceed those that have gone before. Our night in a rancho was without excitement. "I laid me down in peace and slept. I awaked, for Thou sustained me."

It was not much after midnight when the men sleeping on the ground at the door of our biggin began to bestir themselves; at a little after one we were all up, and at two off, one party of two for the South, one of one for the North. The coach had several rent windows, and let in the cold air full freely. But as the air was not very cold, the shawl sufficed for a protector, and I tossed and slept till morning broke. The same level was before me, shut in by the same hills. The light grew rosy in midheavens, then on the western ridge, and then the blaze boiled and steamed up the east, and all was done.

It was a long pull through the unchanging fields of stunted mesquite and palm, varied by equally stunted castor-oil bean, whose very leaves and tiny yellow flower had a slimy and sickly look. At last a miserable cluster of huts appeared, thirty-five miles from our starting place, and we stopped at the rancho with the ornate title of Villa de Gomez Firias. This was once a favorite resort of the Indians for its water, which is bad enough, and shows how the region round about must suffer. It was a favorite fighting-place also, and there were skulls and bones enough to furnish a half-dozen secret college societies, not only with their hideous symbols, but with a secret greater than any of the boyish ones they profess to possess, even that which these embody and express—the mystery of death.

An attempt was made to get up a breakfast here, but it resulted in a fried egg and frejollis, all the intermediate meats being absent. Nice fresh milk made the place of the absent and the present more than good.

A colored boy, lounging at the half-cent grocery, had wandered hither from Texas. He had got on the Mexican white trowsers, sandals, hat, and language, but his pink shirt and black face he had not changed. He is working here for "two bits" a day, living in a rancho with his master. He said he preferred the dollar a day in Texas, but why he does not go and get it he says not. His name is William Henry Griffin. It was a pleasant sight and sound, this American skin and tongue, even as a variety to the universal brown. He was brought up a Methodist, and I hope may yet help these poor people into that liberty, though I fear he is not a shining example to-day of its achievements, whether of faith or works.

Our wide prairie, extending from Mattejuala, here comes to an end. Hills gather around us, and grant no opening; they must be crossed. The level has been not less than fifty leagues, or one hundred and thirty miles. The hills before us are not high, but they are sufficient to conclude that feature of the itinerary. We ascend a hard, handsome road, and wind into a round valley a thousand or two feet across, and shut in by hills. It is well filled with palm-trees that in this high mountain wall are getting ahead of their prairie kindred outside. They are crowned with white blossoms. It is one of the strange contraries of this country in nature, as in men, that such hideous-looking creatures as cactuses and palms produce such marvelous flowers and delightful fruit. This palm bears this tree of white blossoms on the very top of its head; out of the middle of these green spires, like bayonets, rise the tall white plumes, some of them two feet high, and half as tall as the trunk that supports them. Here, too, these trees are uniformly straight, as if, like country people, they are simple and sturdy when at home, but, brought into city society, grow odd and shoddy. Another slope lets us into another park, longer and wider, but not long nor wide. The driver kindly points to a hole in the side of the hill, goes through the motion of cutting his throat, and says that here the coach was once stopped, three men taken out and robbed, and their throats cut, and they thrown into that hole.

This is a comforting word. I ask him if there are any robbers here now. "Oh no; farther on," is his still comforting reply. "Farther on" I saw three men descending a long slope. The hill looked near, and yet I could not tell whether the men were on foot or on horseback. They drew near, and I saw their horses. "These are the men," I said. Stage stops. They part, and pass on each side of the coach. I am up with the driver. I wait to hear the cry to Zaccheus, "Come down!" They chat with the driver, laugh, and drive on. So goes that fear, like all its fellows. Compadres of the driver, they could not pass without saluting him.

Another harder pull yet, and a more beautiful wild orchard of blossoming palms, and we enter a valley of great beauty, with mighty mountains guarding its eastern side and entrance. These are the loftiest peaks that have appeared on the road since leaving the green hills of Mexico. They rise close to the pass, and leave only a narrow path into the valley. They appear as if placed here on purpose to protect the land from invaders, and to that purpose they were put. For we are now close upon the historic ground of Buena Vista. These southern gates are the rear-guard of the land. The real battle was fought some miles to the front, across this valley, and amidst the ravine which opens out of it at almost right angles. But, undoubtedly, this wall was chosen because of its partial protection and defense, and, had the front been maintained, this would have afforded a strong barrier.

The hacienda of Agua Nueva is located at the upper end of this long valley of La Encantada. It is on a dry and rolling rise of ground, well under the tall hills. Here we change our mules, and start on the last posta across this wide sea, whereon we have been cruising these last four days. This is the most exciting of all; for it passes over from end to end the track of that famous battle which more than all others conquered Mexico, as the people of the United States believed, and showed their faith by their works in making its victor President.

The mule-changing Agua Nueva is as hot a spot as one cares to pause on. Yet some decaying buildings, one of which is especially roomy, give us momentary shelter from the storm of heat, as well as the sight of dirty damsels frying their perpetual tortillas. A bit of a chapel, dirty as any of its worshipers, stood among the huts and the larger semi-ruins of a once valuable hacienda. It was, therefore, especially agreeable to see the mozo harnessing up his eight mules for the pull across a famous field, and to a civilized town. It was like that last day out at sea, when the hills of Neversink are almost in view, and you know that to-morrow morning will see you safe in the dear old port.

The mules whiz out of the dusty and decaying plaza, and rush for the gorge that opens straight on to the Gulf. The sweet valley of Encantada, running in the opposite direction, looks fruitful and green as we glance down it, just before the high rocky walls close us in and close it out, perhaps forever, to these eyes.

These walls are like those at the entrance behind, except that the latter run east and west, and these run north and south. The last is the more usual lay of the hill lands. So that the valley of Buena Vista is simply in the same direction as almost every valley we have passed through since leaving the capital. But the previous valleys have been from five to twenty miles wide; this is hardly two. It is well named La Angostura (The Narrows). Its rock forms are very remarkable, especially those on the left, or toward the west. They rise in huge castellated shapes, not unlike the basaltic columns near Velasquo. The range is five hundred to a thousand feet high, and full of surprises in its angles no less than its striated surface. The opposite side is higher, and more after the usual form of mountains.

Between these ranges is a deep dry river-bed that has cut its crooked way through the valley, and scooped out a path twenty feet below the original level, and present roadway of the valley. This *barranca chico*, as they would call it, or little ravine, is not an unusual sight in the country. The hill-sides west of the capital exhibit some of great depth. But this one differs from any I had previously seen in that it is exclusively and evidently a river-bed, and probably is a river itself in the rainy season.

On the eastern side of the narrow valley there are several moraines, as seemingly artificial as is the river barranca. If the one is scooped out by violent action of the elements, the other is heaped up by like violent action. They are as high as the bed of the river is deep. They extend from near the river's edge to the side of the tall rock-hills. How they were cast up is not evident. There are no glaciers to make them, as in the Alpine moraine. They can not have been tossed up from the bed of the river, for they have no connection with the stream. Riding past them, I could not solve their cause. Perhaps some scholarly soldier, who fought on them and under them, may be acquainted with their origin.

They had a use that day. On their summits were placed the American cannon, which did no little to carry the field. Perhaps it was on one of them that the famous order was given, "A little more grape, Captain Bragg," an order which strengthened the American heart, and so helped gain the day.

The battle was fought on this strange field. Along that dry gulf General Taylor's troops made their perilous pause; on these seemingly manufactured hill tops they planted their guns. There was never a better Thermopylæ than this; only it was the invading troops that took possession of it and held it. Santa Anna made the attack. Had the Persians held Thermopylæ, would the Spartans have forced them? I fear not.

Yet the Mexicans ought to have forced these gates. They could not have been flanked; they should not have been routed. But they were wearied with a long march, and the Americans held the position. Pluck and prowess, and, above all, Providence, overthrew them. "Providence," for God was in this war more than most Northern Americans dreamed, and very differently from what Southern Americans dreamed. It was not to give slavery a stronger hold or to hasten its destruction that our war occurred with Mexico. It was to open that country to the Bible and the true Church. It was to Christianize Mexico, not to free or enslave our land, that this war arose. Its fruit, planted then, has been growing since, daily and hourly, and will grow until this land is free from the curse that has so long and so grievously rested upon it.*

---

* General Lew. Wallace, in a late letter to a reunion of the Mexican veterans, thus describes a late visit to the field of Buena Vista: "I have ridden over the old field three times in the seven years last past, and always with the same feeling of wonder at the audacity of the chief who, with his four thousand five hundred, abided there the shock of the Mexican Napoleon's twenty-two thousand, and of admiration at the pluck and endurance of the few who, turned and broken, crushed on the right and left, and, by every rule of scientific battle, whipped oftener than there were hours of the day, knew it not, but rallied and fought on, the infantry now covering the artillery, the artillery now defending the infantry, the cavalry overwhelmed by legions of lancers, and union of effort nowhere —fought on, and at last wrung victory from the hands of assured defeat.

"The field is but little changed. The road to La Angostura is still the thoroughfare across it; winding along the foot of the hills on its left, and looking down into the fissures and yawning gaps which made the valley to the right so impassable even to skirmishers. I stopped where the famous battery was planted across the road, literally our last hope, and tried to recall the feeling of the moment. On the left all was lost; Clay, M'Kee, Hardin, and Yell were dead; where all were brave, but one regiment was standing fast—the only one which through all the weary hours of the changing struggle had not turned its face from the enemy—I mean the Third Indiana. Against the battery so supported,

BUENA VISTA.

This victory gave General Taylor the command of the whole country we have been traversing the last four days. In fact, it gave him control up to the capital. Had it not been for political fears lest his great success, especially if he added to it the capture of the city, would insure him the Presidency, he would have undoubtedly been ordered to advance. As it was, his troops were taken from him, and transferred to General Scott. Among them was a youth who was lowest on the roster, Lieutenant Grant. General Taylor was left idle, while a new fighting to the same city level had to be bloodily carried up Cerro Gordo and like terrible heights, simply to divide the honors between two generals of the same party, and so prevent the Presidential success of either. The Government squandered millions of dollars and many lives for purely political reasons. Mexico was actually conquered at the battle of Buena Vista. Had it been vigorously followed, a month would have seen Zachary Taylor at Chapultepec.

---

along the narrow pass, surged a chosen column of Mexicans. History tells how they were rolled back. In all the annals of war nothing more gallant on both sides, scarcely any thing more bloody and terrible. From the position of the Third Indiana at that moment, away over the plateau, quite to the mountain, reaches a breastwork not there when our comrades fought, but signalizing an incident in the war of the Mexicans against the French.

"The last time I was on the sacred ground, I saw a 'greaser' working with a hoe on the side of a hill by which we identify the position of the Third Indiana at the turning-point of the battle. My curiosity was excited. I rode to see what he could be doing. A moment ago I said the field was unchanged. I was mistaken. The man was conducting a little stream of water from the mountain miles away to irrigate a wheat-field below, in the mouth of the very ravine down which the regiments of Hardin, Yell, and M'Kee had retreated, seeking the cover of Washington's battery—the very ravine where the blood was thickest on the rocks at the end of the fight. I looked down upon the velvet green of the growing stalks, darker from the precious enrichment the soil had that day received, and then at the stream of water which came creeping after the man, like a living plaything. I looked at them, and understanding the moral of the incident, thanked God for the law that makes war impossible as a lasting condition, however it inspires the loves and memories of comradeship, and teaches that each succeeding generation of freemen are as brave as their ancestors."

The hacienda from which this battle takes its name is north of the field, and some two or three miles away. It is a pretty, peaceful spot, its pinkish-white houses girting its plaza showing that it is well kept up. The fields about it are green with produce for the city of Saltillo, which is six miles still farther northward. A pulverized road, broad and usually level, with only slight rises, winds its way through the valley, which widens here to the usual park-like width, five to eight miles. There is no sight of Saltillo. Looking for it, and hastening after it, as I have been doing now this many days, the end, feelingly, of the long and hazardous journey (for no fears affect one beyond this city), still it hides itself from the eye. Where can it be? The mountains throw themselves out before us as a vast amphitheatre, whose diameter traverses a score of miles. But where can the city be? At our feet? We drive along the same dusty and level plain, and suddenly look down, and lo! Saltillo.

There is a lower level out of which that circle of the mountains swings, a hundred feet at least below the Buena Vista plain. At its upper or southern edge, which is as marked as if cut like a cheese against the higher plateau, crowds this Northern town. A glimpse of it, and the diligence plunges down a very rough and noisy hill, leaps past open houses, whose brown occupants hasten to the doors to see the infrequent and much-welcomed coach, and with whirl and dash and snap of whip flings itself around corners, through courts, and comes up, with its crunch, at the hotel door.

The town is enjoying its siesta; our noise awakens it. It drowsily peeps from veranda and hut upon our disturbing mules and coach, and then folds its hands to sleep. It is the hottest hour of the day, three in the afternoon. How presumptuous for the coachman to rush in upon it so early! He would not have done it but for the promise of an extra peso if he made an extra hour; for I could thereby "do" the town before dark.

It was done, and the cool arcade of a pretty hotel welcomed me. Bath and clean linen, the first I had dared to assume since leaving San Luis Potosi, put me in good outward condition, and so, in a degree, good inward also. A big room opened on a broad shaded patio. Singing birds and birds of rich plumage made it all the more home-like. It seemed more beautiful, perhaps, than it was; for the contrast with ranchos and horrid Ceral and dirty Chalcos and wild half-desert living was as sudden as if it had been a new revelation from Heaven.

Especially was it nearer home. One could almost fancy that he was home; for only one day separated him from Monterey, and that was the next town to Matamoras, and that adjoined the United States. It was so near, it seemed as if the dome of Washington must appear over that farther rise of inclosing mountains. But it took long and wearisome days to bring that dome into view.

The clean skin and clean shirt being secured, the town is subjected to inspection. It is soon done. A half-dozen streets run east and west along the upper edge of the plain; a dozen or two, narrow and dirty, cross them. One-story white and tinted adobe dwellings line these streets. There are no sidewalks. The plaza is without ornament. The cathedral is cheap and frowzy. Every thing is asleep.

There is one beauty—the alameda. This lies at the foot of the street, toward the west; it is the prettiest I had seen in all the country. It is lined all around with a hedge of rose-bushes, then in bloom, perhaps always so; its paths are richly shaded. It lies close to the base of high hills, and a river babbles along its edge, which invades its own borders, with its minor streams of irrigation. Outside, the brook gets up a sort of independent alameda, in an open pasture, where it gallops among apple and olive trees at its own wild will.

I find in this city two gentlemen of my own language. One, then far gone in consumption, has since passed away. He had a strange marriage experience. He had remained unmarried till he had reached the ripe age of thirty-five or forty. His master left him in charge, and went to Europe. A rancho beauty came to town, killing lovely. This sober, sturdy, and mature New Englander fell desperately in love with this wild slip of the pueblos. He married her. She appropriated all the diamonds, silver, and whatever else she could beguile her becrazed husband into bestowing. She finally left with a French gentleman. She was captured, brought back, and cast into jail. Getting released, she went as far as Indiana, got a divorce in that State, and married the lawyer who obtained it. Never a word against the wayward wife fell from the sick man's lips. He loved her still. Many waters could not quench, nor floods drown this flame of, in him, purest and most unselfish affection. She had killed him, but he died without saying a word against the rancho beauty that had captured him whole. We read of broken hearts, and usually they are supposed to be of the feminine gender. Here was one of the opposite sort—a sober, sad, modest gentleman, worn to the grave by love and sorrow.

Another gentleman invited the sick friend and myself to dinner. He was an Irishman, but had lived from a child with Jerry Warriner, the famous caterer in Springfield, Massachusetts, thirty years ago. He came out here, and amassed a competence, if not a fortune. His children are all about him, and he is rejoicing in a green old age. It was a delightful evening that I spent in his cheery parlors, among his pleasant family and over his table, that had flavors in its dishes of the old tavern in Springfield.

The change from the wilderness wanderings was more marked by these additions. It was not only reaching land, but home. May every like traverser of that dreary track find like refreshment at these hospitable quarters.

XI.

MONTEREY.

Songs in the Night.—Open Fields near Saltillo.—Effect of Irrigation.—
"The rosy-fingered Dawn."—Gathering together of the Mountains.—San
Gregario.—A Thousand-feet Fall.—Rinconada.—Wonders of Flowers.—
A Hole through a Mountain.—The Saddle Mountain.—The Mitre.—Santa
Caterina.—A Tin God.—A familiar Color.—St. Peter.—No Bathing after
Midday.—The Smallness of Mexican Heads.—Miss Rankin's Work.—Strife
between Brethren.—Its Benefits.—The two Dogs.—The Eye of the Town.—
Revolutions.

Though near the midnight hour, the birds in the court are singing as gayly as at dawn. Hear that clarine! deep and long and swelling and falling are its notes, with a true operatic touch. How that madcap mocking-bird is caroling! They are making a night of it, truly. The day is too hot for their work, as it is for that of men. But, unlike their bigger and featherless biped kindred, they give songs in the night. Only that watchman's whistle replies to their softer and richer note, and a hallooing somebody, who bellows as if mad or afraid, or both. What is his office? To call a revolution? The air is full of that cry.

The roomy court of this hotel is unusually luxuriant. The arcade inclosing it is spacious; flowers, as fragrant as the birds are brilliant, fill the air with odors. Every thing is for coolness and rest. Rest with the pen is a goodly rest: let us take it.

It was at day-break this morning that the coach rattled out of Saltillo with two sleepy passengers, a German and myself. The face of the country in that warm gray dawn looked changed from all behind it. America had touched it with her wand. The huge, high walls of the haciendas gave way to no fences at all. The land lay utterly open. Not the least impediment to your going everywhere, except such as the irrigating water afforded. It was well watered and very green, running up under the lee of the dark mountains, and spreading out in long levels of fertility. Where this water had not come, the soil lay white and dead, a corpse-like look. Where it came, it was overflowing with life.

The plains are about six miles across and ten miles in length, in sight of the white city at their south-western terminus.

A single rosy ray streamed up from behind the easternmost mountain like a finger, an index of the coming sun. Homer's figure, which Milton appropriates, as he does so much of Homer,

> "The rosy-fingered dawn appears,"

was suggested to my mind by this unusual spectacle. Anon a second broad ray joined its fellow, two fingers uplifted by the coming sun. The rose soon changed to yellow, shone through the openings of the hills, and sent its lustre across the lovely plain and upon the high and gracefully moulded mountains that shut that in. The richer line of Tennyson expressed the glory that followed:

> "The rosy thrones of dawn."

I looked and was glad, for I bethought me, that coming light has already risen on my own land. It is not two hundred miles to the border. This rose and gold must have just illumined that fair clime. I prayed the prayer of Alexander Smith for this magnificent land:

> "Come forth, O Light, from out the breaking East,
> And with thy splendor pierce the heathen dark,
> And morning make on continent and isle,
> That Thou may'st reap the harvest of Thy tears,
> Oh holy One that hung upon the tree!"

The road is hard and smooth. Crosses appear quite frequently, and remind us of that long disease of the land, the violent death of its people, while dead mules and asses alike remind us of the late disease of its horses and their kin.

The mountains gather close to us. The open meadows disappear, and the pass assumes its proper place and shape. Three miles these bases stand apart, perhaps more, perhaps less; for distances are deceptive in this clear air. The walls rise a thousand feet and over, and, being so close to us, they seem five times that height. They are black and herbless in the upper portions, but of soft outline that makes verdure no necessity. So we canter slowly, comforting our still sick mules, to the first posta, San Gregario. Leaving here, we begin to descend rapidly. Soon a point is touched from which you gaze downward at least a thousand feet, and into which bottom you could easily roll—all but the easily— by just stepping to the side of the road and putting yourself into motion at the head of the gulf. Passengers usually walk, going up or down this plunge. Our light load lets us ride. The mountains roll up on either side in mighty convolutions, capping their folds with striated columns, now parallel, now perpendicular. They are not altogether lava-like here, but their black robe begins to glow with green. The heat and some moisture of the hills bring out this life.

Down we fly into this defile, which grows more grand with every descent, until we reach the bottom of this plunge, and lift our delighted eyes upon the walls inclosing us. Getting between the banks of Niagara, if the bed were dry, would not be a dull sensation. How much more this gorge, five times at least the height of that ravine, fashioned into artistic shapes, trimmed with gay apparel, and crowned with level strata of piled-up limestone, mother of marble.

This long slide—Yankee boys would call it "coast"—comes to a halt at the hacienda of Rinconada, or Cornertown, an angle made by the mountains, which is level enough to bear culture. It is "a sweet, pretty" spot of fifty acres, *poco mas y menos*, with tall alamo-trees, not unlike a linden, shading its innermost and watermost corner from the intense glare pouring into this horn from that tropical sun. The breeze blows brisk, and tempers the growing heat with its warm March blasts.

A slight rise for two leagues gives us an opportunity to admire, and, in a few instances, to pluck, the brilliant flowers that line our path. Not much chance for the latter is afforded. Once too much, I found, was my getting out of the coach a third time, to gather, if possible, the root of a superb crimson cactus. The driver touched up his horses as I touched the ground, and seemed purposed to push on without me, although the ascent was then quite marked. But it is a law of these diligences never to stop for any thing, a law I respect, and have no desire to see abrogated or weakened. Yet these gorgeous blossoms were a temptation. Especially so were two cactuses, one a round ball, with bits of red flowers, and one a group of small and hidden balls, supporting each a large crimson cup. How can these terribly sharp balls and tubes, so full of spines, burst forth into colors so delicate and deep? For a flower is a fruit of these inner natures. Cut these bulbs, and you find them full of soft, firm, fine fibre, as of lace meshed in cream. They show that the soul of them is sweet. So some rough and thorny exteriors that are human, hide tenderest and grandest spirits. So, especially, does the thorny and self-denying life of faith and patience and sorrow burst forth into the blossoming of heaven. Other flowers abound of less grand style and color: a daisy of the tint of cream; another of yellow, streaked with brown; white daisies, larger and softer than our Northern skies produce; these stand among their cactus superiors in meek yet sweet humility.

The gorge grows in grandeur as you pass over this last ascending point, and begin a descent of ten leagues, almost thirty miles, to the city at its base. The sides of the cliffs are equally fantastic, now hollowed in, now rounded out, now capped with horizontal pillars, now buttressed with a bluff running a half mile out of its side, an enormous roll, but nothing to the wall it seems to support.

Soon, on the left, the steady outline is broken into three separate ranges. The first is short, not over a mile or two in length. It starts up sheer and unbroken from the bottom, a scarped wall of silver gray. On its centre and top two caps are set, of the same stratified rock, whiter than the bases below, of enormous size and regular shape. They look like guardsmens' hats, and well become these watchers of the vale.

The next range is not less than ten miles long, and is more varied in outline, though below, at the city, it looks so like a mitre that it bears that name. Far up its side, close at the edge of that same stratified summit, a bit of a hole lets you into a marvelous cave. But how to get to the hole is the question. It looks impossible, but a gentleman riding with me says he has done it. A safe but very steep path leads up that sheer, swart, hot wall. It was built by an American, who fell a martyr to the revolution a year ago.

The last range is before us, and back of the city, which lies hidden at its base, a huge piece, seemingly cut out of its ridge, making

SADDLE MOUNTAIN.

it look like a Mexican saddle, and hence its name of Saddle Mountain. It is a quaint feature in the scene. More quaint, however, is a hole on the opposite side. Near to the top of that ridge you see a hole clean through the face of the rock, opening to the light opposite. It looks from the valley as of the size of a hat. It is really large enough to let a yoke of oxen and their cart go through, though I have never heard of that being attempted. Whoever should attempt it would "hitch his wagon to a star," as Emerson advises; Charles's Wain, of course, is already thus hitched. My fellow-traveler says you can go over all the world and never see a sight like that, a hole opened through a mountain cliff. It is a hundred feet below the summit; but it is easily attained, if one seeks adventures. The hills on that side, in their ravines, show how intense is the heat; for those hollows, even up to their summits, are filled with green shrubs, and grasses, and trees. Where snow would lie in Switzerland, flowers and grasses of tropical quality grow here.

Santa Caterina is the name of the village at the base of this true "hole in the wall." In a shop in this rancho I find on the counter a picture of the Virgin, framed in tin, for sale, tin and all, for two reals. The engraving puts a crown on her head, and in its corner drawings make her alike crowned, and men her worshipers. I tried my broken Spanish on the vender, saying, "Non Maria, pero Jesu Cristo solo" (Not Mary, but Jesus Christ only). This picture is one of many proofs of the reigning idolatry; for idolatry complete it is; none more so in India. The very term, which this picture recalls, "Queen of Heaven," was the exact ascription given to Astarte, the wickedest goddess of history, lustful as Venus, wrathful as Moloch — that bottom of hell, a fallen woman. Yet her boastful title is given to the sweet, humble, modest "Mother of our Lord." How the mountain views disappear before the condition of this people, revealed in that twenty-five-cent goddess. These also shall perish; they shall not endure; they shall be wrapped together as a scroll, and melt away as these hills have here once melted and stiffened. But of the poor souls that perish here for the lack of knowledge, it is said, they shall never be destroyed — dead, lost, perhaps, but never destroyed. We should forget all sight of earth in the passion for the souls of men.

Here is one at this rancho door, whom I met with at San Gregorio, that I have hopes may yet be brought to serve this people. He is quite black, was once a slave in Kentucky, who fought in our war as a soldier, was transferred to the border at its close, and deserted to Mexico. He is very intelligent and comely; has good employment by the diligence company in shoeing their mules, for which he gets sixty dollars a month. He wears the wide sombrero, silver-mounted and tasteful. He is quite a favorite here, and was promised a captaincy in the last revolt if he would serve Diaz. He was born near Lexington, Kentucky, and his name is Charles Smith. His parents were Methodists, and he ought to be. He can not read or write, because of his early condition. How little his master thought that boy would be riding about in a sombrero, silver-banded and bound and gayly set off, the pet of the owners and passengers of the route.

BISHOP'S RESIDENCE, MONTEREY.

We now pass along the side of the Valley of St. Peter, a very handsome wooded and meadowed plain under the western mountains, among the wild chaparral, the terrible mixture of thorn-bushes of every sort, through which our soldiers climbed to the top of this low hill on our left, where they stormed the bishop's residence on that hill, which is now a ruin. In this charge, Lieut. Grant got his first promotion, but declined it, because another was also promoted, saying, "If Lieut. —— deserves promotion, I do not."

The road still glides downward, amidst blossoming orchards, tall and fragrant, gardens and flower-beds, into the city, down its still slight incline to the plaza and my pleasant quarters.

The heat is intense. It is in a tunnel of mountains that draws all the rays. But the largest and coolest of the hotels of the diligence company refreshes me. This hotel concludes our sojournings of such sort; for only ranchos await us nightly between this city and the Gulf. Its wide porches, and flower-full patio, and plumed and singing birds surpass Saltillo's and all before.

It is Saturday, and the last Sunday in the country is to be passed here. A bath seems the first necessary preparative. So I go to the shop of my German co-traveler, a sombrero manufacturer, and get as near his chamber as a huge dog permits. He tells me, what I tell you, never to take a bath in this country in the afternoon. A gentleman, he says, came up from Matamoras, took a bath after his arrival, and died before the next morning. I content myself with a hand-bath, which is as good as the more formal ablutions.

This same gentleman gives me another bit of information more in the line of his business, yet having an inference wider even than a sombrero brim. He says the Mexican heads average six and three-quarters and six and seven-eighths, hatters' sizes; Americans average seven and an eighth. I had noticed the difficulty of getting hats, in the capital and elsewhere, large enough for the heads of American travelers, and called his attention to it. This fact was given in reply. That is the size of the heads of our boys at twelve. Does it mark, then, a type of civilization, and their relation to the bigger-headed and bigger-brained races of the Teuton type?

I spent the rest of the day in hunting up some of these big-headed brothers. The first I found was as small of head and body as the people among whom he dwelt. He was the missionary of the American Board, the Rev. John Beveredge, a slim, sickly gentleman, whose lungs had driven him first to South America, and then to this everlasting summer. The Master has modes to-day of scattering His apostles, and so increasing His Church, less terrible, but not less certain, than those which prevailed in the earliest times. Then Herod drew his sword, and the Church fled hither and yon, carrying the Word. Now He draws the sword Himself, sends piercing blasts through sensitive lungs and feeble frames; and lo! these saints fly to more genial climes, preaching the Word. Thus the Gospel gets planted in Monterey.

Miss Rankin was its real planter. She came up here from Matamoras, led by love of souls. She had gone to Brownsville, for family reasons. When there she visited Matamoras, and saw the ignorance that settled, a thick cloud, upon the people. She gathered some children into a school, and began to teach them and their elders the way of the Lord the more perfectly. She finally found herself drawn three hundred miles into the country, and Monterey became her chosen seat. She succeeded in establishing over a dozen schools and preaching places, which she supplied with native assistants. The best of bodies break down under such labors, and she had to retreat. She left her work in charge of the American and Foreign Christian Union, and they in turn transferred it to the American Board. Mr. Beveredge was superintending this work. He had several helpers, who came and heard him in the morning, and in the afternoon preached the same sermon in the villages round about. Much good was being done by these efforts. But he had his warfare in his own Protestant household.

A Baptist preacher had come thither and organized his church. He had done his work efficiently, and therefore differences had sprung up among the few and feeble Protestants. A discussion had been going forward between Messrs. Beveredge and Westrup in the form of letters, which had been collected by the former into a pamphlet, and entitled "En Cristo o en Agua" (In Christ or in Water). This title looks like begging the question. Being, as one has remarked, of "impartial bias" in this contest, I visited both meetings. About the same number, not far from twenty-five, were present at each. The Baptists held a Sunday-school, their preacher being out in the villages. After service I talked with them, and found them well watered. They were none the less good Christians for that, and none the more. One lady walked my way homeward. I conversed with her in my broken Spanish, and found her a Close-communion Baptist of the first water. Some complained of this contest. But I went into a Roman Church, and heard the most eloquent preacher I had seen in the country, declaiming with great passion to a crowded house against Protestantism. Mr. Beveredge told me he was very active and violent in his opposition. This conflict of creeds caused his zeal. It showed that somebody in that city was interested in other forms of Christian faith. These despised sects were like two dogs, who might trot along the streets in equal contempt and neglect; but if they stopped and began to fight, a ring was instantly formed, a crowd interested, and the dogs themselves arise in dog rank in their own judgment and in those of their enemies. So Protestantism is growing in and by its own internal and fraternal feuds.

There is need enough of it. The Sabbath is the best business day of the week. The churches, save where the inflammatory priest preaches, are deserted of men, and well-nigh of women. There is no spiritual life in all the people. Surely any breathing is better than death.

In the heart of the town is a fountain of rare abundance, clearness, and sweetness. The Eye of the Town it is called, and those who drink of it, it is said, can never get away from the city. It was near midnight, and the coach was to start in three hours; but I risked it, drank, and got away. It was delicious enough, though, to make me long for it still, and may yet bring me back to its lip.

The Alameda of this city is not equal in rural beauty to that of Saltillo, but as it is the last we shall see, it is not unworthy of praise. Nor is it unworthy in itself. A walled park, with drives, shrubbery, trees, and flowers, well kept, it is one of the loveliest of its sort I have seen. It will be a new and improved era when all our cities have such pretty drives and gardens.

A less agreeable sight are the spots on that blank white wall in a gardenless square. They are the holes where the bullets that missed the men who stood before the wall picked their way into its mortar. It is the place of execution. Even lately has it been

ALAMEDA, MONTEREY.

the scene of such military settlements of political quarrels. That blotted wall bespeaks another trait of the city. It is a fertile field for revolutions.

The air of Monterey was full of revolution. Diaz had held out a year against the government of Juarez and Lerdo, and many were looking and longing for another outbreak. This does not propose to take the old form, but to follow that of Texas: "Independence and Annexation." But Texas warns them that that is submission to the American; and they hesitate, and will. Better work their destiny out in their own lives and language under the guidance of the American faith.

XII.

THE BEGINNING OF THE END.

Rancho de Villa de General Trevina.—A Sign of Home.—A misty Escort.—Blistering Morin.—Chaparral.—The changed Face of Nature.—The Yankee Hat and Hut.—Mesas, or Table-lands.—The bottom Rancho; Garcia.—Mier.—Comargo.—The Grand River unseen, yet ever near.—Last Night in a Rancho.—La Antigua Renosa.

A RIDE since three o'clock this morning is an excuse for sleeping at near the midnight hour, especially as two will find me up again. But the sight of a petroleum lamp is such a novelty that one can not help being kept awake a little season. I have not seen one on a hotel table before since I left the States. It is like the land-birds Columbus saw, harbingers of home. Not twenty leagues off is the Rio Grande. To-morrow's breakfast, if all goes as well as it has gone, will be eaten on its banks. This rancho has, therefore, a value above itself; as a guide-post near your native village, when returning thither, is far more than cross-beams and common letters. It glows with a glory and a beauty not its own. I am getting to like ranchos. This Rancho de Villa de General Trevina, despite its big name, is very cordial. The dinner is good, service amiable, tea *fuerte*, and the bed lies provokingly near, in nice white sheets, too nice and white for this dust-covered form, saying, "Come and rest."

The day broke on me well out of the gardens and grandeurs of Monterey. Three hours I slept, while the sick mules ran out of that paradise, and regained outwardly and inwardly Paradise lost. A thick mist hung around the few low hills, reminiscences of the tall Sierra Madre. The mist was sticky and ocean-like, and I fancied it had come up from the Gulf to escort me thither. It would have badly spoiled the roads had it done so, for the rain and the soil make a black and pitchy mixture which is well-nigh untraversable. I greeted it as an old friend, despite the fear that it might stick a good deal closer than we desire the best of old friends, all the time, to do. But the sun got the mastery of it, and of every thing else, and blazed away without let or hinderance. At the end of eleven leagues we made the town of Morin, a white and blistering place, its sun-dried adobe still reproducing the sun too dazzlingly. No trees, no shaded walks, no pleasant fruit and farm-trading plaza—only a white heat. A cup of coldish water was its only relief.

One hardly expected to find even so agreeable a town; for an almost perfect desolation preceded it for many miles. The chaparral everywhere abounded, tall and briery. A clearing or two showed that the land was fertile, and only wanted inclosing and clearing up to be very fruitful. Cattle and horses and sheep were wandering among the chaparral, finding good herbage. The land did not look like Mexico. It was not high, hilly, or dry. It was moist, bushy, wild, and naturally and easily productive.

Nor did the people look like Mexicans. They had the Yankee hat and look, head-gear and complexion, every thing but the Yankee log-hut; but their ranchos are as bad, so the equality of resemblance continues.

From Morin you begin to get a view of the general lay of the land. Leaving out that low sierra in front of us, which we shall soon circumvent and omit from the scene, you note, as the characteristic, that it slides off in successive terraces, miles wide. It began at Monterey, eight hundred feet above the Gulf. It declines gradually to the sea-level. Probably half of it is made at this place.

The *mesas*, or tables, as these landspreads are called, are broad and level, and from them you see a lower but not low valley, wider than themselves, spreading out for scores of miles, until its green is lost in the blue of the sky. As you descend easily and by very short falls into this lower valley, you find that it is not a complete level, but a succession of slight fallings off. So you dip down, little by little, to the sea. A half-dozen leagues from Morin, we go through a dismal rancho with a grand name, which I have forgotten. All these ranchos have grand names, and nothing else. Its wells are numerous, and have a stone curb and two stone pillars that support the beam that holds the rope that lifts the pail.

This hill we run down amidst chaparral of very fine greenness, but of no present value. Our halt for breakfast is at the rancho Garcia, the bottom of our experiences. Our meal is served under a thatched roof with bamboo sides, with the tortillas frying, and the smoke ascending and descending, especially the latter. The girls are dirtier, if possible, than the food. It seemed impossible to taste their filthy dishes. But hunger, like necessity, knows no law; and a little nibbling carries us on till night-fall.

The trees stand grand about the smoky hut, and the natives lounge under the grandest one. As a dessert, I get up a broken talk with them, and so overcome the cry of hunger within. The still better cry of "*Vaminos*" calls me gladly away from the tree and rancho. The road pursues the same path through an open, empty, thorn-covered country, rich for every manner of fruit, when it can have rest and an intelligent population. Night finds us in a town of huts, whose name I have lost. It was called, as most are hereabouts, for some general of a revolution, and will probably be changed after the next pronunciamento for his name who shall then make a successful revolt of a moment. But the narrow room is cleanly; its hard earthen floor is smooth and swept, and after Garcia its meal is metropolitan.

We are up and off at three, through the same dull landscape, hardly varied now with glimpse of hill, green, flowery, capable, and empty. We are pulling straight for the river; when we reach it we shall turn Gulfward. Open and settled spaces reveal themselves as we get near the American line, and our breakfast is served at noon in the quite bustling Mier. A Frenchman from Paris, *via* New York, gets up a goodly meal of mixed American and Parisian sort. The school is just out, and boys are lounging, in true Yankee fashion, about the coach. The town is half Mexican, half American. Open fields and open windows show the Northerner is here. Adobe houses and blank walls and big coach doors show the Mexican is here also. England and Spain meet and mingle on the outskirts of either realm.

A pull till four, through like expressionless country, brings us to Comargo, the Rio Bravo, and the end of Mexico, though thirty-six hours still remain between being on the one bank and on the other of the Grand and Brave river. This border town is the cleanest and dullest of all between Monterey and Matamoras. An inlet of the Rio Grande, quite a stream, puts up behind the town, and is crossed by a tedious ferriage. The steep bank is pulled up, and the broad plaza stretches out, a third of a mile almost. At its upper end are Government buildings, spacious, pretty, and cool. At its lower end is a covered market, an unseen sight farther inland, swept, garnished, and empty. A few stores inclose the square on its two sides parallel with the two rivers. Here I get my last packet of silver, and the coach proceeds in the gathering sunset hours adown the banks of the river. Its waters are not seen, but I know they are only a mile or so away, and that that Northern sky is over the land of my fathers and my faith.

The trees grow large, the fields are open and cultivated. Every thing is American and fascinating. No matter how much we may admire foreign sights, home sights are ever the tenderer and lovelier. Brilliant Mexico, with its magnificent volcanoes, barrancas, and haciendas; its wonderful flowering and fruit; its orange orchards and banana groves and maguey prairies; its ancient piles and its modern — all are forgotten in the familiar landscape of this semi-northern river. It is near midnight ere we reach our last rancho for the night, La Antigua Renosa.

The rancho is, like its creator man, susceptible of progress. These three nights have demonstrated this. Each good as compared with fears and with maledictions, the present and last is the best. A dozen new chairs of Yankee make, hard-bottomed, brown-painted, are arranged around the room, as if they were expecting a prayer-meeting, or a log-cabin preaching. The table has nice white ware, also of the latest Yankee pattern ; the Yankee candle stands in its shining brass candlestick in a plate in the centre. Surely here is no *antigua* Renosa, but one most modern. But even this word is modernized, for the name they gave me was, Los Renos a Viejo, or some such affair ; Viejo is too old-fashioned a word, and so gives place to La Antigua—"old" to "ancient."

The dinner, at eleven o'clock at night, is being got ready. Not old that ; they never prepare that till the passengers come. The coaches from Matamoras have just arrived, and quite a crowd criss-cross at this out-of-the-way corner. Longfellow's "Wayside Inn" could much more properly have been written of this spot than of Sudbury, where such characters as his could no more have been weather-bound than born.

A good meal follows, and a good sleep, though all too short ; for at four we are off, half asleep still.

XIII.

JOLTINGS AND JOTTINGS.

A Creator and an Imitator.—Church-making and Carriage-writing.—The oldest Church and the youngest.—*Compagnons du Voyage.*—A Brandy-sucker.—Prohibition for Mexico.—Talks with the Coachman and Mozo.—Hides and Shoes.—San Antonio.—Its Casa and Inmates.—Rancho Beauties.—Women's Rights in Mexico.—Sermonizing in the Wilderness.—A Night on Stage-top.—Fantastic Forms.—Spiritual Phantasms.—Light in a dark Place.—Matamoras and Brownsville.

"JOHN WESLEY created a Church," said an ambitious minister not long since; "why may not I?" One effort to imitate that example would have satisfied the aspirant. Many have tried it before and since, but few with such results: Mr. Weinbrenner, Mr. Shinn, Mr. Capers, Mr. Scott, Mr. Campbell; but they did not make such a big thing of it after all. I heard a good story in Mexico of Mr. Campbell and his church. The late Roman Catholic Archbishop of Baltimore was talking with an earnest female Campbellite cousin of his. Said he, "If I was not a Roman Catholic, I would be a Campbellite." "Why so?" asks the lady, delighted at this half a loaf. "Because," he answers, "if I did not belong to the oldest Church, I would to the youngest."

Now, if I can not imitate John Wesley in creating a Church, I can try to copy his example in a hardly less remarkable gift, writing in a coach. If this is so very difficult, as the compositors would affirm could they but see the sheets on which this is penciled, how much more difficult must it have been for his ecclesiastical composition. True, I have not his smooth roads and table fitted to the carriage, but I have a road almost as good, and a slow and easy-going coach. The last day in Mexico I may well be treated to this luxury. I am nearing Matamoras, having been for twenty days,

Sundays excepted, an occupant of a locomotive house, which, though changing itself regularly, has never really changed. It has ever been the self-same vehicle, of a faded red without, a dirty and dusty leathern buff within. Along its upper edge has always been printed, "Empresa Diligencias Generales," or General Diligence Company. Here I have laid off, sometimes on nine seats, almost always on three, slept much, seen much, talked little, read less, and written least. I have had many talks with myself, because I had no better or worse companion, if worse there could be; sad talks and pleasant, worrysome and worryless.

As it was the only seat taken through, so not many others have been occupied for even an occasional posta. One started from Mexico with me, whom I left at Queretaro, as my going forward would have necessitated my riding on the Sabbath, and from that, my edition of the Litany reads, "Good Lord, deliver us." And He has so far delivered me. He has also added a favor not especially asked, and allowed me to speak in every city of Sabbath sojourn, save one, the words of His grace. That one, Queretaro, I strove hard to get three English-hearing people to arrange a service. I failed, perhaps because I did not ask the lady of the trio. She would have let me in, I think.

I took up one and another companion for short stages, one of whom I recall as a very polite gentleman, who gave me much information, talking slowly and distinctly, so that my untrained ear might distinguish the words, a gift my untrained coachman never could attain.

His successor, for a posta, was of another type. Bringing a leathern bottle with him, with a very small faucet, he kept steadily sucking brandy out of that tiny hole, leaning back his head to catch the oozing drop, slowly descending, as if it was ashamed to leave the upper leathery bag for the baser human one below. I was rejoiced to see any such sign of a not utterly fallen sort of brandy. It does harm enough to more than offset this only symptom of a better nature. It is the drink of all foreigners and the better-off class of natives. I have seen Germans nearly drain a full flask in a single day's ride ; and an Englishman pour a half-tumbler, undiluted by water, down the throat of a six-year-old daughter. Of course, they themselves set the bigger example : for our English brothers are the hardest drinkers in the world, or are only excelled by their American cousins, who excel them in debauchery, since these trample conscience under their lust of appetite, or more usually, fear of man ; for it is love of fashion, rather than love of liquor, that makes the American drink. How glad I was to read in Monterey last Saturday that Massachusetts had repealed the Beer Act, and by such a grand majority. The fall of '66 is the rising again of '73. Though she may fall again, it will only be to a perpetual struggle until she shall attain a permanent deliverance. How far shines that good deed in this naughty world ! Away across the country, and into this land, that no more dreams of Prohibition than it does of Protestantism, burns this ray of the coming sun that shall renew the face of all the land and of all lands.

But the few people of the coach have not interested me so much as the coachmen themselves. They and their mozos have been a constant study. The one that took me across the battle-field of Buena Vista was a vehement talker, especially after he had been promised a dollar if he would deliver me at Saltillo two hours earlier than his accustomed time. He described every mountain, some of them, I have no doubt, for the first time, and with a nomenclature of his own creation. He described the plants and their qualities—this for soup, and that for medicine ; went over the whole battle-field and battle as though his side had conquered, just as our guides do to British visitors at Bunker Hill.

Yesterday's drivers were of a younger sort. They were near of an age, not far from twenty-four. Usually the mozo is a lad, the driver a man of forty. These, boys as they looked, drank muscat, a strong liquor of the smell of whisky, lashed and stoned the tired mules beyond boyish enthusiasm, sang, and were jolly exceedingly. They knew but little, and seemed glad they knew no more. The driver was smart, dark, fine-looking, and would make a good general or preacher, if he had had the chance of the one, or the grace of the other.

To-day's mozo is of another type. The driver slept all the morning under his seat, and I acted the part of the mozo, plying the lash to the rear mule, and the stones to the leaders, as if anxious to show my zeal in order to get promoted. The poor fellows were so sick with the epizootic that they could hardly move. And the only response they made to my applications, not sermonic, was a kick or two occasionally from the off-mule. Or was it the nigh one? My horsemanship can not answer that conundrum. They did right to kick. As Balaam's ass was wiser than he, so these, his half-brothers, were wiser than the half-brother of that prophet. For they had dragged the coach in on the last night's posta, and then, with only four hours' rest, had been compelled to drag it back again; and sick at that. No wonder they were *no quiere* to any request for them to urge their step beyond the slowest walk. I beg their pardon for my stony salutations. They made the five leagues in five hours, less than three miles an hour, and they did well.

Between the beatings with whip and stones, in which latter I became quite expert, I talked to the mozo on all sorts of subjects: home, business, prospects, religion. He said that he was thirty-seven years old; married at thirty. His wife was then fifteen. He had one child, Thomas, aged four. He had no more children; it cost so much to support them, and they all took to drink. He said ladies were called young at twelve, thirteen, and fourteen, and as late as fifteen, but old at twenty. His wife attended church, but he was kept at work on the road Sunday, and rested Monday, just in order to break the Sabbath. He thought I must be rich: worth not less than two hundred thousand dollars, and was surprised to see that fortune dwindle to naught. What could I be? he asks. "*Predicado*," I say. It was a sort of Spanish he had never heard, nor I either before I used it; but it was a guess at "preacher." A "*padre*" he knew too well, and a friar; but a preacher was a new vocation. So I added, for his illumination, "a missionary." "Romanista?" "No! Metodista." "Protestante?" "Si." He is a little surprised at this, and ready to draw back, for his wife's faith has a hold upon him. He soon recovers, and tells me about a señora who had often passed over this road. "Señora who?" "Señora Protestante—Señora Virga," he adds. A new phrase to me, as I had supposed that señora was only applied to married ladies, señorita being the unmarried title. He showed that the Spanish followed the English custom, which very properly calls unmarried ladies of mature age after the married ladies' title. Yet, as a maid with them is old when past fifteen, this remark is not as sure a proof of advancing years as it might be in higher latitudes.

I thought he was trying to say something about the Señora of Guadalupe; so I sought in this direction. But I found I was off the track. It flashed upon me. "Señora at Monterey?" "Si! si!" "Señora Rankin?" "Si!" This lady's work and fame have thus made her known to the common people. And well she deserves to be, for hers is by far the best work in all this part of the country.

We pass a load of ox-hides. "How much are they worth?" "A real apiece, here. In Matamoras, a real and medio." "How much do your boots cost?" "In Matamoras, four dollars and a half; in Monterey, seven dollars." So they sell the hide for twelve and a half cents, or get eighteen and three-quarters by carrying it a hundred miles, two weeks' journey (fifteen miles being a good day's journey for mules and oxen), and then pay from four and a half to seven dollars to get that same hide transformed into a pair of boots. So much for the difference between Mexico and Massachusetts. No more duty protects the latter than the former. Not so much, probably; for every thing here is taxed, and taxed horribly.

He asks which I like best, Mexico or the United States. "Both," I diplomatically answer. I try to describe the beauty and wealth of Mexico, and the comfort of the people of the States, especially the poor; floors to their rooms, not earth, as here; chairs, tables, beds, all nearly unknown. His eye flashed with longings for that goodly land. When will ours be altogether such, and this be like it?

I asked how long it would take to reach the next posta: "An hour?" "Two." "No, one." "Two." He drew out a dollar, and offered to bet. So I had the privilege of resisting no severe temptation, especially as there was not even a watch among us three; and therefore it would not have been possible to prove either true. I had also the better privilege of setting forth the evils of gambling; how it made him lose all his wages, leave his wife and child without bread, and otherwise destroy him. I was astonished at my liberty of prophesying in the unknown tongue, and could almost see how that the love of Christ, without a miracle, under the mighty breathings of the Holy Ghost, could make the disciples speak with other tongues. The Spirit gave them utterance.

The village of San Antonio is reached at length, a blazing speck of white on a low hill overhanging the Rio Grande. It looks almost as pretty as a New England town, as you approach it through the interminable groves of mesquite. But enter it. Only a perpetual fire, a perpetual desolation. The huge plaza is without shrub or speck to mitigate its whiteness. Not a flower to relieve the white heat of the houses. Many of the houses are in ruins. The church has a skull near its entrance, an appropriate symbol of the town.

Yet here I found several things of a contrary sort. There are a custom-house and its officers; for this is a smuggling port, and each nation has its officers to protect its rights, or its claims rather, for rights in customs there are none. People have as much right to carry their wares across the line as to cross it themselves. It looks as if these officers had killed the town, for smuggling was its life.

The place where we had our breakfast was another novelty. It was a casa with three rooms, the first large, with a wide bed in the corner of the American type. All Mexican beds are single. It also had high-posters, after the old American fashion. Its dirty pillow-cases suggested livelier dirt below. A fashion-plate and a fancy girl of the period—a bright-colored Hartford print—set off the walls, evidently showing travel on the part of the ladies of the house or desire for it, there being no room for fashion-plates in the rebosa and skirt, which compose their usual costume.

I glanced into the kitchen, and concluded to take a nearer view. It was a farmer's kitchen, larger by far than any rancho or peon could boast of. Its high thatched roof looked cool, and the smoke from its tortilla frying-pan wandered unharmed and unharming among the rafters. The good lady, young at forty, sat on the ground, busy over her stew-pans. A daughter, of the overripe age of sixteen, was frying the tortillas, which a twelve-year-old young lady was kneading. A taller miss, between the two, was walking about in a very draggly pink skirt, and a very old daughter of, possibly, eighteen, sat on the ground, assisting her mother. Three younger girls were sitting or toddling around, and a ten-year-old was chatting with a boy of like age, while also busy with kitchen duties of the vegetable sort. I was surprised to see so large a crowd, and they were doubtless more surprised to see me, with my unwashed and unshorn face, huge sombrero, and dusty garments, peering into their common room.

But they were too near the border to be disturbed by this Yankee freedom. The good lady told me that these were all her daughters. The boy was not hers; he was an outsider. She has eight children, seven daughters. They were unusually comely, and the one just a little year beyond "young," according to our mozo, would make an impression in any society. She was as beautiful as the ragged and almost naked Apollo lad whom I had seen as near the beginning of the trip as I had this industrious and modest Venus near its end. I could easily see how my Vermont brother in Saltillo had been swept from his bachelor moorings by a rancho beauty. As she sat there on the ground frying tortillas, she made one think of Thackeray's "Peg of Limovaddy:"

"Hebe's self, I thought,
Entered the apartment:
. . . . . .

> As she came she smiled,
>   And the smile bewitching,
> On my word and honor,
>   Lighted all the kitchen.
> See her as she moves;
>   Scarce the ground she touches,
> Airy as a fay,
>   Graceful as a duchess."

This maiden of San Antonio had like natural graces, and was doomed to a like wasting of them on this desert air. What would not this group of superior girls do with the advantages of superior society? Culture and Christ would make them all beautiful within. Now they were comely of countenance; then, also, of soul. Yet perhaps they are safer and happier in this humble obscurity than if exposed to a city's culture and a city's shame. May this family be kept as godly as goodly.

The dinner was hardly equal to the handsome, youthful cooks who had prepared it. In variety it was sufficient. Four ways of preparing meat, and two of eggs; but its ways were too new for me. Soup, made by stewing fat meat in water, was eagerly drank by the coachman, but was too greasy for my palate. The two fattest parts of the meat, served up separately, were pointed out by the gentleman of the house as especially excellent. Solid junks of fat they were, and each was eaten by the cochero and his mozo as confirmatory of the landlord's judgment. The fry, and the tortillas, and the unmilked coffee, and the poor water, just made the dinner passable, and that only because I was comforted with the thought that one more meal, and Brownsville and a beefsteak were mine. The handsome cooks spoiled the broth, and a plainer face and better *cuisine* would have been more agreeable. Thackeray wisely omits the description of Peg's dinner.

A sign of the esteem in which the fair, fat, and forty lady of the house is held by her husband, or a token of the manner in which she rules him, is made manifest to all visitors; for is it not printed in good round letters on one of the beams that crosses the ceiling of the dining-room?

"Cedo, yo, Francisco, esta Casa a mi Sposa, Maria Lucia Zepada de Conclingo."

(*I, Francisco, give this house to my wife, Mary Lucia Zepada de Conclingo.*)

How many husbands have the courage to make like proclamation? "Very uncommon in Mexico," says the American custom-house clerk; very uncommon anywhere. Yet the fact is not uncommon. In a town adjoining Boston, a gentleman said his was the only house that was not deeded to the wife of the occupant. Better put the fact over the door. Still, though the wives own all the best houses in that large town, and can sell them, and be sued for them, they can not vote to protect them, to keep out the liquor-shops which injure their property, and to create a government which shall improve it. I read in the coach to-day that the Maine House of Representatives had voted woman the ballot. The Senate should follow its example. It is the seal of assurance to her liquor legislation. It is the only salvation of the ballot-box from the stuffing and bribing abominations of to-day. Señora Maria Lucia Zepada, etc., is a sign of the coming woman in the State, in all save her cooking. She looks as if able to bear her honors, with her large and healthy and handsome family; not a solitary and sickly unit, to which social ideas now diminish and degrade the household. With her abundant kitchenly ways, owning her casa and honoring it, shall she not also jointly own and honor the State?

Much more, the Church; for there her heart is, and her treasure also. Let not the Church lag behind the State in opening every door to her admittance. Let her be welcomed, especially when she is knocking at these doors; nay, when the Lord has Himself come down from heaven and opened these doors, not by sending His angel, but by the abundant outpouring of the Holy Spirit with signs following. Not more clearly was Paul thrust among the unwilling Peter and his ten—the vacancy in the apostolate being kept open by the Head of the Church for his admission—than is the sisterhood of the Church thrust by the same Head into like fellowship with their elder, but not superior, brethren. He that hath ears let him hear what the Spirit saith unto the churches.

"*Buen!*" (Well), as they say here, the same as we; our bad dinner has given us a good long dessert in the shape of a dull sermon.

> "Now good digestion wait on appetite,
> And health on both."

Good-bye to the hung beef, a clothes-line of which is stretched across the yard; to the poor cooking and pretty faces; to the casa and its owner; and, it must be confessed, to the somewhat henpecked-looking husband and father; to the custom-house friends; and to San Antonio.

The hot day drags to its close. The mules onward "plod their weary way." Gray's ox is not slower. How their prancing fleetness is changed.

The same green wood everywhere embraces me that has embraced me for this last two hundred miles—mesquite, mesquite, mesquite. It sometimes rises to the height of an apple or willow, very rarely to that of a maple. Brush is its proper level. Grass, weeds, thorny bushes, ground-flower cactuses of yellow and purple and magnificent crimson, humble, but hardly less beautiful, thornless pink, and daisy, and dandelion—very old, dear, homely, and homeful creatures—and chiquitite, tiniest flowers of every sort, a bed of beauty; such is the rich, green desolate valley on the Mexican side of the Grand River of the North.

For three hundred miles it is practically without inhabitant. Not less so is the American side. Every inch fertile, and capable, like the ground of a certain rich man, of bringing forth abundantly. Why should so many starve and pinch and toil when this abundance goes untouched? How alike is the God of nature and of grace! Ever thus He spreads His table of salvation in the wilderness, and ever thus man prefers starving in sin to sumptuous fare at His overladen board. For four thousand years has He said, "Ho, every one that thirsteth, come ye to the waters, and he that hath no money; come ye, buy and eat; yea, come, buy wine and milk without money and without price." Still they come not; they dig out their own broken cisterns; they eat their own tasteless food.

Shall it be always so? Will every generation thus treat the Lord and His royal feasts? Many have come; more will.

These lands are filling up. Those superb white Roman Campagna oxen that just passed us are driven by a new settler. That pretty log-hut, with its half-dozen Yankee-looking men and women at its door, is the first I have seen in Mexico. How like Minnesota it looks. Only Minnesota does not have such a soft spring garb on this second day of April. They are the indices of the coming myriads that will make this lovely desert lovelier with human life and love. So shall the overflowing and ever-neglected gifts of God in Christ, this wilderness of grace, this prairie ocean of salvation, be more and more appropriated by the sinful, sensual heart of man, famishing for bread, hungering and thirsting after the righteousness of Christ. They shall reject alike the crudities of superstition and of false and haughty self-sufficiency, the religion of idolatry and of a spurious humanity, and, sitting at the feet of Christ, Creator, Saviour, Brother, shall grow up into Him who is the head over all things, blessed forever.

The sun is gone; the shade is coming. Matamoras is a long sixteen miles off, at our slow walking pace, but the first jotting in a Mexican coach is ended. Not so the joltings; they continue till day-break. The musings with the pencil end at dusk at a rancho by the roadside, the last and worst of all. Still the tortillas and the coffee, as being the last, were kindly entertained, the children duly patted and pennied, the parents praised; and gladness unspeakable filled the heart as the slow mules pulled slowly away. No more starting off in a whirlwind rush; that is reserved for city taverns, where glory and gain go together. It is night-fall ere they leave, and six leagues (sixteen miles) are to be dragged over. Midnight they are due, and in expectancy thereof I foolishly mount on the top of the coach. The woods grow denser as the sky grows darker. The branches brush my head, but I am no fly, and not to be brushed into the empty coach below. I sit it out, seeing fantastic forms in every shadowy clump, riding up to vast walls that bar our way, straight, smooth, and high? How is it possible to penetrate them? Yet as we approach them they vanish, or move back to a more defiant position.

It is the mist of midnight, or of sleep, that plays such fantastic tricks with my eyes and with the scenery. Which? Lights glimmer in front; surely these are the city lamps. They come near, and disappear in approaching, either as will-o'-the-wisps or as camp-fires. Again is darkness; again the damp mesquite strikes the dizzy head; again the walls, high, and huge, and false, arise; again the fires flicker and go out. The coachman cries "Kutchah! Kutchah!" to his bedraggled mules, and tells me we are almost there. The hours drag on, and so does the coach. I think of the Light that shineth in a dark place, and wish for like illumination. But it comes not. No more does that come to the soul, wading through earth's midnight. How that soul is beset with false guides, bewildering lights, fictitious gates and walls, and still is out in the wet woods and fields, homeless and guideless. What a lesson that last night in Mexico taught me! Never shall I forget it. Through all its hours I watched and waited on the top of that coach. It was almost day-break—four of the clock—ere the real gate was touched, the real city entered. The guardsman searches sharp, because no fee is offered. The mules spurt and make their finish; the drowsy clerk of the hotel is not too drowsy to forget how to cheat. A score of dollars is my due. He tries to pay me off with worn-out quarters smoothed to twenty cents and less. I protest. He proffers smooth dollars. I still protest. He declines any better currency. Nervous with long vigils, and anxious to get to Brownsville for breakfast and a couch, I entreat better treatment. He is incorrigible. I surrender, and snatch with a benison that burns, not blesses, I hope, my degenerate dollars, and strike for the river. The stream is crossed by ferry in the glowing morning; Mexico is done.

Matamoras and Brownsville represent in name as in nature the two civilizations. The nomenclature of Mexico is soft, flowing, enervating; that of America, short, sharp, energetic. Matamoras in pronunciation is like lotus-eating; Brownsville like the crack

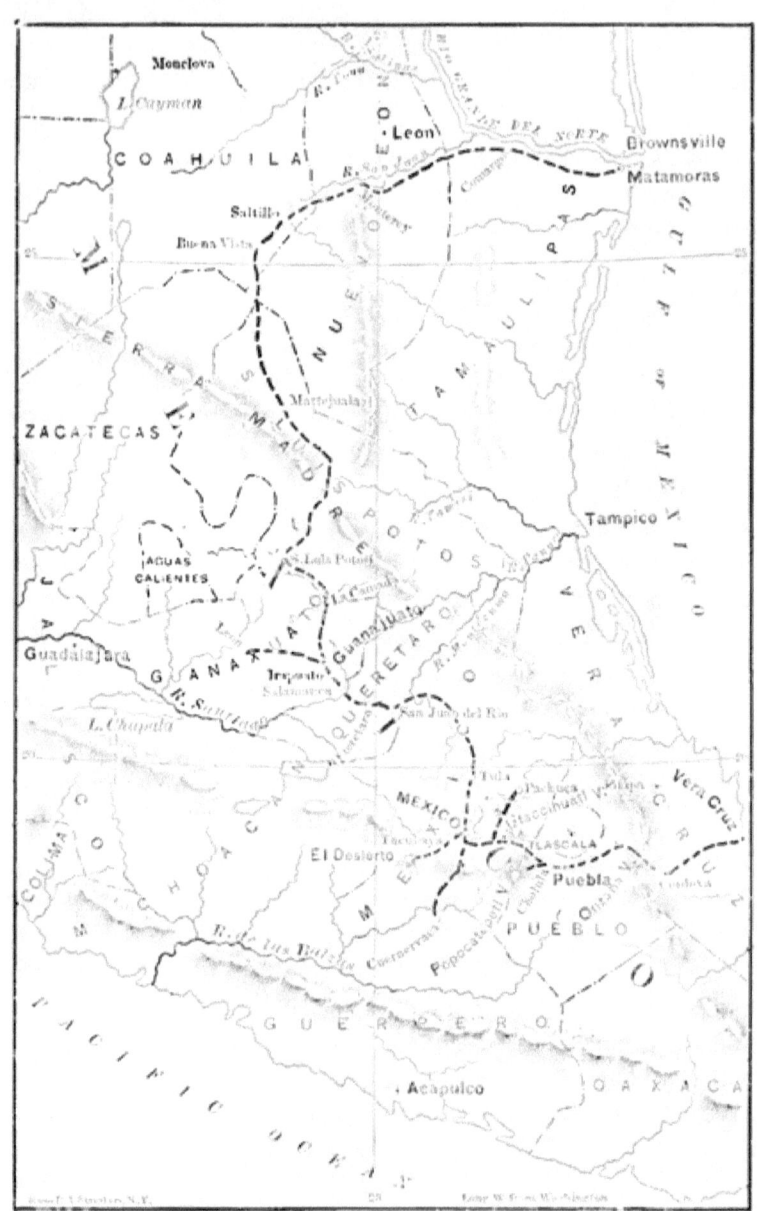

THE ITINERARY—FROM VERA CRUZ TO MATAMORAS.

of a pistol. So are the civilizations they represent. Idle and incurious, letting things go as they come, is the one; obtrusive and ever-moulding is the other. The cities are like their nations. The old-style house, barred windows, barred gate-way, narrow street, dead wall, plastered and tinted, is Matamoras; open windows, narrow door-ways, no coach-doors, no city walls nor gates, wooden houses, painted sometimes, wide streets: Yankee of Yankees is Brownsville. The two, when blended and built up in Christ, will be a beauty and strength, husband and wife, one "entire and perfect chrysolite."

XIV.

THE FINISH.

Coach, not Couch.—A new Tread-mill.—Rascality of a Sub-treasurer.—The same Country, but another Driver.—Live-oak *versus* Mesquite.—A sandy Desert as large as Massachusetts.—Not a complete Desert.—A dirty, but hospitable Rancho.—Thousands of Cattle on no Hill.—A forty-mile Fence.—A Patch of four hundred square Miles.—Mr. King's Rancho and Pluck.—Perils. —Mr. Murdock's Murder.—Corpus Christi.—Indianola.—Good-bye.

It was a coach, and not a couch, that awaited me. Neither beefsteak nor bed, on each of which I was so much doting, did I see or feel or taste in Brownsville. Reaching the hotel, I find a few servants just opening and sweeping its hall; for the time of breakfast is not yet. Inquiring as to the best means of reaching Galveston, I learn that no steamer is due for a day or two, and it will be several days before she leaves. A stage is to leave for Corpus Christi in a few moments. It will reach there to-morrow night. Thence I can catch a mail-boat for Indianola, perhaps a steamer, and so swing round to Galveston.

It seems strange that one on a stage-coach for three weeks should crave it again so soon. But Holmes describes a tread-mill prisoner who was so pleased with his punishment that he determined, at his release, to "have a round or two for fun," and, after he had got home, to set up "a tread-mill of his own." I have no expectation of going into the stage business myself; but I did feel so glad at escaping from that three weeks' imprisonment in a tossing, racking, galloping prison, that I felt willing to add nearly two hundred miles more to it, and not hesitatingly mounted the coach of rest.

Two things helped forward this feeling—a dislike of the sea, and the fact that I was moving homeward; so, like every other motive or act, it was mixed.

> "Joy and moan
> Melt into one."

This is a new route, hardly yet opened. The first change noticeable was not in the country, but in the drivers and driving. The country remained the same. The Rio Grande is no more a natural boundary than the St. Lawrence. The same woods of mesquite; the same cactus (called here prickly-pear), with its varied and rich blossoming of crimson, yellow, and many-tinted hues; the same humbler but not less beautiful flowers—these testified to a common country. The fields grew a little more open, but not vastly different from those the other side of the tiny stream which I had traveled beside for a day and a half, and only seen a corner of once, and the narrow, muddy brook which I crossed at Matamoras. But the driving told me that I was in a new country. The four large horses, the calm driver, the unused whip, the unheard screech and yell, the square, steady trot, no spurts of a run and long blanks of walking, hardly even walking, the absence of mozos and stones, were all new features in horsemanship. The intelligent driver talked mildly, and showed also the calming influence of character and success. These elements grow with success, and America is fast becoming as phlegmatic as England or any other well-to-do people.

I had been a little excited at Matamoras. The administrador, or agent, of the Diligence Company had put upon me, despite my protest, a lot of smooth and cheapened silver, what was left of my deposit in Mexico. Fortunately, it was only ten dollars. It was a rascally robbery, and I urge all who cross the country to take up their deposit, what remains of it, at Comargo. It is a good way of traveling, as you can put your money in the office at Mexico, and draw it out at every place where you stop for the night, what you wish of it. But do not leave any of it for the man at Matamoras. Señor Don Rumaldo, I think they call him; *mal do*, a giver of evil, he surely is. He attempted to shove forty quarters on me, not six of which could show both faces, and most could show none, and some never were worth more than pistareens, or twenty cents. When these were refused, he denied he had any more money, but afterward offered a chipped gold-piece. This could not be changed. He then offered ten dollars, only two of which were of full weight. This, of course, would have prevented the sale of the silver at its full value. He was robbing the depositors, and should be instantly removed. The other agents acted excellently.

I had to run to catch the coach after this vexing debate, had been up all night, and had no chance even for a cup of coffee or a cup of milk; so I was not in the best of conditions. But a glass of cold water, buttered rolls (butter had been a thing unknown for weeks), and a good nap put me to rights.

The country became more open, and cattle began to becloud the broad prairies. The woods changed from the light, thin-leafed mesquite to the dark, thick, short, John-Bull leaf of the live-oak, an evergreen of beauty in this spring-time; how much more in the yellowness of winter! It stands in groups and bunches on the open sea of grass, at times stepping out by itself to show us how perfectly it can round itself into shape when it takes the notion. Then it is almost as lovely as a New England elm or a New York maple. I have not yet seen the Southern rival of these twain, nor the Western, unless this live-oak be he. It comes near it—so round, so compact, so green. It is handsome enough, anyway.

Half-way of the trip we cross a sandy desert, forty miles wide; and, with the passion for push that possesses the modern traveler, the slow dragging of the horses over it seems like a forty years' journey in the wilderness. It takes all the night, and more. From five at evening to nine in the morning we pull through this heavy sand. But this soil is not barren after the Israelitish pattern. Rains keep it moist, and certain black specks in it keep it rich. Is black always the base of richness? Greenness, therefore, does not desert it, nor cattle, nor live-oaks, nor flowers. Some of the finest groups of trees are on this space, which is as wide and long as the State of Massachusetts, and yet hardly noticed in this

State, forty times her size. Many beautiful flowers cover it. I gathered over a dozen different varieties round one rancho, and comforted and strengthened the wavering heart with that apostolic promise, "If God so clothe the grass of the field, which to-day is and to-morrow is cast into the oven, shall he not much more clothe you, O ye of little faith?" These lovely grasses of purple, and scarlet, and blue, and pink, and lustrous white, and golden yellow, and variegated, how brief their life! That beautiful soul far surpasses these creatures in original excellence, infinitely more surpasses it in that its day is eternal.

It is hard sometimes to realize this, as you step into one of these dirty ranchos and see these unwashed, uncombed, almost undressed women and children, and imagine the change that Christ would make if fairly seated in their hearts. He will come, and the flower that fades be excelled, even at its beginning, by the flower that grows in beauty forever and forever. They are kind and hospitable now. How generously a mother and three girl-children, who seemed to have never known a comb or a towel, feasted me on thick milk and delicious coffee, and Spanish chats and smiles! Won't they take to Sunday-schools and all their cleanly accompaniments, when they get out of their Spanish and their Romanism into the light of English and Protestantism?

The fields show great herds of many cattle feeding. Wordsworth thought, when he said, "There are forty feeding like one," that he was describing a good-sized herd. What would he have said had he seen these hundreds and thousands? The prairies, rolling slightly, and dipping down into the sky on every side, are sprinkled with kine. There are thousands feeding like one. Well, it is only multiplication. He first said, if he did not first see, the fact of the silent feeding of great flocks and herds. The prairies would have amazed him more than the cattle. That forty, to his petty and pretty Rydal meadows, were vastly more than these hundreds to these prairies, actually boundless to the eye. They are lost on the ocean. The cattle on a thousand hills are here transformed into thousands of cattle on level plains.

Near noon we drive near a fence, the first I had seen, save of the corral sort for the coach horses. "That fence is forty miles long," says an employé of the road on the coach. Our Mexican driver (we have changed drivers) knows only to lash and scold his horses, run them and walk them by frequent turns. "Forty miles now; that is its beginning. It will include twenty miles square when finished." The owner is Mr. King. We enter the gate, itself nearly a mile from the house, which looks close by, and drive to the barn. Mr. King generously provides a cold cut of beef and cold cup of milk—rarities indeed. He has about sixty thousand cattle, and ten thousand horses and mules. He will get them all in his "patch" when the fence is completed, which will be, he says, seventy miles in length. He intends to improve his stock, and will slaughter twenty thousand this fall, to make way for the better quality. He keeps a hundred men racing down these herds, which are now wandering all the way from the Rio Grande to Austin. That is a specimen of the stock-breeding of the country. He is one of many such—only two or three quite as big, and only one bigger—Mr. Conner, who has not less than one hundred thousand cattle. A passenger had smiled an "Ah Sin" smile when I spoke of a hacienda in Mexico with its five thousand cattle and forty thousand sheep. I saw it now.

They say Mr. King's life is threatened by the Mexicans; but he is brave and daring. Once they shot at his ambulance, and killed a German on the box with the driver. His house is an open one, broad veranda, one story, wood—excellent for a fire, if the Mexic is so disposed. But he would sell his life dearly, and they do not want to buy at such rates; so he will probably live a while yet.

Not far this side, a small fenced inclosure, with trees and gardens, was the abode of Mr. Murdoch, who in the autumn of '72 was caught in bed by these savages, chained down, covered with tar and kerosene, and the house set on fire. He was an easy prey to the flames. So these prairies are not Paradise, except as it was after the devil entered it.

Corpus Christi receives us at night-fall. It is a live, pretty town, lifted up slightly from a livelier and prettier bay. It is only a night we stop there. The mail-boat thence to Indianola drops down the bay at six in the morning. The wind is splendid, and the run also. The boat sits on the wave without a wave. The breeze is as soft and warm as it is strong; so the more of it the better. I hoped it would get us to Rockport before the steamer left, but I was out of luck. The stars began to fight the other way. I had made every connection up to this time; now I was to make none. The steamer left just before we arrived. She passed us, majestically scornful. Another left Indianola just before we came in sight. So we were left stranded at that port for a day, when the steamer transported us to Galveston, and so to New Orleans, our point of departure. The path to our door is reached. Let us shake hands, and Good-bye.

28

XV.

CHRISTIAN WORK IN MEXICO.

Not yet.—The First Last.—A Telegram and its Meaning.—Perils and Perplexities of Church purchasing.—Temptation resisted.—Success and Dedication.—Curé Hidalgo and his Revolution.—Iturbide and Intolerance.—Beginning of the End.—The Mexican War, and its Religious Effects.—The Bible and the Preacher.—The first Revolt from Romanism.—Abolition of Property and of Institutions.—Invasion of the Papacy through France and Maximilian.—Expulsion thereof through America and Juarez.—The Constitutionalists the first Preachers.—The first Martyr: "Viva Jesus! Viva Mexico!"—Francisco Aguilar and the first Church.—The Bible and his Death.—First Appeal abroad.—Response.—Rev. Dr. Riley and his Work.—Excitement, Peril, Progress.—President Juarez, the first Protestant President.—The chief native Apostle, Manual Aguas.—His Excommunication by and of the Archbishop.—A powerful Attack on the Church.—His Death.—The Entrance of the American Churches in their own Form.—Their present Status.—The first American Martyr, Stephens; and how he was butchered.—San Andres.—Governmental Progress.—The Outlook.—Postfatory.

Not quite yet Good-bye. A journey undertaken solely for Church purposes should not omit the consideration of that work from its pages. It has not been largely thrust into the body of the work, brief and infrequent references only having been made to the subject. The aim has been to give a transcript of the land and people, apart from all especial views or ends, so that those who sought light upon the country or sought the country itself should not have too much, to them, extraneous matter set before them. It seemed better to put such matter in a chapter by itself, so that those who wished it not might avoid the dish entirely, and those who wished for it might enjoy it all by itself. At the risk of slight repetitions in minor points, let us glance at the story of Christian Work in Mexico, and put that which was first in its appropriate place, the last.

CHURCH OF SAN FRANCISCO, CITY OF MEXICO.

At the very close of the journey, in the little village of San Antonio, where the grateful husband acknowledges the lordship of his lady in the painted confession along the ceiling of his casa, I received a telegram, which drew my eyes and soul far away from the handsome family, obedient husband, and horrible breakfast. It was an electric shock in which was more than magnetic currents; for it foretold a future of unmeasured and immeasurable vastness, a future of spiritual currents of divine magnetism, that shall permeate, thrill, revive, and renew this whole land. Its enigmatic words were these : " Puebla business closed. Mexico will be to-day."

The brief line was inexpressibly grateful; for doubt had hung over the last purchase. Foes were many and sharp. One effort had failed through treachery, a priest appearing before the judge the day the papers were to be passed, and getting the property (the Church of Santa Inez, then used as a cotton warehouse) transferred to minor heiresses, and another portion of the estate set off to the youth to whom this church had been already assigned, and who was going to sell it to us. What might happen between the beginning of the effort to purchase these more central quarters and its completion, even to the frustration of that completion, it was impossible to tell. Had any priest suspected the possibility of this attempt, every member of his guild, and, primarily, its primate, the archbishop, would have put forth every effort to have prevented success.

And such efforts could have hardly failed of success ; for there were so many parties to negotiate with, that it seemed well-nigh impossible to preserve the secret. The real owner was in Paris. His administrador was a warm Papist. The holder of the first mortgage was a widow lady, residing in San Luis Potosi. The holder of the second mortgage was a carpenter in the city. Besides these proprietary interests, a person held it under a written lease for two years, for a theatre. Here were four, if not five, parties to be consulted ; for possibly the administrador might not have power to sell without a legal authorization from the actual owner.

A more perilous adventure was never more successfully executed; thanks, and thanks only, under God, to the sagacity and shrewdness and patient push of Dr. Julius A. Skilton, our consul-general, James Sullivan, Esq., and Señor Mendez, their attorney. To them the whole business was intrusted. A glance at the spacious quarters on the Monday after my arrival, which was the previous Saturday night, was sufficient. I have never seen them since. I hardly dared glance at them as I passed the street, for fear some Jesuit looker-on might notice a too fond expression in the eyes, and report the danger to the high-priest. So great is this peril, that Bishop Keener, of the Methodist Episcopal Church, South, who was at the same time negotiating for suitable quarters, informed me that he had made his selection, but only by riding by the place in a carriage, he not daring to inspect it more thoroughly. I regret to add that he failed in securing this spot, perhaps because the man he rode with or the man who drove him was in his secret, and put the priest on the track. The difficulties in my case were increased by the distance at which the first mortgagee lived, and the fact that it was a lady who held the claim as a portion of her husband's estates. She must be corresponded with in the slow process of the mail. A telegram would have quickened her fears and her covetousness. She must consult her compadre and all her family. The least conception that it was being bought for the Protestants would have probably cut off all negotiations at the start, or would certainly have leaked out and cut them off very soon thereafter.

The lessee was left out of the transaction. His case would have to be managed after the purchase was completed. The other three parties were slowly and softly approached, and after nearly three months from the date of that ten minutes' visit, and the issuing thereupon of the order to secure, if possible, the property, I had the supreme satisfaction of receiving the above telegram at the hot and dusty and desolate San Antonio. Is it any wonder the spot blossomed into beauty? The white dust turned to lilies. The hot sun tempered its blaze seemingly to the most genial warmth. Perhaps this event increased the comeliness of the family, and

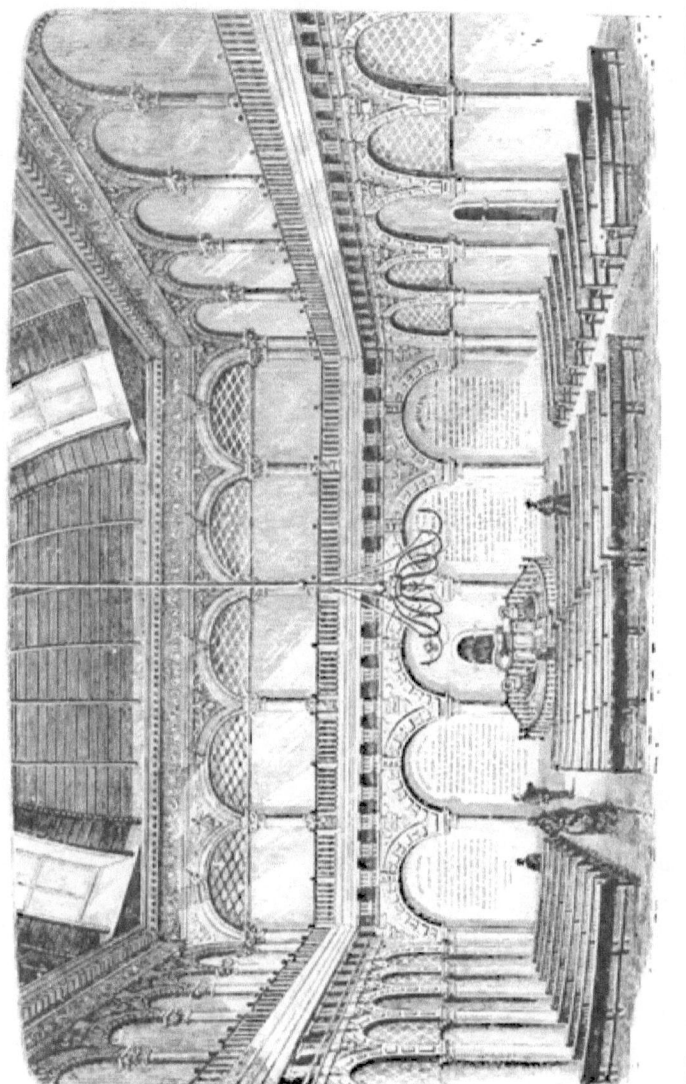

FIRST METHODIST EPISCOPAL CHURCH, CITY OF MEXICO.

made Peg of San Antonio more beautiful than she really was. It was not powerful enough to transform the *almuerzo* into a breakfast of delights. There were limits to even its ability.

The end of the journey and its objective end are reached at one and the same time. The cause of our coming puts its doxology and benediction in at the end of our going. Against unseen and unnumbered foes, against Mexican procrastination, against possible treachery, against perils without and fears within, success is assured.

How great this peril was, a single fact illustrated. Mr. Sullivan was approached, the very day he had consummated the purchase, and when he yet held the titles in his own name, by the leading native broker of the city with an offer of five thousand dollars for his bargain. The offer was undoubtedly from a higher source, for the property had laid idle for years, and was of no possible use to the broker, there being acres of like convent ruins at his command over all the city. It was instigated by the archbishop, undoubtedly, who had watched the coming and going of these invading ministers, and who had supposed as they left the city, with no possessions secured, their mission had failed, and who only woke up to the fact after their departure, when, the papers having all been passed, it was allowed to creep forth that this Irish gentleman, the fear of every brigand, whom he had more than once made to know the accuracy of his shot, and whose protection at El Desierto showed like skill and pluck, the successful rebosa manufacturer and silver operator, had bought this central and spacious property for a Protestant Church.

But he mistook his man. The splendid bribe was spurned, and in due time the property was transferred to the real owners. It was soon fixed up as the residence for its missionary, school for girls, and the beautiful audience-room of the Trinity Church. The Christmas following saw the joyful consummation of this undertaking in the dedication of this church by the services of Rev. Drs. Butler, Carter, Cooper, Ramirez, Guerro, and Señors Hernando, Pascoe, and Morales. A large audience filled its handsome auditorium. The dome of wood and glass lifted itself over the once open patio, erected by the first purchaser for his circus performers. Screens inclosed the area behind the pillars. The desk and platform and melodeon, with its simple style of sacred service, reminded the auditors that a new day had dawned in Mexico, or, at least, that a new hour of the day had struck. That day began to dawn and to shine before this glad hour arrived. Other men labored, and we were entering into their labors, not in any spirit of envy or strife, but with a desire for their enlargement, and with a purpose to unite with them in common love and labor for the recovery of this heritage to our common Lord and Master.

The Church planted by Cortez on the ruins of the Aztec superstition, with its horror of human sacrifices, existed unchallenged, so far as organized effort went, over three hundred years. From 1523, when Zaragossa, appointed to the headship of the Mexican Church, two years after the subjugation of the state, had exterminated the ancient worship, unto 1823, there had not been an organized, hardly a visible protesting to the absolute sovereignty of that Church. Men had been burned at the stake, but more because they were Jews and Portuguese than as heretics, though heresy was the charge under which they were slain. The native had no disposition in his peonage to assert his religious liberty, not even his civil. And but few Spaniards ever emerged into the heights of faith and of martyrdom; though undoubtedly some, brethren of those whom Torquemada burned in Spain, avowed here like precious faith, and received like honored torture and burning.

Out of sheer malice they slew those that dared profess a higher and better faith; nay, they slew them on suspicion of such faith. The history of the Inquisition in Mexico remains to be written. We hope some missionary or native Christian will give to the world the story of this tribunal from year to year, its victims and its crimes.

In 1811 the Curé Hidalgo raised the standard of independence from Spain; but though of the priesthood, he had no countenance from the Church; and so, after terrible slaughter, his enterprise failed. He is remembered now, and a superb statue of heroic size, "in form and gesture proudly eminent," stands in the walls of the Church of San Francisco, executed by two young brothers, awaiting its transfer into marble or bronze. It is most apt and fit that the moulded form of this earliest hero of emancipation and independence should be placed in the walls of a church which has also secured its independence from an oppressive and foreign faith.

The cause of independence lay sleeping, but not dead, for a dozen years, when the General, Iturbide, who had been chief in suppressing the revolt, headed it, and made it a speedy and almost bloodless triumph. But he succeeded because he recognized the supreme authority of the Church. His declaration of independence began after the Jeffersonian sort: "Mexico is and of a right ought to be free from the throne of Spain." His second declaration how different: "The Roman Catholic Church is the religion of the state, and no other shall be tolerated." Had that been in our Declaration, our path upward had been equally slow and bloody. It, however, secured him the alliance of the Church, and was a wise political measure, viewed in the exigencies of the moment; unwise, viewed in the light of the future.

So rigidly was this state of intolerance maintained, that in a treaty made with our Government ten or twelve years after, while we granted perfect liberty of worship to their citizens resident in our territory, Mexico granted such liberty to ours only in their own private residences, and then "provided that such worship was not injurious to interests of state." And that treaty, I am told, on high official authority, remains unmodified to this day; so that now, were Romanism in power, it could suppress even private worship in an American family, and there could be no redress under our treaty stipulations. So rigid was the grasp of the Church over the whole state.

The first ray that shot its solitary light across the dark was the bold act of Mr. Black in burying the poor shoe-maker, assassinated for not sufficiently respecting a kneeling Mexican's prejudices, in his prostration before the passing priest and wafer.* This occurred in the year of Iturbide's successful revolution against Spain and more successful subjugation to Rome. But the real gray of the dawn was the American war, twenty-three years after the proclamation of dependence as well as of independence. Before that event not an open Bible could have been seen in the whole realm, which then included California, Nevada, Colorado, up to, if not across, the line of the Pacific Railway; nor could a minister conduct worship other than after the form of the Roman Church.

That war carried the Bible and the Protestant Church into Mexico. The soldiers brought the Book in their knapsacks or pockets, and falling out by the way, through cowardice, capture, or sickness, they dropped this seed of the Gospel along these new paths. They could easily talk with the natives after a few weeks, and in their hours of sickness, sometimes unto death, they translated its tender words into the common tongue. Thus the thirsty peon tasted the first drop of the Water of Life. Then, too, the Bible Society sent its agents with the armies, who carried and scattered the Word wherever the troops marched. I have met with several since my return who engaged in this work under the shelter of our flag.

Besides the sowing of the seed in this form, was the more noticeable though not more valuable revelation of it in the shape of public worship. To that hour, no Mexican in his own land had seen any Christian worship, except the celebration of the mass and its attendant ceremonies. The gaudy array of the priests, the mumblings in an unknown tongue, the prostration before a carved image, the uplifting of the Bread and Body of God, the swinging of incense, and ringing of bells, and beating of breasts, and wailings of people, and mournful and triumphal music of the organ and choir—this was their only daily food. The extras were after the same sort: preaching that fostered the follies of superstition and

---

* See page 257.

fed the fires of persecution, and processions that made the materialized service more material.

It was a new sight, the standing of a gentleman in the garb of a gentleman, among soldiers and civilians, the reading of a hymn in their own language which all join in singing, the utterance of a prayer in the same language, in which all reverently bow and join, the reading of the Bible in their own tongue, and the deliverance of a discourse upon its passages; only this, and nothing more. They had never seen it after this fashion. A gentleman said to me, "The first time I ever saw Protestant service conducted was in the palace of the President, by the chaplain of General Scott."

The effect of this was heightened from its being performed by these foreign invaders and conquerors under their own flag. The inquiry shot from mind to mind and heart to heart of the on-gazing multitudes, what is the new mode of religion? The Spanish conqueror's form of worship was no greater novelty to the Aztec, than the American conqueror's was to the Mexican. And each was associated with the victory of the worshiper. "Had this religion," they were compelled to ask, "any thing to do with the sudden and complete overthrow of our armies? Is this anti-Roman faith so much greater than the Roman, that a dozen thousand men can carry the fortified and well-defended gorges of Cerro Gordo, march, over the volcano passes, storm Chapultepec, and capture the city in less than half the time it took Cortez to subdue the land, and that against a people of our own European nationality, trained in every art and weapon of war with which we are conversant?"

What can the answer be, but that the cause of the conquest is Religion? And as the Montezuma and his men recognized sadly that their faith caused their overthrow, so the rulers of Mexico acknowledged that like slavery was the reason of their subjugation. So will France yet confess that it is her religion that made her sink before the German arms, and that only the highest faith can produce the highest race.

The revelation of this conviction appeared in a very few years after the American conquest. Our withdrawal from the land delayed the revelation; but it came. The first proclamation of independence from Rome was made by Comonfort in 1856, less than ten years after our coming and going. The Bible had been allowed to stay, and was steadily, though slowly and almost imperceptibly, leavening the lump. The street that went out from the western end of the plaza, parallel with the Street of San Francisco, was intercepted by the Convent of San Francisco. Comonfort saw that if he was to improve the city anywhere, it must be begun here. This splendid suite of buildings must be pierced. The archbishop resisted. "Touch that, and all is touched." He was right. He touched that, and all was touched. That fell, and all fell. The convent was cut in twain, and the street opened from the plaza to the gates. That was Mexico's first proclamation against Rome. On one side that street to-day you will see parks and dormitories of the convent; on the other, the patio, chapel, and church, with several blocks of private dwellings, two chapels, used for a stable and a blacksmith shop, and the former library, now used as the chapel for American service, and blocks of residences.

That was the key-note of the revolution. On it went, sweeping out the friars and nuns, and cutting their superb estates in pieces. It was Protestantism in the State, blindly destroying, but not building up.*

Juarez followed Comonfort, and the war prevailed yet more. Confiscations of convent property became general. Schools were established without the control of the Church. The institutions of friarhood and sisterhood were abolished, and the claims of the Church, formerly loaned on the estates of the people, were declared of none effect. As this claim covered almost all property, it was a proclamation of universal financial emancipation. The disruption of Church and State was violently going forward. Had no religious influence come in to build up a better Church and State, that conflict would have resulted in the resubjugation of the State to

---

* See Madame Calderon De La Barca, for animating descriptions of these institutions at the height of their prosperity, hardly forty years ago. Her travels are still the best description of the people and their pastimes.

A DISTANT VIEW OF THE CHURCH OF THE EX-CONVENT OF SAN FRANCISCO, CITY OF MEXICO.

the Church, as has always been the case in France and Spain, and, but for the very active Protestantizing of Italy, would be the case there also. The Church saw this, and took advantage of our civil war to revive her fallen fortunes. Maximilian and Carlotta, two bigoted Papists, were imported and upheld by the arms of Napoleon and Eugénie, the last the most bigoted of Papists, in order to bring the State again at the feet of the Church. Not Napoleon, but Pius IX., is the instigator of that war. He who alone of temporal sovereigns recognized our slave power as a nation, sought to help that rebellion to succeed by getting up this rebellion in a neighboring state, and fostered that for the sake of making this triumphant. He succeeded. The French army subdued the republican, and from Vera Cruz to Paso del Norte freedom in religion and in government went down. Rome was mistress of Mexico.

Not until our war was ended did the Papal dominion cease. Juarez enters. Maximilian is captured, and justly and wisely shot, and Mexico is delivered from Rome, as she had been nearly half a century before from Spain. Her progress from that hour has been steady and rapid. But this progress has been because of the increase of the leavening power of the Bible and the Church. This has a story of its own.

Papers lie before me, prepared by a Mexican Protestant at the request of Rev. Dr. Riley, which give the story of the rise of the true Church. From this unprinted pamphlet I am permitted to make up this narrative.

It declares that Mexico was groaning under the hard yoke of the Roman clergy; that after a war of many years, and after long and cruel sufferings, the republican government was established, and freedom of religion. "How much blood was shed," it plaintively cries, "in settling these laws! How many families are still weeping for their fathers, how many mothers for their children, slain in the wars of the Reformation!"

After the first election of Don Benito Juarez to the Presidency, and before the last civil war, that is between 1858 and 1863, some clergymen, called Constitutionalists, established a new worship like that which is to-day performed by the anti-Romanists. To these ministers the President gave the use of two of the confiscated churches, Mercy and the Most Holy Trinity.

When the French came in, the monarchical government, at the instigation of the priests, seized one of these ministers, and having scraped his hands, and his clerical tonsure on the top of his head, in order to degrade him of his priestly character, they led him out to execution. When about to be shot, seeing the rifles leveled at his breast, he cried out, just as they fired, "Viva Jesus! Viva Mexico!" (Long live Jesus! Long live Mexico!)

This vivid expression of devotion to the Lord Christ and his country is the inspiration of the whole movement. The scattering of the Bible resulted in the conversion of Rev. Francis Aguilar. After the expulsion of the French in 1867, he opened a hall for public worship in San Jose de Real, in the old convent of the Profesa. He was the first preacher of the true faith. His meetings were well attended. He also translated a book entitled "Man and the Bible," which had a large circulation. In a few months he became sick unto death, and in the last hour, taking his Bible, pressing it tenderly to his bosom, he said, "I find in this peace and happiness," and fell asleep in Jesus. The second dying witness was as serene and triumphant as the first. "Jesus," "the Bible," were their several words of victory. Francisco Aguilar circulated the Scriptures with great zeal, and helped greatly to extend and establish the true faith.

On his death, his church, being without a pastor, sent a committee to the United States to seek aid from the Protestant Episcopal Church. This Church, through its bishop in New Orleans, gave them pecuniary help, but could not aid them farther. Rev. H. C. Riley, a native of Chili, born of English parents, but conversant with the language from his birth, was preaching at that time to a Spanish congregation in the city of New York. He listened to the cry, gave up his congregation, and in the spring of 1871 started for the country. The American and Foreign Christian Union supplied means for the furtherance of the cause, and his own purse, and his father's, with the gifts of William E. Dodge and others, gave him the necessary sinews for the war upon which he was entering.

That war quickly broke out. Almost as soon as he had arrived and taken quarters at the Hotel Iturbide, there was a conspiracy formed for his murder in that very hotel. He saw the band meeting to plot against his life. He escaped to safer and less noticeable quarters. He fought fire with fire, bringing out pamphlet after pamphlet, the first of which was called "The True Liberty." He wrote and arranged many of the hymns and tunes that are still in use. He also prepared a book of worship, with Scripture readings and prayers, after the form of the Episcopalians.

The excitement grew, and the priests thundered against the new worship which had so speedily assumed form under the experience and energy of the new apostle. An American Spaniard, versed in their whole style of procedure, versed equally in the opposite and better style, with singing and Bible reading, and praying and preaching, and publishing, was making himself felt and feared throughout the city and surroundings.

This uproar drew attention of politicians and priests to the new man and his work. His friends at home seconded his zeal. Private persons gave largely for the purchase of two church edifices, that of San Francisco, and that of San Jose de Gracia. The latter was chiefly, if not solely, the gift of his own father. Rev. Dr. Butler, secretary of the Society, traversed our country, eloquently pleading for the new enterprise, and aiding its extension by liberal and especial gifts of many gentlemen. The Chapel of San Francisco and the Church of San Jose de Gracia were fitted up and occupied by large congregations. The latter is a comely church within, though possessed of but few external attractions. Among the worshipers at the latter place were President Juarez and his family.

Meantime the pamphlet and pulpit war went on. But Dr. Riley was not left alone on the field. Out of the eater came forth meat. The most popular preacher in the cathedral and the Church of San Francisco, over whose eloquence thousands had hung entranced, who was a violent persecutor of the rising faith, a Dominican friar, Manuel Aguas, read the pamphlets, was convinced, withdrew from his pulpit and from the mass. He read the Bible, distrusted his former teachings, visited the "Church of Jesus," as the new church called itself, and at last confessed unto salvation.

It made a great stir. He became very bold in his preaching, and aggravated his former associates by his ability and enthusiasm and popularity. The archbishop excommunicated him in the cathedral in the presence of an immense crowd. But the deposed priest did not fear the anathemas. He stood in the audience, and even sought debate while the terrible curses

CHURCH OF SAN JOSE DE GRACIA.

were being solemnly recited—anathemas that a few years before would have been instantly attended with burnings on the plaza of his own convent, and in which also, a few years before, had it been another of his brethren who was being thus accursed, he would himself have taken part joyfully in the burning. He waxed bolder, and wrote to the archbishop a powerful paper, in reply to his excommunication, showing up the follies and falsehoods of the Romish Church.

It is worthy of being scattered over our own land. It professes to give a conversation between Paul and the archbishop. The former visits the cathedral, witnesses the performances, condemns the heathen idolatries, and learns, to his surprise, that he is finding fault with what some assert to be the most ancient Christian ordinances. He inquires farther, and finds no Bible permitted to be read, marriage of the clergy forbidden, idolatry observed in the worship of the mass, the bread of sacrament alone being distributed to the people, the wine being denied because, as Aguas says, one council affirms, "the blood of the Lord would be squandered by adhering to the mustache." In these charges he utters some truths not so well known to Americans as they should be, and in a masterly, sarcastic manner. He declares "Prohibition of matrimony has driven many unfortunate proselytes to commit great immoralities;" that fastings are not very painful, the rich on such days fasting over tables laden with delicacies and wines for four hours, "rising very contented, not to say inebriated;" that the God whom the priest creates in the mass "has been deposited in the abdomen of mice, when these mischievous little creatures have eaten the consecrated host, a misfortune which has often happened, though kept secret from the faithful." He charges the priests with stealing the alms deposited to pray souls out of purgatory, and mocks at their saints for every thing, declaring that "it is a very fortunate arrangement to ask Saint Apollonia to cure us of the toothache; Saint Lucy, of cataracts on the eyes; Saint Vincent Ferrer, of pains of childbirth; Saint Anthony the Capizon, 'so called on account of the large head the sculptor has seen fit to place on his shoulders,' to find lost things; Saint Caralampius, to keep our houses from being burned; Saint Dinias, to preserve us from robbers; Saint Judeus Thaddeus, to deliver from slanderous and lying tongues," although he sarcastically adds, "the nuns have multiplied the prayers to this saint in vain, since Padre Aguas will not leave Mexico, nor cease invading the Holy Cathedral." He notes what was mentioned as being absent from the catechism sold at Leon, the erasing of the Second Commandment. He also sarcastically refers to the priest's family as "nephews who are the legitimate sons of their uncles," and presses home on the archbishop not only these unwelcome facts, but the severest denunciation of the apostle for permitting and approving them. Pitifully he concludes with the story of her cruelty, and describes her great inquisitor, Dominic de Guzman, as surpassing all others in cruelty, and yet canonized and worshiped by the Church. Nowhere in modern history has there been a severer, sharper, more sarcastic, and more effectual rebuke to the pretensions and career of Papacy than in this powerful pamphlet. Can not our tract societies give it to our people?

MANUEL AGUAS.

The separation was complete. The most popular of her preachers, confessor to the canons of the cathedral, doctor and teacher of divinity, giving medical advice to multitudes of the poor of the city, was so cast out by the greater excommunication, which was nailed on the doors of the churches and announced in the papers, that all his friends forsook him, and, had it not been for the police, the boys would have stoned him in the streets.

He preached to large houses in the two chapels, and superintended the work after Dr. Riley's departure. Sickness seized him, some think poison, and he died in the spring of 1872, when only about fifty years of age. His last sermon was on the text, "Blessed are ye when men shall revile you, and persecute you, and shall say all manner of evil against you falsely for my sake. Rejoice, and be exceeding glad, for great shall be your reward in heaven." He was so ill he could scarcely finish his sermon. He was taken from the pulpit. Soon he was dying. A friend asked him, in this solemn moment, "Do you now love Jesus?" "Much, very much," was the answer.

As memory commenced to fail, so that he was forgetting his nearest friends, one of them stooped over the dying man, and in his ear asked the question, "Do you remember the blood of Christ?" He had not forgotten that. He exclaimed, "The most precious blood of Jesus!" On breathing his last, a smile rested on his countenance, which abode still upon it when it lay in state in the Chapel of St. Francis. A great multitude attended his funeral, among whom were many Romanists. His hearse had properly upon it the emblem of an open Bible. By that he had conquered.

There is no doubt that Manuel Aguas is, so far, the chief fruit of the Mexican Reformation. Whether he would have proved the Luther, can not be known. Probably its Luther must come from abroad, or from the youth now growing up in the faith.* More probably it will have, as it will need, no Luther.

The congregations were not confined to the two chapels of the "Church of Jesus," or to any organization. Laymen and clerics began to talk where opportunity offered. I attended one such meeting, held by R. Ponce de Leon, near the Tulu gate. It was a charming morning when we walked through dust and degradation to the preaching place. It was in a quadrangle occupied by a gentleman who acted as an interpreter to the Indians.† He was a grave man of sixty. He led me into his library, and showed me books in different languages still in use. The Indians had come to the gate to do their trading. A few, in their blankets and wretchedness, sat on the clean floor of the little room, while the interpreter and a few of his sort occupied chairs. Señor Ponce

---

* See Appendix B. † See Appendix C.

read prayers and Scriptures; his wife and daughter sang superbly, and he talked earnestly. It was an impressive and profitable hour.

With the death of Manuel Aguas the movement assumed a new departure. The American and Foreign Christian Union abandoned the field. The Presbyterians, encouraged by Dr. Porteus, of Philadelphia, for many years a resident of Zacatecas, accepted the mission in Villa de Cos, in the State of Zacatecas, and sent their missionaries there in the fall of 1872. They have now flourishing missions at Toluca, Zacatecas, Vera Cruz, and in and around the city of Mexico. Rev. Mr. Hutchinson at the capital is very efficient and successful.

The Baptists flourish in Monterey under the supervision of the Rev. Mr. Westrup. A native preacher introduced their form of faith. The Congregationalists at Monterey and Guadalajara have already had precedence of all other missionary churches in the seal of martyrdom to which they have attained, in the brutal massacre of Rev. Mr. Stephens, by a mob incited by a Romish priest.

This martyr, John Luther Stephens, deserves especial mention. Born at Swansea, Wales, October 19, 1847, murdered in Ahualulco, March 2, 1874, he had barely passed his quarter of a century ere he captured this crown. His father, a sea-captain, was drowned at sea in 1850. His mother went to live in Petaluma, California. In 1866, when nineteen years of age, he joined the Congregational Church in that place. He spent nearly five years in study for the ministry, graduating in May, 1872. That fall he entered Mexico from the West. He staid at Guadalajara, doing valiant service with his colleague, Mr. Watkins, printing the Biblical and Roman Ten Commandments, and placarding them over the city, distributing Bibles, and holding meetings. Great was their boldness of speech toward their malignant enemies of the Roman Church. Several times they were threatened with assassination; but their would-be murderers were baffled. Mr. Stephens visited Ahualulco in the fall of '73, sixty miles from Guadalajara. Here he had great prosperity, though also great peril. One attempt was made to shoot him, but the man was prevented. At last they succeeded.

This is the story as told by Mr. Watkins, his colleague, and printed in the *Missionary Herald:*

"For three months he labored with success far beyond our most sanguine expectations, winning many souls to the truth as it is in Jesus. He had gained, through his labor of love, the favor of the majority of the people of Ahualulco. This grand success infuriated the cura, and the day before Mr. Stephens's death he preached a most exciting sermon to the numerous Indians who had gathered there, from the various ranchos and pueblos near by, in which he said, '*It is necessary to cut down, even to the roots, the tree that bears bad fruit. You may interpret these words as you please.*' And on March 2, at one o'clock in the morning, a mob of over two hundred men, armed with muskets, axes, clubs, and swords, approached the house where Mr. Stephens lived, crying, 'Long live the religion!' 'Long live the Señor Cura!' 'Death to the Protestants!'

"The house which dear Stephens occupied was fronting the public plaza, and on the opposite side of the plaza were a few soldiers, acting as guard to the prison and to the town, from whom he expected protection. But we have learned that these soldiers, instead of giving him protection, aided the enemy to carry out their evil design of murder and robbery. As soon as Mr. Stephens and the two brethren that were with him saw that the mob was fast breaking down the front door they entered an open square, which was in the centre of the house. From this square, Mr. Stephens and Andres, one of the brethren, made their way into the back yard, seeking there a place of shelter. Here they separated. Mr. Stephens taking a pair of stairs that led to a hay-loft, and Andres making his escape by climbing over the wall of the back yard and letting himself down among the ruins of an old house, from which he made his way, unseen by the mob, to the mountains.

"Mr. Stephens had been in the hay-loft but a few moments when the furious throng entered, and he, seeing in the crowd the soldiers alluded to, ran to meet them, thinking they had come to his help; and when he cried out, 'Protect me! Protect me!' they replied, 'They come! They come!' and at the same time soldiers and others discharged their muskets and other fire-arms on our beloved brother, killing him instantly. One shot entered his eye, and several his breast, and as soon as the villains reached him they used their swords, cutting his head literally to pieces, and it is said, *taking the brains out with sticks.*

"Nor was it enough for these ferocious assassins to take his life away so inhumanly, and commit such barbarities on the dead body, but they afterward robbed his body of every article he had on, and the house of every thing he had in it. They took all his books and burned them in the public plaza. The small English Bible that was in the dear martyr's hand when he died shared the same fate. And, lest the awful crime should fail to prove the utmost barbarity, they entered the church, and announced the deed well done by *ringing twice a merry peal of bells.*

JOHN L. STEPHENS.

"We are left to weep and mourn the loss of one so dearly beloved, but his tears have been all wiped away. Stephens, the protomartyr from among us, doubtless ere this has been welcomed by Stephen, the protomartyr from among the disciples of old, into the company of those who have laid down their lives for Christ's sake, and our brother now, with them, wears his crown in glory, the crown that belongeth to the martyr, a 'crown that fadeth not away.'

"It was an absolute impossibility to bring the body to Guadalajara, on account of the great heat and the insecurity of the roads, so it was secretly buried Monday night, by five of the brethren, in a place only known to them."

A letter from Mrs. Watkins narrates this incident:

"The theme upon which he dwelt for some time before his death was 'Sanctification,' as though in unconscious preparation for that life before him upon which he was so shortly to enter. During the last evening of his life he sang several times, in company with others who were present, in Spanish, 'I am traveling, yes, to heaven I am going.' Sooner by far than he expected did he enter the heavenly port, where he is enjoying the bliss prepared for him."

This is the favorite hymn, referred to previously, "Voy al cielo, soy peregrino" (page 93), and shows how wide-spread is that familiar melody, and how befitting it proved itself to be in this supreme moment.

The Church that slew him hailed his death with the same gladness that it did the like and larger massacre of Saint Bartholomew. A priest in the theological seminary of Guadalajara told his students that when Stephens was killed "the Church had one enemy, and the world one thief, the less ;" and "would to God that the other one" (Watkins) "were destroyed." The local government arrested two priests and nine of the people, but all were liberated. It is as impossible to hang one yet, or to punish him in any shape, for murdering a Protestant. Mexico prevents, sometimes, these murders, but is powerless to punish those who may commit them. But their commission will yet be followed by punishment, and Mexico be redeemed from this horrible sin and crime.

The Methodist Episcopal Church South has initiated work in the capital, having secured the Chapel of San Andres, and is preparing missionaries for other sections. The Chapel of San Andres is in the rear of where the Church of St. Andrew stood, which church received the body of Maximilian, on its way to Europe, and where it lay in state. Juarez, consequently, leveled the splendid structure with the ground, and opened a street over the very spot where Maximilian lay.

The Episcopal Church, though not formally present, is the chief patron of the work of Rev. Dr. Riley, which is called the Church of Jesus, and in an indirect, if not direct, form will probably continue to support that organization. The Methodist Episcopal Church has flourishing missions at Orizaba, Cordova, Pachuca, Miraflores, and other places, and in the city itself, where it has four missions as well as its central quarters. So that from the seed-germ of Consul Black, fifty years ago, watered and replenished by the American war, and nurtured by the martyrs who suffered unto death not ten years ago, there has sprung already a goodly harvest, while promises of yet greater harvests beckon the Church to yet greater sacrifices. It is reported that sixty-nine churches are already organized and flourishing throughout that land. It is probable that this number is less than the facts will warrant.

The state, meanwhile, is progressing in the ideas of a proper distribution of the powers and prerogative of itself and its co-ordinate, the Church. Getting clear of the terrible tyranny that so long held it down, and striking blind blows at all ecclesiasticism, in its efforts to free itself, it is settling down calmly and strongly to a proper discrimination of its own functions. It has protected the new Church in many places from danger, and will not do less, but more, in that direction in the future, if need shall be.

Meantime, the enemy rages and rises at times into ferocity of hatred. At Toluca it assailed with riotous bands the little congregation, shouting "Death to the Protestants!"* At Tirajaen a gang set on fire the house of a family, while all were sleeping, and wounded the father severely with the sword. At Cuernervaca a Romanist stabbed one of the brethren with a poniard, and killed him. At Capulhuac they killed one and wounded three. At the capital, earlier in the movement, one was assassinated. At Acapulco a mob killed and wounded a dozen. It was suppressed by volleys discharged into its midst by the commandant of the place, which resulted in several deaths. Other persecutions have occurred, and may occur; for the country has hardly yet been penetrated, and the pagan, which is the village population, may rise fiercely on the teachers and preachers of a better faith. But rise and grow that faith will. The labors of Riley, the martyrdoms

---

* See Appendix D.

TOWN AND CASTLE OF ACAPULCO, MEXICO—SCENE OF THE RECENT MASSACRE.

of Aguilar and Stephens, the heroism of Aguas, the vigor of the present workers, shall not be in vain. To-morrow shall be as this day, and much more abundant.

Another topic, touched upon in the beginning, deserves notice at the end. I had the privilege of going out in the same steamer with railroad managers, abode in the same hotel with them, and rode with them over the same paths. Success has attended efforts in that direction. Mr. Plumb, former secretary of legation, and a son, I believe, of a missionary, has succeeded in getting an agreement signed by the Government which insures a railroad to Leon and to Texas. He was not the representative of the party I was most conversant with; but it is with railroads as with Christian churches: it is not of so much importance who build them as that they be established. His bland manners, admirable tact, elegant bijou of a house, fine command of the language, and knowledge of men, with a constant perseverance that was not to be put by, secured him the precedence. Undoubtedly, the parties behind both leaders will be united in the prosecution of the gigantic enterprise. Railroads and religion have an affinity. They come from the same land, and for the elevation of the people. Together they will develop and regenerate the nation.

A correction may find place here. Reading, since these pages were written, the interesting work of Judge Wilson, I find a suggestion there, which I am inclined to adopt. It is that the Pyramid of Cholula is natural, and not artificial. He explains the adobe stratifications that were noted, as buttresses to preserve the road. There is some plausibility in this; but only a thorough research can verify it. Nor does this prove the other pyramids near the city to be natural. His views as to Cortez and his conquest I do not support. It is, therefore, with pleasure that I admit this suggestion.

I have carefully abstained from giving any information that I had to learn from books. All such information is better found in its own place. I have not told you the number of the states, their names, their boundaries, their populations, their trade, or any thing belonging to that valuable department of Mexican knowledge. I could have easily written out from books the facts that Mexico has 9,176,082 inhabitants, not one more, nor less; that it is as densely populated as the "United States of the North;" that it is made up of twenty-three states, one territory, and one district, whose names I could write in, but you would not know any more then than now. All this and more you will find in cyclopædias and gazetteers, and chiefly in a coming guide-book which has never yet been gotten up, but which I learned that an enterprising gentleman was engaged in. I have not discussed the various tribes and tongues of the Indians. That has been done, and is being done, by expert and accomplished hands.

I should also add, that I know of no previous itinerary of the tour from Mexico to Matamoras, a French brief military journal to Saltillo being all I have seen. This part of the journey, therefore, is entirely without any aid from other sources than my own eyes. The rest has been once and again spread before us on other canvas. Yet a new picture of an old, familiar landscape may convey new and agreeable impressions. May this have that fortune.

The work is done. It remains but to thank the many friends who have aided in putting it into this comely shape. Mr. Kilburn, of the firm of Kilburn Brothers, Littleton, New Hampshire, whom I met in the capital, has kindly allowed the use of many of his superb photographs. Messrs. Skilton, Butler, Riley, and others have aided with their superior knowledge. The secretaries of the several missionary boards operating here have kindly supplied me with the data at their command. How patiently the compositors and proof-readers, and that chief, unknown of men, who superintends them, have gone through the obscure manuscript, and brought it forth in comeliness, only they and the writer know. They, at least, shall be gratefully remembered. To all, thanks. Not the least to you, brother reader, for having accompanied me thus far on this long journey. May you break the icy monotony of our long winters by a visit to our Next-door Neighbor, and forget this story in the delights of your own experience. Hail and farewell!

APPENDIX A.

THE PROTEST IN LEON.

[Translated from the *Revista Universal*, Mexico, October 28, 1873.]

"*Doctor and Master Don José Maria de Jesus Diez y Sollano, Bishop of Leon by the Grace of God, to our beloved Diocesans, Health and Peace in our Lord Jesus Christ:*

"Following the illustrious example of our Most Holy Father, Pius IX., who, full of sacerdotal firmness, in the midst of the most cruel enmities against the Church, incessantly raises his pontifical voice to admonish the faithful on each occasion as to the duties that are incumbent on them, and explicitly declares all the Catholic doctrines which it is their duty to follow, intimating what censures the Church would pass on any act contrary to said doctrines, according to the canons that were lately published in his allocution of the 25th of the past July; we, in the fulfilment of our episcopal duty, do not wish to criminate ourselves before God (before whose tribunal we have all to appear) by not raising our voice on the present occasion, when our faithful ones, seduced by the dread of humanity, protect a constitution and laws which involve many underhand heresies condemned by the Holy Church, and others nominally condemned in the Encycli *Quanta y Syllabus* of the same most high pontiff, Pius IX.

"We declare: That the protest which newly exists, and which is added to-day, the 25th of September, to the Constitution of 1857 by decree of the General Congress is unlawful, and those who protect it simply commit a mortal sin, and the crime of heresy, and those who comply with the feast of its externals will require absolution from the Holy Father.

"We equally declare: That for the same reason the Mexican Episcopate declared that he could not absolve those who had taken the oath of allegiance to the Laws of Reform, without previous retractation from the scandal and from the heretical propositions which are involved in this protest, and that no one who has protected it can be absolved sacramentally without previous retractation and reparation from the scandal, and from the form and manner of swearing to said laws.

"The Holy Apostolic Roman Catholic Church, following the footsteps of the holy apostles, Peter and Paul, and the expressed doctrines which are evident in their canonical epistles, has been the first to teach obedience to the people, respect and submission to the authorities and civil laws, not only through fear, but for conscience' sake, *non solum propter iram, sed itiam propter concientiam*, and still more through the disjunctive of obeying God and obeying man, and has incessantly proclaimed the maxim of the prince of the apostles, Peter, '*obediro oportet Deo magis quam hominibus*' (it is necessary to obey God rather than man), and in such an extreme the answer of a Catholic ought to be that of the same apostle when before the Sanhedrim, '*Non possumus*' (we can not, it is not lawful); and a man can not do these things without showing that he acts contrary to the authorities who respect the authority of God, according to the judgment of St. Paul : '*Non est potestas nisi a Deo*' (There is no power but of God).

"We exhort, therefore, our faithful diocesans, and admonish them, and even supplicate them, '*in vinculis Cristi*,' to enliven their faith, and remember the precept of our Lord Jesus Christ, which to-day urges us in a special manner to confess before men, in order that they may prove us in the name of their Heavenly Father, and that we might flee resolutely from the risk of incurring that terrible sentence which the same Jesus Christ adds, 'He that denieth me before men, him will I also deny before my Father and his angels.'

"And, in order that this notice might reach all, we command all the rectors of our diocesans that the first religious act after the reception of this be, in order that all may read, to fix it on the doors of the chancels.

"Given in the Santa Visita de Silao, on the 14th of October, signed by my hand, and countersigned by our Secretary of Visita.

"José Maria de Jesus, *Bishop of Leon.*

"José H. Ibarguengoitia, *Secretary of Visita.*

APPENDIX B.

The following letter of Manuel Aguas, written only six months before his death, illustrates his spirit and the soundness of his conversion. It is a touching cry from the chief of the fathers of this better faith. It should yet be heard.

"Mexico, October, 1871.

"I have learned that you take a sincere and practical interest in the propagation of the Gospel in this Republic of Mexico—a nation until now sadly unfortunate—unfortunate because it has not enjoyed the blessings of true religion.

"The Lord has, most clearly and signally, blessed the Christian efforts that you have made in our behalf. Let me tell you how: You contributed funds in behalf of Gospel work in this, my native land. Part of these funds were employed in the publication of Christian pamphlets, which were widely distributed here. These publications were the instrumentality that the Lord selected, in order that I might begin to realize the spiritual blindness in which I found myself. I was a presbyter in the Roman Church, and most anxiously longed for salvation. With all sincerity did I follow the errors of that idolatrous sect, and imagined Protestantism, or true Christianity, to be, as it were, a pestilence that was coming to make us, in Mexico, more unfortunate than ever. I consequently opposed its doctrines with all my power. I sincerely thought that in so doing I not only did good service to my native land, but also gained merits to aid me in obtaining everlasting glory. How unfortunate was I! I knew that Jesus Christ had died for us; but that most precious belief was to me obscured, because from childhood I had been taught that, in order to obtain salvation, besides the merits of the Redeemer, the meritorious works of men were also needed. As if, forsooth, the sacrifice of Calvary was not enough to save the soul that truly trusts in it. Being imbued with these Romish errors, it is not strange that I should oppose and attack true Christianity; that I should frequently declaim against it in the pulpit; that I should go to the confessional in search of a remedy for my spiritual evils; and, as one precipice often leads to another, I prayed to the Virgin Mary and to the saints, and endeavored to gain all the indulgences possible; all which practices offend and tend to dishonor Jesus, our generous Saviour.

"As a natural consequence, I had not obtained peace for my soul; I doubted of my salvation, and I never believed that I had done sufficient work to obtain it; and I was truly unfortunate, because I observed with sorrow that, after all I did, my heart remained unconverted, and dragged me often into sin.

"I was in this sad state when there reached me the pamphlet called 'True Liberty.' I read it most carefully; and, notwithstanding that I tried to find in the arsenal of my Romish subtleties arguments with which to answer the clear reasoning that I found in this publication, a voice within—the voice of my conscience—told me that my answers were not satisfactory, and that perhaps I was in error.

"I commenced to reject the errors of Romanism, and dedicated myself to the study of all the Protestant books and pamphlets that I could lay my hands on. I carefully read the 'History of the Reformation of the Sixteenth Century,' by Merle D'Aubigné, and, above all, I commenced to study the Bible, without paying any attention to the Romish notes and interpretations. This study, from the moment that it was accompanied by earnest prayer, led me to true happiness. I commenced to see the light. The Lord had pity on me, and enabled me to clearly understand the great truths of the Gospel.

"I first realized that it is false, most false, that salvation is only found in the Romish Church, as the Romanists pretend. But what completely convinced me of the falseness of the Roman system was the finding that, after I distrusted my own natural strength and trusted in Jesus alone, abandoning all other intercessors, and believing that true safety, salvation, and the remedy for our guilt, are alone to be found in the sacrifice of Calvary, I felt a great change in my heart; my feelings were different; what formerly pleased me now was repugnant to me; I felt real and positive sentiments of love and charity toward my brethren —sentiments which before were fictitious and artificial in me; in a word, I found the long-desired peace of my soul. By the grace of the Lord, I was enabled to resist temptations, and passed a quiet, peaceful, and happy life. As I had dedicated several years to the study of medicine, I was able to maintain myself by this profession. In the evening I read the Holy Scriptures to my family, and prayed with them.

"Although all this was very agreeable to me, it was not just that I should continue inactive in the Gospel cause. I soon commenced to think that I was in conscience bound to participate with my brethren the happiness I enjoyed, and especially so, as I had much facility in speaking to multitudes, from my long practice and experience in preaching that I had had while yet a Roman Catholic. I determined to manifest publicly that I had separated myself from the Roman Church, and that I had joined the true Church of Jesus. But, in order to take this step, I found myself laboring under great difficulties, which the devil would fain have me believe to be insurmountable. The idea of poverty from want of a livelihood presented itself to me with all its deformity; as I was aware that the moment I made such a declaration the Roman Bishop would excommunicate me, and, as I lived among an essentially fanatic people, I felt sure that not only my patients would abandon me immediately, but that all my friends would turn a cold shoulder upon me and also abandon me, and that my life would be menaced and attacks made against it. These and other considerations entered my mind, and I imagine that Satan augmented them, so as to try and swerve me from accomplishing the holy resolution that I had adopted.

"Nevertheless, my resolution was unshaken, and I commenced to attend the Provisional Protestant Church, which had been established in a large hall situated in the Street of San Juan de Letran. Being short-sighted, I there began to know my dear brother, the Rev. Henry Chauncey Riley, solely by his voice. It filled me with comfort to hear him speak of Jesus and his precious blood; the liturgy and hymns which the congregation used enchanted me, as they were full of the pure faith of the primitive Christian; and I anxiously desired the arrival of Sundays, because in our church services I enjoyed delicious moments of peace and joy—Christian emotions that I had never felt in the Roman sect.

"I had for some time been thinking how to become personally acquainted with my brother Henry. One night, as I was at one of our churches, I heard my brother preach with so much valor and faith that I became quite ashamed of myself, and was filled with a holy envy of that Chilian who, in Mexico, in the midst of the most loathsome idolatry, and surrounded by enemies, presented himself as an intrepid soldier of Jesus, ready to lay down his life for his divine Captain. I then was determined to present myself to him alone, and to give him a fraternal greeting, exclaiming, 'We are brothers; our cause is the same: let us unite our efforts, and, strengthened by our adorable Saviour, let us contend for the faith of Jesus, even though we perish in the contest.'

"Various persons had spoken to my brother Riley about me. I was presented to him by an elderly gentleman, who is a Protestant. We had a long interview, in which we were convinced that we were brothers in the faith; we loved one another; and, since then, we worked together unitedly. Our Lord God has deigned to bless our work: for notwithstanding the intense and furious persecution that the Romanists have raised against me, the number of true Christians is increasing most marvelously in Mexico. In Central Mexico we have many Christian congregations, and their numbers are increasing rapidly, even among the smaller towns, where our brethren often suffer the most terrible persecutions from the Roman Catholic curates and fanatics. The Romanists have burned the houses of some of our fellow-Christians, wounding men, women, and children in their efforts to check the progress of the Gospel in Mexico; but, in spite of all their efforts, we have the consolation of knowing that the sacred light of the Gospel, which is now so brightly shining in my native land, and increasing in splendor every day, will not be darkened, even with all the efforts that our persecutors, the fanatical Roman Catholics, are making against it.

"Allow me to heartily thank you for what you have done in our behalf. Part of your contribution for Mexico was converted into Christian pamphlets, that were widely and effectively circulated here. One of these arrived at my sad dwelling, where I was despairingly suffering, because I had not been able to find peace for my soul, finding myself, as I then did, in the darkness of Roman idolatry; but from the time that I read that Christian pamphlet—little esteemed by the worldly, but most precious to me as containing the Divine truth—the Lord commenced to lead me, little by little, in a manner at once sweet and powerful, without in the least wounding my free-will, until He guided me into the glorious light of faith, where I find myself so happy, and where, by the Lord's help, with the Bible in my hand, I have succeeded in making the Roman magnates in this capital tremble with dread and consternation.

"By what I have already said, you will clearly understand that these are solemn moments for my native land, as these may have much to do with her future happiness. The admirable religious movement that is now making such rapid progress in this republic, is likely soon to spread the Gospel in its purity far and wide throughout this nation, and lead to a great reformation in the Mexican Church. This reformation is absolutely needed. Our society is divided between

'Liberals' and 'Conservative Romanists.' The 'Liberals' have abandoned the Roman Church. The Romanists, who have imagined from what is taught them that they can live a life of dissipation, and yet, provided they confess themselves in their dying hour, be saved, remain in the heretical sect of Rome.

"The 'Liberals' have plunged into the dark horrors of infidelity, and are the slaves of their evil inclinations; the Romanists are the slaves of the tyrant of Rome. In a word, true religion has not been the foundation of our society. The results of this want have been fratricidal wars, insecurity, avarice, poverty, and misery. Scenes of wickedness have been the schools where our Mexican children have been educated.

"Such a heart-rending picture ought to fill Christians with sorrow. They ought to ask themselves: 'Why should Mexico find itself on the border of a precipice where deepest ruin threatens?'

"The answer is a very simple one. Allow me to point it out with frankness, but without meaning to give the slightest offense, for I love you for Jesus Christ's sake. Having made this observation, I must say that all you who compose the true Church of Christ in that country neighboring to ours are partly to blame for our misfortunes. I know that you are true Christians; I know that you have imparted to Spain your generous protection; I know that you send your missionaries to remote parts of the world, such as Syria, where you generously and disinterestedly aid the Gospel work. Why, then, have you for so many years forgotten your brethren, who, by your very side, have been without the bread of the Divine word? Why do you allow them to perish, and to sink, day by day, into deeper ignorance and fanaticism? It is well and good that you should exercise your charity with those people to whom you send the light of the Gospel, however distant they may be; but this is no reason why you should leave the Mexicans by your very side in the darkness of idolatry. I am sure that you and your friends will agree with me that it is necessary to do what is possible, in order that true religion may be extended throughout this, my native land. If you think on this subject with earnest prayer to God, your consciences will call upon you to fulfill this duty as Christians. God has not in vain bestowed on your wealthy Church riches, nor in vain has He endowed you with generous hearts.

"MANUEL AGUAS."

APPENDIX C.

THE INDIAN TRIBES OF MEXICO.—THEIR ACTUAL CONDITION, SOCIAL AND SPIRITUAL.

Mr. James Pascoe, an English Wesleyan, for many years residing in Toluca, now doing admirable service in the Presbyterian Church, gives in this article in the monthly *Missionary Journal* of that Church an excellent view of the past and present of the Indian.

"The Indians form three-fourths of the entire population of Mexico, and are divided into three distinct classes: 1st, the subjugated tribes; 2d, the Pinto Indians of the Tierras Calientes; 3d, the untamed Comanches, Apaches, and others. At present, I will speak only of the subjugated tribes, as being most numerous, most important, and as those who are likely to be first brought under Gospel influence. These Indians are the broken-down and despised remnants of the old Aztec, Texcucan, Tlascaltecan, and other nations, who, only three hundred years ago, were the ruling powers in Mexico. Three centuries of the withering influence of Romanism have sufficed to degrade these noble tribes to the level of beasts of burden; stamping out almost every spark of liberty or virtue, and steeping them in superstition, ignorance, and fanaticism of the grossest kind. These tribes still retain their ancient dialects, although, in many cases, corrupted and mixed with many Spanish words; but still they are so distinct that an Indian of one tribe can not understand the dialect of another; and the gulf that separates the Spanish-speaking Mexican from the Mexican or Otomi, or Mazahua-speaking Indian, is as great as that which divides the English and Chinese.

"As a rule, the Indians have their towns apart from the Mexicans, and the lands belong to the whole community, each man having a right to cut fire-wood or boards, etc., and to sell them, or to till any part he pleases; but no one can sell land without the consent of the whole town. Also, each man is obliged to render general services, gratuitously when required, and the expenses of religious festivals are defrayed from a general fund, to which all contribute. The Mexican Government has endeavored to break down this system of clanship; but the Indians, generally, have been shrewd enough to evade the laws and remain in their old ways.

"These towns are not grouped in any order. Here will be a town of Indians, speaking Mazahua; close by may be another of Spanish-speaking Mexicans; a little farther on a village of Otomies—this medley being seen in the neighborhood of all large cities, and each town preserves its distinctive language and customs, and even style and color of dress—the women of one town adopting one uniform shape and color of garments. But, at a greater distance from the cities, we find large districts occupied wholly by Indians of one tribe or another. The Indian lives generally in a rude hut of shingles, or of sun-dried mud bricks, and roofed with shingles or grass according to the supply at hand; but such huts are low-roofed, the bare earth the only carpet, and wind and rain finding free entry by a thousand openings in walls and roofs. The one room serves for every purpose, and often affords shelter to pigs and poultry, as well as to the family. The staple food is the maize cake (tortilla), the Indian very rarely tasting animal food—many not once a month, and thousands not once a year. Their costume is also simple. The men wear a simple shirt and a pair of cotton drawers; the women, a thin chemise, and a colored 'enagra' (skirt) rolled around their waist; and the children, as a rule, in unhampered freedom. A 'petate' (rush mat) for a bed when obtainable, and a 'zerape' (blanket) as overcoat by day and bed-clothes by night, complete the Indian's outfit. These Indians supply the towns with poultry, vegetables, pottery, eggs, mats, and other similar corn materials, which they carry for many leagues.

"For instance, an Indian starts from his home loaded with goods weighing, on an average, five arrobas (one hundred and twenty-five pounds), and sometimes eight arrobas, and will travel a week, and often two or three weeks, before disposing of his wares. He calculates how many days the journey will last, and takes a stock of tortillas to last the whole time, allowing six tortillas a day, which he divides into three portions of two tortillas each, for morning, noon, and evening meal. And this is his only subsistence. So ignorant and stubborn are these Indians that they oftentimes refuse to sell their goods on the road. I have seen many carrying fowls, for instance, to sell in Mexico city; I have met them a week's journey from Mexico, and have proposed to buy the entire lot at the same price they hoped to realize at their journey's end; but no, he was bound for the city, and all my arguments were vain: not a chick would he sell. This has occurred on various occasions. Charcoal, plants, etc., are all supplied to the towns by the Indians, and it is astonishing to see their patient endurance. A man will spend, at least, four days in the mountains burning the charcoal; then carries it on his back a day's journey, sometimes more, and sells it for thirty-seven cents, thus realizing from six to seven cents a day. In the same way the poor creature fares with all else. If he sells planks or 'vigas,' he has first to pay for liberty to fell timber, if he happens not to belong to a town rich in forests. Felling the tree and hewing out the log with his hatchet occupies a day. In four days he has four 'vigas' ready. The whole family is then assembled, and the logs are dragged down to the plain and placed on two rude wheels—

also the work of the hatchet. The donkey is now hitched on, and husband, wife, sons, and daughters, each lending a hand, away they travel, one or two days' journey to the nearest city. On reaching it, they must pay an entrance-fee, generally only three cents on each log; and at length they sell their logs at thirty-seven cents each, and oftentimes for less.

"The Mexican can not do without the Indian. Farms would be deserted, lands untilled, cattle unattended, and the markets entirely deserted, were it not for the poor, patient, despised Indian. Worse still, the poor Indian is the staple food of the cannon, and without him the Mexican would be unable to sustain his revolutions.

"It may be asked, how is it that the Indians, being in such a great numerical majority, allow themselves to be down-trodden by the few Mexicans who rule them? It is because Romanism has so effectually blighted and crushed out their old chivalry and love of liberty, and has steeped them in a degrading and profound ignorance. Excepting the few who, within the past few years, have become acquainted with God's word by means of Protestantism, we shall be safe in saying that not a single soul among them has ever read a line of the Bible.

"Very few of the men can read or write. National schools are found in some of the villages, but only for boys. Schools for girls are almost unknown. Perhaps a few are found in the cities; but in the smaller towns and villages they are unheard of. Thus the Indian women are kept in profound ignorance; a vast majority of the men are the same. This mighty engine of darkness, wielded by the skill and cunning of Romish priests, has produced the fearful uncleanliness of body and soul, the stupid superstition, and bloody fanaticism which now characterize the Indian of Mexico.

"Underlying this patient humility and subjection to their Mexican lords, the Indian nourishes a deep-seated and ever-augmenting hatred of his whiter countrymen. The Indian and the Mexican races do not mingle, except in isolated and exceptional cases. The Indian, in his necessary intercourse with the Mexican, naturally acquires a knowledge of the Spanish language; but they jealously avoid speaking that tongue unless compelled by necessity. In their homes not a word of Spanish is heard; the women scrupulously avoid learning it, and of course the children grow up without understanding a word. I have gone through whole villages and not found a single woman or child who could speak Spanish. I have also observed, on large haciendas, where hundreds of Indians are employed, and where they daily hear Spanish spoken, many of the women, who come weekly to the pay-office to take up their husband's miserable salaries, although understanding Spanish, nothing will induce them to speak it; and some bailiff or head workman, an Indian also, always acts as interpreter. His aversion to speaking Spanish is also seen in religious matters. The Indian refuses to confess to the priest except in his own native tongue. Very few priests understand those tongues; and to surmount the difficulty the priest has a list of written questions and answers, which he learns to pronounce like a parrot. When the Indian presents himself, the priest reads question No. 1. If the Indian replies in accordance with the written answer, well and good; but if not, the priest reads again, until, by good luck, the right word is uttered, and the hitch overcome. The priest who explained this ingenious mode of confessing was somewhat perplexed when I remarked: 'But suppose the Indian confesses to some sin not down on the list; what then?' The Indian is always treated as an inferior creature. The priest requires his Mexican parishioners to confess and receive the sacrament very frequently; but the Indian is not expected to confess oftener than once a year, and, as a rule, he receives the communion only at marriage and when about to die. Once in a lifetime is considered enough for *him*. The march of Liberalism has done much to alter this state of affairs; but not many years ago the Indian might confess, but could not commune without a special license. So great is the chasm which separates the Mexican from the Indian, that the title of '*gente de razon*,' or people of reason, is given to the former. Nothing is more common than the expression, 'Is he an Indian?' 'No, he is "de razon;"' thus making the Mexican to be a reasonable being, in contradistinction to the poor despised Indian, who ranks only with beasts of burden. The Mexican Indian is essentially religious; his whole life seems devoted to the service of the priests and saints; his earnings are all devoted to wax-candles and rockets to be burned on feast-days, and he seems to think of nothing but processions and pilgrimages to some distant shrine. Since the days of his Aztecan forefathers, the only change which the Indian has undergone in religion is that of adoring a San Antonio instead of his ancient god, 'Huitzilopochtle;' and, with this slight change in the objects of his worship, he continues to adore on the same sacred spots, and with many of the ceremonies, and with all the ignorance and superstitious zeal as did his pagan forefathers.

"The Roman Catholic priests, in days gone by, in order to divert the Indians from their Aztec idolatries, adopted the ingenious plan of going by night to some heathen temple, removing the old idol, and placing in its stead a crucifix or some Catholic saint. The next day the Indians were amazed to find a new god instead of the old one, and at once accepted the change; they continued their worship as before. Cannibalism and human sacrifices have died out; but, if we view the Indian's present religion from his own stand-point, we shall see that really *he* finds not one single point of difference. In his old Aztec religion he had a water baptism, confession to priests, numerous gods to adore, and whose aid he invoked under various circumstances. He worshiped images of wood or stone; employed flowers and fruits as offerings, and incense also, and offered fellow-beings in sacrifice, while he also worshiped a goddess whom he styled 'Our Mother;' and in his worship dances and pantomimes took a prominent rank. In his new Roman Catholic religion he finds baptism and confession; a great host of saints to adore—saints for every circumstance or ill of life; he finds images better made, and of richer material than the old ones; he again employs fruits, and flowers, and incense; worships another goddess as 'Mother of God,' and 'Queen of Heaven,' and 'Our Lady.' He is also taught to believe that not a mere fellow-being is sacrificed, but his Creator Himself—as the Romanists declare, in real and actual sacrifice, thousands of times every day; and, as of old, the Indian still dances and performs pantomimes in his religious festivals. Where, then, is the difference?

"As a proof of some of my assertions, I will mention a few facts. In the large town of 'Yinacautepec,' distant about two leagues from Toluca, I visited the annual feast on various occasions. It draws an immense number of spectators from all parts, and for several days bull-fights, and cock-fights, and religious processions hold sway. The procession is a very gorgeous affair, and issues from the church. Banners, and wax-candles, and images in great number; music by the band, and rockets whizzing; but the greatest feature of all consists of a number of Indians dressed in grotesque attires, with skins of animals, bulls' horns, cows' tails, and some with their heads helmeted with the entire skin of game-cocks—altogether forming a wildly fantastic mob, shouting and dancing around their priests and saints like so many imps from the lower regions. The famous church of 'La Villa de Guadalupe,' near the city of Mexico, is built on the site of an old Aztec temple, and the Roman Catholic priests adopted their usual plan of removing the old and replacing it with the new one, and by means of a pretended apparition have made 'Our Lady of Guadalupe' become the patron saint of Mexico.

"The far-famed convent of 'El Señor de Chalma,' about fourteen leagues to the south of Toluca, is another instance. It is the favorite shrine of all the Indian tribes of the land. Formerly, before the convent was built, the place was occupied by an Aztec idol, located in a cave. This idol existed long after Roman Catholic churches had been built in neighboring towns; and the Indians, when they wished to have a child baptized, would first carry the infant to be blessed by their Aztec god, and from there would go to the Romish church and complete the ceremony. To make the most of this propensity, the Catholics, in their usual fashion, stole the idol from the cave and placed there the present 'Lord of Chalma,' which is a crucifix, the Saviour being painted copper-color. This apparition gave rise to a convent being built; and all the year round the Indians, whole families, and whole towns, make pilgrimages from all parts of the land to the said convent. The sales of candles and the Popish requisites are enormous. A shop is attached to the convent, where the poor Indians buy their candles, which they carry to the priests, who remit them by a back-door to the shop again, where they are sold and sold again many times over. But here, also, the chief feature of the Indian worship consists in dances inside the church, which is of great size. Eye-witnesses assure me that at one time can be seen as many as sixteen distinct groups of dancers, each group with its separate band of music, all playing different tunes at the same time, and the worshipers tripping it merrily in different dances, producing a Babel confusion and a grotesque pantomime, which baffles description.

"These are of daily occurrence, and are a true and faithful specimen of the spiritual condition of the Mexican Indians of to-day."

APPENDIX D.

The following placard and commentary show something of the perils our cause has to undergo. Their dates are late, and they, or others like them, we fear, are not yet concluded.

[Translated from *El Monitor Republicano*, September 27, 1873.]

"*DEATH TO THE PROTESTANTS!!*

"To the People of Toluca,—Either you are Catholic by name, or Catholics in fact. If you are Catholics in faith, give a terrible blow to these savages, intruders, and adventurers, who, to make themselves appear wise and important, and to assure to themselves a future without labor, attempt that which they do not understand—that band of filthy scoundrels, deluded sons of all the devils. Let us rise *en masse* to finish at once this accursed race, whose proper place is in hell, which is not complete without them. With one sure blow insure their death and the death of their families. Let a fiery death exterminate this sect of accursed wretches, who attempt to overthrow the Apostolic Roman Catholic religion, in which we will live and die.

"Unfurl proudly the standard of the Faith, and shout, 'Long live the religion! Viva la religion!! Death to the sons of Satan!!!'"

[Translated from the *Revista Universal*, Mexico, October 29, 1873.]

"*ACTIONS OF GOOD CATHOLICS.*

"*ASSAULT ON THE HOUSE OF A PROTESTANT.*

"*HE AND HIS AGED PARENTS ARE WOUNDED BY THE PSEUDO-CATHOLICS.*

"*LAUDABLE CONDUCT OF THE GOVERNOR OF THE STATE OF MEXICO.*

"A few days ago we published a placard, which was circulated in Toluca, directed against the Protestants of that city, and exciting the 'good Catholics' to try to kill all the said Protestants in those parts.

"So it seems that the excitement is extending. We have tidings from Toluca in which we are informed that a Mr. Valero, an invalid, was attacked in his own house in Metepec by a party of 'good Catholics,' who, armed with swords and muskets, entered the dwelling of said Protestant, wounding him, and then left him nearly dead.

"Of course those barbarians did not make their incursion without insulting and using filthy words toward the Christians, and the unfortunate Valero's mother, whom they also wounded.

"The aged father was also seriously wounded by the 'bandidos religiosos,' and it is greatly feared that his son will die shortly.

"The Governor of the State has put forth energetic measures for the apprehension of these invaders, and those upon whom the responsibility rests of executing justice with them will fulfill their duty; these infractors will see that such perpetrations will not escape the power of justice."

THE END.

www.ingramcontent.com/pod-product-compliance
Lightning Source LLC
Chambersburg PA
CBHW051858300426
44117CB00006B/443